FOR OUR SOUL

FOR OUR SOUL

ETHIOPIAN JEWS IN ISRAEL

Teshome G. Wagaw

WAYNE STATE UNIVERSITY PRESS   DETROIT

Copyright © 1993 by *Wayne State University Press*, Detroit, Michigan 48201. All rights reserved. No part of this book may be reproduced without formal permission. Manufactured in the United States of America.

The publication of this volume in a freely accessible digital format has been made possible by a major grant from the National Endowment for the Humanities and the Mellon Foundation through their Humanities Open Book Program.

LIBRARY OF CONGRESS CATALOGING-IN-PUBLICATION DATA

Wagaw, Teshome G., 1930–

For our soul : Ethiopian Jews in Israel / Teshome G. Wagaw.

p. cm.—(Jewish folklore and anthropology series)

Includes bibliographical references and index.

ISBN 978-0-8143-4410-1 (paperback), 978-0-8143-4394-5 (ebook)

1. Jews, Ethiopian—Israel—History. 2. Ethiopia—Emigration and Immigration—History.

3. Israel—Emigration and immigration—History. 4. Immigration—Israel—History.

5. Israel—Ethnic relations. I. Title. II. Series.

DS113.8.F34W34   1993

956.94'004924063—dc20   93-7494

DESIGNER | S. R. TENENBAUM

Exhaustive efforts were made to obtain permission for use of material in this text. Any missed permissions resulted from a lack of information about the material, copyright holder, or both. If you are a copyright holder of such material, please contact WSUP at wsupressrights@wayne.edu.

http://wsupress.wayne.edu/

FOR *TSEHAI WOLDE-TSADIK*

Jewish Folklore and Anthropology Series

GENERAL EDITOR
Raphael Patai

Contents

Preface ix

1 Introduction and Historical Background 1

2 Israel as an Absorbing State 30

3 The Journey and Settlement 53

4 The Beleaguered Family in Transition 72

5 Setting Up Home 91

6 Crisis in Communal Integrity and Identity 108

7 Primary Education 130

8 Postprimary Education and Training 154

9 Adult and Continuing Education 191

10 Community, Race, Modernity, and Work 215

11 Epilogue 233

Notes 245 *Glossary* 272

Bibliography 275 *Index* 287

❖

Preface

❖

My family and I left our homeland, Ethiopia, in the summer of 1974, just for a year of sabbatical leave from Addis Ababa University (then known as Haile Selassie I University), where I had held various positions as professor and administrator for eight years. We never went back. A week after we left Addis Ababa, the Emperor was deposed by a military junta, as we had expected, but that did not matter, we thought. What mattered was the continued worsening of the political situation under the new military regime which later declared that it had adopted the Marxist-Leninist philosophy for the country. Among many other professional and family affairs, several of my research projects were interrupted.

I have been hoping to return to Ethiopia "next year." Next year was to arrive seventeen years later in the summer of 1991.

Deprived of the opportunity to serve the society that has a legitimate claim on me directly in the areas of my qualifications, I had felt on several occasions emotionally, if not professionally, unfulfilled. When the news of the Beta Israel migration began to filter, I saw an opportunity to get involved. I had been to Israel in 1969 at the invitation of the Government, and I had long standing appreciation for the unique development efforts exerted by the people of that brave little country, but I had never seen an opportunity to stay there and work. That awareness came at the beginning of 1980 with the mass immigration of Ethiopians to Israel.

When I first visited the migrants in Israel in the summer of 1985, I felt I had come home. These were people I could understand and with whom I felt at home. Although not Beta Israel myself, I am from the same area and similar rural conditions most of them come from. Our language and general culture are similar. I grew up knowing some of the kids in the fields where we played together and tended our cattle. Later on, I had taught in a region in which some students were Beta Israel. At high school some were my classmates, later at college level I came to know some as my students. The sentiments derived from such experiences eventually led me to undertake the present investigation. I found the venture very rewarding.

Undertakings such as this require the cooperation and support of many experts. I was fortunate in having been able to enlist the support of so many talented people from both the United States and Israel. An attempt to list them all will, I am certain, remain incomplete. I will mention only the major ones. I would like to thank the late professors Wilbur Cohen and William Haber, deans emeriti in the School of Education and in the College of Literature, Science and the Arts of the University of Michigan, respectively. They were kind enough to commend and introduce me enthusiastically to Israeli officials, which proved to be invaluable. Once in the field, I was lucky to secure the support and mentorship of Professor Chaim Adler of the Hebrew University. His active support and encouragement during the fieldwork and continued interest since proved very valuable for the success of my work. I'd like to thank Dr. Steve Kaplan, also of the Hebrew University, a specialist in the history of Ethiopian religions, for his support and help in paving the way for my research. Dr. Haim and Esther Rosen were constant friends and confidants during my long months of work in Israel. We traveled together to the fields on several occasions, and their knowledge of the many issues the immigrants were facing in Israel was invaluable to me. Dr. Zev Klein, then director of the School of Education of the Hebrew University, was very helpful. Dr. Shalva Weil, Pnina Golan-Cook, Jemaneh Yosef, and Joan Chase also were of much help. Ato Rahimim Yitshak, an educator of long standing in both Ethiopia and Israel, contributed to my understanding of the issues of the Beta Israel in the area of education. Ato Akiva Elias, one of the young men who had obtained his education in Israel in the 1950s, had returned to Ethiopia to work for twenty-one years in many capacities, and now was back in Israel doing valuable work among his own people, was very generous in putting his deep understanding of the many issues confronting the migrants at my disposal. Yani Elchanan, director of the Kiryat Arba group, was both generous with his time and very pleasant as a colleague and friend. Above all, I would like to record my lasting gratitude to my friend and former colleague, constant adviser, confidant, and supporter, Dr. R. B. Schmerl, formerly of the University of Michigan and now with the University of Hawaii, who generously shared his vast knowledge of Israel and his editorial skills. Dr. Mary R. Achatz, then my assistant at the University of Michigan, went beyond the call of duty by applying her many scholarly talents and technical skills to stimulate and help refine my thinking regarding methods and instruments of investigation; at a later stage, she was the first person who saw the draft pages as they came off my word processor and gave them acceptable form. I owe her a debt of enduring gratitude. My wife, Tsehai Wolde-Tsadik, once again bore much of the family responsibilities during my long absences. I thank her for her forbearance and support.

At the institutional level, I am proud to acknowledge the generous support of my own institution, the University of Michigan, which provided invaluable support through the Office of the Academic Vice President for Research. The monies I received at critical times enabled me to undertake timely fieldwork and raise additional funds to carry out even bigger projects. The grant of the Senior Faculty Scholarship I received from the Fulbright program helped me to stay in the field for a period of one year. The School of Education at the Hebrew University of Jerusalem where I was located for most of the year provided essential office space, supplies, and some funding towards a student assistantship. I thank the Annenberg Institute of Philadelphia which afforded excellent opportunity during my fellowship there to devote considerable time completing the analysis of data. I am indebted to these institutions. I also thank my editor at Wayne State University Press, Lynn Trease, for her gentle guidance throughout the long process of publication.

Finally, my thanks to the Beta Israel immigrants themselves who graciously admitted me fully into their world. It stands to reason, however, that any shortcomings found in this volume are the responsibilities of none other than myself.

CHAPTER ONE

❖

Introduction and Historical Background

❖

In the central part of northern Ethiopia, mainly around Lake Tana—the source of the Blue Nile—as well as in the surrounding Semien Mountains and in parts of southern Tigray and Wollo provinces, live small communities of Jewish people who throughout history have been known by a variety of names. The people among whom they have resided have called them *kayla* (a Semitic term that is not necessarily derogatory), *taib* (a name perhaps derived from the Amharic term *tebib*, meaning one who is skilled or clever, but, as we shall see later, associated with another expression, *buda*, a person with the "evil eye"), *bale-ij* (meaning one who is clever with his or her hands), and, in more recent centuries, *Beta Israel* (of the house of Israel). To most outsiders, they are known as the *Falasha*, a term derived from the Ge'ez or Amharic (the ancient and modern languages of Ethiopia) root of *meflas*, meaning to uproot. Given their historical claim to descent from King Menelik I, the son of King Solomon and Queen Makeda, the queen of Ethiopia or Sheba who came from Jerusalem, the term might be appropriate. But in recent years, educated members of the group have rejected it, preferring to be called either Beta Israel or simply Ethiopian Jews. That preference will be respected in this volume except when historical explanation requires other terms.

Over the period of 1977 to 1992, practically all Ethiopian Jews have migrated to Israel on the basis that they, like all other Jews of the world, were entitled to take advantage of the Law of Return.[1] This book analyzes their immigration to and absorption into Israel. The analysis is based on original data collected during fieldwork over a period of several years, updated to 1992.

FRAMEWORK OF INQUIRY AND ANALYSIS

The definition of migration includes the act of physical transition from one social setting to another and different setting. For religious, political, economic, or cultural reasons, an individual, alone or with others such as family members or people with similar identities or objectives, abandons one society in favor of another. This transition involves a complete change and disorganization of the individual's role system, including his or her social identity, status, and self-image.[2] In other words, the individual leaves that which is cognitively, emotionally, and socially familiar for another setting that is either unknown or vaguely imagined and in which the psychological realities are markedly different from those left behind. Migrants face the formidable challenge of unlearning past roles which the new situation has rendered obsolete; modifying their self-images, perceptions of their status, and future expectations; and otherwise learning new sets of attitudes and skills that will enable them to assume new roles as required by the receiving society. Depending on what other experiences have preceded migration, such as some prior knowledge of the language or some other cultural acquaintances or affinities with the receiving society, upon arrival migrants must begin to reorganize their cognitive as well as emotional maps and learn new sets of cultural codes, language, and conventions as though life were beginning for the first time. This is done at a time when their accustomed circles of contact, and roles (the vehicles of social interaction that anchor individual and social identity as well as self-esteem), are shrinking. Their self-images of competence, ability, and responsibility regarding work, family, and community shrink or become altered. The degree of disorientation and confusion depends on their previous experiences, level of education or skills, age, degree of aspiration propelling them toward the receiving society, and the quality of their reception upon arrival in the new setting.

The literature on migration, immigrant absorption, and human adjustment or transformation suggests a variety of theories and paradigms one might use to structure an inquiry. Most incorporate, with varying degrees of emphasis, the concepts of role and identity, cognitive mapping, learning and unlearning, or socialization and desocialization, as well as social transformation. The works of Eisenstadt,[3] Erikson,[4] Merton,[5] Bar-Yosef,[6] and others have some bearing here, though none is singularly complete with respect to all aspects of migration and absorption. The analytic framework adduced by Eisenstadt,[7] with modifications as necessary for the specific purposes of this inquiry, will be adopted to analyze the migration and absorption processes of the Beta Israel. The variables that may be helpful in the study of the sociological and psychological nature of the processes of immigration and absorption include: (1) the nature of the initial crisis in the society of origin which gave rise to the feelings of inadequacy or insecurity that precipitated motivation to migrate; (2) the social structure of the immigration process, the formation of the group in which that process is realized, and the basic orientation as well as roles of the members; (3) the process of institutionalization of immigrant behavior in the new country, including the new roles and values accepted and performed by the groups and the various degrees to which they participate in and are identified with in the new social setting (attention should also be given to the characteristics and platforms of the various leaders who emerge as a result of the transformation of the immigrant groups); (4) institutionalization of the immigrants as viewed from the vantage point of the absorbing society, description of the range of possibilities open to the immigrants and the institutional demands made upon them, and estimation of the compatibility of these with the immigrants' role expectations or abilities; (5) the extent to which the pluralistic structure of a specific type of immigrant community or communities emerges—its scope and direction should be considered and then reviewed from the point of view of the types of roles (universals, particularisms, and alternatives) allocated within the absorbing society; and (6) the extent to which different types of disintegrative behavior or normlessness develop on the part of both the immigrants and the inhabitants of the absorbing society, and what the provisions or possibilities are for institutional reorganization and change in the absorbing society.

Measures of progress toward successful absorption include the extent to which the immigrants become dispersed in the new setting along the continuum of social and economic life in the society; the degree to which they participate in and contribute to the economic, social, or religious life of the larger society; and the extent to which they are able to achieve an increasing sense of accomplishment and self-fulfillment. These do not suggest, however, that the immigrants will abandon their primary group. Rather, the primary group, while fulfilling certain expectations, also makes it possible for the immigrants to reach out and become an integral part of the larger society. In the course of this process, one can expect that individuals will vacillate between the primary group for shelter and sustenance, especially in times of personal crisis, and the larger, absorbing society, toward which they will continue to move. Note that these premises are based on the conventions and expectations of the particular society—in this case, that society is Israel, which as a rule measures absorption in terms of the unitary or "melting pot" framework as opposed to the pluralistic framework increasingly accepted in other societies such as Canada and the United States.

IN THE LAND OF ORIGIN

In the context of Ethiopia, which is known as a "museum of people," the existence of any community of people, exotic or otherwise, large or small, is not unusual. Simply stated, there are scores of groupings across the land speaking a wide variety of languages, practicing different religions, worshiping different gods, and engaging in different occupations. Perhaps for this reason, Ethiopian writers have not said much about the Jews in their country. Most references are to the effective resistance they put up throughout history to the nation's central powers as well as to those occasions when they assumed power over the nation. Their unique identities in Ethiopia are based first, on the type of religion they had followed for more than two and a half millennia as Jews (although this specific appellation is not necessarily known or understood by most of the local non-Jewish community) who also happened to be black, and, second, on the kinds of occupations they practiced, although they were not alone in those occupations. But it is more logical to say that their occupational identities followed the religious one, since religion (in this case, the practice of non-Christian religion) was the excuse used for the treatment they received at the hands of the majority of the society which eventually led to their adoption and practice of certain occupations. For all practical purposes, except for their religion, the Beta Israel are indistinguishable from the other people among whom they live in physical appearance, and the way they dress, prepare their foods, construct their houses, and otherwise conduct their daily lives. Ethiopian records document, albeit scantily, their social, religious, and political history; the battles they fought and won or lost against various medieval rulers in Ethiopia; and the military and political techniques they deployed in their efforts to preserve their identities. Once conquered on the battlefield, however, they were denied ownership of land, vital in a peasant society. In their efforts to survive, they became artisans producing goods and entering occupations necessary in the community but whose practitioners were despised. In the course of time, economic circumstances emanating from their landlessness forced them to become an occupational caste and outcasts as well. As alluded to above, however, neither the larger Ethiopian community outside the immediate areas where the Beta Israel lived nor the outside world knew very much about them. What follows is a brief sketch of their origin, history, and religious and occupational practices in the context of Ethiopia. Readers wishing to learn more about the life of the Beta Israel, or about Ethiopia in general, are referred to the bibliography at the end of the book.

HISTORY AND ORIGIN

The history of the Beta Israel is surrounded by controversy and legend. Much of what they claim is not in accord with historical facts, but those facts themselves are either inconsistent or unable to elucidate many of the difficult questions. The task here is briefly to review what is known, what is claimed, and what is uncertain, and to indicate what is perhaps plausible.

The Beta Israel position regarding their history is in accord with that recorded in the *Kibre Negest* ("Glory of the Kings"), which

MAP 1. Ethiopia in relation to its African and Middle East neighbors

Ullendorff[8] refers to as the Ethiopian equivalent of the Talmud, the legendary source that seeks to trace, account for, and legitimize the history of the Ethiopian version of the Solomonic dynasty.[9] According to that account, the legendary Queen Makeda (Sheba), the queen of Ethiopia, in union with King Solomon, conceived a son who became Menelik I, the king of Ethiopia. The young man was raised and trained in Jerusalem. When the time arrived for him to return to assume the kingship of Ethiopia, his father arranged for some Jewish nobles, priests, and guards to accompany him. The Ethiopian Jews, then, are descendants of these people, who presumably intermarried with indigenous local people. The legend of King Solomon and the queen of Sheba is, of course, woven into Judaism, Christianity, and Islam. The Ethiopian version adds that when the priests were asked to leave Jerusalem to accompany young Menelik, they stole the original tablets containing the Ten Commandments (the Ark of the Covenant), which they then placed in the holy city of Axum, where, according to legend, it remains to this day.[10] While most of the Ethiopian kings and emperors trace their lineage to this source, so do the Beta Israel. Perhaps it is this belief that led them time and again into trouble, defeat, and humiliation as they tried to wrest their freedom from the rulers of highland Ethiopia during the Middle Ages.

The legend goes back to about 900 B.C., when King Solomon was ruler of Jerusalem. The prophet Zephaniah, a contemporary of the prophet Jeremiah who lived more than six hundred years before Christ, refers to Jews living beyond the River Nile and its tributary the Atbara (the Tekazai River of modern Ethiopia).[11] This description fits well both the geographical location where the Beta Israel are found and the historical claim made by them. For the most part, the main centers of the Beta Israel were around the Semien Mountains, just south of the Tekazai River.[12] In addition, there are several references in the Old Testament to the region of Cush, which included what is today modern Ethiopia. One account describes Miriam, the wife of Moses, as Ethiopian. The account relates that Moses' sister was "angry" that he married. But was she angry simply because he married, or was she angry because he married an Ethiopian, someone ethnically different? The story of the Ethiopian official who was baptized by the apostle Philip while he was on an official visit to Jerusalem also indicates the existence of a Jewish community in Ethiopia before the Christian era.[13]

Documentary and archaeological evidence suggests that before the Axumite Kingdom accepted Christianity as the religion of the court in the fourth century, Judaism and heathenism (worship of the serpent) existed side by side. It seems heathenism was rampant among the upper classes while Judaism was strong among the *agew* (indigenous people) and the lower classes.

Historians are not in agreement about the authenticity of the legends, for there are other possibilities to account for the existence of a

Jewish community in this part of Africa. One is that the Beta Israel are descendants of local people who converted when they came into contact with Jews from southern Arabia, particularly from Yemen, where there was a thriving community of Jews and where Ethiopia ruled for some time. Considering the very close proximity of Ethiopia to Yemen and the similarities in many cultural and physical referents, this seems very plausible. Some others adduce the existence of Jews in Elephantine who were either remnants from the old Israelites of Egypt or latecomers who traveled throughout the Horn of Africa and converted some Ethiopian *agew* to Judaism. This, too, is a possibility.[14]

RELATIONS WITHIN ETHIOPIA

Ethiopia long has been considered an anomaly among nations. Along with Japan and Iran, it is one of the oldest continuous nations in the world. This long and independent life, however, came with a price which included isolationism—both forced and self-imposed. Ethiopia is located in northeast Africa in close proximity to Middle Eastern nations that have contributed to its culture but in recent centuries also have become increasingly hostile because of Ethiopia's religion and affiliations with Christian powers. It has been subjected to intrigues from European powers during the scramble for colonies in Africa. Its many internal conflicts and civil wars kept it busy and alone for a long time. Ethiopian religious and political institutions tended to become defensive, ossified, conservative, and unresponsive to emerging realities around them. Ethiopia's monotheistic religious institutions—Judaism, Christianity, and Islam—must be viewed in this light.

Ethiopian calendars often are reckoned in terms of victories and defeats in war and battles usually associated with the reigning monarchies. Therefore, Ethiopian chronicles record the existence of the Beta Israel in the context of the many skirmishes and battles they engaged in against the rulers of the day. Seldom have the Beta Israel been studied by Ethiopians in their own right. This pattern of neglect also applies to many of the other religious and ethnic or linguistic groups of the country, including much larger ones.

Ethiopian history relates that during the tenth century, the Jews under the leadership of Queen Judit (Gudit, or "the monstrous one")

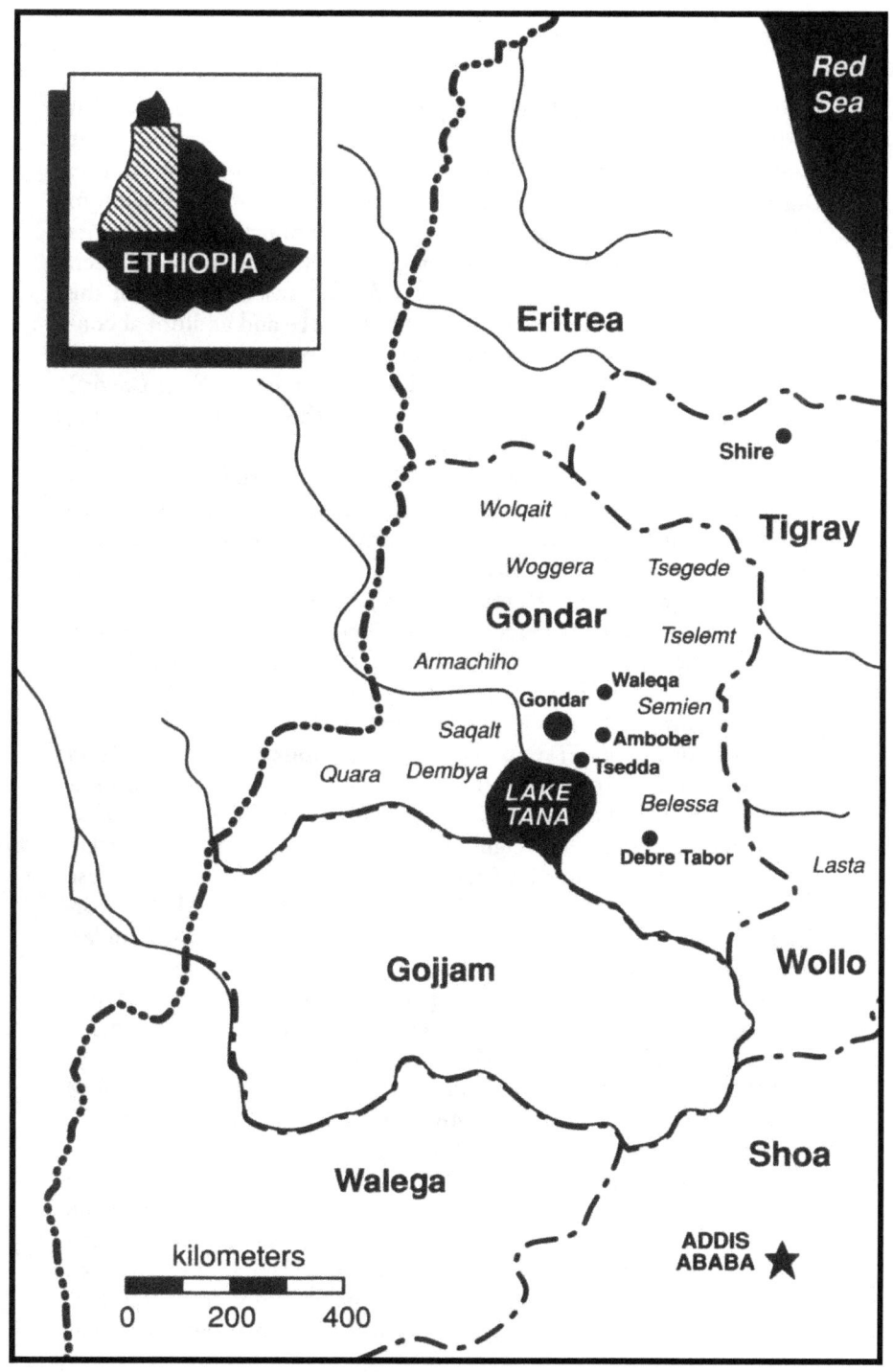

MAP 2. Villages of Beta Israel origin in Ethiopia

destroyed Axum and pillaged many of the monasteries and Christian institutions in other parts of highland Ethiopia.[15] This was not their only major rebellion, nor was she the only leader of high stature. During the reign of Amede Tsion (1314-1344), when the kingdom was involved in a war against a group of Muslim principalities on its eastern and southern boundaries, a group of Beta Israel who had been forced to convert to Christianity rebelled and caused trouble for the king, whereupon he responded with further force and additional conversion. Other Beta Israel groups continued to resist the king and provided sanctuary to dissidents. Thus, during the reign of King Dawit I (1382-1411), the Beta Israel accepted into their fold a dissenting monk by the name of Qozmos who abandoned Christianity to adopt the Jewish faith. Eventually, the apostate monk introduced monasticism, an honored institution among Ethiopian Christians but alien to the Jews. Difficulties between the emperors and the Beta Israel continued throughout the next two centuries.

It appears that during the reign of Yeshaq (1412-1429), the Beta Israel gained control over much of Begemider and Semian (present-day Gondar region). Following that, during the reign of Zara Yakov (1434-1468), one of the most learned if not one of the cruelest kings, conflict continued to rage when the Jews gave refuge to one of his rebellious sons, *Abba* Tsegga, apparently a monk, as the title *Abba* indicates. Zara Yakov was a fanatically religious man who did not hesitate to put his own children to death for suspicion that they worshiped idols. During his reign, many pagans and Jews alike were forced to convert to Christianity. Apparently many of these "converts" resorted to their original religions, forcing the king to order his armies to march against the Beta Israel of Tselemit, Gondar, and Semien.[16]

During the ensuing years, Ethiopia was embroiled in war against the lowland Muslims, which eventually led to the Portuguese being invited to come to the rescue of a Christian monarch. During the wars against the Muslims, the Beta Israel seem to have played ambiguous roles—at one time resisting the Muslims, at another time banding together with them to undermine the king. The coming of the Portuguese, however, seems to have restored the upper hand in favor of the king. When the king ordered and received cannons from Portugal, the fate of the Beta Israel was sealed. Some decades later, when King Minas assumed power (1559-1563), the Beta Israel rebelled once again. This time, however, they not only successfully defended their stronghold of Semien but also, for a time, occupied Woggera further south. Mina's son and successor, Sarsa Dangal (1563-1597), continued the wars against the Beta Israel, who stubbornly fought back and burned their crops rather than let them fall into enemy hands.

The reign of Sarsa Dangal continued to be problematic. He eventually ordered and received men and cannons to fight against the invading Muslims under the leadership of Ahmad ibn Ibrahim el Ghazi (nicknamed Gran, or the "left-handed one") from Portugal. Although the Beta Israel continued to fight with tenacity using the mountain as their shield, their efforts were increasingly futile. In the meantime, Za Dangal was killed in a battle against a rival from Dembia and after some skirmishes was finally succeeded by Emperor Susenyos. In 1615, Susenyos (1607-1632), who, like his predecessor Za Dangal (1603-1604), was suspected of having accepted the Roman Catholic faith under the guidance of the Jesuits who had come in the footsteps of the Portuguese expeditionary force to fight against the Muslim invaders on the side of Ethiopia, was being attacked from several quarters and was having great difficulty holding the empire together. The besieged ruler decided to administer a decisive blow against the Beta Israel. This time, the excuse was that the Beta Israel had provided sanctuary to one of his rebellious sons. The Beta Israel fought back against a weakened king and nearly succeeded. Later, the emperor ordered the extinction of the Beta Israel from Lake Tana to the borders of the Semien. Battles with the Beta Israel continued, off and on, until the forces of Susenyos finally prevailed and the Beta Israel surrendered. There is no way of knowing the extent of the massacre, but it must have been massive. One wonders how much of this phase of their persecution was the result of influences from Europe. The Portuguese Jesuits surely had brought their views of the proper relationship between the Church and the Jews, especially in the Iberian peninsula, with them to Africa. It is not impossible that this king decided such measures were what he needed at this juncture, for prior to this contact there is no information of large-scale massacres against the Beta Israel. At any rate, although the Jews obviously were not entirely wiped out, the massacres and defeat led to their dispersion over a wider area. They spread to Quara, Aramchiho, and Damot, where hitherto there had been only small communities. Large numbers remained in Dembia, Wolqait, and Woggera, and other isolated groups of Beta Israel were scattered over large areas in the region. Emperor Yohannis I, who reigned between 1668 and 1678, granted some religious freedom (or at least tolerance) to the Muslims and the Jews and it is during his reign that members of these two minority religions settled in the newly founded capital city of Gondar. Each religious group occupied a different part of the city.[17]

When the Beta Israel finally lost the fight, they also lost their right to own land. In Ethiopia, land is considered more than the source of economic well-being. It is the basis of self-identity, the definition of one's roots and essence. But life had to continue, and the Beta Israel began to learn and perfect other skills. They became artisans in a country where such skills were needed but the practitioners were despised. As Payne rightly observes, "Ethiopians have respect for the farmer and the priest but not craftsmen nor traders. Most of all they admire the warrior, and their highest titles are military in origin."[18] He could have added that the vocation of priesthood is also respected. At any rate, the Beta Israel played important roles as artisans in the building of the new capital city of Gondar and continued to become potters, blacksmiths, weavers, and the like.

A question must be posed here: Were these struggles between Ethiopian Christians and Jews based on their religious differences (which surely played a part in the history of Europe's treatment of the Jews among them), or were they just another manifestation of a feudal society whose internal upheavals and realignments were assumed to be religious among many other sources of conflict? It is beyond the scope of this book to answer such a question in detail. But it can be said that the usual concept of anti-Semitism or even of anti-Jewish feeling does not enter here. To begin with, the Beta Israel are similar in physical characteristics to any other Ethiopians among whom they live. Second, the Ethiopian Christian tradition is passionately attached to the traditions of the Old Testament (Orit) and prides itself on this connection. At the political level, most of Ethiopia's emperors and kings have sought to trace their lineage through Jewish lines to the Solomonic root. Even recent kings such as Emperor Tewodros, who rose to power during the first half of the nineteenth century, would not tolerate the notion that they were not connected to the Solomonic line. Tewodros spent considerable energy and talent in pursuit of establishing his legitimate claim to the Ethiopian crown, and it is possible that this search contributed to the untimely conclusion of his reign in 1868. Menelik and Haile Selassie included in their royal appellations *Mo-Anbessa Ze-imnegeda Yihuda* ("the Lion of the Tribe of Judah"). This, of course, does not mean that the anti-Semitism of Europe might not have crept into the thinking of some rulers in the sixteenth and seventeenth centuries. The Jesuits ridiculed the practices of Ethiopian Christianity for being closer to Judaism than to

Christianity as the latter was practiced by the Catholic church in southern Europe. Emperor Susenyos, as a suspected convert to Catholicism, may have fallen under their spell when he determinedly campaigned to "exterminate" the Beta Israel. But on the whole, I believe the Beta Israel suffered severe persecution because they were stubborn, because they happened to practice a religion that was different from others around them, and because they practiced an exclusionary life or *atinkugn* ("do not touch me") mentality. This, in turn, bred suspicion, mistrust, and hatred. The Beta Israel were not the only ones regarded in this way.[19] There are other religious, ethnic, or linguistic communities, including Muslim, Kimant (akin to the Beta Israel yet different from them), Protestant, Catholic, and other small Christian denominations who practiced exclusion from one another and who were from time to time subjected to persecution by the dominant group. One community would not partake of meat slaughtered and prepared by the other. Even now, when they come together at the wedding of a mutual relative or friend, each community keeps to itself, and food and beverage are served separately. Perhaps because the Beta Israel had lived in Ethiopia longer, were fewer in number, and were more strict in their observances of exclusion, the intensity of suspicion and mistrust that led to animosity and persecution was stronger. For that they suffered much.

CONTACT WITH THE OUTSIDE WORLD

By the seventh century, Islam had overrun the Middle East, parts of Europe, Iran, Egypt, and the northern portion of Africa. Ethiopia, however, was spared the onslaught, temporarily at least, because the king of Ethiopia had provided sanctuary to the persecuted followers of the Prophet. But when the Muslims eventually occupied the southern portion of the Red Sea, they cut off the Axumite Kingdom from the rest of the world, making it increasingly difficult for Ethiopians to maintain and conduct diplomatic as well as commercial intercourse with the larger, outside world. Hence, for some nine hundred years between the ninth and seventeenth centuries, Ethiopia was almost completely isolated, prompting English historian Edward Gibbons to declare that Ethiopia slept for nearly a thousand years, forgetful of the world that had forgotten it.[20] However, these centuries were not uneventful. For one thing, both Christians and Jews were forced to look inward regarding the problem of maintaining and advancing their respective religious principles. The Christians stayed with the many tenets of the teachings of the Old Testament, as they also developed their own literatures on the interpretation of these and the New Testament teachings. The Jews did the same with the Orit (Torah). Also during these centuries of isolation, it is likely that these two monotheistic religions continued to borrow many religious conventions from each other. Outsiders, both Christians and Jews, remarked about the primitiveness of these religions, meaning that their practices were much closer to those of earlier times—in the case of the Jews, the Temple period; in that of the Christians, the practices of the second through fifth centuries A.D. This certainly could not be denied. But in addition, both communities did create or adopt works of interpretations and were involved in theological expansion.

For centuries the Beta Israel thought they were the only Jews in the world. They yearned for their return to Jerusalem which they thought would be possible after the coming of the black Messiah, who would reign in Ethiopia and later establish his kingdom in Jerusalem, where final fulfillment would be consummated.[21] Likewise, for centuries, the outside world was hardly aware of the existence of these Jews in the heart of Africa. The first person from outside Ethiopia to mention the Beta Israel was a Jewish traveler, Eldad the Danite, in the ninth century. He thought the Beta Israel were part of the Ten Lost Tribes of Israel. This report was followed by other travelers such as Benjamin of Tudela in the twelfth century and Elijah of Ferrara in the fifteenth. Most of the reports were based on hearsay and lacked historical bases.[22] Throughout the Middle Ages, Ethiopia was known as the country of the legendary Prester John and was also where the Ten Lost Tribes were supposed to be residing.

The Scottish traveler James Bruce interviewed some Beta Israel during his travels in Gondar between 1770 and 1771. When he returned home, he wrote an extensive report concerning what he had learned about the society in the Gondar region, including the Beta Israel whom he identified as black Jews. His report, which was not published until 1790, aroused the curiosity of many in Europe. But the next report, that of the Frenchman Antoine d'Abbadie, did not appear until 1840.

The reports of black Jews generated considerable interest among the Christians of Europe. In particular, the initiatives of English missionaries such as Stern, and Flad energized the study of the Beta Israel. The Christian Missionary Society (CMS), organized in England in 1799, had as its sole purpose to energize the Christian churches in the Middle East in order to evangelize among the Muslims. Its branch, the Church's Ministry among the Jews (CMJ), was established in 1809 and was joined by the Basel Missions from Switzerland and Germany, who had similar objectives. The first man to travel to Ethiopia under such missionary sponsorship was well-known church leader Samuel Gobat. He was followed by Flad and then Stern (a Jewish convert to Christianity and one of the most successful ones in the field).[23] The English missionaries concluded an agreement with the Ethiopian government to be permitted to proselytize among the Beta Israel. The converts would be taught according to the traditions of the Ethiopian Orthodox Church and would become part of the membership of that church. The missionaries established several schools in different parts of the region and made their first converts—twenty-one Beta Israel—in 1861.[24] Meanwhile, the reports the missionaries sent to Europe aroused some concern among European Jews about the survival of Beta Israel.[25]

In 1867, the Alliance Israelite Universelle sent the noted Semitist Joseph Halevy to study the situation. He reached Ethiopia when that country was undergoing one of its hard times. The local princes were rebelling against Emperor Tewodros II, and the British were considering a military expedition to liberate their diplomatic and missionary citizens who were imprisoned by the emperor following some misunderstandings with Queen Victoria. Halevy did manage to reach the Gondar region, where he visited extensively with the local Beta Israel people. He listened to what they said about their conditions and the threats presented by the missionaries. He assured the Beta Israel that their coreligionists in Europe were very concerned about their continued viability as Jews.[26] Although he entered the country incognito and was at first suspected of being a Christian missionary, a Turk, or an English spy, he soon was able to win confidence, as he reports the many pleasant exchanges of religious views he had with the Beta Israel. He notes: "I sat all night with my brother Israelites, and we read the Bible in the Amharic language."[27] He made notes on their daily lives and religious activities, including how they prepared their food, the types of homes they lived in, their literature, forms of local religious and secular governance, and so on. However, his contact with the non-Jews of the community must have been indirect or very limited, and what he writes is consistently very derogatory or simply could not have been true. Nonetheless, his experience was the antithesis of that of the Christian missionaries, and on balance the information we get is useful, the assertions of Leslau[28] and Ullendorff[29] to the contrary. Halevy concludes: "It was a great pity that the Falashas should have forgotten the use of the Hebrew text, as the Ge'ez is crowded with errors and mistranslations, disfiguring the sense of the Scriptures. In order to purify the religious ideas of this sect it is absolutely necessary to introduce among them the study of the Hebrew language, an advantage which they themselves much desire."[30]

This favorable evaluation that the Beta Israel were indeed Jews, that they did desire to be in close contact with their coreligionists elsewhere, that their viability was endangered by both the Christian missionaries and the local conditions, and that European Jewry should come to their rescue and help them to revive themselves was received skeptically. As a result, the sponsors decided to send another group of fact finders headed by a Turkish Rabbi Haim Nahum. This mission, however, reported that the Beta Israel people were not Jews, that they were happy the way they were, and that no further concern was needed from Europe.[31]

In 1904, one of Halevy's disciples, Jacques Faitlovitch, traveled to Ethiopia. His report of 1905 was similar to that prepared by Halevy and promoted much interest in the Jewish community, in both Europe and America. Faitlovitch was to play a very important role in the history of Ethiopian Jewry. He stayed in the country, teaching and working, and made representations to Emperor Menelik II on behalf of the Beta Israel. He established schools for them and sponsored a group of young men to study in the Middle East and Europe. These young men later became leaders in their own communities and in the country.

In the years after World War II, one of the first to travel to Ethiopia for the specific purpose of studying the Beta Israel was Wolf Leslau of the University of California. He did much to enlarge knowledge of Beta Israel people. Based on information collected in the course of his fieldwork, he published numerous articles and monographs that remain landmarks in the field.

In recent years, since mobility has become relatively easy, Beta Israel children and youth have been traveling to other parts of Ethiopia in search of schooling and employment. They have been exposed to the larger issues pertaining to the national community as well as to their own specific identity. I have seen them in school situations at all levels as both students and teachers. I know of no way that they were singled out for discrimination.³² Both before the revolution that brought down the Haile Selassie government and since, the Beta Israel youth participated in their share of activities together with young people from other parts of the country. Had they remained in Ethiopia, it is quite possible that voluntary assimilation on the part of the Jewish youth would have threatened the survival of the group. Perhaps this would have accomplished the long-held objectives of both the Christian missionaries and the Ethiopian government.

RELIGION AND CULTURE

Whether they live as a community by themselves, as most do, or among the majority, Beta Israel are not distinguished by their physical characteristics, the clothing they wear, the food and drink they consume, or the style of their houses. Rather, the differences lie in their religion and specific religious cultures.

The Beta Israel believe in one supreme God, the God of Israel, or Egziabher (Lord of the Earth or Creation). They accept not only the Pentateuch (the five books of Moses) but also the entire Old Testament as Orit (Torah). Over the years, they also have developed their own books and have adopted some from Ge'ez, Amharic, Arabic, or Greek sources. They are innocent of the Talmud or Mishna (the oral laws) which are accepted and practiced by most other Jews (the Samaritans and Karaites are in a similar position, but for them it is out of choice), for the Talmud was developed in Babylonia and Palestine between the second and fifth centuries of the Christian era when the Beta Israel were cut off from contact with outsiders. They used no Hebrew until recent years, which also makes them unique among other communities of Jews. Their Bible and other religious works are written in Ge'ez or, more recently, in Amharic, as is the case for their Christian compatriots. Some of their religious works include Tezaz Sanbat (Commandments of the Sabbath), Book of the Angels, Testament of Abraham, and Death of Abraham.³³

The Beta Israel were until recent years the only Jews who continued to offer animal sacrifices for the forgiveness of sins. The sacrifices, which are no longer made, included most of those mentioned in the Old Testament.³⁴ The Sabbath, which is celebrated on Saturday, is strictly observed as commanded in the Orit. The people wash and get ready by Friday afternoon; special foods are prepared and served cold, since it is not permitted to make fire on the holy day. All work ceases from sundown on Friday to sundown on Saturday. In contrast to the practice of other Jews, sexual intercourse is forbidden on the Sabbath. Indeed, the Beta Israel have given the Sabbath a personality that is actively engaged on their behalf. They have given it the special attributes of a woman who is crowned by the angels in heaven each Sabbath, plays major roles in delivering souls from hell, and acts as chief mediator on behalf of believers.[35]

In addition, they celebrate Passover, Day of Atonement (a day of fasting), the Festival of Booths which lasts for a week (although they do not live in booths), and the Pentecost or harvest. The commemoration of Skewed is purely their own, which they continue to celebrate, even after their arrival in Israel. The Beta Israel have never commemorated any of the postexilic Jewish holidays such as the feasts of Purim or Hanukkah. Nor do they use prayer shawls or wear the kippa. They do not practice the bar (or bat) mitzvah when a Jewish boy of thirteen becomes initiated as a son of the Law. However, the Beta Israel do have their own traditional initiation of boys. When a boy reaches the age of fourteen, he offers gifts of money to a priest, who then becomes *ynefis abat*, or the boy's soul father, for life. In this way, the boy is initiated into adulthood and accountability.

Nearly every village has a *mesgid* (place of worship) with one or three compartments, where villagers, led by their *kes* or *kahin* (priest) and *debtra* (deacon or cantor), come to worship. The priesthood is not hereditary and is not restricted to a particular family, as was the case in the days of the Old Testament. Instead, a priest is elected by the community and appointed by the high priest. Much of the education for the priesthood is carried out under the supervision of the monks and the high priest.

Days of fasting occur from morning until night. At the end of the day, they can eat anything, including animal products, which is contrary to the practices of the Christians in Ethiopia, who do not touch milk, butter, or meat during periods of fast. In matters of food, the Beat Israel strictly follow the teachings of the Orit and do not eat the meat of animals that do not chew their cud or have a cloven hoof. However, they do not follow the rules of not mixing meat and dairy products as other Jews do.

Jews, Christians and Muslims in Ethiopia do not eat the meat of an animal slaughtered (*yetebareke*) by a nonmember of their religion. Like the others, the Beta Israel are very strict about this.

Ritual purity is of great concern to the Beta Israel, and as a community they are very clean. As documented by Leslau,[36] the Beta Israel consider the following people unclean: a woman during the time of her menstrual period, a mother in childbirth, a midwife, people who perform circumcision or excision, people who touch or bury a corpse, people who touch a grave, people who touch a dead animal, people who come in physical contact with a non-Beta Israel, and a priest and his wife after sexual intercourse. People considered unclean must stay outside the community for a specified number of days, depending on the degree of impurity. When the period of seclusion is over, individuals wash themselves, and their clothes and in some instances shave their heads. For example, during the menstrual period, a woman is secluded in a special hut known as *yemergem gojo* (hut of curse or malediction) or simply *yedem gojo* (hut of blood) for seven days. At the end of the seclusion, she washes her clothes and herself and shaves her head before rejoining the family. The same is done following childbirth. For the duration of forty days if the child is male and eighty days if female, the mother is confined to a special hut. During the confinement, she is supplied with food and other necessities by members of the family, but no one is allowed to touch her. If this happens by accident, the affected person is required to go through a ritual of purification. At the end of the period of confinement, the woman washes her clothes and body before rejoining the family.

Regarding marriage, the practices of the Beta Israel are similar to those of others in surrounding areas. The parents and relatives of the groom select the prospective bride, usually at a very early age, and the groom and bride as a rule do not see each other before the wedding night. Although divorce occurs frequently, there is no special Beta Israel law that governs divorce. Divorce for a priest is a sin. When it is discovered that a bride is not a virgin on the wedding night, divorce is justified, even for a priest, and is sufficient grounds for excommunication from the community. Virginity is certified either by a group of elderly women who examine the bride on the night before the wedding or by the groom himself on the wedding night.

The Beta Israel practice magic, as do other Ethiopians. They do not consider it evil or especially improper when it is practiced on a Gentile.

HOW NEIGHBORS LOOK AT THE BETA ISRAEL

Since the nineteenth century at least, much of the suspicion and persecution of the Beta Israel has come not from the central government (once they were vanquished in the military field they were not considered a threat) but from the communities in which they have lived. It seems misgivings arose primarily for reasons of (1) secretiveness, (2) absence of communication, (3) practices of despised occupations, and (4) religion—perhaps in this order. There was mutual exclusiveness among the communities. The Beta Israel felt their religious teachings required them to avoid any contact with non-Jews. The Christians (the Ethiopian Orthodox Church) and Muslims felt the same way. However, in highland Ethiopia, where the Orthodox Church has the strongest grip on the population and where that religion is traditionally associated with national patriotism, Ethiopians who believed or practiced different religions were suspect. Intolerance and contempt followed, and persecution was rampant against the Beta Israel and practitioners of other minority religions in that part of Ethiopia, including the Muslims. In addition, out of necessity, the Beta Israel perfected their skills as artisans in blacksmithing, weaving, carpentry, masonry, and the like. Although these skills were valued in the larger society, the practitioners were themselves despised. Some scholars believe the term *taib* is a corrupted form of *tebib* (or tebiban, plural), the Amharic word meaning skillful or wise. This term when applied to the Beta Israel came to mean one who is not merely skillful but also possessed of an extraordinary power which could be used for evil as well as good.

Another concept further complicates the matter. The term that explains this concept is *buda*, meaning one with the "evil eye." The *taib*, then, is one who is a *buda* or one who could cast an evil eye on someone who is not a member of that community. It is held that the *taib* can change into a hyena at night and, after going through some rituals, turn back into a human being. The *taib* also can cause someone's death and after the burial can secretly remove the body and turn it into a slave. That slave is not aware of its original identity and simply does as it is commanded. If relatives of the slave drop by unexpectedly, a slave can be turned into a household utensil by the stroke of a magic rod. Stories such as these are rampant among the non-Beta

Israel communities and believed by young and old. These beliefs have prompted terrible mistreatment of the Beta Israel in some communities. It should be noted, however, that the *buda* concept is not applied to the Beta Israel alone; there are other communities in different parts of the country whose members are also practitioners of the despised vocations and also suspected of being *buda*.

Because the Beta Israel's religion forbids them to eat food prepared by outsiders, they do not travel far from their home bases. Some have thought this was because their religion forbade them to engage in trade, but this is not so. They do go to the local markets to sell or exchange their products. This inability to travel farther also might have contributed to the misunderstandings of their true identity as skillful, religious, and good people.

Since the nineteenth century, the Ethiopian emperors have sought to discourage prejudices against the Beta Israel. Emperors Tewodros, Yohannis, Menelik, and Haile Selassie all sought to dispel the notions held against them. These emperors were aware, for one thing, of the destructive nature of the attitudes highlanders held toward nonfarming and nonsoldiering vocations. The emperors knew the traditional attitudes against manual labor and laborers were counterproductive since the country needed artisans and merchants for modernization. But they also knew that the Beta Israel were very few and practiced their religion in a highly prejudiced, intolerant society. They sought to find some solution. They must have concluded that as long as the Beta Israel persisted in their practices, the problems would continue. Therefore, they allowed the missionaries to work among them with the hope that they would convert to the Orthodox Church. Even those who sympathized with their situation never saw the community as anything but part of an expanded, monolithic, national agenda. On the other hand, Menelik issued a proclamation protecting artisans and traders and encouraging the practice of these occupations by others. In the proclamation, he expressed his bitterness against those who berated artisans who, he thought, were the backbone of his modernization efforts.[37] The emperor did not mention the Beta Israel by name, but it was clear that he had them in mind. He was, after all, fully aware of the tremendous contribution they had made in building his capital city of Addis Ababa, as they had done centuries ago when they built the beautiful city of Gondar.

After Word War II, with the introduction of an expanded system of education, things changed rapidly for all segments of the Ethiopian population, including the Jews. At first cautious but later in droves, the children and youth of the Beta Israel began to attend public school. To attain a high school or college education, most had to travel away from home. At first, the villagers of Beta Israel tried to seclude those who had lived away,[38] but later they must have come to realize that they were fighting a tide that could not be stopped. As was true for other Ethiopians, the thirst for education was very great among the Beta Israel children and youth.

As the young people tell it, they were subjected to insults from some students in the public high schools in Gondar. But, they said, they were defended by the teachers and as the years passed the insults subsided.[39] Outside the Gondar region, of course, there were no insults of any kind from any quarter. It is therefore not surprising that within a generation the schools had effected socialization in relation to the national community to the extent that when Ethiopian students initiated organized movements against the central government of Haile Selassie, Beta Israel youth were among the vanguards. Since the movement was against feudalism and sectarianism and in support of the common people, the depth of their involvement is not surprising. Later, when the student movement presented an organized and active resistance against the military regime that replaced Haile Selassie, Beta Israel youth were out in force. As a result, when the backbone of the student movement was broken in 1977, many sought refuge in neighboring African countries, from which they were later taken to Israel. It is now easy to hypothesize that, had the trends of the 1960s and early 1970s continued for a while longer in Ethiopia, assimilation among the educated would have become total, which in the long run might have affected the continued viability of the Beta Israel community.

SIMILARITIES AND DIFFERENCES AMONG THE BETA ISRAEL

The Beta Israel live in communities scattered throughout the Semien mountain regions, around Lake Tana, Tselemit, Wolqait, Woggera, Shire (southern Tigray), Lasta (Wollo province), and the northern part of Shoa Province. This latter settlement must have taken place some time after their final defeat in the seventeenth century at the hands of Susenyos. The Jews might have come there in search of better jobs as artisans, or perhaps they were brought by some of the rulers to help build their ever changing headquarters, which was the pattern for a long time. In addition, I have seen small communities of Beta Israel living in remote, isolated places in Gondar and Tigray, perhaps unaware of the existence of larger groups elsewhere. These small isolated groups have no designated places for worship. They lead isolated lives, and their primary contact with the larger community is for business purposes only. As a rule, they are the only ones in the community who know how to make and maintain plowshares, sickles, and other metal parts a peasant farmer needs for work in the field. Especially during the sowing and harvesting seasons, one can see long lines of farmers waiting their turn to be served by the Beta Israel blacksmith. Payment may include blocks of salt, raw cotton, and sacks of grain. Although they raise cattle, the Beta Israel I am describing here do not typically engage in farming. In addition, their women seem to attract men from the Gentile world. I have seen men traveling considerable distances to visit them. It is likely that they were aware that the others talked about them behind their backs, but there is no evidence of open persecution against the group or any evil intentions toward them. The non-Beta Israel, however, did suspect them of possessing the powers of the *buda*.

Otherwise, the Beta Israel are for the most part indistinguishable from the others among whom they have lived. There are differences, however, in the perceptions and social interactions among the Beta Israel themselves based on their different ethnic backgrounds. Thus, there are long-standing presumed differences and interests between the people of Gondar and those of Tigray. As far as language is concerned, at one time they spoke one of the variants of the local *agew* (indigenous) languages such as Kuarigna or Kemantigna, in addition to the other languages spoken in the host societies. By now, the old languages have nearly disappeared, and Amharic, the national language and Tigrigna, another important language, are the languages of communication. Many of the Gondar Beta Israel speak only Amharic, while those living in Tigray speak Tigrigna as their first language and some Amharic as a second language. Those living in the border areas between Gondar and Tigray, such as Tselemit, Semien, or Wolqait, speak both Amharic and Tigrigna. Most of their religious works are in Ge'ez, the ancient language of Ethiopia from which both Amharic and Tigrigna are derived. In recent years, however, some works have been rendered in Amharic.

The Beta Israel from the Gondar region are more numerous, are relatively better educated, and also have provided most of the leadership for the community. Over the years, this group also has enjoyed more of the educational, religious, health, and other benefits that came from overseas Jewish organizations. Reflecting the situation at the national level, these differences (tribal or class) exist among the two major Beta Israel groups, the Tigray and the Amhara. Even in Israel, friction between the two groups continues to be a problem.[40]

The crisis that led to the 1974 revolution in Ethiopia is one of six or so similar traumatic events that have taken place in this ancient and still troubled land. But this latest one, the most profound of all, has fundamentally and irrevocably altered not only the socioeconomic and political aspects of the society but also its most fundamental values, its psyche, and its consciousness which has defined it for centuries. A series of droughts, pestilence (cholera), famine, civil wars, and, over the last eighteen years, savage, brutal misrule by a clique of incompetent, ill-equipped, ill-trained young military tyrants known as the Derg ("Committee") under the leadership of Lieutenant Colonel Mengistu Hailemariam (who later named himself president) are all responsible for the misfortunes that have befallen this ancient land. Even after the overthrow of the brutal regime in the spring of 1991, the country continues to struggle to redefine its new identity and its ethnic, linguistic, and religious borders. As of late 1992, the political and social condition of the country could be summed up as in a state of undefinable flux.

TRADITION OF EMIGRATION IN ETHIOPIAN MILIEU

In Ethiopian history, some individual citizens and communities might have ventured to travel beyond their borders for purposes of establishing residence. But they are comparatively rare. One such rare but very significant exception is a community of monks and nuns of the Ethiopian Orthodox Church who have continued to live in Jerusalem since the twelfth century. King Lalibela, of the Agew dynasty who was the force behind the building of the famous series of rock-hewn churches in Roha which he renamed Lalibela, was able to persuade the famous Arab general Saladin, who had expelled the Crusaders from the holy city, to give him a portion of the Holy Sepulcher for his church.⁴¹ Since that time, although they had lost some of their holdings, a community of Ethiopians have lived in the Holy Land. Later, when Ethiopia was invaded by Fascist Italy in 1936, many of the Ethiopian notables, including the late Emperor Haile Selassie and his family, had stayed in Jerusalem. So when the Beta Israel began to arrive, they were not necessarily alone or the first Ethiopians to establish permanent residence in the Holy Land. It should be added here that the two communities, the Christians and the Jews, have very healthy and supportive relations in Jerusalem.

Otherwise, in the annals of Ethiopian history, the concept of migration of citizens hardly exists. No convention, no law, and no expectations for it exist. In Ethiopia's long history, a few individuals may have wandered from time to time to foreign lands, and some may have lingered, but these were the exceptions. Even in the post–World War II era when "brain drain" was a problem for many developing countries, the moment Ethiopians received their diplomas from colleges and universities overseas, they rushed home. For a long time, it was believed that Ethiopian nationalism and attachment to the cultural milieu were so strong that citizens would not consider making their homes outside the country. But in the wake of the 1974 revolution, severe economic and political upheavals occurred. The brutality of the military regime, which later claimed to have converted itself to Marxism-Leninism, as well as severe drought and famine, compelled hundreds of thousands of Ethiopians to leave their country for foreign shores. It is estimated that three and a half million left, though no one knows for sure. The first wave of migration was drawn primarily from among intellectuals and professionals. The younger generation of schooled people followed when they found life untenable after their attempt to topple the military regime failed. They felt their own safety and the lives of members of their families were in jeopardy. They left in droves for safety and security in other countries. Soon it became known that there was hardly a country in the world where an Ethiopian emigre could not be found.

Although there are important qualitative differences, the waves of migration of the Beta Israel must be considered in this context. In addition to their victimization and persecution as a minority religious and cultural group prior to the revolution, they also suffered, like other Ethiopians, as a result of conditions prevailing in postrevolutionary Ethiopian society. Unlike other Ethiopians, however, their migration involved most of the families in their villages and was directed toward a specific destination ready and waiting to receive them. That home was Israel. From the mid-1970s onward they journeyed to Israel. In the beginning, they were able to travel directly and secretly from Ethiopia to the Middle East, but later circumstances demanded that they enter third or fourth countries en route to their destination.

PERSONAL VIEW

Like many others, I became interested in the whole dramatic episode of the Beta Israel immigration. I was especially interested to learn how the Ethiopians would fare in such a profoundly different society as Israel. After all, most of the Beta Israel came from one of the most conservative, rural regions of Ethiopia, where modern means of communication and transportation were undeveloped, illiteracy among the adult population was more than 90 percent, and isolation has been the norm for centuries. Furthermore, for the Beta Israel, the migration process included most of the families of the community—women and children as well as men. One's ability to survive in a foreign land was not the issue. Finally, as one who was born and brought up in the region, I was curious to learn how "we"—meaning rural Gondar-Tigray Ethiopians—behave or cope with this kind of situation. After all, such a phenomenon on this scale has never before taken place in Ethiopia. Equally important, perhaps, as an emigre myself, now living in the United States for near two decades, and always feeling that I was deprived of the exciting opportunities of continuing to work, live, and find fulfillment in my own society, I decided to seize the occasion to study the conditions of the Beta Israel in the context of Israel. In addition, I was brought up in religious community, and the Bible in its historical context holds an abiding emotional and intellectual interest for me. I have always been interested in the traditions of Judaism and later in Israel. My visit to the land in the 1960s deepened my interest. As it turned out, and perhaps not surprising, the experiences of living and working with the immigrants for a total of fifteen months proved rewarding beyond my expectations.

In 1969, as a guest of the Ministry of Foreign Affairs of the Israeli government, I had visited Israel for a period of two weeks. At the time, I was an officer at Haile Selassie I University in Ethiopia. I enjoyed the experience of visiting Israel's institutions of education and research as well as the exchange of ideas with policymakers, academics, and teachers. I was impressed by how the state had organized itself to achieve its goals and by the dynamism of its institutions and people. In 1974, I left Ethiopia on sabbatical for a year. I didn't return until the summer of 1991, for a short visit, right after the Mengistu Hailemariam regime was ousted by the Ethiopian Peoples Democratic Revolutionary Front.

I have been following the developments in Ethiopia, of course, including the migration of the people. In the mid-1970s, I was paying particular attention to the movements of the Beta Israel. However, I was not able to make the trip to Israel or to the Sudan until the summer of 1985. With some assistance from the Office of the Vice President for Research at the University of Michigan, I made an exploratory visit to Israel to acquaint myself with the issues concerning the policy, procedure, and patterns of settlement of the Ethiopian Jews in Israel and to get a general but firsthand impression of the issues from the perspectives of both the immigrants and the larger Israeli community. My primary concern was to determine how the phenomenon could best be studied, analyzed, and documented so that verifiable knowledge would be available to the scholarly community, policymakers, and service providers as well as to the *olim* (immigrants) themselves.[42]

This visit was followed by another in the summer of 1986, when I returned to discuss some of the logistics, methods, and instruments with Israeli colleagues and friends (recent Ethiopian immigrants and veteran Israelis). After returning home and having refined my thinking on the tools needed for the project, I returned to Israel one more, this time under the auspices of the Fulbright Senior Scholar Program and the Hebrew University of Jerusalem for the duration of a ten-month period between September 1986 and June 1987. I made my headquarters at the Hebrew University in Jerusalem as a visiting professor and research fellow at the Truman Institute for the Study of Peace. From there, I traveled at least once, often more, to nearly every place the Beta Israel were to be found. In collaboration with some colleagues at the University of Michigan, I had originally developed highly stratified and structured instruments for the research. This involved questionnaires and projective techniques which involved a lot of written responses. But once in the field, I came to learn that the community to be studied was in a situation of very high flux and that the language problems were quite involved and perhaps insoluble. Many of the people were not literate even in their own languages; the children and young people were in transition between learning the new language, Hebrew, and forgetting their own native languages, Amharic and Tigrigna. Although I am a native speaker of Amharic and am conversant in Tigrigna, I became convinced that methods other than those I had developed would yield better results. During the year of fieldwork, the majority of the Beta Israel were in transition from temporary absorption centers where they had stayed during the previous year to permanent apartments; some of the young adults were beginning to enter the labor force; and those between twelve and eighteen years of age were being transferred to boarding schools. In the same year, those in the age groups spanning four to eleven years were being "mainstreamed" into regular schools. Given these circumstances, I decided the best option was to follow the people wherever they went —to talk with them and listen and to observe what was being said, done, or considered in the context of the respective locations from the points of view of the immigrants as well as the agents of the absorbing society. Therefore, participatory observation and interview methods were utilized. Although the immigrants were scattered in more than fifty different locations, Israel's small size made it possible to travel from one location to another in a matter of a few hours. I visited, talked with, and observed all kinds of people in schools, training centers, absorbing centers, permanent homes, workshops, employment centers, and wherever else Beta Israel parents, families, and students could be found. I also observed and talked to many teachers, social workers, physicians, psychologists, anthropologists, school administrators (including officials at the Ministry of Education, absorption administrators, and politicians at the highest level), house mothers, food supervisors, rabbis, administrators, and academics who had contact with the *olim*. I sat in classes, conferred with school personnel, participated at playgrounds, and visited workplaces, homes, dormitories, clinics, and synagogues. The objective was to get as much information as possible by means of direct observation and interaction from as many angles and sources and sources as possible. To aid my senses, as well as my span of attention, and to capture some of the finer nuances, such as gestures, tones of voice, mealtime rituals, and other more subtle but important expressions, I employed video tapes, tape recorders, and still camera. As a supplement to my extensive field notes, the information collected with this system of modern technology proved a boon. The analysis of data incorporates information collected and recorded from all these sources. Where I felt necessary, and in order to protect personal and institutional identities, I have refrained from disclosing full names in all instances.

Initially, it was suggested that I might encounter some difficulties from the Beta Israel because I am a non-Jewish Ethiopian and the community, on the whole, might be suspicious regarding meeting and interacting with outsiders. I gave these suggestions little credence. I knew that given adequate knowledge of my intentions and my own personal feelings toward the whole episode that had precipitated their departure from Ethiopia, they would accept me readily. Outsiders often tend to underestimate the strength of the ties that bind Ethiopians of all persuasions, in spite of the many differences we may have based in religion or ethnicity. In addition, when we meet one another outside our country, special feelings emerge which serve to draw us closer together. So once the initial formalities were over, the reception I received from all quarters could not have been better. The immigrants showed tremendous warmth and generosity toward me, which helped the research to proceed smoothly and made the process enjoyable. The project demanded long hours of work, but given the atmosphere that prevailed, it was an experience that made the inconveniences less important. The veteran Israelis—and this includes all categories and levels of people who had something to do with the Beta Israel immigrants—were cooperative and generous. There was a readiness to facilitate the kind of project I was undertaking. I was fortunate. I hope they all will be able to see a part of their efforts in this book.

CHAPTER TWO

❖

Israel as an Absorbing State

❖

The purpose of this chapter is to provide some brief historical background to our main concern, the absorption of the Ethiopian Jews into Israeli society. It does not aim at providing an extensive account; there already exists a rich body of materials on the social, economic, and political history of Israel. Our intention here is to present a panoramic view of the history and people of Israel to assist those readers who may not be familiar with Israel but are interested in the present topic. The bibliography at the end of this book will help those readers wishing to pursue the subject in greater detail.

Modern Israel is truly a land for Jewish immigrants. It was conceived and built on the fundamental Zionist principle that ultimately the Jews, who until recently have been scattered over most of the face of the globe, are to find a place of "ingathering" in their original home, the land of Israel. Furthermore, the concepts of ingathering and settlement were based on the fundamental Zionist and European socialist ideologies that held that the Jewish people who had sojourned in different parts of the world among strangers, as minorities, and in the process had acquired modes of behavior and of making a living not always compatible with traditional Jewish ideals, would become rehabilitated once in the land of their ancestors, where they would build an egalitarian, social-democratic state. On the whole, Israeli society was built on the quadruple principles of social democracy, modernization, integration, and Zionism. But first let us go back to the pre-state period and examine how these ideas germinated and developed.

THE *YISHUV* (JEWISH PALESTINIAN) SOCIETY

Palestine was ruled for some four hundred years by the Turks until the end of World War I, when, because of their alliance with the Axis powers, they lost control of the territory. During the period of Turkish rule, no census seems to have been taken of the population of Palestine or of its composition and characteristics. However, even from the incomplete records available, it is possible to gain some idea about the various communities, including the Jewish one, that inhabited the land. Some historians support the notion that some Jews had continued to live in Palestine since ancient times, and certainly some Jewish communities have lived there since Medieval times, side by side with Christians and Muslims. The estimate is that in 1800, out of a total of 300,000 persons, 5,000 were Jews, 25,000 were Christians, and 270,000 were Muslims. The Jews of the period were mostly of Sephardic (Spanish) origin and lived in the four holy cities of Jerusalem, Safed, Tiberias, and Hebron. The Christian community, largely comprised of Greek Orthodox and Greek and Roman Catholic, lived in Jerusalem, Nazareth, and Bethlehem.[1] Because of improved health and living conditions and a continuing trickle of immigrants, the Jewish population had grown by 1982 to 24,000.[2] Also by that time, a Jewish community of considerable size had established itself in the port city of Jaffa, today a suburb of Tel Aviv. This Jewish community consisted, by and large, of extremely orthodox people whose lives revolved around their synagogues, religious schools, and charitable organizations.

Following a series of large-scale pogroms in czarist Russia in 1881 and 1882, mass emigration of European (largely Russian and Polish) Jewry began. First by the thousands, then by the hundreds of thousands, Jews migrated to the United States, to central and western Europe, and to Latin America. In 1882, a group of young Russian Jews calling themselves Bilu, supported by a movement known as Hovevei Zion ("Lovers of Zion"), emigrated to Palestine and later established agricultural settlements there. Despite the many hardships they encountered, this group of young pioneers persisted and later were joined by other immigrants of similar persuasion. This continued until 1903 and constituted the first of the five waves of *aliyot* (immigrations). During this First *aliyah*, between twenty thousand and thirty thousand Jews migrated to Palestine. In the meantime, the Dreyfus trial in France and the change it helped to bring, about in a young Viennese Jewish journalist—Theodor Herzl—led to a growing interest of western European Jews in the idea of establishing a Jewish settlement in Palestine. Herzl, regarded as the father of modern Zionism, worked hard and long to marshal the sympathies and support of Europe's powerful and wealthy for the idea. He organized the first World Zionist Congress, held in Basel in 1897, at which the World Zionist Organization (WZO) was founded, with Herzl as president, to facilitate the immigration and settlement of Jews in Palestine. Between 1904 and 1914, the second *aliyah* brought between thirty-five thousand and forty thousand Jewish immigrants to Palestine, largely from Russia (Poland was, of course, part of Russia until the end of World War I). These waves of immigrants, consisting of organized Polish and Russian Jews, arrived in Palestine with new social and political visions which ultimately left an indelible mark on the development of the state and affected the environment that subsequent waves of immigrants were to enter. In search of solutions to the economic, political, and social problems in their countries of origin in general and to the problems of Jews in particular, many of those who arrived during the second *aliyah* had been associated with socialist movements in eastern Europe prior to their arrival in Palestine. Their hopes for social change in their lands of origin had failed. The renewed anti-Jewish pogroms and the failure of the 1905 revolution to address their many problems must have convinced them that their best recourse was immigration to Palestine and the hastening of the organization of the Zionist movement. This group, consisting mostly of young, unattached, highly motivated people who had rebelled not only against the conditions of the Jewish people in Europe but against their own parents and elders as well, brought with them what they considered the contemporary ideals and sought to fuse them with the precepts and traditions of a nationalistic Judaism in which religious orthodoxy played no significant role. As mentioned earlier, their influence on the shaping of the eventual state of Israel was enormous. As Judah Matras observes: "This wave of immigrants did become the political, social, economic, and ideological backbone of the Jewish community in Palestine, and large sectors of life in Israel today are organized around institutions created by immigrants arriving in the Second Aliyah."[3]

Then came World War I, which disrupted immigration. The World Zionist Organization, now led by Chaim Weizmann, a chemist whose inventions had been of military importance to the British, continued actively to promote the aspirations of the Zionist movement. Weizmann's patience, persistence, and usefulness eventually led the British government to recognize these aspirations in the form of the Balfour Declaration. The declaration, issued as a letter on November 2, 1917, to Lord Rothschild by Arthur Balfour of the Foreign Service, stated: "His Majesty's Government view with favour the establishment in Palestine of a national home for the Jewish people, and will use their best endeavors to facilitate the achievement of this object, it being clearly understood that nothing shall be done which may prejudice the civil and religious rights of existing non-Jewish communities in Palestine or the rights and political status enjoyed by Jews in any other community."[4] The declaration, which was endorsed by President Woodrow Wilson of the United States, signaled the beginning of a British vision of Palestine. Within a month, the British had forced the Turks to withdraw. In 1922, the declaration was incorporated into the League of Nations' Mandate for Palestine. The mandate identified the WZO as the representative of Jewish interests to advise and cooperate with the British government in matters pertaining to the "establishment of the Jewish National Home."

Soon after the conclusion of the war in 1919, the migration of Jews to Palestine resumed, now under British supervision. Between the years 1919 and 1923, the third *aliyah*, an estimated thirty-five thousand immigrants, arrived in Palestine. This was made possible by the favorable climate that prevailed during the first part of the mandate period and by the Bolshevik revolution which exerted pressure on Zionist Jews to leave Russia. Like the previous two groups of immigrants, this third group arrived primarily from Russia and Poland. However, these immigrants were different from the two earlier groups: prior to their departure from their respective lands of origin, they had formed groups and had undergone training to prepare them for life in Palestine.

The waves of immigration continued. Between 1924 and 1931, some eighty-two thousand new immigrants arrived in Palestine. Roughly 86 percent of this fourth *aliyah* came from Poland. Primarily middle class, this group came to Palestine partly to escape the economic depression. But anti-Semitic sentiment was increasing, partly because of hard times in Poland, and the United States refused to accept more migrants from eastern Europe regardless of the unique situation of the Jews. Two other characteristics of the people comprising this *aliyah* are especially noteworthy. First, some two thousand were Jews from North America. Though small vis-à-vis other nationalities, this number represents the first significant wave of migration from North America. Secondly, ninety-two hundred, or slightly more than 11 percent of the immigrants who arrived between 1924 and 1931, came from non-European countries such as Yemen, Iraq, Persia, and Turkey. Compared to their relatively small representation among the third *aliyah*, (5 percent), this is a marked increase. But during the same period, twenty-three thousand people left Palestine primarily for economic reasons, reducing the total Jewish population to one hundred seventy-five thousand.

During the fifth *aliyah* of the pre-state period, yet another group of immigrants arrived. The years 1932 to 1938 witnessed the rise of the Nazis to power in Germany, deterioration of economic conditions in Europe, and the accompanying search for scapegoats. As this was happening in Europe, economic conditions also were worsening in the Middle Eastern countries. The net result was that many Jewish communities found themselves in very untenable positions which eventually prompted them to migrate to Palestine. During this period of the fifth *aliyah*, more than two hundred seventeen thousand Jewish immigrants arrived in Palestine. They came from Germany, Austria, Poland, the Soviet Union, Romania, Greece, Yemen, and Aden. In addition to the diverse origins, this aliyah was unique in other respects. The immigrants were older, relatively fewer were single, and the ratio between males and females was nearly normal for the first time, that is, there were proportionally more women in this group than in earlier ones. This aliyah also brought many people with skills and capital. There came experienced and well-established businessmen and members of the liberal professions. Upon arrival, they established many businesses and enterprises as well as commercial and cultural institutions. By 1938, the Jews in Palestine numbered four hundred thirteen thousand. These figures probably include illegal as well as legal immigrants.

Toward the end of the pre-state period, and with the onset of World War II, the rate of immigration slowed down considerably. Conflicts between Jewish settlers and the indigenous as well as other Arabs had existed for years, but these conflicts grew in number and seriousness in the 1920s and 1930s. As the number of Jews in Palestine increased, local Arab leaders expressed their opposition. As a result, the British Mandatory Government issued its 1939 White Paper on Palestine, which restricted the number of Jewish immigrants to a total of fifteen thousand during the ensuing five-year period. It also stipulated that at the end of the five years, no more Jewish immigrants would be allowed to enter without the consent of the Arab population. The policy was in force throughout World War II, while millions of Jews were trapped and suffering in Europe. Despite efforts to control the number of immigrants, some forty-six thousand European Jews were permitted legal entry, and another twenty-nine thousand entered illegally. In addition, another seventeen thousand arrived from non-European countries.

IN THE AFTERMATH OF THE HOLOCAUST

At the close of World War II in 1945, some two hundred thousand Jews from Russia, Poland, Germany, and other countries were among the many people classified as "displaced persons" by the Allied powers. Temporary measures were taken to shelter and feed them in refugee camps. The Mandatory Government stood by its decision to restrict the number of Jews allowed to enter Palestine legally. Other means were found. One way or another, most of the immigrants from the refugee camps in Cyprus and elsewhere eventually found their way to Palestine. The process was, however, not without intrigue and controversy, involving as it did the United States, Great Britain, and the Arab governments as well as Jewish organizations. Altogether, during the period of the mandate (1919–1948), some four hundred eighty-seven thousand Jews set up their new homes in Palestine, including some fifty-three thousand who had arrived initially as visitors but stayed on. Of the world's total Jewish emigrants between the years 1919 and 1948, about 30 percent came to Palestine. Of these, 80 percent came from Europe, 10 percent from Asia, and 3 percent from North and South

America, Africa, and Oceania.[5] Most Jews in Palestine were concentrated in the three largest cities of Tel Aviv, Haifa, and Jerusalem; only about 15 percent lived in rural settlements. This pattern of settlement would have repercussions on the dispersion of subsequent immigrants, particularly those coming from Africa and Asia, for whom successful absorption and integration were major goals.

The preceding analysis shows that the formation of the *Yishuv* (the Jewish community of Palestine), which took place over a relatively short time, was a community created by immigrants as well as one absorbing them. The axioms often made that the quality of immigrant absorption is a function of immigrant role expectations on the one hand and the demands made on them by the established society through its institutions on the other could not hold true here since the Yishuv community did not have sufficient time to institutionalize its demands. In other words, the requisite institutional framework through which immigrants could be absorbed was not fully organized or established. It was only through the interaction between the succession of immigrants, mainly between the two world wars, that such institutional structures emerged. In addition, except for the relatively few immigrants from Africa and Asia, most of the immigrants were of European background who presumably had some broadly shared cultural, political, and ideological reference points as well as similar aspirations informed by the harsh economic, political, social, and cultural realities of Europe. Whatever differences existed, members of this European majority must have had a relatively easy time communicating with one another about the type of society they wished to create and the strategy or means for establishing the framework. At any rate, unique in the history of immigrants, a complete dispersion took place, with only a few exceptions such as the Orientals and some Jews from central Europe. Dispersion is considered one of the most important elements in the absorption and integration of immigrants in the host society. For the Yishuv this happy coincidence occurred, but it would not repeat itself when immigrants from the non-European regions began to arrive en masse. By the time state sovereignty was achieved, the Jewish community was well solidified; the institutional frameworks it wished to develop and behavioral norms it desired to cultivate in the new state were defined. Those arriving later were required to conform to the norms and role expectations of the "establishment."

ISRAEL AFTER 1948

In the aftermath of World War II, the Jews of Palestine and their allies elsewhere concentrated their efforts on addressing the issues of Jewish immigration, the fulfillment of the Balfour Declaration, and the provisions adopted by the United Nations. Such nationalist aspirations and activities were the rule of the day, for following the war, many heretofore colonized countries were seeking their independence and freedom from European powers. But what distinguishes the Jewish claims from the others is that the Jews were not agitating for equal rights, independence, civil rights, and so on, as most of the others were doing. Rather, they were agitating for an ingathering of Jewish immigrants to Palestine to colonize it and establish the right to enjoy their Zionist or national aspirations there. Eventually, the Mandatory power, Great Britain, was forced to bring the matter before the United Nations, which led to the decision to partition Palestine between the Jews and the Arabs. It is not surprising, therefore, that in 1950, two years after the attainment of statehood, Israel enacted the Law of Return, declaring the right of all Jews everywhere to immigrate to Israel. This policy of *kibbutz galuyot*, or ingathering of exiles, was in complete accord with the cardinal aim of Zionism: to reestablish a Jewish state on the land of ancient Israel, which would serve as the instrument for the fulfillment of the Jewish.[6]

The migration of world Jewry to Israel is best understood when viewed in the framework of the total demographic perspective. Since the dichotomies between the different subcultures within the communities are pivotal in our analysis of ethnicity, pluralism, and equality, we will take some space to highlight some of the more outstanding characteristics of the different groups. For one thing, the dispersal of the community at the global level is very interesting. Although the division of Jews into different categories of Ashkenazim, Sephardim, and Orientals presents some methodological problems, the following statistical patterns emerge. The total Jewish population in the world in the year 1500 was one and a half million.[7] Of this total the vast majority (67 percent) were of Sephardic-Oriental origin. In the same year, some five thousand Jews were living in Palestine, of whom 80 percent were of Sephardic-Oriental origin. By 1800, the world's Jews numbered about two and a half million, of whom the Sephardic-Oriental sect or comprised 40 percent. In the same year, the Jewish population living in Palestine was eight thousand, 60 percent of whom were Sephardic-Oriental. From 1895 on, the global Ashkenazim population increased dramatically; in that year, the global total stood at ten million, of whom only 10 percent were Sephardic-Oriental. In Palestine, the total Jewish population was forty seven thousand of whom 40 percent were Sephardic-Oriental. From then on, the Sephardic-Oriental population continued to shrink relative to the global total until in 1975 it constituted only 17 percent of 14,145,000. However, as the relative number decreased at the global level, it increased in Israel. Of the approximately three million Jews in Israel in 1975, the Sephardic-Oriental group constituted 55 percent of that total. Thus, although the total Sephardic-Oriental population in the world is now less than 17 percent, in Israel it constitutes a significant and growing majority. By 1985, 58 percent of the Jews in Israel were of Sephardic-Oriental background. Although there has been some moderation in recent years, the birth rate of the Sephardic-Oriental segment of the population in Israel is higher than that of the Ashkenazim (except for the ultra-Orthodox, who tend to have large families). With these facts in mind, we now return to Israel proper.

At the time of the creation of the state of Israel in 1948, the total Jewish population stood at 716,678. Of this total, 35 percent had been born in Palestine. Of those born abroad, 85 percent had been born in Europe, America, or Oceania; 12 percent in Asia; and only 3 percent in Africa. Of those who had come from Europe, at least in the earlier *aliyot*, many were single persons, while most from Asia and Africa already had formed families before their arrival. Those Ashkenazim who came as single persons then eventually met each other in the context of forging a Jewish state in Palestine, indicating bonds of shared aspirations and experiences. When children were later born to these couples in Palestine, the parents were in the position to inculcate in their offspring the spirit of pioneering Zionism. The same cannot be said for the Oriental groups, since families were already formed and in all likelihood children were born both in the land of origin and after arrival in Palestine.

Upon attainment of statehood, the migration of Jews to Israel accelerated. Within the first two and a half years, the Jewish population doubled, and by 1960 it had tripled, most of the increase coming from immigration.[8] Between May 1948 and the end of 1984, more than one and three-quarter million immigrants arrived in Israel, in contrast with fewer than five hundred thousand who came to Palestine between 1882 and 1948. This great influx of immigrants, of course, overwhelmed the new state. The number, the diversity of immigrant backgrounds, and the speed with which the migration took place all would have significant consequences for absorption and integration. Transporting, settling, and caring for the influx of mostly poor immigrants placed an inordinate burden on the receiving society, which on the whole shouldered it heroically.

Soon after the attainment of statehood, priority for migration was given to the Jews of Europe who were in displaced persons camps in Germany, Austria, and Italy. When the camps were emptied of their initial occupants, they continued to be used as transit points for others waiting to migrate. In addition, those Jews whom the British had interned in Cyprus as "illegals"—Jews trying to enter Palestine without their permission—now were brought in as well. Also during this mass immigration period of 1948 to 1951, one hundred thousand Polish and one hundred twenty thousand Romanian Jews migrated to Israel. During the same period, non-European Jews began to arrive in unprecedented numbers. Between 1949 and 1950, during what became known as Operation Magic Carpet, forty thousand Jews from Yemen were flown to Israel. During the same period, almost the entire Jewish community of Libya was transferred. In the following year, 1950-51, one hundred twenty-four thousand Jews from Iraq and twenty-seven thousand from Persia immigrated. The differences in geographic origin, and hence the sociocultural differences, were very pronounced, obviously. Of the total number of Jewish immigrants to Israel of the 1948-51 period, only about half were from Europe, about 35 percent were from Asian countries (mostly from Iraq, Yemen, Persia, and Turkey), and another 14 percent were from North African countries (primarily Morocco, Tunisia, Algeria, and Libya); that is, about half were from what are known as the Third World countries of Asia and Africa. The pattern continued. Of the total number of immigrants who came between 1948 and 1975, 50 percent were from African and Asian countries (Orientals). During the years of 1952 and 1953, there was a slight decrease in the number of immigrants primarily because Israel's altered policy to give first priority in aid to those individuals and communities whose security was threatened, second to those whose skills were required by the state, and only as the third priority to others. But even during this time, only 29 percent were of Ashkenazi background. The largest group was of African and Asian origin, 42 and 28 percent of the total, respectively. This is in sharp contrast to the 90 percent of Ashkenazim immigrants who came during the Mandate period.

The explanations for this profound change in the origin and cultural backgrounds of Jewish immigrants to Israel are not obscure: the wholesale destruction of the masses of European Jewry outside Russia between 1939 and 1945; the refusal of the Russians to allow Russian Jews to emigrate in any significant number; the general satisfaction of the remaining large communities of "western" Jews—in the United States and Canada, South America, England, and South Africa—with their conditions and opportunities in their countries; and, on the other hand, the low status of, and quite often marked discrimination against, Jews in Asian and African countries. But the point to be emphasized is that the very pronounced shift in the kind of immigrant who now entered Israel, as distinguished from the kind of immigrant who had come to what had been Palestine, was not just a shift from one kind of culture to another but also a shift in expectations. Jews now were coming to a country in which Jews were in charge—and it was still foreign, alien, and frustrating. Also, most of the Oriental Jews who came now had lived among Arabs for centuries and found that the Jews in charge in Israel knew comparatively little about them. These differences, too, had profound repercussions, not only for Israel but for its Arab neighbors.[9]

There were still other complications. The birth rate of people of Asian and African origin was much higher than that of the Ashkenazim. For instance, in 1960, the Jewish population stood at 1,911,000, representing a 267 percent net increase over the 1948 population; 69 percent of this growth in population was a result of net immigration, and 31 percent was natural increase. During this twelve-year period, the number of children younger than ten quadrupled. The Jewish population of Asian birth increased five-fold and that of African birth increased fifteen-fold. New centers were opened for settlement to accommodate this influx and the rural population quadrupled. Immigrants came from 89 different countries.[10] Because of the great pressures to accept and settle this influx, of new immigrants, insufficient thought was given to the long-term implications for absorption and integration of these settlements. Those arriving from the developing countries came as groups and wished to settle in close proximity to one another in Israel so that they would not lose the kind of communal traditions they had enjoyed in their lands of origin. The Orientals also expected not only to practice their Judaism as they had developed it but also to maintain their other communal, cultural, or economic values from their lands of origin. This was a major difference between the Ashkenazim and the Orientals in the Yishuv and it remained critically important in Israel. As a result, the form and substance of the Zionist dialogue within the Jewish state became altered, perhaps irreversibly. The Orientals were perceived by the Ashkenazim as coming from underdeveloped, semi-feudal, and traditional societies, with different types of aspirations (primarily religious Zionism) and different expectations and perceptions of political goals.[11] Moreover, the Oriental immigrants had large families and were mostly poor, without education and without modern skills. On the whole, they were generally unprepared to participate fully in a modern, Westernized society such as Israel. The existing society perceived the coming of the Orientals as a challenge. They had to be socialized, trained, and acculturated to Western modes of behavior, which was considered imperative for modernization. Perhaps it is fair to say that as far as the Orientals were concerned, the only things they had in common with the predominantly Ashkenazi society existing then in Israel was their Jewishness as defined in broad terms, a common desire to develop and use the Hebrew language, and an abiding concern for the security and survival of the Jewish state.

The concern for security, survival, and viability is, of course, in the heart of every Jew in Israel. This is made imperative by a number of realities emanating primarily from the historical circumstances surrounding the founding of the modern state. Israel is a pluralistic state in religion, ethnicity, culture, and nationality. Of the 4.3 million people living in Israel at the end of 1985, for instance, approximately 3.5 million were Jews, representing 81 percent of the total; of the six hundred fifty thousand Israeli Arabs, who constituted some 15 percent of the total population, more than three-fourths were Muslims, 15 percent Christians, and 9 percent Druze. The rest, about 4 percent of the population, were made up of other communities such as members of the various Christian representatives, and the Armenians.[12] In addition there are the two and a half million Palestinian Arabs whose territory was seized from Jordan in 1967 and has since been under Israeli occupation.

To complicate the pluralistic nature of the society of this small state even further, serious divisions exist within the Jewish community. Among the Jews, 70 percent consider themselves to be nonreligious (secular); the remaining 30 percent are religious (different shades of Orthodox). Among the latter are people who not only do not believe in Zionism but actively oppose the instruments set up for the state's existence. Yet the latter are the ones who set up the rules that govern most of the fundamental aspects of life such as the initiations of children, marriage, divorce, and holiday observation. As one might expect, the relationships between the religious and the nonreligious communities are in many respects at cross purposes. Yet there is also an understanding, or so it seems, that one cannot exist without the other. For in Israel, there is no separation of state and religion, even while there are serious disagreements about the reasons why this should be so. The magnitude of the immigration, especially from the African and Asian countries, over a short period of time and the many economic, occupational, and educational challenges it represents must be viewed in this context.

As far as the state was concerned, the greatest challenge was how to marshal the resources needed to address the many problems represented by the immigration of the Orientals. Many other nations, at one time or another, have been confronted with similar problems, but never on the scale Israel faced in the 1950s. The young state was overwhelmed by immigrants who were different in many respects—poor, unskilled, and with different aspirations and worldviews. These important differences made the successful absorption and integration into existing communities problematic. When the immigration of Orientals to Israel was at its zenith, the culture was still being formed, and the institutions were in the conceptual stage and not yet organized. The Orientals came in as the institutional infrastructures for absorption were being put into place. But they were given little opportunity (or perhaps they were unable or not sufficiently mobilized to seize the opportunity) to participate in the shaping of the infrastructure to suit their purposes or even to leave the imprint of their thoughts, hopes, and concerns on these institutions. Instead, the Orientals accepted what existed in the country and tried to align their economic, political, and cultural lots, hopes, and aspirations accordingly. Later they came to regret those lost opportunities.

THE "ORIENTALIZATION" CHALLENGES AND RESPONSES

The mass migration of Oriental Jews to Israel was perceived by the receiving Ashkenazi society as the Orientalization of Israel, a formidable challenge to the concept of *mizug galuyot* (the fusion and integration of exiles). As was alluded to earlier in this chapter, the African and Asian Jews—the Orientals— were perceived as backward in their economic, cultural, educational, occupational, and technological backgrounds as well as in their general sense of civic responsibilities. To the Ashkenazim, this implied that a massive program of modernization had to be undertaken at once.[13] Their orientation had to include aspirations for the "national" culture and solidarity. The possibility that certain aspects of the Afro-Asian cultures might be worth keeping, perhaps fusing them with the best ones in existence, was not entertained. Instead, the Orientals' traditions were considered obstacles to modernization. It was imperative to wipe out the inferior traditions of the Oriental immigrants and replace them with Ashkenazim traditions and Western attitudes and behavior. The primary objective was to achieve behavioral assimilation. Structural assimilation was also sought, though pursued with much less vigor.[14] The key word was *assimilation*, reflecting the vision that Israel could become a "melting pot" for Jews from a wide range of backgrounds.[15] This same vision once was held for the United States.

The task involved the desocialization, socialization, and resocialization of the Orientals.[16] The Orientals were expected to abandon those values and traditions that were considered incompatible with and indeed obstacles to the modernization they were to achieve as they learned and accepted new attitudes, behaviors, and skills in line with the conditions and expectations of life in Israeli society. However, many scholars say that while the efforts to resocialize and educate the Afro-Asians were necessary and indeed commendable, the premises on which these efforts were based and the way they were carried out left much to be desired. In several ways, the policies were similar to those of the European colonialists toward their Asian and African subjects up until the first half of this century. As Klaff made clear, in the 1950s (and even today), there were strong convictions among the Ashkenazi settlers and a good segment of the academic community of Israel about what social and cultural characteristics should become dominant in the future of Israeli society. The Ashkenazim "believed the absorption of new immigrants required giving up previous habits, customs, etc., and adopting the traditions of the veteran community, approach similar to the 'Anglo-conformity' concept in American literature. This assimilative perspective has tended to persist in Israeli sociology with the issue of ethnic integration seen as a problem of modernization of immigrants from Asian and African countries."[17]

Voices arguing the opposite views were not lacking, however. For instance, Selzer[18] maintained that the positions taken by the veteran Ashkenazim were nothing less than deliberate discrimination against the Asian-African communities which led to the destruction of the latter's culture. He claimed that all cultures have equal validity and that in a democratic state cultural pluralism should be encouraged and cherished. Selzer's position was, criticized however, by Cohen,[19] who argued that the cultural traits brought and maintained by the Afro-Asians were neither endemic nor desired by the people concerned and that these cultural traits are not suited to the life-style of a modern technological society.

The affected groups on their part could not be faulted for not trying to accept and internalize the roles assigned to them. Shuval, in her study of an ethnically mixed housing project, found that the Ashkenazim were ranked highest and the Moroccan group lowest in status. The same study also showed that the Moroccans ranked themselves lower than the Ashkenazim. Shuval added that in their desire to gain acceptance, the northern Africans were conforming to norms and values defined by the dominant group of the society, even when they saw evidence of discrimination against themselves.[20] Weingrod further elaborated on the depth of perception of the hierarchical status symbols: "To come from Poland or Britain is, ipso facto, to be more prestigious than to have one's origins in Egypt or Iraq. This rift is fundamental, and it runs throughout the [Israeli] society."[21]

After studying the residential pattern of ethnic distribution, Bachi reached a similar conclusion. He generalized that "the most marked contrast was found between the geographical distribution of people of Polish and Russian origin (who constituted both the largest group among veteran settlers and the largest European group), and that of people from Morocco, Tunisia and Algeria (being both the largest non-European group and the largest group among new immigrants)."[22] Klaff added that the evidence demonstrates that ethnic distribution patterns in Israel represent a "mosaic of segregated people."[23]

Inequalities, real and perceived, could have been minimized if it had been possible for the communities to live in proximity to one another so that they would interact and hence come to know and understand one another's habits and values. But this was not possible. The Yishuv had settled mostly in the major cities, and, as pointed out already, there was no congregation of immigrants based on country of origin. The European immigrants, even when they came from different parts of Europe, were able to communicate with and understand one another. But the Orientals arriving after the establishment of Israel were increasingly brought to settlements far removed from the cities. Moreover, they were also settled by groups based on their association in the land of origin. The Ashkenazi immigrants placed in settlement towns later moved out to urban environments and better opportunities while the Orientals stayed on. In summarizing the residential patterns studied, Klaff concluded that "the data confirms that the closer the geographic and cultural character of the country of origin, the more similar the residential distribution of two populations [Ashkenazim and Orientals]."[24]

EDUCATION

Educational institutions often are thought to be the best agencies for the absorption and integration of immigrants. They are able to draw people from diverse home backgrounds. They try to impart common values, goals, ideology, and skills as no other single institution can. The development and progress of institutions of education in the absorption of immigrants therefore deserve separate consideration.

The Jewish people have been known as "people of the book," indicating their rich traditions and the great respect held by families and individuals for high literacy, learning, and scholarship. The home, the synagogue, and formal learning institutions are the major means of perpetuating that tradition. However, the amount of dedication to learning and scholarship varied among the Jewish people during the centuries of the Diaspora. Whereas European Jewry was, in the main, dedicated to the pursuit of religious and secular education, Jews living in the Middle East, Asia, and Africa associated education with religion—to be pursued by religious leaders or those aspiring to assume some kind of leadership in aspects of religion. Mass literacy and aspirations to achieve intellectual eminence in secular fields were not necessarily a part of all Oriental or Sephardic traditions. This was mostly a reflection of the largely Muslim host countries. To a large extent, these differences between the Ashkenazim and Oriental groups were carried to Israel and persist to this day.

In Israel, educational and training enterprises are operated by several governmental, quasi-governmental, and nongovernmental agencies such as the Ministry of Education, the Jewish Agency, the Histadrut (Labor Federation), the armed forces, and other independent religious or secular organizations. Throughout the Yishuv, primary schooling was maintained under the auspices of the different "trends" —namely, the general, religious, and labor. Each of the trends was associated with a political party, and each espoused a variant of the traditions of eastern and central European Jewish education. Each tried to use its influence to inculcate its nationalist, religious, or socialist brand of ideology and party politics. This diversity of approaches to national education was further complicated by the organization, control, and administration of the secondary school system. The secondary schools were not affiliated with any political party; they were independent and primarily under private ownership, with the exception of a very few vocational schools similar to the gymnasia type in central Europe. The British Mandatory Government tried on several occasions to unify the elementary and secondary school systems along lines similar to those adopted by the Arab Palestinians, but their proposals were rejected out of fear of British cultural domination.

The demise of the trend system began to occur with the influx of immigrants from northern Africa and other Middle Eastern countries in the late 1940s. Immigrants had always been courted for their affiliation with the political parties. The schools and youth movements were means of political recruitment and indoctrination. But now, since most of the Oriental immigrants were religious, the labor trend, which was not religious, rushed to patronize them—going so far as to establish a subreligious system. This political step aroused open rivalry and accusations among the political parties supporting the trends. The matter was referred to the Knesset resulting in a coalition crisis and the resignation of the government. Finally, after two years of negotiations, the State Education Law was put into effect in 1953. This law abolished the trend system and replaced it with a unified system under the purview of the Ministry of Education and Culture. The primary education system was divided into two categories: state schools and state religious schools. With the exception of emphasis on religious studies, the curricula, under the supervision of the Ministry of Education, were standard across schools. This legislation brought some relief, but dissensions arising from party politics, especially between the religious and labor or socialist wings, continued under numerous pretexts.

Since the establishment of the state, education has been conceived as a major tool for the cultural, political, and social integration of the olim and for the forging of a unified society out of the disparate ethnic groups. However, as already noted, the underlying assumptions or principles of immigrant absorption were based on two of the valued premises of political Zionism: the collective particularism of the Jewish aspirations for an independent national state and the universalism of modern Western civilization (the ultra-Orthodox wing of the religious party, Agudut Israel, has its own agenda which is completely at variance with these principles). With these premises in mind, the absorption of immigrants was conceived as a complete reeducation or resocialization of the newcomer, who in the process was to become a new person.[25] The Oriental immigrants were expected to forgo and forsake their past, including their Diaspora traditions, values, and cultures. Although in the majority, as latecomers who suffered from high rates of illiteracy, low skill levels, and lack of democratic experiences, they were required to adopt European standards and characteristics in order to become participating members of Israeli society. The challenges of absorbing immigrants from Europe were not so formidable, since their cultural values were close to those being promoted in Israel. With the passing of time and the increased influx from Asia and Africa, this unitary concept of absorption and integration became increasingly untenable, so much so that it was explicitly challenged by the affected groups as unrealistic and discriminatory to the Orientals.[26] These challenges gave rise to a realignment of thinking in an accommodationist mode.

Returning specifically to education, the gaps between the Orientals and the Ashkenazim widened. The Orientals lagged seriously behind in completing even their primary level education. Only a few were able to pass the seker, the examination used for admission to the second level of education. At the secondary level, the dropout rate was very high, and very few Oriental students were admitted to postsecondary or tertiary institutions. As the Ashkenazim moved into the first-rate academic high schools that fed the universities, the Orientals were channeled into the previously deserted second-rate technical and vocational schools.[27] In other words, the Orientals were not getting very far with their education, and they knew that without higher education they were not going to get anywhere in Israeli society. In response to these challenges, a series of laws was effected between 1953 and 1978. In many respects, the problems of the Orientals were similar to those which black Americans were experiencing in the

United States. But in the United States, cognizance was taken of the fact that the black minority was not benefiting from the status quo due because of historic racial discrimination. In Israel, the problem was attributed to differences in ethnic background, and the more threatening factor of racial discrimination was not mentioned. In Israel, emphasis was placed on the Diaspora backgrounds of immigrants which, with time and compensatory efforts, would be overcome. In other words, the difficulties were attributed to the environmental rather than genetic backgrounds of the immigrants and were therefore not a result of resistance of the dominant society. At any rate, the specific goals of these laws were to encourage the enrollment of more children in the school systems, to encourage youth to stay in school as long as possible, and to provide extra help for children from disadvantaged backgrounds to enable them to participate as fully as possible in education. More specifically, in 1949, the state provided free and compulsory education for children between the ages of five and fourteen years and for youth ages fourteen to seventeen who lacked elementary education. In 1953, the state abolished the politically oriented trends system in favor of a uniform curriculum for all. The rationale for this law was that it would facilitate the assimilation of the immigrants into the economic, social, and cultural structure of the state.[28] This kind of legislative action was consistent with the "melting pot" paradigm of absorption. But it soon was discovered that universal education and uniform curriculum did not guarantee equal outcomes. Although more students were being admitted to the schools, many were not graduating as expected. For instance, in 1956 to 1957 the ratio of Orientals in the age category of fourteen to seventeen was 55 percent of the total, but their proportion in the secondary schools was only 18 percent; in the academic secondary schools, their representation was even lower, 13 percent. The authorities had to admit that the low achievement of Oriental students was a result of "cognitive deprivation" during their early childhood. This was followed by legislation to provide for "compensatory" education along the lines followed for minorities in the United States. Throughout this period, the aim of education was to "change or adapt Oriental students to the existing structure of the educational system which was elitist and largely responsible for the failure of many Oriental students."[29] The goal of equality of outcome, however, remained elusive. In 1968, the School Reform Law provided for the change of the educational structure from eight-plus-four to six-plus-three-plus-three. The intention was to provide for articulation at each stage so that the performance of students would improve successively at each stage and to encourage social integration. The law also provided for more qualified teachers in the middle schools; a shift in teaching methods which emphasized inquiry rather than verbalization; democratization of the secondary schools through elimination or minimization of formal selection; and introduction of guidance and counseling, provision of kindergarten education, encouragement of parental participation in school endeavors, and fostering greater social interaction with the introduction of busing, rezoning, and the like. But despite these reforms, the gaps remained, especially at the secondary and college levels, with the result that even the self-perceptions of the Oriental children were damaged.[30] Since 1975, there has been some acknowledgment that the problems of relatively poor performance and negative self-image among Oriental students might have to do with the way they are instructed. Specifically, it was concluded that the problems may have more to do with the nature of cultural or ethnic pluralism and less with material inequality between the Ashkenazim and the Orientals.

This recognition gave rise to the concession, hitherto a taboo concept, that ethnic pluralism was a legitimate reality in Israel's life. In 1976, the Ministry of Education announced its intention "to integrate the spiritual heritage of Oriental Jewry into education and culture." Though there remained a general tendency among educators and politicians to negate ethnicity, it was felt that "in order to foster a positive self-image of Oriental children, the culture, traditions, customs and literary heritage of Oriental Jewry should find its place in the one-sided European curriculum."[31] It was alleged that these actions would restore pride among Oriental students, mitigate their feelings of inferiority to the culturally dominant Ashkenazim, and minimize feelings of alienation in Israeli society. It is too early to evaluate the outcomes of this shift in thinking. Casual observation of teaching methods and classroom activities, however, suggests that little real change is occurring. One might conclude that even in the State of Israel, which was created to achieve an egalitarian and just society based on social-democratic principles, the traditional Western ethnocentrism seems to persist.

The education system in Israel today is highly centralized under the Ministry of Education and Culture headed by a cabinet-level officer who is a member of Knesset. This central administration is responsible for the training and certification of school personnel and the curriculum.[32] The country is divided into six regions, each administered by an inspector. The regional offices report to the cabinet minister through the director of education, who is appointed and is typically a professional educator. The responsibilities of the director include the formulation and administration of national policies and supervision of their implementation. The Ministry of Education has two major branches: the state secular branch, which handles the nonreligious education system, and the religious branch. Although both branches have set minimum professional qualifications for teaching staff and administrators, the certification requirements are not exactly the same in both cases. The National Religious Party, which is responsible for the maintenance and operation of the religious branch, guards its schools closely. It is rare that one finds secular professionals working in the religious schools. The secular branch maintains criteria of professional status and employs qualified teachers whether they are religious or secular.

Each branch has its supporters in the Knesset who negotiate politically tight situations. Moreover, the political and religious factions persist in their efforts to recruit individuals or groups of immigrants into their own rank. Recruitment is facilitated by political clubs, youth organizations, kibbutzim, and so on. Recruitment of new immigrants is a very interesting aspect of national politics which, as we will see, affected the Beta Israel.[33]

With this brief background, one can see that even before the arrival of the Beta Israel, the culture, goals, aspirations, and expectations of other Asian and African immigrants challenged the state apparatus and philosophy for absorption and subjected the educational system to severe pressures. As Eisenstadt observes, "The educational system was faced with the fact that the pioneering ideology had lost much of its vividness and drawing power for the new Israeli generation, that it could not be upheld by the teachers, did not appeal to the new immigrants, and did not provide enough common bonds between the old and the new parts of the population."[34]

In conclusion, then, it may be argued that to perceive the Ashkenazim—their values, skills, and achievements—as superior and, in contrast, the Orientals—what they stand for and their traditional values—as inferior is to accept Western criteria of modernity. These include such constructs as income, occupation, education, and power. By these measures, the Orientals are indeed very far behind the Ashkenazim. In other words, inequalities as measured by income, levels of educational achievement, and status attainment are glaringly apparent. The question is how to explain the longevity of the phenomenon, despite the society's serious efforts to rid itself of it. There are, of course, various answers. For instance, Chaim Adler of the Hebrew University, who has studied these issues in depth over a long period of time, points to the fact that the "population dispersion" policy—the settlement of Oriental Jewish immigrants in remote parts of the country—while it may have political and military importance, has tended to aggravate the isolation of this disadvantaged category of citizens.[35]

If, as postulated, social integration in heterogeneous societies such as Israel is to be achieved, one of the primary efforts should be directed at achieving a structural dispersion of the various ethnic groups so that they could interact at the institutional as well as individual levels and thereby come to understand and learn from one another. Behavioral assimilation would be impossible to attain without structural dispersion. In other words, unless the different ethnic groups live in close proximity in residential settings, social integration would be very hard, if not impossible, to achieve. The vexing issues of inequalities or perceived inequalities would persist, which, in turn, would lead to communal friction and disharmony.

As things stand, inequalities among the various ethnic groups, most importantly between the Ashkenazim and the Orientals, continue to exist in educational attainment, employment opportunities, power and status. Why the groups thus negatively affected are not going to the streets in protest as they do in other societies has to do with the external threat Israel is always confronted with. If that threat were reduced, many Israeli scholars think there would be social disruption.

Researchers rule out the notion that such manifest disparities between the two major subgroups of the society leading to inequalities could be explained in terms of biological factors. Rather, they attribute the disparities to the different cultural backgrounds of the two groups. It is admitted that to overcome the deficiencies represented by the cultures and circumstances of the Orientals, massive educational, training, and socialization efforts should be mounted.

Sociologist Sammy Smooha of Haifa University, himself an Oriental Jewish scholar, observes that the founders of it had sought to make Israel as homogeneous and egalitarian as possible. This nonpluralistic vision has led the nation for a long time to assume an ostrich-like stance. "The time is overdue," Smooha asserts, "for Israel to come to grips with its structural pluralism, intergroup inequality and conflict and to do justice to its disadvantaged groups. Israel's most cherished political stability and national cohesion are in danger unless firm measures are taken to redress structural inequalities."[36] Other societies, such as the United States and Canada, have abandoned the melting-pot theory as nonfunctional in a multiethnic society. In Israel, for many reasons, this would be very hard to accept. But if, on the other hand, the status quo continues, will the society continue to grow into a harmonious whole?

Such questions are raised here primarily because the coming of the Beta Israel, the most conspicuous minority group, may help to sharpen the debate. Fortunately for the Beta Israel and the host society, there are forces at work now to change the situation in the right direction. The policymakers are increasingly aware of the need not to overlook background factors of populations in education. Students different ethnic backgrounds do attend schools together, and more of the disadvantaged youth are proceeding to advanced levels. Annually, up to 25 percent of marriages in the larger society are inter-ethnic. Some of the Ethiopians already have begun to intermarry with the veterans. Changes such as these augur well for the possible successful integration of the newcomers.

ILLUSTRATIONS

Beta Israel boys at the praying (Wailing) Wall.

Two boys at a bar mitzvah in front of the Praying Wall.

Sons and fathers at a bar mitzvah in front of the Praying Wall.

Nursery school children in Kiryat Arba (Hebron).

Yani Elchanan, absorption center director, Kiryat Arba, with a Beta Israel girl.

Elders in council, Kiryat Gan.

Youth Aliyah World Director Uri Gordon chatting with T. Wagaw in front of school Miqveh Israel near Tel Aviv.

Adult students in Mevasseret Zion near Jerusalem.

Vizunisky, in charge of Youth Aliyah programs for the Beta Israel, with the author in Vizunisky's office, Tel Aviv.

Workers at their tasks, Kiryat Arba.

Four generations of a Beta Israel family attending class with immigrants from other lands.

Nurse's aids at graduation.

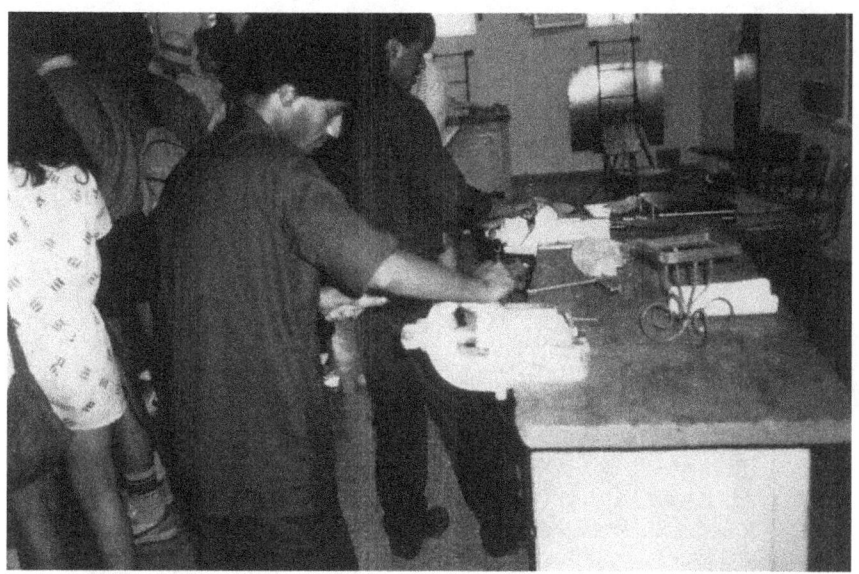

Beta Israel young men at a metal workshop.

Young men at a workshop.

Recently arrived parents, their son who had come earlier, and his wife.

Demonstration in front of the prime minister's office demanding reunification in Israel with relatives left in Ethiopia.

CHAPTER THREE

❖

The Journey and Settlement

❖

As the Beta Israel left their African home for Israel, they must have anticipated that the move would not be easy. But it is doubtful whether they, or anyone else, expected the magnitude of the ordeal awaiting them. They were caught up in actual and latent local, regional, and international rivalries and animosities in and among Africa, the Middle East, and the superpowers. Their flight from Ethiopia was exploited as a political lightning rod in attempts to channel public attention away from the ills of these other societies. In the process, the Ethiopians paid a heavy price arising from their membership in a particular group of people in the Middle East, involving their religion, race, and level of modernity. This chapter describes and analyzes the many intrigues and political machinations encountered by these people and the eventual triumph many of them achieved in reaching their ultimate objective. The chapter also indicates the extent to which the experiences of the Beta Israel may affect their quest for successful settlement and integration in Israel.

In the winter of 1984, massive airlifts that came to be known as Operation Moses effected the transfer of more than eight thousand Ethiopian Jews from Africa to Israel. Operation Joshua, brought nine hundred more. Together, these were the climax, not the beginning, of the exodus of Ethiopian Jewry from its home of more than twenty-five hundred years. The magnitude of the escape of entire families from religious, political, and economic oppression has as precedent in African history only the exodus of the ancient Hebrews from Egypt to the land of Canaan some three thousand years ago under Moses and Joshua. This latest episode galvanized the attention of most of the world across all spectra of beliefs, political orientation, and ideology. Up to that time, the world, which for the most part had been unaware of the existence of African Jews, began to look into the meaning of the whole drama. Some people were alarmed by the political and economic significance for the region from which the Jews came, as well as for their destination. Even non-Jewish Ethiopians, living outside the immediate areas of Gondar and Tigray, were, for all intents and purposes, ignorant about Ethiopian Jewry. In the long and turbulent history of Ethiopia, even those people among whom the Jews had dwelled for so long were not able to conceive of any association between the Ethiopian Jews they called *Falasha, taib, bale-ij, kayla*, or even *buda*,[1] and world Jewry or, since 1948, with the people of the State of Israel.

After the birth of the State of Israel, productive relationships in commerce, security, education, and culture were forged and nurtured. Following the Arab-Israeli war of 1973, Ethiopia, with other members of the Organization of African Unity (OAU), broke diplomatic relations with Israel. However, some tacit relations were maintained off and on thereafter.

These positive dispositions had their roots in the religious and political persuasion of Ethiopians. To begin with, the Orthodox Christian faith, for long the state church, more so than other forms of Christianity, is based on the tenets of the Old Testament, or Orit, and on the other books that are considered apocryphal by most other Christians but are accepted by Ethiopian Christians and Jews alike. (The only extant book of Baruch is found in the Ge'ez language in Ethiopia.) In addition, deeply ingrained in the ethos of Ethiopians is the legend of the queen of Sheba, or Queen Makeda, and her union with King Solomon of Jerusalem in the tenth century B.C. Their son, Menelik I, was the founder of the Ethiopian Solomonic dynasty.[2] This union also gave birth to the legend that copies of the tablets (the Tabot) on which the Mosaic Ten Commandments were inscribed, together with some priests (*kesoch*) and cantors (*debterawoch*) were transferred to Ethiopia. According to that legend, the Tabot was de-

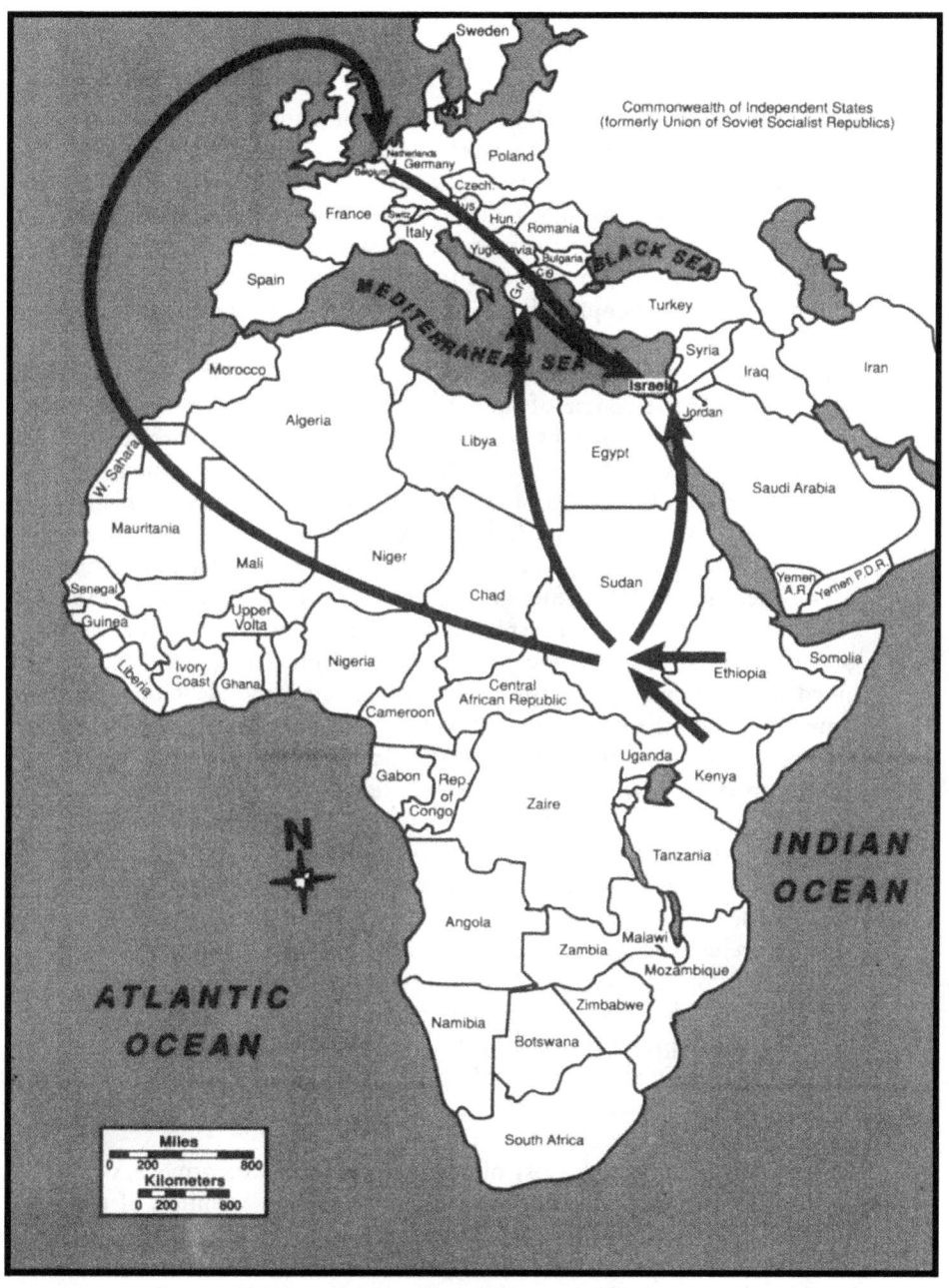

MAP 3. Approximation of routes followed to Israel

posited in the historic church of Aksum Tsion (Zion).[3] This and similar stories are enshrined in the highly revered book of the *Kibre Negast* ("Glory of the Kings"). Such legends legitimatize both political and religious claims, as they are intended to do. But it is surprising, with this background of intimate relations with Judaism, to learn that the Beta Israel have been subjected to harsh discrimination and persecution by the very people who trace a good part of their intellectual or religious beliefs and cultural, linguistic, and political traditions to Judaism. The most plausible explanation may be the following combination: (1) In the course of time, the larger community of Ethiopians was unable or unwilling to associate the Beta Israel with mainstream Judaism or even Judaic traditions.[4] (2) The maltreatment of the Beta Israel at the hands of others was based neither on ethnicity nor on anti-Semitic feelings. Indeed, the dichotomy that some have drawn between the Beta Israel and the Amhara is misleading. The Beta Israel are for all intents and purposes Amhara. Moreover, the Christians in the area were suspicious toward any non-Orthodox religion or peoples, not just the Jews.[5] (3) Over time, orthodoxy combined with jealousy of the special skills the Beta Israel developed to compensate for their forced landlessness.[6] But the subjection of the Jews to severe persecutions by the Orthodox majority, whose religion for centuries enjoyed political and material support from the state, was not unique. For instance, most of the Muslims, who are another minority in the parts of Ethiopia of concern here, are also landless and survive by engaging in trade, handicrafts, and weaving, as do the Beta Israel. Roman Catholics and Protestants have been viewed with grave apprehension and from time to time also were subjected to ostracism, expropriation of property, and physical harm, until recently. For smaller Christian sects operating in the country, such as the Pentecostals and Baptists, termed *addis mette* ("newcomer"), the situation during the Derg era (1977–1991) was very bad. Persecution was coming not only from the local communities but also from zealot forces of the Marxist central government.

In light of their long history of persecution and maltreatment, why have the Jews in Ethiopia only recently come to the attention of the world? More specifically, why, after having lived for more than twenty-five hundred years in Ethiopia, did mass migration to Israel become necessary? Were conditions worsening for them? Or have they been maintaining the long-range goal of a return to the Holy Land all this time? The reasons for recent mass emigration have to do primarily with the current (post-1974) political, religious, and economic conditions of Ethiopia. Their departure also was facilitated by change in the political situation of Israel and countries in northeast Africa such as the Sudan, Egypt, and Kenya, as well as in the United States and, to some extent, Western Europe and what was then the Soviet Union. Some of the political and economic entanglements of these countries and their effects on the conditions of Ethiopian Jews are examined below.

POLITICAL AND ECONOMIC CONTEXT

The immediate reasons for the mass exodus of the Ethiopian Jews include (1) the drought and the consequent famine which has become increasingly acute since 1973; (2) the civil strife and military activities within Ethiopia which continued to get worse following the 1974 revolution; (3) the increased awareness on the part of religious or ethnic groups of their political, cultural, or religious rights within the Ethiopian union following the 1976 Declaration of the Democratic Charter;[7] and (4) just as important as any of these for the Beta Israel, the availability of another viable home in Israel.[8] To escape to Israel, however, the Jews had to mingle with the other refugees from the famine in the northern and northwestern regions, from Eritrea, Tigray, Gondar, and parts of Wollo. In the process of departure and resettlement, political groups within and outside Ethiopia and the regimes of many African and Middle Eastern countries played interesting roles whose consequences still reverberate across Africa and the Middle East. Needless to say, these groups and regimes pursued their own political or economic ends unrelated to the interests of the Beta Israel. In 1973, after a long, drawn-out debate, the Sephardi chief rabbi of Israel, Ovadia Yosef, ruled that the Jews in Ethiopia were in fact descendants of Dan, one of the ten lost tribes of Israel, and were therefore entitled to avail themselves of the 1950 Law of Return which affirmed the right of Jews in the Diaspora to return to Israel as full citizens. Two years later, the Ashkenazi chief rabbi expressed agreement with the decision, and on April 25, 1975, the government made it law. Through a variety of channels, this decision was communicated to the Ethiopian villages. We will return to this theme, but first let us further analyze the factors that precipitated the emigration.

Famines and attendant diseases have been with the people of highland Ethiopia, off and on, for some time, especially in the Tigray and Wollo regions, where a smaller number of Beta Israel are found. In southern Gondar, the home of most of them, the drought was not so severe. But the fighting between the rebels and the central government was severe enough for the young people and peasantry of these regions to want to leave.

Since December 1960, when the first well-known unsuccessful attempt to oust the Haile Selassie government was made, the educated generation of Ethiopian youth organized and staged various political actions against the conservative and increasingly oppressive government. Schools and college campuses became centers for political mobilization and demonstrations in favor of land reform, equitable distribution of economic opportunities, more education for all, and the like. The cumulative effect of these political agitations and actions by students, who were later joined by people from organized labor and professional unions, was the popular revolution of 1974. Haile Selassie was deposed, the constitution was suspended, and the parliament was abolished. At all levels and in every direction in the political, social, and economic sectors, fundamental and perhaps irreversible changes were imposed on the country.

The military, which subsequently assumed power, tried to forge coalitions with various civilian groups. But most of these, once again led by the politicized student organizations, insisted on establishing a civilian, progressive, "democratic" government of their choosing. The military government, led by the Derg (committee), refused. Soon after, the civilians, led by the students, decided to reorganize themselves into an entity that later came to be known as Ethiopian People's Revolutionary Party (EPRP). EPRP, as a first stage, decided to launch a guerrilla war against the Derg and its representatives and supporters under the campaign known as "white terror." This was a fatal mistake. The Derg retaliated against the EPRP with its own "red terror." The terror campaign against EPRP and its suspected sympathizers was carried out in 1977 and 1978.[9]

In spite of its considerable organizational and tactical skills, the EPRP was no match for the government. Eventually, it was forced to retreat from its major centers of activity, Addis Ababa in particular and the Shoa region in general, to the northern regions of Gondar and Tigray. In the meantime, the Derg's pursue-and-destroy tactics resulted in the deaths of thousands of young people. Many were captured; some were executed, others suffered long terms in prison, and still others were coopted to serve as informants and collaborators with the Derg against their erstwhile compatriots. Among the captured and persecuted were children as young as ten. The brutality inflicted by the government's forces on their victims is beyond description. The EPRP was forced to regroup in the north, where it found support from young Jews, among others. Retreat forced some of these young people to seek temporary shelters in such neighboring countries as Kenya, the Sudan, and Djibouti.

To satisfy its ever-growing need for military manpower, in 1979, the Ethiopian government instituted a law of conscription—the first ever in modern Ethiopia—forcing young people to serve in the armed forces for up to three years.[10] Thousands of ill-trained or untrained peasant youth were perishing in the civil wars raging in the north. This decision on the part of the government added impetus for young people and their parents to leave the country in droves.

As for the Jews, most of whom have been landless for decades, if not for centuries, the announcement of the Land Reform Law in 1975 by the Derg was a welcome event. From now on, they could own land, they thought, and make their livelihood. However, the peasant associations newly established by the government across the country continued to operate along traditional, discriminatory lines. Committee members, at least initially drawn from the older generation, tried to assign marginal or nonproductive lands to the Jews. Better lands were taken from them and given to others. In addition, with the importation or local development of new technologies of farming and manufacturing and the emergence of a new class of artisans among the non-Jews, the economic conditions of the Jews went from bad to worse. The Beta Israel's initial joy at the prospect of owning land must have been replaced by deep disappointment and helplessness. Once again, it was made clear that since, for the most part, discrimination against and persecution of the Jews were based at the community level, a change of government or law did not appreciably change their condition. In their search for alternatives, the possibility of migrating to Israel must have seemed more and more attractive.

THE PROMISE OF ISRAEL

Beginning in the 1960s, with the cooperation and material and technical support of European and North American Jewish organizations, and with some help from the Israeli government,[11] the Beta Israel operated some education and health-care programs in Ethiopia. These programs included instruction in Hebrew and religion. Encouraged by some changes in Ethiopia, the Jewish ORT (Organization for Rehabilitation and Training) initiated educational, religious, and medical programs in the Gondar region, not only for the Beta Israel but for all Ethiopians living in the immediate vicinity.[12] Convinced that the ORT programs supported what the Derg was trying to institute across Ethiopia, the government first extended a welcoming hand to the programs. ORT operated them effectively through 1980. Then, quite suddenly, they were ordered to cease and desist. Among the reasons adduced were that the agency was serving as an arm of the CIA and of "world Zionism," anathema to a Soviet-supported regime that belonged to the Organization of African Unity whose membership includes the Muslim states of North Africa. ORT was further accused of either encouraging or facilitating the departure of Ethiopian Jews for Israel.[13] Moreover, Payne asserts that the Israeli government feared their development activities were inculcating notions of the possibility of mass migration to Israel among the Beta Israel—a dream Israel was not prepared to fulfill.[14]

So, as the Ethiopian Jews struggled to cope with the rapidly shifting socioeconomic circumstances within their country, and as many of their young people were being persecuted relentlessly, the news of the availability of a viable option filtered to their several villages. This was indeed news. Except for a brief episode in 1836, the Beta Israel generally have believed that their redemption had to await the coming of the Messiah, who would gather the faithful together in the Holy City of Jerusalem in eternal peace, justice, and harmony.

Some Beta Israel youth had gone to Israel in the 1950s primarily as students to receive vocational and religious training. Most returned to Ethiopia to work for the government or in the Jewish villages as teachers or religious instructors. But the influence of these teachers, traveling back and forth, was very limited and affected only a small

The Journey and Settlement

number of young people. Despite both ancient and more recent cordialities between Ethiopia and Israel, permanent emigration of Ethiopians, no matter how subjugated or despised, was never any part of Ethiopian culture. Not only Ethiopians but leading European and North American scholars as well documented that the Ethiopian Jews were busy trying to improve their lot within Ethiopia. The concept of aliyah, the ingathering of Jews of the Diaspora, did not apply to them.[15]

Nevertheless, political and economic conditions in Ethiopia continued to deteriorate rapidly. World Jewry's influence became palpable. The new government of Menachem Begin approached the Derg to discuss the legal emigration of Jews to Israel.[16] Given the Ethiopian tradition regarding emigration of citizens, and especially the then-prevailing domestic and international political situation, one would have expected the Derg to refuse. But that is not what transpired. Pressed as it was, the Derg instead decided to use this leverage to obtain weapons and munitions from Israel to use in its fight against Somalia and the local rebels. The two governments concluded agreements in 1977. Two Israeli aircraft flew to Addis Ababa loaded with weapons and ammunition. On their way back to Tel Aviv, they transported 121 Beta Israel people from Addis Ababa. It is probable that such arrangements might have continued were it not for the unfortunate (some say deliberate) and premature disclosure by the minister of foreign affairs of Israel, Moshe Dayan, at a press conference in Switzerland in 1977 that Israel was indeed helping Ethiopia's war efforts through the provision of essential armaments. As could be expected, this disclosure was viewed as extremely embarrassing and politically damaging by the Derg, which vented its anger not only by denying the whole story but also by expelling all Israelis from Ethiopia. Legal migration was frozen. From then on, in the face of the worsening condition of the Beta Israel group, and under mounting pressure from the American Association for Ethiopian Jews (AAEJ) and other individuals and similar organizations elsewhere, other means of escape had to be found for the Ethiopians. With the cooperation of Kenya and the Sudan, small groups of people began to slip out from Africa to Israel. Still, the total number of Ethiopian Jews who settled in Israel up to 1979 may not have been more than four hundred. Thousands more were waiting.

Toward the end of 1979, a new and dramatic phase began. With stepped-up rebel activities in Tigray, Eritrea, and parts of Gondar and Wollo, cooperation to facilitate the passage of the Jews to neighboring countries and from there to Israel improved. At the same time, Israel's increasing hospitality was becoming more widely known in the villages and hamlets of the Ethiopian Jews. Ethiopians in Israel wrote letters home, and some were even smuggled back by the Mossad, the Israeli secret service, to help establish escape routes.[17] Now hundreds of people from the southern parts of Tigray and from Wolqait left their villages for the Sudan en route to Israel. By 1980, when nearly half a million Ethiopians were in the Sudanese refugee camps, about three thousand Jews were among them. The agents instructed the Beta Israel people about the opportunities for escape and how the journey could be facilitated to the Sudan. The villagers were assured that if they made it to the Sudan or Kenya, the trip from there to Israel would be relatively simple. Some of these Israeli-Ethiopians served as guides along prearranged routes where provisions were hidden. Other cooperating agents on both the Ethiopian and the Sudanese sides were recruited to help.

THE SUDANESE

The person and the country that played significant roles in the flight of the refugees need to be described at this point. The Sudan, Africa's largest country, has had a history of shifting alliances in regard to regional politics as well as relations with the superpowers over the last twenty-five years. Colonel Gaffar al-Nimeiri came to power in 1969 in a Soviet-supported coup inspired by the Egyptian revolution of 1952 led by Gamal Abdel Nasser. Two years later, in 1971, Nimeiri's efforts to reduce Soviet influence in his country led to an attempted coup against him which he soon crushed with the support of Colonel Muammar Qaddafi of Libya. But subsequently, when Nimeiri stalled on the proposed merger of the Sudan with Egypt and Libya, a perpetual dream of Qaddafi's, the latter began to plot to overthrow Nimeiri. In 1976, yet another coup was attempted. Organized and financed by Libya, it was led by Sadik el-Mahdi, a descendant of the Sudanese hero by the same name. This time, Nimeiri turned to Egypt for help and was able to defeat Sadik el-Mahdi and the Libyans. It was inevitable that events such as these continued to play pivotal roles regarding the political alliances and policies affecting the conditions of the Ethiopian refugees.[18]

The decision of the Sudanese government to open its borders to thousands of Ethiopian refugees may have been influenced by the realization that the border of more than six hundred miles between the two countries could not be sealed. And, as some have claimed, the government's reasons also may have included Nimeiri's mother's origins in northwestern Ethiopia. Nimeiri himself has cultivated a deep friendship with many Ethiopians from different walks of life. Whatever the underlying reasons, his manifest attitude was that the Sudan could not turn away hungry women and children. But the Sudan is an Arab state and a member of the Arab League. It was forbidden by law to do anything that would promote or facilitate the policies or actions of Israel. Handling the Beta Israel issue was a political as well as moral dilemma for Nimeiri. At the initial stage, at least, his policy was to let the Beta Israel come to the Sudan like any other refugees and to let them proceed to Israel as long as this was done with great care and discretion. For a time, this policy worked. Groups of Beta Israel arrived in Israel via the Sudan by air. The Israeli public as well as the local and international press knew of these operations but cooperated with the government's request to maintain secrecy. To a large extent, a remarkable degree of discretion was exercised for a long time.

However, the influx of Jews to the refugee camps accelerated. By 1983, the number of Beta Israel in the camps greatly exceeded the number of people departing for Israel. Hundreds of people were dying daily from diseases, malnutrition, or starvation, and from maltreatment at the hands of camp officials and inmates.[19] Between 1983 and 1984, an estimated three thousand to five thousand Beta Israel perished during the flight and from disease and privation in the refugee camps. According to those who survived and made it to absorption camps in Israel, beatings, imprisonment, robbery, and rape were also part of the ordeals en route to and in the camps.[20] Survivors related in 1985 that robbery came at the hands the *shiftas* (vagabonds) as well as government officials. In many instances, they thought the *shiftas* and government officials worked together. They reported that they were robbed of clothing, food, and whatever little money or personal effects they had with them.

As the refugees tell it, within Ethiopia, the attitude of the Derg was stubborn and oppressive. Local officials such as Major Melaku Teferra (his name means "angel" in Amharic), the governor of Gondar region,[21] stood firmly against letting them go. At first, those Beta Israel who were captured as they tried to escape were beaten up, imprisoned, and told not to try again. This seems to have worked initially. But with the passage of time and the increased worsening of their conditions, more and more of them attempted to get out. Many succeeded. Eventually even Melaku Teferra was forced to admit it was futile to attempt to stop the flight. What seems to have followed was a policy of denial, ignoring the whole effort as if it did not exist.

In the meantime, in the Sudanese refugee camps, the situation for the internees was growing worse. As reports about camp conditions reached the outside world, pressures mounted on Israel to find alternative, even unorthodox, means of getting the Beta Israel to Israel. The Nimeiri government, on the other hand, fully aware of the political implications, refused to let a mass exodus to Israel take place directly from its soil. The Israeli government now turned to a mutual friend, the U.S. government,[22] to apply whatever pressure it could on the Sudan. In response, the then-roving ambassador, General Vernon Walters, discussed the need for a massive lift of the Beta Israel with Nimeiri early in 1984 on a visit to the Sudan. In March of the same year, Vice President George Bush followed this up during his visit to the Sudan. In the meantime, the AAEJ, the strongest advocacy organization on behalf of the Beta Israel, was letting the world know the Israeli government was stalling and urged the U.S. Congress and administration to supply needed material and human resources.

In Israel, the Shimon Peres government was becoming increasingly aware of the urgency of the matter but was also convinced it could do very little without the full cooperation of the Sudanese government. Accordingly, Peres dispatched his deputy prime minister and minister of foreign affairs, Yitzhak Shamir, to Washington to plead with Ronald Reagan's administration to prevail on the Sudanese to cooperate, and to do it quickly. The U.S. administration in turn already was feeling pressure from Congress and lobbyists to do something on behalf of the Jews. Accordingly, the United States instructed its embassy in Khartoum to do whatever was necessary to cooperate with the Israeli and Sudanese governments.

The worsening political and economic conditions of the Sudan, like those of Ethiopia, continued to play a significant role affecting the welfare and eventual fate of the Beta Israel. Sudan had a debt burden of more than nine billion dollars, food production was low, drought and famine were realities in the daily lives of millions of its citizens, and it was fighting a prolonged and debilitating civil war against the Sudanese People's Liberation Army (SPLA), led by Colonel John Garang, who was supported by Ethiopia and Libya. Fighting to survive and to bolster his sagging prestige, Nimeiri promulgated the Sharia, or Islamic Law, in 1985. This might have gained him some friends in the Arab world but did not help improve his relations with the SPLA, which is made up of Christians and animists. As he well knew, Nimeiri was in troubled waters. He did not need additional problems. But given the urgent economic conditions on top of the political ones, he was bound to respond positively to the demands for facilitating the departure of the Beta Israel, even if that could lead to further trouble. It was American financial aid, more than $197 million in 1984 with a promise of $250 million for 1985, which was later doubled, that persuaded him. As was later brought out during the trials of former officials, some monies from Israel and from other Jewish sources might have been promised and delivered as well, either to compensate the Sudan for its efforts or to purchase and equip transport vehicles, provide safe houses, and meet security expenses.

Even now, however, Nimeiri resisted Israel's wishes to move the Beta Israel to Israel through the port of Sudan by boat or by any direct means.[23] However, Nimeiri did agree to the use of civilian airlines to transport the refugees, but he insisted that this, too, had to be done discreetly, on a small scale, and indirectly, to some location other than Israel. Finally, the Belgian-based, Jewish-owned European Airways was identified, agreements were secured, and the major operation was ready. Commenting on possible economic retaliation by the Arabs, the owner of European Airways, George Gutleman, is reported to have said, "There is no greater obligation than the redemption of captives."[24] The Nimeiri government could not have been more cautious. It tried to plug all loopholes, cover all tracks of complicity, and avert the wrath that would inevitably erupt in the Sudan, other Arab countries, even the larger Islamic world. The Sudanese tightened security around the camps where the Beta Israel were concentrated. Visitors to the camps were barred. Certain government officials, trusted only incompletely, and some individuals representing international aid organizations were removed from positions where they might be able to observe or interfere with secret operations. For instance, in October 1984, the Sudanese commissioner for refugees was summarily fired on the grounds that he had defied the Sharia by drinking hard liquor. The truth was that he knew too much and was about to know a great deal more of what was to transpire around the camps.

Israeli agents continued to infiltrate the Beta Israel camps as spotters to identify, round up, and bring the emigrants together at designated centers. At about this time (October 1984), a Sudanese diplomat is reported to have traveled to Switzerland to meet with representatives of the Mossad and the Jewish Agency. There monies were exchanged for the Jews' safe departure and perhaps to reward individual or collective official efforts for cooperation.[25]

Finally, on November 21, 1984, one of the biggest ventures of its kind in recent world history, later to be known as Operation Moses, got under way. Between that time and January 6, 1985, Boeing 707s made at least thirty-five flights between Khartoum and Tel Aviv via a number of western European countries. The planes flew over Egypt, stopping in several European airports for refueling, rest, and exchange of flight personnel. Most of their charges were in terrible mental and physical condition. In case of trouble that might have interrupted the operation, it was decided to transport the weak, the children, and the elderly first.

The operation was going well and might have taken care of nearly all who needed to be removed, but the secret was leaked by an officer of the Jewish Agency and later officially confirmed by Peres in a press conference in Tel Aviv. The disclosure of the venture embarrassed the Sudanese and Ethiopian governments and the operation was brought to an abrupt halt. After a delay of some three months, with the help of American military and CIA resources, an additional eight hundred to nine hundred people were airlifted to Israel. Known as Operation Joshua, this got most of the remaining Jewish refugees out of the camps. The few left behind migrated to other countries, returned to Ethiopia, or died in the Sudan. Official doors have been closed since then, but a trickle of Beta Israel continue to find their way to Israel. In May 1991, a huge airlift brought nearly fifteen thousand Beta Israel from Addis Ababa to Tel Aviv. Since then, most of the remaining have joined their relatives in Israel. For all practical purposes, Ethiopian Jewry is totally uprooted from that country which had been their home for centuries.

REPERCUSSIONS

For a period of at least six weeks, Israeli officials and newspapers as well as international agencies had agreed implicitly to honor the request of the Israeli military censors to refrain from discussing any aspect of the operation. However, some mayors began to raise questions regarding their ability to absorb the newcomers, religious leaders were concerned about the Halakic implications of the new arrivals, and parliamentarians were dismayed at both. When the leak finally occurred, it traveled through a very unusual route.

The director-general of the quasi-governmental Jewish Agency, Yehuda Dominitz, revealed the existence of Operation Moses in an interview with a very inconspicuous right-wing newspaper, *Netuda*, published by a small group of West Bank Jewish settlers.[26] On January 3, 1985, early in the day, two big daily tabloids, *Yediot Ahvonot* and *Ma'ariv*, played up the story on their front pages. It is still a mystery how the story got through the censors. *Netuda* was not censored, but the story was picked up by the Itim news agency on Wednesday, January 2. When the two papers played up the story the next day, the floodgate was opened. The international news agencies spread the reports worldwide, and, as the article "An Unfinished Rescue" in the *Jerusalem Post* on January 6, 1985, observed: "The dike was in shambles. . . . Certainly no international, no African and no humane interest can be served by any interruption of this exodus. It must be hoped . . . that once the present hue and cry subsides the effort can be resumed and the remaining refugee Jews of Ethiopia reunited with their families here." But the repercussions of the disclosure reverberated worldwide, including in the United States, Africa, and the Middle East. The Peres government held a press conference on the January 4 to confirm the existence of the operation. This was more than other governments could stand. Whatever tacit or explicit help had been given, they did not expect it to come back at them this way.

Senior American White House and State Department officials as well as American Jewish individuals and spokespersons of various organizations claimed to have been shocked and deeply annoyed by Israel's decision to lift military censorship of the sensitive operation Israeli officials claimed they had permitted publication only of the absorption of the Jews, not the details of the airlift. Indeed, on January 7, 1985, the *Jerusalem Post* reported in an article entitled "Ethiopians Upset and Bitter over Airlift Halt" that the Jewish Agency chairman hoped the worldwide publicity, on the contrary, would ensure continuity of the scheme. While sending messages to the American administration that the disclosure forced it to bring the operation to a halt, the Sudan government accused Ethiopia of selling its Jewish citizens for twenty million dollars in spare military parts. The Ethiopians retaliated by labeling the Sudanese Zionist sympathizers who had abducted the Ethiopians for money. Libya demanded an emergency meeting of the Arab League to discuss the operation. Within Israel, the opposition parties in the Knesset threatened a motion of no confidence in the government, charging that by officially confirming the news reports, the Jewish Agency had jeopardized thousands of Beta Israel still trapped in Ethiopia or other Third World countries. The severest critics, however, were the veteran Beta Israel in Israel. A crowd of two hundred fifty demonstrators marched in Jerusalem to demand punishment for those responsible for the disclosure. "This is sabotage. . . . This is calculated murder," they thundered. In the "Unfinished Rescue" article in the *Jerusalem Post* on January 6, 1985, some others reportedly accused Israel of trying to back out of its commitment to bring all those who wanted to come to Israel. Prime Minister Peres tried to reassure all those who would listen. He insisted that the airlift would continue. "No economic difficulty, no internal distress, no geographical distance and no political obstacle will halt the effort," he said. "We shall not rest until all our brothers and sisters from Ethiopia come home."[27]

The Soviet Union, picking up the rehearsed lines from Ethiopia's Mengistu, opined that the United States had misused the funds designated for relief to "abduct" Ethiopians. Mengistu appeared on television shows in Canada, insisting that the Ethiopians were not Jews, that they were abducted and held in Israel against their will, and that, given the chance, they would like to return to Ethiopia. In that May 1985 interview, he claimed that since they were not permitted to do so, many were committing suicide.[28]

The Sudan, because of its strategic location relative to the Persian Gulf, is of vital economic interest to the West. Its geographic significance is strategically complicated: it borders on Egypt, Libya, and Ethiopia, all of which are of vital importance to the global jockeying of the United States, and it bestrides the Arab and sub-Saharan cultures on the continent of Africa. Nimeiri had balanced the various conflicting pressures quite successfully, securing needed support and assistance from both East and West. But from the early 1970s on, he tried to align his government more with the West and received a substantial amount of military and economic assistance over the years. Now, when the West tried to call upon his assistance in the migration of the Beta Israel, he delayed, fully aware of the repercussions sure to follow once his complicity was revealed. And when the disclosure did occur, his regime was indeed vilified by the Arab League, Ethiopia,

The Journey and Settlement

Libya, and a number of other Third World countries. His government was seriously undermined, so much so that his erstwhile allies were already counting him out. The United States, for instance, was withholding promised aid, and Egypt was apprehensively watching the accelerating process of decline.

The occasion of Nimeiri's state visit to the United States via Egypt was seized by some of his military officers, led by his defense minister, Lieutenant-General Suwar al-Dahab, to stage a successful coup on April 4, 1985. Nimeiri stayed in Egypt. What transpired in the Sudan as well as in other Arab countries following the coup demonstrated political duplicity and intrigue of unusual proportions, highlighting once again the fragile nature of the regional and international economic, military, and cultural alliances.

The new military council led by al-Dahab and the civilian cabinet headed by Dr. Gizzuli Daffa-Allah, as prime minister, must have taken stock of the conditions of the Sudan they inherited—the wrecked economy, the drought and famine, political polarization among the citizens based on religion and ethnicity, and a civil war that had been festering for more than two years. They also knew that these conditions had grown worse while the Sudan was still enjoying the material and political support of its erstwhile principal allies, the United States and Egypt. The Sudanese decided to realign themselves with their neighbors without, they hoped, alienating their traditional allies. They approached both Ethiopia and Libya for reconciliation. These two countries had up to now supported the SPLA in the south. If Ethiopia and Libya could be persuaded to see the new government as meriting reconciliation, the Sudanese thought, then John Garang, leader of the SPLA, would have no chance of survival and would soon be forced to the conference table for negotiation and accommodation. The Sudanese also sent a high-level delegation to Moscow to plead for Soviet help to persuade Ethiopia not to support the SPLA.[29]

In the meantime, the new leadership wanted to rally its citizenry in support of its initiatives. This, they thought, could be done by putting members of the former government on trial, thus diverting attention from other problems. The main crime with which these former government officials were charged was Sudan's participation in the airlift of Ethiopian Jews to Israel. As a member of the Arab League, the Sudan had statutes prohibiting any kind of dealing with Israel. The four-month trial in the fall of 1985, which was broadcast daily over radio and television, tried to highlight what were considered Nimeiri's failures and looked closely at the activities of American officials in the Sudan, in particular Ambassador Hume A. Horan. In the trial the attorney general charged that the airlift had been supervised by the U.S. embassy in Khartoum and that the CIA also had played an active role.[30]

The former first vice president, who was also in charge of the State Security Forces, Major General Omar Mohammed el-Tayeb, was the major figure in the trial. Attorney General Omar Abdel Ati charged, for the state, that Tayeb was a culprit in undermining the constitution and instigating war against the state and was guilty of treason and spying. The charge added that the Sudanese penal code and constitution prohibited dealings with Israel and that the airlift constituted strategic support for Israel. In the meantime, the occasion was used to highlight the complicity of the American embassy in the activities. Tayeb was sentenced to two thirty-year terms, the equivalent of two life terms.[31] The attorney general had wanted a death sentence and said he would appeal. Tayeb also said he would appeal. While the trial lasted, the Sudanese radio and TV public was entertained daily with the detailed reporting of the Beta Israel airlift and the roles played by the former officials and the U.S. government. Apparently the public enjoyed it.[32] But the government's hopes that the trial would serve as a lightning rod were of short-lived. Sudan had to face the realities confronting it.

The Ethiopians' response to the Sudanese quest for reconciliation consisted of two demands: (1) that the Sudanese government expel the Eritrean and Tigrean rebel forces from the Sudan, and (2) that the Sudanese culprits in the airlift should be brought to trial. Libya, on the other hand, was eager to establish diplomatic ties and concluded military agreements with the Sudanese. Libya also gave three hundred thousand metric tons of free oil as well as two military aircraft to Sudan and provided employment opportunities for thousands of Sudanese laborers in Libya. Libya did not seem to have any hesitation about abandoning the SPLA, which it had been supporting against the Khartoum government. The United States, for its part, continued to provide economic, military, and famine assistance (four hundred fifty million dollars for 1985 fiscal year) but reduced its staff in the Sudan significantly, charging that the political climate in that country threatened the security of American personnel.[33] Egypt found itself in a very precarious situation. After some hesitation, it, too, came up with some fourteen million dollars in military aid, which was substantially increased later.

The Ethiopian Jews long have maintained that they have been used as pawns in the games of Ethiopian and foreign politicians. It is indeed clear that they were caught in political webs and that their victimization was irrelevant to the players of the games. For the Jews, the end does not yet seem to be in sight.

SUMMARY

The flight of Ethiopian Jews from Ethiopia to Israel has been full of drama, conflict, tragedy, and triumph. The Ethiopians, when they eventually decided to leave their country of origin en masse for the Promised Land, ran into a complex of problems they could not have imagined. They might have been familiar with corrupt local government officials and with bandits who robbed and plundered them, but how could they have anticipated that they would become an issue of such grave importance to leaders of African and Middle Eastern countries, let alone the superpowers?

The repercussions of the events must be viewed not only in global terms but also in human terms for the sake of the immediate and long-term well-being—mental, physical, and social—of those who survived the ordeal and those who are still trapped in Ethiopia. In the course of the whole episode, it must be recalled, many families were separated. Parents departed with only some or none of their children; children left their parents. Under Operation Solomon most of the remaining Beta Israel have come to Israel. Now, the question for those who survived the long ordeals is not separation from loved ones but surviving and eventually flourishing in the new home. The question must be, once again, what will be the future of this ancient, proud, and battered people?

CHAPTER FOUR

❖

The Beleaguered Family in Transition

❖

      This chapter deals with the family in its various forms, compositions, and relations. It presents briefly the traditional goals and practices for conducting life before coming to the new land and proceeds to discuss how family members once in Israel are coping, collectively and individually, with the tremendous challenges; the types and quality of resources provided by the host society to facilitate the survival and adaptation of the family; and the immigrants' perceptions of the service providers and material resources. The chapter concludes with consideration of some of the main problems—technical, human, and perceptual—that have emerged how these challenges and issues have been handled, and the consequences of decisions made and actions taken.

THE SETTING

      Organized immigration to Israel from Ethiopia began toward the end of 1979. Before that time, there were approximately four hundred Ethiopians in Israel. They had come over beginning in the mid-1950s individually or in small groups, primarily for purposes of education, to accompany a spouse, or for other individual interests unrelated to *aliyah*. The only exceptions were those 121 people who came in 1977 under a bilateral agreement between the governments of Ethiopia and Israel. As indicated already, that event had no precedent and was halted abruptly when an Israeli politician carelessly made it public. Following that episode, legal or open emigration visas were denied to the Ethiopian Jews. Alternative strategies were devised. Most of the sixteen thousand (1988 estimate) immigrants now in Israel escaped from Ethiopia in two stages between 1980 and 1985.

The first stage began sometime in February 1980 and continued through November 1984. In these years, some seventy-five hundred immigrants, mainly from Tigray province and adjoining districts, arrived in Israel. The second stage, known as Operation Moses, began on November 21, 1984, and ended on January 6, 1985. Operation Moses, together with the mopping-up operation in March 1985, brought approximately eight thousand more immigrants. Although dramatic, massive airlifts were interrupted for a long time, small groups of Beta Israel continued to find their way to Israel through different channels. Between 1980 and 1985, some fifteen thousand immigrants had arrived in Israel. Since 1985, approximately five hundred more Ethiopians have come in small groups, making a total of sixteen thousand Beta Israel immigrants.[1] However, these latecomers tend to differ from earlier emigres. Many are from urban areas such as Addis Ababa and had attained (or their parents or spouses had attained) significant positions in teaching, the health professions, or the civil service before leaving Ethiopia for Israel. The rest are young people with considerable formal educational background. This group, then, is comprised of Beta Israel who had become well integrated into the mainstream of Ethiopian society. As the general conditions in Ethiopia worsened, they came to see Israel as a viable alternative and began to claim their erstwhile dormant rights.[2]

When we consider the conditions and characteristics of the Beta Israel in this chapter, we have in mind those who arrived in the two stages between 1980 and early 1985. Most of those who arrived in the first stage were from the Tigray administrative region. The Tigrean group constitutes about 20 percent of the estimated thirty thousand total Beta Israel population, including those still in Ethiopia. Their native language is Tigrigna; Amharic is a second language.

Those from Gondar and districts adjoining Tigray province, on the other hand, generally speak both languages and are more versatile in relating themselves to or dealing with the two major ethnic groups of Tigreans and Gondares (Amharas). As a result of the Italian invasion in the 1930s and the consequent movement of populations, a considerable number of intermarriages have taken place between people living in the border areas.

According to the Jewish Agency, the total number of families was estimated at three thousand, and an additional two thousand adults were singles. Many of the families were broken up through separation or death, either on the way to third countries, such as the Sudan and Kenya (mostly the latter), or in the refugee camps. Between three thousand and five thousand people are believed to have died.[3]

Although as a whole there were more men than women among the immigrants (56 percent men, 44 percent women), in 1986, the Jewish Agency estimated that nine hundred, or about 30 percent, of the three thousand Ethiopian families in Israel were single-parent families. This is a reflection of the toll the hardships had taken. Moreover, 80 percent of these single-parent households were headed by females. Among these females who headed households, 44 percent were divorced, 24 percent were widowed, 30 percent were married but had husbands who were left in Ethiopia or had abandoned the family since coming to Israel, and 2 percent were unwed mothers. About 60 percent of these women were younger than forty (36 percent of whom were younger than thirty). In light of the fact that the female population is the less literate or skilled and traditionally has been restricted to the home, families headed by females present formidable challenges in skill development, employment, socialization, and adaptation.[4]

Table 1 depicts the age structure of the immigrants.[5] It can be seen that 7,620, or more than 52 percent, of the immigrants were younger than eighteen. Of the remaining Beta Israel immigrants, 27 percent were between 19 and 34; 8 percent, or 1,120, were between 35 and 44; 7 percent, or 1,080, between 45 and 64. Those 65 years of age and older number only 860, 6 percent of the total.

Among those thirty-seven years of age or older, more than 90 percent were illiterate; very few females were literate. Among those younger than twenty-five, about 37 percent had at least six years of some kind of formal education. Nearly all of the adult population are of peasant background and unskilled, and most had never traveled beyond the immediate environs of their respective villages.

TABLE 1

Beta Israel immigrant population characteristics

Age group	Number	Percentage
0–3	992	6.8
4–6	1,442	9.9
7–12	2,598	17.8
13–14	782	5.3
15–18	1,806	12.4
19–24	1,970	13.5
25–34	1,950	13.3
35–44	1,120	7.7
45–65	1,080	7.4
66+	860	5.9
Total	14,600	100.0
Children and youth	7,620	52.2
Adults	6,980	47.8

Source: Jewish Agency of Israel and the Ministry of Immigration, Government of Israel.

The demographic picture clearly shows that the immigrants are overwhelmingly young and in need of tremendous amounts of training, education, and socialization in line with the requirements of the new realities. As a result of the traumatic experiences the immigrants went through to reach Israel and their encounter with what must seem to be an alien, confusing, complex, and overwhelming modern technological society, the immigrant community is in serious crisis. It may continue to deteriorate, unless determined, well-conceived interventions are made at the different stages of the absorption process. The Jewish Agency, the Ministry of Education and Culture, and the Labor Federation or Histadrut have the challenge and opportunity to organize the institutions of learning and training—the family, the schools, and the numerous training institutions sponsored by the government—and to address the many needs of the group in terms of skills, knowledge, and attitude formation.

CONCEPTUAL CONSTRUCTS

For immigrants, surviving and prevailing in a new society are facilitated by strong ego identity which may be derived from strong primary group and family identity and family support.[6]

In addition, I suggest that the speed and quality of integration and adaptation of immigrants are a function of the policies and orientation of organizations—secular, religious, democratic, socialist, etc.; the quality of the leadership in the organization(s) and the circumstances under which they operate, at least at the initial stages; and the ratio of the new immigrants to members of the receiving society. If the number of newcomers is relatively large in relation to the population of the veteran community, the latter come to feel they are required to carry too heavy a burden relative to their capacity to help the immigrants without jeopardizing their own legitimate interests. In other words, competition for limited resources tends to breed negative attitudes toward the newcomers. Hence, a prudent policy provides for a fair distribution of national burdens or responsibilities for the immigrants among the receiving communities in proportion to the resources at their disposal. If not, resentments build up, and eventually the immigrants get hurt and form negative attitudes toward their new country, while the host community remains bitter and divided and may have to live with a residue of guilt. Also important are the age structure and educational attainments of the immigrants. The younger and more educated immigrants have more opportunities and are therefore more likely to adapt successfully. Finally, the tempo of immigration, settlement, and transition are vital ingredients in the quality and speed of adaptation. If too many immigrants arrive within a short time without adequate advance information and preparation on the part of the host society, the newcomers tend to put too much strain on available local capabilities and resources. As a result, either the quality and amount of services suffer, or the absorbing society is compelled to reach beyond its borders in search of additional assistance. Such assistance may not be forthcoming, or it may come too late.

THE MANNER OF HOMECOMING

To come to the Promised Land, most of the Ethiopian *olim* experienced many hardships and much suffering at the hands of government officials, vagabonds and bandits, and inmates. They suffered hunger and disease and witnessed the deaths of many relatives at refugee camps. Since they left Ethiopia secretly, decisions had to be made about which family members should leave first. Usually the young, who were more likely to survive the arduous and dangerous journey, were encouraged to leave first. An estimated three thousand to five thousand people perished in the process. Those who did manage to survive were in horrible condition by the time they reached Ben Gurion Airport in Tel Aviv. At first, there was some relief; the ordeal was over. But gradually, remorse and guilt set in as they realized family members left behind would not be able to follow soon and conditions in Ethiopia were worsening. Nearly everyone who emigrated from the Gondar region left some close family member or members behind. Reports coming from Ethiopia regarding the drought and famine in general, and the continued mistreatment of the Jews left behind in particular, further aggravated the conditions of the olim. They tried to pressure the government of Israel to try new means to free their mothers, fathers, sisters, brothers, sons, and daughters from Ethiopia. Demonstrations ensued, and promises were made. But the situation did not improve, making adaptation all the harder. More than anything else, the plight of the relatives they left behind continues to be a constant concern.

THE CHANGING ROLES

Ethiopian Jewish society is based on patriarchy. At the turn of this century, Faitlovitch made some insightful observations about their family life. His remarks on divorce, for instance, may be somewhat exaggerated, but otherwise the conditions he describes are remarkably similar to those found today. He noted: "I speak . . . of their life, which has preserved the patriarchal character of the ancient Jewish family life. Polygamy or divorce are things unknown among the Falasha. Their families are fairly numerous; on the average they have six children."[7] The male, usually the father and husband of the household, is the dominant figure. He sets the rules governing how the family should function, gives orders and assignments to each member, and otherwise assumes the position of unquestioned authority. In matters of spiritual and judicial activities, the village elder, usually a *kes* (priest), is expected to provide guidance and render justice. The woman, on the other hand, is expected to obey or otherwise fully recognize the authority of her husband; she has certain responsibilities within the household and is expected to discharge her duties with the assistance of other women in the household, such as mature daughters or daughters-in-law. In public life, the woman has the right to initiate divorce. If successful, she takes half the wealth accrued in the family during the marriage. Custody of minor children is awarded on the basis of the age, gender, and inclination of the children as well as the ability and fitness of each parent to look after their well-being. During his visit to the Ethiopian Jews in the Gondar region in about 1867 on behalf of Alliance Israelite, Halevy, a Jewish Orientalist from France, observed that the women of the villages participated fully in public discourse on matters related to religious and village life. He noted: "Women . . . take part in public gatherings as well as men. . . . They state their views on all questions, and their opinions, especially on the subject of the laws of purification, prevail over those of men. . . . They are all very religious, and do not omit to recite their morning and evening prayers."[8]

The mainstay of the family's economy was subsistence farming and craft work of many types. In this endeavor, all members of the family, including children age seven and older, contributed labor. But the central figure was the father. The rest of the family looked to him as protector, provider, and leader in all spheres of family life. The mother was primarily responsible for the upbringing of both male and female children. When sons reached the age of five or so, the father assumed full responsibility for them. The mother continued to be responsible for the daughters.

On the whole, both parents, assisted by members of the extended family, such us grandparents, uncles, and aunts living in the same village or in one of the nearby villages, recognized the gravity of their responsibilities in raising their children. On all occasions, skills, morals, and appropriate deportment were deliberately taught to children at all stages of development. Some of these tasks, expectations, and deportments in the educative processes were gender-linked, and parental roles were delineated by sex. As far as the parents were concerned, to fail in the full discharge of their responsibilities would not only deprive the child of his or her rightful place in society, but, if the child failed to master developmental tasks and age-appropriate deportments, he or she would bring shame to the family. Thus, in addition to an intrinsic interest in the well-being of the child, concern for the opinions of others prompted parents to be diligent. The following terms and sayings in Amharic illustrate not only the general thrust of societal expectations and parental role assignments but also the different tasks and role expectations for males and females. *Libam*, a very inclusive term, refers to a girl who is wise, well versed in matters of proper deportment, and a skillful cook, or, in more general terms, one who skillfully manages her several roles as a daughter, wife, mother, and mother-in-law. *Enatitwan ayteh lijitwan agiba* means "Marry the girl only after you have known or observed the mother"; as the mother is, so is the daughter. In the same vein, society expects that the boy should be appropriately brought up by his father. Failing to do so results in the display of inappropriate behavior on the part of the child, who is ridiculed, reproached or shamed for it. The term *yeset lij* literally means "child of a woman." It means that although the individual's body is male, his expressions and behaviors are womanly, which further translates to mean cowardly, fearful. This insult denotes that a male child was not brought up by a man and therefore his deportments display womanly characteristics. This shames both the individual and the family. In a society that places a high premium on manliness,[9] this kind of appellation is taken very seriously by the person to whom the insult is directed. Many other expectations apply to both males and females. On the positive side, the boy who has been brought up well is described as *yejegina lij* or "son of a brave parent" (father), once again showing the importance not only of proper upbringing according to societal expectations but also of parenthood and the appropriateness of gender roles. Still another term that applies to both genders is *yechiwa lij*, or "a child of proper or gentle upbringing." The opposite is *balege* or even worse, *yebalege lij*, which means "an uncouth child" or "the son of an uncouth parent." When the child has done something seriously wrong, the strongest term, *assadagih ayideg*, is applied, meaning "May the one who brought you up be destroyed (cursed)." These expressions illustrate the tremendous forces of the community not only in mapping out the parameters of appropriateness but in specifying the contents thereof as well. Families wishing to maintain respectability in the community and wanting their offspring to be respectable must and do take child-rearing very seriously.[10]

Often, the father—or, in his absence, another male relative such as a brother, grandfather, or uncle—concentrates on imparting to the growing male child the imperatives of manhood, including moral fortitude and physical courage in support and defense of the family and clan; and the art of being a good provider, with emphasis on farming, cattle breeding, handicrafts, knowledge of the seasons, the nature of the crops, the soil, and the like. The mother, on the other hand, concentrates on teaching her daughter to become *libam*, wise and thoughtful in matters of the family and the community. The mother teaches the daughter how to cook nutritious and appetizing meals, how to sew, how to serve the husband, and how to relate and interact with the different segments of people in the family and community. There is much to be taught and learned. Often, to achieve the goal of inculcating proper behavior, parents or parent surrogates resort to methods that demand obedience and imitation. Complete obedience to one's parents and elders is the time-tested, quickest way of instilling what is considered desirable. Traditional expectations and roles do not leave much leeway for individuality or individual differences and creative approaches to problem solving. It is not that effective solutions are not appreciated when they can be had, but the tacit assumption is that there is no time or tolerance for innovation. One has to work hard within the prescribed parameters of behavior and find his or her fulfillment in that context. When one fails to do so, the punishments are severe and bring shame to one's self and family.

With the coming of modern schooling in the post-World War II decades, some children—even those in remote rural areas such as where most of the Beta Israel lived—began to attend modern, secular schools. The primary schools were located near the villages so schoolchildren could continue to live at home. Secondary schools, on the other hand, often were located some distance away, and those few who were qualified and could afford to attend had to leave home and take up residence in towns or cities. In the process, the traditional responsibilities and expectations of the homes were diluted and eroded. For one thing, as parental contact and influence diminished, the influence of schools increased. In schools, the better ones at least, the modes of thinking and behaving that were taught and reinforced ran contrary to the methods and goals of traditional family education, such as the values of independent thinking, rationality, the proper place of authority, and the roles of family, government and the individual in the scheme of building a society. Concepts such as these are for the most part at cross purposes with the traditional values outlined above. Also, because relations between the homes and the new schools were not close, there is little doubt that children experienced some confusion about expectations and roles. Yet, since the number of those who had access to schooling was relatively small and the innovation of schooling based on secular values was of recent origin, major problems and conflicts between the expectations and value orientation of the two generations remained for the most part submerged. When they did surface, traditionally sanctioned means were used.[11]

In this regard, the Beta Israel community's situation was not much different from that of other communities of similar modernity within or outside Ethiopia. It has been demonstrated several times that modern, secularly based schooling tends to encourage divisions between families, between the old and the young, between the educated few and the illiterate many, between the time-tested wisdom of traditional values and freedom, and between absorbing received wisdom and engaging in an active search for new ways of knowing and learning.[12] Such tendencies toward dislocation are usually handled within the communities, though often at great pain. As long as the contending parties are on their own ground and traditional institutions are still in place to provide moderating influences, complete dislocation or confusion does not usually result. But when that society is also confronted with complete physical, social, or psychological dislocation, as happened to more than half of the thirty thousand Ethiopian Jews, the challenge is very different.

In Israel, as immigrants to a new land and culture, the *olim* found that the familiar arrangements regarding role expectations, the structure of the family, and the status of its members were all drastically changed. To begin with, the new arrangements called for both the husband and the wife to receive equal shares of income in the form of either pension or wages. The man discovered that in this new environment, he no longer had special skills or other attributes which traditionally provided him with an aura of status and power vis-à-vis other members of the family. For the first time, the woman was in a position to own and control her own income. She was encouraged by social workers and others at the absorption centers and in the permanent settlements. While the man's skills in subsistence farming, crafts, or any of the other similar areas had no value in the new society, the woman was still able to teach weaving, sewing, cooking, and basket making to her daughters.[13] Unlike men, then, the women could continue to receive some kind of psychological reward for continuing to be useful along traditional lines, even as they began to enjoy the new power derived from their new sources of income. The ensuing conflicts led to the development of destructive behaviors such as fighting in the family, drunkenness, and abandonment of the family altogether for another town or woman. Knowledgeable Israeli informants estimate that the divorce rate among the Ethiopians is five to six times that of Israeli society as a whole.[14] In the Jewish population in Israel, 6 percent of the families are headed by single parents; among the Ethiopians, the figure is 38 percent. Of the single parents, 80 percent are female. The same sources estimate that before the Beta Israel left Ethiopia, only 23 percent of their families were headed by single parents. But these same sources add that the rate of divorce among the Beta Israel immigrants may not be any higher than it was in Ethiopia. It is possible that the higher incidence of single-parent families is a result of separations and deaths that occurred en route to Israel from Ethiopia. This has been challenged, however, by others, including the Ethiopians themselves, who assert that the rate of divorce or desertion has increased significantly since arriving in their new home. At one time, the problems of divorce and desertion were so worrisome that one of the ministers in charge of welfare appointed a committee to investigate the problem and make recommendations to his ministry for action.[15]

Yochi, a woman about forty years of age, married to an Ashkenazi physician, is director of a community center of Afula where there is a large concentration of Beta Israel (sixteen hundred of them at one time, reduced to fourteen hundred by the time of my visits in February 1987). The town is divided into three zones. Two are development zones where, among other things, housing is controlled by the government, similar to public housing projects in the United States. The American-Israeli "Project Renewal" scheme was in operation. It aims to rehabilitate poor neighborhoods so they have better chances to be on their own after the termination of the five-year project. The third segment of the town is of high socioeconomic status—the houses are individually owned and very expensive, and the people who live there are doctors who work in the local large hospitals and others of similar socioeconomic status. Yochi belongs to this latter group. The community center is large and provides opportunities for people of all ages to learn a wide range of basic skills. In addition, it provides some facilities to local schools to enhance their programs. I wanted to learn what Yochi thought about the Ethiopians. To begin, she complained that there were too many of them in this one town, which is not good for their integration and adaptation; they are unwilling to transfer to other towns—they like to be together. She added, "If the Ethiopians want to live like that [in segregated settlements], they will never become like the Israelis." She said it is not always the Ethiopians' fault that they stay where they are. The government wants to move them, but some communities do not want them; in others, houses are not available. In other cases, Beta Israel have declined the suggestion that they resettle in Kiryat Yam or Jerusalem. "It is to the advantage of none to let them stay where they are for a longer time," Yochi said.

Responding to specific family situations, Yochi continued: "Unless the Ethiopians change their attitudes regarding the role of the men, women, and children, there are bound to be problems because family members have different roles in Israel and the Ethiopian personalities can't stand what exists here. The families are in trouble. In Israel, Ethiopian Jewish women work outside the home; as such, she may be running too fast for the man. Also, parents are not as important here as they were in Ethiopia. The same holds for the elders of the community." As far as religion was concerned, Yochi felt the Beta Israel "are confused about their religious feelings or activities. They are a very suspicious people. If you take their children for school picnicking, they suspect that you are taking them to a *mikveh* [ritual immersion] for conversion [here she is referring to the controversial issue of mass immersion mandated by the chief rabbinate of Israel which the Ethiopians were resisting]. On the other hand, she adds, "The Israelis want them [Beta Israel] to behave like them, and the Ethiopians are not ready. Even if they want to do what is expected of them, they cannot do it all at once."

What about the spiritual conditions of Beta Israel? Yochi responded: "No one knows. They are not a part of the community. They are very suspicious. They got more promised than could be delivered. . . . Ethiopians do not have confidence in other Ethiopians [veteran Ethiopians]. Maybe they have to be told the truth." A reliable Ashkenazi informant who was present at the interview added that she had heard on several occasions that the older generation of immigrants have said they are glad they came to Israel for the sake of their children—even though it may be hard for the older generation. They said they are happy with what they already have begun to see over a period of a year.

Yochi related that the community center she headed was trying to help the Beta Israel children as well as adults, but with emphasis on the children, to acquire academic as well as vocational and social skills. Here the Ethiopians and other people from the community come for recreational and learning activities. The students come for supervised afternoon studies. Volunteers go to the apartments or settlements of those who don't come to the center to provide supervised after-school activities, such as homework or recreational, social, or cultural activities. In addition, the community center brings together representatives of government departments to plan and coordinate policies and programs for the Beta Israel. I asked whether she had tried to get help from the veteran Ethiopians, and Yochi replied: "Here in Afula, we do not have the right kind of Ethiopians to get involved. . . . We do not have educated Ethiopians in this town. Even when we tried to recruit people for social work training, we could not find one. For some reason, educated Ethiopians do not come to Afula. I am actively looking for one. We want to help them help themselves. So far, we have been having so many problems with the Ethiopians that we did not have much time to think about anything else."

The problems of the family are compounded by the absence of sources of emotional or spiritual support. The traditional sources of spiritual and legal support, the *kesoch*, or religious leaders, have lost their significance in the new order of things.[16] They cannot be counted on. New sources of spiritual succor have not been discovered, cultivated, or utilized successfully . Here linguistic as well as cultural differences are the culprits. The few who have tried to use the local rabbi, a *vatkim* or veteran Israeli, found that absolutely unworkable.

Let us take the case of Yalganesh (not her real name). I visited Yalganesh in her two-bedroom apartment in one of the larger settlement centers. Two female social workers who were familiar with both Yalganesh and the center were also present. One of the women had worked at this center for a year as a social worker and assistant to a researcher. Let's call her Rachel. Rachel speaks good Amharic and very good English as well as Hebrew. Although she had been transferred to another center before the interview took place, she returns to this center periodically, primarily, she said, to visit Yalganesh and her family. They're very close. The interview took place in Amharic and English. Yalganesh and Rachel spoke to each other in Hebrew. Yalganesh is an attractive woman in her late 30s. She lives with her two small children and a sister. She was divorced from her Ethiopian husband. Yalganesh was a little inhibited when it came to talking about intimate personal matters. Her close friend Rachel did much of the talking. Rachel said that Yalganesh, being young, single, and a divorcee, was subjected to a lot of suspicion by her Ethiopian neighbors. She was controlled by what others thought of her. Yalganesh's sister, Asrat, who said she was eighteen years but looked at least ten years older, worked in a factory in the same town. Rachel related that Asrat had had an abortion, and as a result of this and similar experiences, Rachel was giving instructions to both women regarding methods of contraception. Asrat recently had had an affair with the interpreter of the center. But Rachel and Yalganesh put pressure on Asrat to terminate the relationship because the man was much older than Asrat and had a wife and children. Rachel said that the two Beta Israel women are not inhibited in asking her about methods of contraception. They even asked Rachel what kind of devices or methods she used. She told them. But, added Rachel, when she asked the Ethiopians how they protect themselves, they became evasive. They would say *atkkelidge* (Amharic for "You must be kidding",) or they would evade the issue by asking another question. In spite of this inhibition to discuss the subject in public, however, contraceptive information and the technologies that go with it are sought and provided formally or otherwise in certain of the high schools as well as at the clinics.

On the subject of family planning, we should note that there are no open official sanctions in Israel. This is so for any one of the following reasons: (1) the state needs to increase its Jewish population vis-à-vis the rapidly increasing numbers of non-Jews in and around Israel; (2) birth control is not acceptable to the religious leadership; and (3) at least the non-Ashkenazim segment of the population frowns on birth control. The fact of the matter is that, as one visits settlement or absorption centers, one comes across many small children playing on the sidewalks and the streets, and most of the young Beta Israel mothers are carrying babies on their backs or pushing trams. It also appears that, among the Beta Israel, many older men are married to younger women, in which case the women continue to bear children even when the men seem to be unwilling to have children at their age. This perhaps is explained by what some social workers call the factor of *yenjera lijoch* or stepchildren. The extent of separation through divorce or death within the community must have made it possible for many older men to marry younger women and hence to continue to have children well into their later years. The total number of children in a family, including all children from the previous marriages of both partners, would thus be larger than normal. At any rate, a number of the men reported to me that they would like to stop, but that either the available methods of birth control were not suitable to their spouses or the younger spouses wanted to have more children from the marriage. On the other hand, many young women of high school age became pregnant unintentionally while still in school. This is a very delicate matter which the authorities do not talk much about, but it is a real problem. For many of these young Beta Israel women, this is their first exposure to men of their age without adult or parental supervision. Up to now, either they had married earlier, say at nine years old or so, or, because most of them did not attend school, they did not have the opportunity to meet men. Temptations or opportunities did not arise. In contrast, opportunities now exist, and controls are very lax. Many young women have no parents or, living in youth villages (Youth Aliyah), are far away from them. Desirous of human affection and closeness (like anyone else), they are not well versed in coping with the consequences. In other words, they may not know how to enjoy sexual intimacy without unwanted pregnancy. When pregnancy occurs, however, the young father is encouraged to acknowledge paternity and, if possible, marry the woman. But when a marriage does not take place, the woman is taken to one of two centers in the country where she can receive proper medical care. Once she gives birth, she transfers to another school to continue her studies The child remains at the center and is raised by the caretakers there. One administrator told me that when one of the young women was asked why she was not careful, she denied that she had had sexual relations with any man—"it is only that God must have willed it."

In spite of the lack of official sanctioning or the unwillingness of authorities to discuss the subject in public, family planning and provisions for sex education are available at some of the high schools and at clinics for those who want them. Since 1986, family planning education was formally instituted under Dr. Emanuel Chieger, who serves as director of medical and psychological services for the Youth Aliyah system. Using carefully developed audio-visual materials, instructors try to teach young students about reproduction and sexuality, including the social and psychological consequences of lovemaking. There are other clinics where some family planning advice and assistance are available to those Beta Israel who are not attending school.

Emotional and spiritual support for Yalganesh came primarily from her immediate family—her two children, her sister, and her friend Rachel. There is one Sephardic rabbi in the area, but "he is useless," said Yalganesh. He even lost her divorce papers. There is no trained Ethiopian rabbi, and the traditional leaders, or *kesoch*, have lost their significance since arriving here. Interviewees at other centers also reported that they were unable to find an understanding, interested, and competent rabbi. In light of their backgrounds, it is reasonable to assume that men find it even harder to reach out for spiritual or other types of counseling.

In general, real friendship between the Ethiopians and the veteran Israelis is either rudimentary or nonexistent. This is not surprising given the linguistic, cultural, and other important differences. When friendships between members of the two groups do develop, it is a phenomenon in and of itself. Such is the case between Rachel, a veteran Ashkenazi Israeli, and Yalganesh and her family. Although now working at another center some distance away, Rachel still comes twice a week to visit her Ethiopian friends. "When I first met them, I thought that the Beta Israel women were unfriendly and suspicious; their health habits were not acceptable to me. When I first met Yalganesh, she would not even sit facing me. Instead, she gave me her side profile. But gradually I came to discover that the reserved attitudes were just external facades. Underneath, I discovered warmth, caring, and genuine friendliness—they care for me."

The preceding case illustrates how some family problems are tackled. Obviously, human ingenuity continues to inspire hope where one does not expect to find it. Another case was related to me by the head of a regional Ministry of Absorption office, division of social services. According to Offir, a Beta Israel woman who came to Israel without her husband subsequently got pregnant by another Ethiopian man. When the child was born, there arose the question of how to register him for social service purposes. If they tried to register him under the real father's name, the father would abandon the child and the mother because he did not want the relationship to be known. Eventually, the matter was settled, at least temporarily, by registering him in the mother's name. This provides immediate relief, but in Israel, where the rabbinate does not accept or recognize children born out of wedlock as legitimate, the future life of the poor child may become practically untenable. "There are many cases such as this one," Offir concluded.

Another practice should be noted. However, because it has not been well investigated, it is not easy to draw conclusions regarding its effect on the family. It is the practice of ritual purity followed by the devout Beta Israel. This includes, among other things, the seclusion of a woman when she is menstruating. In Ethiopia, the menstruating woman is secluded in a hut apart from the household. At the end of each menstrual period, she immerses herself in a river before rejoining the family. The woman is also secluded after giving birth. Postpartum seclusion lasts forty days if the child is male and eighty days if female. Here again, when the prescribed seclusion is over, the mother dips herself in a river before she returns to the family. In the Israeli context, the Talmudic traditions do not include these practices. But for the Ethiopians, dropping the practice, which they think is mandated by the Torah, is very hard and painful. In addition, it is practically impossible to find a running river in Israel. Conflicts within families and between families and the authorities have been reported.[17]

As for the children, they may be divided into two categories: (1) those up to eleven years of age who attend one of the neighborhood schools and most of whom live with at least one of the parents or a guardian, and (2) those between the ages of twelve and eighteen who attend boarding schools (youth *aliyah*) and who visit their families only once every three or four weeks. The contact between the latter group and the home is very insignificant and may be dismissed as nonexistent. Following the experiences at boarding schools or youth villages, most of the able-bodied male youth join the Israeli armed forces for three years. (For religious reasons the Ethiopian females are exempted from service.) While in the armed services, they receive additional training in vocational, linguistic, and civic skills. During leave times, they are expected to visit their families. A question that may arise regarding this latter group is, how are they going to relate to their parents in a few years from now? But for the younger children who stay at home, several sets of challenges already have begun to emerge. To begin, many of the children younger than seven were born after their parents left Ethiopia—either on the way, in refugee camps, or in Israel. For all practical purposes, these children have forgotten their home languages (Amharic or Tigrigna), making even simple communication between the non-Hebrew-speaking parent and the child who is fluent in that language extremely limited and difficult. The older children (nine to twelve years of age) speak Hebrew with their siblings and peers, though they still speak the home language with their parents. So, in theory, communication should not be a problem. But it is. The inability of the parents to speak Hebrew is not only considered a lack of skill but also denotes a lack of modernity in the eyes of the child. Also, seeing that the father's skills are irrelevant in the new setting and that he has no position of dominance in the family, many of the children ignore him; at worst, they remind him of his loss in status—and they do it in Hebrew. One social worker observed that "of all categories of immigrants, the father has lost the most."

Here emerges the question of ego identity. Some fathers have become strong enough to understand the new realities and try to live with it as best they can. Others are not so fortunate and resort to abusive methods in their attempt to regain lost prestige and control, for instance, by assigning children tasks that interfere with their schooling, asking them to stay behind from school to do the cleaning in the apartment, or sending them to buy some groceries when they are supposed to be in school.

There are parents who are concerned with their children's schooling. Also, some children, such as Odium, are concerned about their parents. Odium is one of the best students in her fifth-grade class. Unlike most of her Ethiopian age-mates in Israel, she attends a secular public school. She said she prefers to speak in Hebrew, but for the sake of her parents she always tries to talk to them in Amharic except when she wants to help them to learn Hebrew. At the regional center, an administrator showed me a letter Odium had written to the housing administration pleading with them to assign her family an apartment near a good school so that her goals would not be stifled. The letter, written in Hebrew, impressed the administrators, and they told me it is the kind of phenomenon that helps to keep them going.

An Israeli psychologist who has worked and studied Beta Israel youth said, "By coming here [to Israel], the position and authority of the parents are weakened." The parents realize this and, for the most part, have accepted it well. Although parents may regret leaving their country of origin, their sacrifices seem worthwhile when they consider the opportunities their children will have in Israel. One father who was nonliterate when he arrived in Israel six years ago but is now literate, has eight children. His regret was that he and his family did not come to Israel fifteen years earlier (the age of his oldest son). His children would have been able to start their education earlier. This kind of sentiment is almost universal among families with children, even as they express reservations about their own personal future.

CHAPTER FIVE

❖

Setting Up Home

❖

The Ethiopian Jews were, of course, not the first *olim* to come to Israel. In a state conceived and built around the idea of providing a home for all Jews in the Diaspora, even before its creation in 1948, mechanisms and institutions were put in place to encourage and facilitate the arrival, settlement, and continued survival of Jewish immigrants. Beginning in 1882, small and large waves of immigrants, a vast majority of them from Europe, have been arriving in Palestine. Since the formation of the state in 1948, even larger waves of Jewish immigrants continued to arrive, primarily from the developing regions of Asia and Africa. The rate of immigration reached its peak in the early 1950s with the arrival of thousands of Jews from northern Africa and Asia. The Ethiopians were the last of the large waves of immigrants from the developing part of the world. In fact, by the 1970s, the rate of immigration from the traditional sources of Europe, Asia, and other parts of Africa was tapering off very drastically, with the result that institutions, facilities, and personnel had become idle. Therefore, when the Ethiopians began to arrive, they could not have done so at a more opportune time. Addressing this topic, the dynamic director of Youth Aliyah,

Uri Gordon, was prompted to declare that "this was the era of the Ethiopians."[1]

The two waves of Beta Israel that immigrated to Israel between 1980 and 1985 (or most of others since, for that matter) were not selected based on any criteria other than their desire to come and their willingness and ability to endure the long, arduous process of leaving home, traveling to the camps in third countries, and eventually reaching their destination in Israel. Thus came people who were young and old, preliterate and literate. The vast majority were people of peasant background who had never before ventured beyond their immediate communities; they were devout but unlettered people. They came from parts of Ethiopia unexposed to outside influences, where modern means of communication, commerce, and education were very undeveloped, to settle in Israel, a technologically and scientifically advanced Western society with no previous experience with people from sub-Saharan Africa claiming to be Jews and entitled to set up homes in the Holy Land. The Israeli authorities had ample time to prepare for the arrival and reception of the Ethiopian Jews long before they were overwhelmed by events in the 1980s.

IMMIGRANT RECEIVING CENTERS

The policy, now formulated, was to take the immigrants to receiving centers in two stages before they were released into the larger society. This policy took into account the very poor physical and mental condition of the Ethiopians at the time of arrival and their peasant background. The need to educate the Israeli public about the Ethiopians in such a way as to minimize, if not totally forestall, formation of negative impressions was also recognized. Therefore, the decision was made to settle the immigrants in sheltered centers until they had mastered at least the rudiments of Hebrew and met the basic requirements of setting up home in the context of Israel.

It was also anticipated that through the utilization of the media, the Israeli public would come to know and appreciate these Zionists who had suffered so much for the sake of their faith and Jewish culture. As will be detailed later, considerable effort was made to depict the Ethiopians as heroic, which they were, but, more importantly, as a people who for centuries had longed to be united with their coreligionists in Jerusalem. Moreover, they were presented as a people who considered themselves aliens in Ethiopia, seldom participating or wanting to participate voluntarily in the development or protection of their land of origin. Their languages—Ge'ez, Amharic, Tigrigna, or any of the others—were depicted as uniquely their own. In other words, the Ethiopians and their Jewishness were packaged and presented in a way that resembled the historical conditions experienced by Jews in Europe, the Soviet Union, and to some extent in Arab countries in the hope that the Israeli public would understand and identify with them.

While this was going on, the immigrants were living in sheltered or absorption centers, where they could be prepared for gradual release to their own apartments in communities throughout Israel. The hope and expectation were that eventually they would become accepted as functioning and contributing members of such communities like any other immigrant group. This was the objective.

There was some recognition, nevertheless, that for some time to come, the immigrants would be receiving far more than they could give to the local communities, which would have some problems accepting them. Therefore, efforts would be made not to place too many immigrants (in proportion to the veterans) in a given apartment block, neighborhood, or town. The authorities did appreciate, overall, the magnitude of the task at hand. For "by its very nature . . . a comprehensive long-term [plan] that seeks to grant destitute immigrants a basis for integration in the normal Israeli life is expected to be costly."[2] By all accounts, indeed, the Ethiopian immigrants, have been the most costly *olim*.

The coming of the immigrants was the responsibility of the Israeli government at the first level. The assistance of international Jewish organizations and other governments such as that of the United States were crucial at certain stages of the process but not indispensable. It was imperative that many of the governmental agencies such as the ministries of foreign affairs, interior, absorption, labor and social welfare and the security apparatus play their respective and unique roles efficiently. But once the immigrants were in Israel, and at least for the duration of their first year, the responsibility for their processing and welfare was that of the quasi-governmental Jewish Agency for Israel (JA). After the immigrants had completed their year at the absorption centers, the Ministry of Immigrant Absorption would move to center stage. Assisted to some extent by other private organizations such as the Joint Distribution Committee, and in cooperation with other relevant governmental departments, the Ministry of Absorption assumed responsibility for coordinating the immigrants' housing, training, employment, and socialization functions.

At the initial stage, they were received in a care center known as the Absorption and Sorting Base. Here, the immigrants were identified, registered, and assigned new Hebrew names, authorities having decided this would resolve immediate and long-term problems for the absorbing society and the immigrants. The 1984–85 arrivals also were reconverted (they had to go through symbolic circumcision in the case of males and immersion in water for all), reunited with families if any, and in general allowed time to recover from the hardships they had experienced. Immigrants were provided with clothing, medical care and were otherwise prepared for referral to other centers. Immigrants could stay from a few days to up to three months, depending on their readiness and the availability of proper absorption centers. When they stayed longer, they were taught Hebrew and learned housekeeping and some rudiments of life in Israel. Except for some organizational difficulties, according to those who had a chance to evaluate the procedures and accomplishments, the quality of care and reception provided was very good.[3] At the next stage, however, when the immigrants were to pass a year in absorption centers before being placed in permanent quarters, there developed organizational, administrative, and personnel problems that would affect the quality and efficiency of the absorption processes and would have serious consequences for the immigrants in the first instance and the absorbing society in the second.

During the period of this study, there were more than thirty-three centers of absorption scattered throughout Israel and at least one on the West Bank.[4] In most instances, immigrants stay for only about five to six months in absorption centers, but in the case of the Ethiopians, this was extended to about a year. The Ethiopians, it was recognized, were unique cases in the annals of immigration to Israel. They had long been separated from the bulk of the Jewish people and their history. They came from a traditional, developing society to an industrialized, Western society, and there existed a huge gap in all aspects of life-styles between the two. Their deteriorated physical and mental conditions rendered them unfit to confront life in the new society.

Another set of factors that needs to be considered is the crumbling family structure that began en route and continued after arrival.

But perhaps what set the Ethiopians apart from the other Israelis most of all was their color—their blackness. The Yemenites and the Benei Israel (Jews from India), who had preceded them in coming to Israel, are darker than most of the other Israelis, but the Ethiopians, or at least most of them, stood out much more because of the color of their skin. These were some of the Ethiopians' differentiating characteristics to be taken into account when planning for their absorption in Israel.[5]

The objective, then, was to create conditions that would bring the two groups gradually together. The immigrants were to be prepared for the requirements of the absorbing society at the absorption centers. They were then to be placed in permanent settlements that would allow the continuation of communal life but avoid the creation of "ethnic pockets," as had happened with earlier immigrants from Asia and Africa. The immigrants ultimately would be placed in areas neither too strong (from the point of view of culture and economics) nor too weak, and dispersed among the absorbing local communities. In other words, the objective was to maximize interaction between the immigrants and the members of the local communities without jeopardizing communal life or straining the capacities of the local communities to handle the absorption of immigrants. That is why it was imperative to plan the stages of absorption at different levels carefully and to monitor them closely.

The immigrants who arrived between 1980 and 1984 were accommodated by themselves in centers that were empty. However, when the number of immigrants increased because of Operation Moses, other temporary shelters such as hotels and guest houses were used. But when it became clear that the latter type of accommodation was not suitable, attempts were made to place the immigrants in existing centers alongside immigrants from other countries. What emerged from the various arrangements in the fall of 1985 was the following: 5,377 Beta Israel were placed in seventeen centers owned by the Jewish Agency; 2,552 were placed in nine centers made up of hotels and guest houses; and seventeen other centers accommodated another 2,552 Beta Israel mixed with other immigrants. Most of the immigrants were accommodated in centers of their own.

Different categories of personnel were recruited and deployed in the centers. They included veteran Ethiopians (*vatikim*) who acted as interpreters and instructors and served as effective bridges between the newcomers, the care givers, and the local society. Homemakers, recruited from the local community, guided the immigrants in ways of life, health, and household management, a service absolutely essential for the newcomers. The most important groups of professional personnel were the social workers and the medical practitioners (nurses and doctors) who worked under the supervision of a center director. Later on, other professionals such as anthropologists and psychologists were added. These constituted the core group of personnel whose skills or lack thereof molded the nature of at least the initial processes of adaptation and absorption of the immigrants. In other words, the immigrants were entirely dependent on the skills, knowledge, and attitude of the personnel assembled to guide them through the strangeness of their new environment. At this stage, the immigrants were taught in *ulpanim* (formal and informal centers for learning the Hebrew language) the rudiments of Hebrew, how to set up homes using unfamiliar utensils and furniture, how to shop, how to manage the household budget, how to prepare meals using local ingredients, and the many other things vital to existence in a modern society. As the immigrants learned skills that would help them to survive, they also acquired and developed attitudes toward life in Israel, mostly as reflected through the people they came in daily contact with—the care providers at the absorption centers. Before examining the degree of success these people had, as seen from the immigrants' point of view, let us review some of the accomplishments primarily from the organizational and administrative points of view.[6]

At the height of the initial absorption activity, there were about one thousand employees of the Jewish Agency, both permanent and contractual, some working in the headquarters but most in the field working with the immigrants. About eighty were social workers, 113 were instructor-interpreters (veteran Ethiopians), and the rest were teachers, house mothers, block supervisors, health-care providers, and so on. In their respective spheres of responsibility, these people were the gatekeepers between the new immigrants and the veteran society. Most of them did a commendable job, working hard to establish good relations with the immigrants and to gain their confidence. The social workers were especially commended by both the immigrants and official reports. The instructor-interpreters had a number of problems with the immigrants, as will be described. But there were also serious oversights that could have been avoided or, once apparent, could have been corrected earlier, whose effects were untoward for the immigrants as well as those working with them.

There had been no comprehensive search within the Jewish Agency to identify people with qualifications and experience in immigrant absorption, although such people did exist. Nor was the possibility considered of recruiting retired employees who had extensive experience in absorption of immigrants. They were not even asked to work as volunteers. The steps taken to recruit workers were not made public, the positions were not advertised, and the recruiting committee was drawn mostly from junior employees. Such shortcomings also applied to the recruitment of the most crucial persons, the directors of the absorption centers. The result was that quite a number of unqualified persons were retained which resulted in several disturbances, including open demonstrations by the immigrants in a number of centers. The homemakers, who were recruited locally, on the whole seem to have worked hard and effectively. But even here, when the internal organization in the absorption center was deficient, the homemakers were not adequately utilized.

At another level, conflicts occurred within the absorption centers among the professional and staff people as well as people working under one of the two wings of the Jewish Agency. There was confusion regarding the lines of command. The homemakers and instructor-interpreters were moved from one line of command to the other so frequently that they became confused. Lack of sufficient orientation at the start of employment regarding the nature of their charges and the policy of JA and absence of guidance once on the job may have contributed to the failure of some of the directors. Of course, the JA department responsible for the immigrants pointed out that, among other things, they could not have announced many of their efforts to the public because the arrival of the immigrants was necessarily secret. This is true, but it does not explain all the shortcomings of those efforts over a relatively long time. It seems traditional bureaucratic inertia, narrow self-interest, and red tape were at work full-time, despite the most urgent and important needs of the immigrants.

The immigrants, then, had to go through the experiences of the absorption centers. The ways and conventions of the new society had to be learned gradually, and during the process the immigrants were to be accommodated so that their encounters with the larger society would not be awkward for either side. There were many obvious advantages to this concept, but important questions remain. How much time should have been spent at this stage? What might have been the optimal mix of shelter and exposure to the real environment so that adaptation could begin? These are hard questions, and this study provides no answer for them. What might be said here is that living in the absorption centers entailed a dependence on the care providers for even routine duties (shopping, getting children ready to go to school, being escorted to the clinics and banks, etc.) incompatible with steady progress toward adaptation. Postponing the time when reality has to be faced creates more dependency, distorts family structure, precludes interactions with local people, and might lead the immigrants to think that their sheltered existence and the provisions made on their behalf were normal and would last indefinitely.

The JA was challenged for not asking whether the premises on which the absorption center concept was based were tenable. At one stage, there was a conflict among members of the two major ethnic groups (Amhara and Tigray) in one of the absorption centers in the Negev which led the authorities to remove some of them to regular apartments. Later follow-up revealed that the people mainstreamed earlier had made faster progress toward adaptation than those who stayed behind. The agency was criticized for not following up on that experiment by trying to mainstream as early as possible most of the rest of the immigrants.[7]

Unfortunately, the care providers apparently did not encourage their charges to lead increasingly independent lives (which would have made their services unnecessary). Instead, the immigrants became more and more dependent on such personnel, even to the point of seeking authorization to leave camp. When some of these untoward side effects were revealed and the agency was criticized for them, it wanted to terminate its role and responsibilities. This created additional problems and further complicated the issues.

In the winter of 1986, the Jewish Agency announced termination of its operation of the absorption centers, saying it was time for the Absorption Ministry and others to locate the immigrants in permanent houses. The agency said the original plans called for the immigrants to stay in temporary centers for only about a year, and that period was over. Further, the agency had run out of money, and the immigrants were becoming too dependent on the care providers of the centers. As long as they stayed in absorption centers, had their bills paid and stipends delivered on time, and sought and received direction from the care providers before making any simple move, the immigrants would never be able to stand on their own, negating the fundamental objective of gradual adaptation to Israel. The agency's termination of its role included removal of the telephones, mailboxes, furniture, and utensils on which the immigrants had come to rely. No alternatives were provided. The agency wanted to get out quickly and dismissed practically all workers, except a few social workers in some of the centers. The residents as well as most of the workers protested the agency's sudden decision to withdraw, saying the move would create hardships for the immigrants and that more time was needed to make the transition—but to no avail.

To determine if there were motives other than the stated ones for this sudden decision, I interviewed different people I thought were in positions to know. One senior official of the agency's department responsible for the centers gave the following account of the sudden withdrawal. It is true that there had been an agreement among the governmental bodies that the agency would get out at the end of the first year or before, but the real reason was that the immigrants' situation was becoming increasingly afflicted with problems and controversies and was not a glamorous front-page news story anymore. Instead, the news media were carrying accounts of strikes, fights, and similar stories of rancor among the immigrants, between the immigrants and certain sectors of care providers, and among the various categories of workers. So it was decided to get out at once. For whatever reasons, this informant added, there was no doubt that this decision created a lot of problems for the Absorption Ministry, which had to get in now and assume the many challenges, and for the workers and *olim*. Other administrators supported the agency's move, saying that continuation of the efforts would have served neither the interests of the immigrants nor those of the absorbing society. The Ethiopians were receiving distorted impressions of Israel, they said. The overall reaction was that the agency had to pull out sometime anyway and it already had met its contractual obligations. They did regret that the agency did not see fit to give advance warning so that adequate provisions could have been made for all concerned. More than half of the immigrants were still in the centers, and for them the abrupt weaning was a shock and suggested that they were being punished for things done or undone by others over which they had no control. The immigrants were disappointed or bitter about the decision. Most seemed to blame the lower echelon staff in the agency for prompting the action. It is still too early to find out what impact this action had on the process of adaptation. The possibility that it may result in psychological regression for the immigrants cannot be ruled out.

MEASURING SUCCESS

For most of the Ethiopian Jews, 1986–87 (which coincided with my fieldwork) was a year of *gojo mewttat*, or establishing a home, striking out on their own. Usually, the term is used in connection with a married son living with his wife in his parents' household until he is financially and otherwise secure. When the time comes to set up his own home, he does so with the blessing and support of his parents. The new home usually is established on the same premises as that of his parents. The transition from being an integral part of the family to becoming fully independent takes place gradually. In Israel, the immigrants applied the expression *gojo mewttat* to their situation, which at first sounded strange for adults but on second thought was quite appropriate. They were striking out on their own for the first time. This was also the beginning of the test of their readiness, of the adequacy of their preparation during the previous year(s) at the absorption centers. For the first time since their arrival in Israel, they were confronted with choices in housing, employment, training, and schooling; they were expected to pay grocery and utility bills fully and on time, travel to the municipalities without an escort, pay taxes, and otherwise forge their niche in the larger community. This was also the year most of the school-age children were mainstreamed into the regular schools and began to interact with members of the absorbing society. For the parents, this was another challenge. They were now expected to encounter not only the teachers and administrators of the schools but, through the schools, the general adult population. New sets of rules, procedures, and activities had to be followed by both the children and their parents. The extent to which the immigrants would be able to perform the myriad routines of daily life in the new society independent of center supervision could be considered a measure of the effectiveness of the absorption program and immigrant adaptation.

Arrangement for housing and permanent settlement were high on the list of priorities. For this, the Absorption Ministry required the coordinated efforts of the various ministries, including housing, finance, and labor. The cooperation of the immigrants was also very crucial, especially in light of their natural desire to stay near relatives and close friends. The government wanted to disperse the immigrants among Israeli communities that were neither too weak nor too strong and where different ethnic groups and persons of different ages and marital status are represented in a way that the *olim* could maintain some relations among themselves. Strong communities would be too much for the immigrants to cope with, since the class structure would make the immigrants feel inadequate; communities that were too weak, however, would be unable to help immigrants make the necessary progress toward independence and long-term well-being. Access to good schools and opportunities for employment were part and parcel of the prerequisites taken into account.

As sound and as logical as these objectives appeared, when it came time to implement them, other practical problems emerged, most of which had to do ultimately with money, though that was not the only problem. For instance, there were empty apartments built earlier for other immigrants which had been empty for some time. Because of their location, nobody wanted to live in them. Some were located where there were no possibilities for employment; others were located in weak communities. The Absorption Ministry tried to urge the building of additional structures at the desired locations but was told by the Housing Department and the Jewish Agency that there were no funds to do this. Negotiations among the various agencies resulted in considerable compromise, and the final outcome was not always what was desirable. Finally, some of the absorption centers were converted into permanent settlements. Large groups of immigrants were thus settled in communities of their own, thereby abandoning the goal of integrating them into the larger Israeli society. Others remained in the absorption centers on a temporary basis while the search continued for permanent apartments. Still others were placed in permanent apartments according to the original plans. As time passed, differences in the progress toward goals of absorption and adaptation of the groups settled in these different ways became apparent.

Setting up home, or *gojo mewttat*, proved difficult for many of the immigrants. During the absorption period at the centers, social workers and others had assumed many of the family's responsibilities. The image of destitute immigrants that had been presented on television when the immigrants first arrived left an overwhelming emotional impact on the minds of the public. As a consequence, many people had volunteered to work for free, others for nominal pay, and still others as full-time employees to help the immigrants. Naturally the tendency was for these well-intentioned people to do too much for too long, depriving the immigrants of the opportunity to learn to do things for themselves and thereby gradually become self-reliant. When the time came, serious problems developed. For one thing, the Ethiopians had no idea about Israeli expectations. They could not anticipate what they should or should not do on those rare occasions when they encountered outsiders. More importantly, this was the year the children of the immigrants were sent to schools attended by other Israeli children. Here was a critical test of the level of understanding the Ethiopian and veteran Israeli populations had of each other and of how effectively they could work together to resolve issues without the mediation of absorption center personnel.

For instance, in one of the largest centers where some Ethiopians still were waiting to be assigned permanent apartments and where others already had settled, I heard a lot of complaints from the teachers, social workers, and school administrators that the Ethiopian parents were not participating, as any parent should, in preparing and sending their children to school on time. They complained that the Ethiopian children often came to school untidy, ill clothed, ill shoed (barefoot or in sandals even in winter), with unwashed faces, runny noses, and some with shaved heads. This shocked Israelis especially when they saw sores on the child's head which might have been one of the reasons for shaving. Further, the children were said to be full of lice, disorganized in personal appearance, coming to school without notebooks or school bags, and often lethargic, perhaps indicating lack of proper rest the previous night. The Israelis felt the Ethiopian parents did not care how their children presented themselves or, more generally, were disinterested in the overall well-being of their children, including their education. In an achievement-oriented society such as Israel, they argued, this kind of behavior was intolerable. Such complaints were so frequent, intense, and widespread that in one instance I asked the head volunteer social worker at one of the large centers who spoke some Amharic and was well accepted by the Ethiopian community as well as the school authorities if she could arrange for me to talk to the parents in groups. A month or so later, on December 8, 1986, I was again in the area and made the same request. In a matter of thirty minutes, a meeting was arranged. The social worker, some of her colleagues, and I met with the Ethiopians in a packed hall with some overflowing into the corridors. Parents and nonparents, young and old came. Most of the people either had seen or heard of me before in different contexts in both Ethiopia and Israel, so they had a fairly good idea of what I was doing.

I briefly introduced myself, highlighting my background, experiences, and work in Ethiopia and the United States. I told them I was a visiting professor at the Hebrew University for a year. I added that I was at this meeting to tell them what the complaints against them were and to serve as an honest broker by listening to their side of the story which, if they so wished, I would convey to the authorities on their behalf. Then I presented the litany of complaints I had heard leveled against them. From the beginning, it was apparent to me that the people present were starving to talk to someone in their own language, especially someone they saw as being of some consequence. I spelled out what I had heard already and let them respond to the charges. I had not expected their reactions to be as serious, heartfelt, and articulate as they were. As happens often in such gatherings, a few tended to talk more than others. But speak they did, for the better part of two hours. From what I observed, there was no inhibition on their part, which is also a measure of their adaptation, since they felt that they could express their anger against the authorities without fear of retribution.

At the root of their problems was a lack of money. Whether they are employees or pensioners, their income was not sufficient for their many needs. They were unable to purchase new clothing for themselves or their children and certainly had no money for parties. Some of their clothing had been handed to them at the time of arrival more than a year earlier. As far as the complaint about their parties was concerned, there were no parties. In accordance with their customs, at the time of *merdo*, the breaking of the news of the death of a family member in Ethiopia; at *gizret*, the circumcision of a child; at *tezkar*, the remembrance of a dead relative; or, at the time of weddings, the death of a relative or close friend, and the birth of a child in the family, friends and family members get together to mourn or rejoice over the event. Usually, each adult contributes either food, soft drinks, or money. The expenses are small and distributed among the family and friends. These occasions make it possible for them to get together and give one another emotional support. They asserted that these were some of the cultural components they cherished and were not willing to give up. "These are the things we used to do in our country. We are not ready to abandon them. As it is, we have modified many of our customs already. *Endenesu mehon anfelgim bet zegitew yemibelu; yenesun bahrye memar anfeligim.* [Amharic: "We do not want to be like those who close their doors when they eat—meaning they are uncaring."] We do not want to learn their culture."

"We [here] are oppressed people," another elder added.

It was apparent they felt unjustly treated and were going to demand redress for their grievances. At one stage, the settlers had been promised that people with large families would be able to buy washing machines at reduced prices. As instructed, they filled out the forms. A few months later, they were told to come again and fill out another set of forms because the former ones had been lost. They filled out the second set. But the promised machines did not arrive. The people continue to hand-wash their clothes in an environment that is not suitable (back in Ethiopia, they also washed their clothes by hand, but in the rivers where the natural contours and stones were more suitable). The result is that they cannot wash the clothes as often as necessary. In the winter, it takes longer to dry them, and they do not have enough clothing for changes.

The adults also had been told they would receive some clothing if they came to the centers and signed some forms. They did. Later they were told they would receive the clothing through the local schools. When they reported to the schools, they were told that the money intended for clothing had been used instead to purchase school supplies for the children. (Actually, the clothing had been donated for the Ethiopians by persons and organizations outside Israel. The local authorities, I was told later, decided to sell the clothing and use the money to purchase school supplies. This is directly related to the complaint that the parents were unwilling to invest money on behalf of their children for school-related expenses. One way of getting the money was to use the proceeds from the sales of donated clothing. Obviously, the parents were furious that they had been given a runaround and were not trusted to handle their own affairs. The immigrants, in fact, strongly suspected that the money from the proceeds went into the pockets of local officials and that this was not the first time that had happened. They repeated that the local officials were dishonest, including the very detested *astergwami* (Amharic for "veteran") Beta Israel instructor-interpreters. The immigrants were convinced that other food and clothing which had been sent for them from abroad had been appropriated by the local authorities and interpreters.

Several of the speakers repeatedly emphasized how their lack of language proficiency worked against them and how the local authorities were getting away with murder. They said this was the first chance they had had to express themselves collectively and fully in their own language. For this they were grateful.

They moved to the provision of day-care, another point of contention a number of the younger parents complained about. One young father of two small children related that the local day-care center had a policy of accepting only one child per family and that there was no other center in town for his other child to attend. What could he do with the second child? The mother, when she does not work outside the home, has to take care of household duties, including doing the laundry by hand. They needed to find a place for the child.

The immigrants also complained that they were ignored when they went to visit the clinics. Other people, they said, were given priority by the health-care providers. Sometimes, after spending an entire day waiting for treatment, they would be told to go home and try again tomorrow. They said they also were denied ambulance services even when there were emergencies such as childbirth and acute cardiac attack. One elderly woman added that it was because of their religion that they suffered this kind of indignity and insult. She meant that if it were not for their religion, they would not have come to Israel.

In brief, the immigrants had come to distrust the local authorities as well as the employees of the Ministry of Absorption and the Jewish Agency. Immigrants questioned the intentions and actions of these personnel. They also questioned their integrity in matters of finance. (There were a few exceptions, and most of them were volunteers.) They emphasized that the money they either earned or received from pensions was very inadequate. Without articulating why, they thought they deserved better treatment than what they were getting. It should be recalled that this was their first year out of the absorption centers and for most of them their first attempt at independent living, *gojo mewttat*. Some were still waiting for permanent housing. Their condition may be described as one of transition. Their bitterness and anger emanated from their experiences in the absorption centers as well as their first year of independent living. They related their experiences to me with deep feeling, clear thinking, and great eloquence. Even as a native speaker of Amharic, intimately familiar with the manner of thinking and speech of the people, I was profoundly moved by the way they were able to express their thoughts and experiences. I only wished that the authorities could hear them as I did.

Unfortunately, because the authorities do not understand Amharic or Tigrigna and are unfamiliar with the immigrants' culture, they, as well as the Israeli public and even the care providers, see the Ethiopians as awkward and incompetent as they try to do things for themselves in everyday life. Had they heard what I did that evening, they would have understood the Ethiopian *olim* much better; more importantly, they would have accorded them much more respect than they have done so far. It is apparent that the local authorities acted on the assumption that the immigrants were, for the most part, simple folks of peasant background who would not and could not understand much of what was good for them. Consequently, the authorities seem to feel that whatever decisions were made on their behalf should have been accepted, even appreciated. I find it hard to believe that corrupt practices by local representatives are as prevalent as the immigrants report, but at the same time, the appearances of corruption are there. If clothing had been sent to the people, they should have participated in decisions regarding its fair distribution or alternative uses. What transpired was that since the immigrants were allegedly wasting money on "partying" (which was a misunderstanding of their concepts and practices) and seemed unwilling to contribute money for extracurricular activities and school supplies, the authorities took it upon themselves to sell the clothes and use the proceeds to purchase the needed items. Apparently, no effort was made to account for the money to the satisfaction of the immigrants. Misperceptions ensued which in turn solidified into mistrust and confrontations.

Following the meeting, I briefed the non-Amharic-speaking workers who had helped organize the meeting and were present throughout the lengthy discussion. They told me they were electrified by the way the grievances were articulated. On the following morning, I traveled to the other side of town to meet with the regional representatives of the ministry and the Jewish Agency, including the top administrator in charge of the Ethiopians. At first, she told me how things were moving smoothly in finding housing and employment opportunities for the immigrants. But I told her I was duty-bound to relate to her what I had learned from my previous contacts and especially the meeting from the previous night. She was visibly shaken. Perhaps she was concerned about whether an outsider could be trusted enough to be told all these things. At any rate, she said it was true that they had many problems with both the immigrants and the workers. She also admitted that, because of language problems, some mistreatment, including at the health clinics, might have taken place as described. She and others also admitted that the reports regarding the disposal of clothing were true, though they insisted the proceeds were put to good use in helping children with their education. She added that some of the other complaints also might have been justified. But then she gave her side of the story.

Setting Up Home

She said the Ethiopian Jews had declared that they want to be Israelis, that they want to learn, and so forth. "We would like to help them achieve those goals," she said. "At times, we find that their wishes are incompatible with what we think is in their long-term interest. They want to live in places such as Petah Tiqva or Haddera where there are already too many Ethiopians. We want them to go where the jobs are and where they can become integrated with veteran Israelis. We urge them to travel with us and visit some of the other places, but most are not willing to move even a distance of a mile. They all want to stay together in this one place. Since the *merkaze klita* [absorption centers] are not their own, they do not look after them well. After we have told them repeatedly of our positions, they keep coming with the same requests."

"Personally," she continued, "I like to go to their houses to talk to them instead of having them come to the office. But they do not seem comfortable. If they keep coming here, how can I go there? I sit on this side of the table [in her office] and they on the other, and it is not possible to establish rapport, trust, and understanding. But if I do go to their houses, they may expect that they will get everything they want. This is not possible. Administrators have to say no sometimes."

What seems to be working here is a cultural assumption on the part of the immigrants: if you do not get what you want the first time, try again until you convince the official that your cause is justified. Eventually, the official will get tired and grant your wishes. This is known as *dejmettinat* in Amharic. Literally, it means "waiting at the gate"; in other words, after you have made your request, keep showing up in person at the gate until you succeed. For some, this works even in Israel, but nonetheless the officials get baffled when the Ethiopians do not take no as the final answer.

Regarding the condition of the Ethiopians, this administrator thought there was too much generalization. "They were depicted to us as destitute, poor, and severely persecuted because of their Jewishness. Now we know differently. But the depiction of them as such was helpful in precipitating a lot of dialogue that led to the mobilization of public opinion which in turn led to their coming to Israel."

By way of summary, then, it could be said that the Beta Israel's first year in Israeli society—their new home—was full of challenges and surprises, not all of them pleasant. How these initial experiences will color or influence what lies ahead remains to be seen.

CHAPTER SIX

❖

Crisis in Communal Integrity and Identity

❖

If it is assumed a healthy ego identity and a sense of continued belonging to the primary group are essential for successful absorption of immigrants,[1] then it is important to identify clearly some of the major factors that fortify the ego and bind the group together. This chapter delineates some of these factors as they relate to the Beta Israel and examines how they are functioning in the context of Israel. The analysis considers the conditions and demands imposed by the absorbing society, or significant representatives of it, on the immigrants and how the immigrants have tried (or, in some instances, have refused to try) to respond to the demands.

RELIGION AS THE CENTRAL ISSUE

Whether Ethiopia's social, economic, and political hardships had much to do with the Beta Israel's flight to Israel, or whether they had deeper motives, is the subject of debate. Delineating the push and pull factors in the migration of the

Beta Israel is a very complicated and sensitive task. Most Ethiopians would say that they left for Israel at the time preordained by God and foretold by the prophets. They say: *"Lenefisachin sinil new yemettanew"* ("We came for the sake of our soul [religion]"). No doubt, some came for more mundane economic or political reasons. Certainly, Israeli society and many other supporters of the Diaspora Jews considered the rescue of the Ethiopians a religious act to be accomplished on the same bases as that of other Jews from Asia, northern Africa, eastern Europe, and the Soviet Union. So on both sides the religious reason was compelling. Perhaps it is precisely for this reason that the ensuing controversies may seem contradictory and illogical to the Ethiopian Jews and to others outside the Israeli rabbinate and Orthodox circles. It must be remembered that, as far as the Beta Israel were concerned, at this juncture they were confronted with two very important challenges. At one level, they were Ethiopian citizens and Ethiopian Jews just as there are American or Indian Jews in their respective countries. But by immigrating to Israel, they were suddenly Israeli citizens and Israeli Jews. Their previous identities in the land of origin counted very little if at all. In other words, their civic as well as religious identities underwent dramatic transformation at the very time that they were trying to recover from the ordeals and traumas of their very debilitating journey.

As far as their Jewishness is concerned, the Ethiopians maintain that for twenty-seven hundred years they led an authentic Jewish life in accordance with the principles and guidance of the Orate and supplemented by their own religious works which evolved over the centuries.[2] In matters of ritual purity, marriage and divorce, circumcision, and observance of holidays, they followed the injunctions of the Holy Writ. They tried to live an isolated and uncontaminated life vis-à-vis other groups in their native country and as a result suffered much persecution, discrimination, and injustice.[3] For the vast majority, coming to the Holy Land fulfilled a long-cherished hope; it was not a special favor to them or dispensation on the part of anyone.

For the most part, the Ethiopians had remained ignorant of the existence of other Jews, just as other Jews knew nothing about the Ethiopians. In the latter part of the sixteenth century, some Ethiopian Jews did try to find their way to the Holy Land.[4] Later, similar attempts had no appreciable results.[5] At the time when Joseph Halevy visited Gondar, he told the Beta Israel community that there were other white Jews, like himself, who were interested in the well-being of the Ethiopians. Upon his return, he urged the European Jewry to respond to the plight of the endangered Ethiopian Jews. Jacques Faitlovitch, following in the footstep of his mentor in 1904, established an enduring relationship with the Beta Israel that contributed greatly to the continued viability of the community. Among other things, Faitlovitch was instrumental in establishing the first Jewish school and synagogue in Addis Ababa, and in sponsoring some promising young people from Gondar to study in Palestine, Germany, Switzerland, and other places. He also presented the cause of Ethiopian Jewry at the courts of Emperor Menelik II and his successor, while advocating their cause in Europe to gain the sympathy and understanding of Jews there. Later, the young people he had helped to obtain Jewish education overseas returned to Ethiopia. Men such as Emmanuel Tamarat and Yona Bogale became outstanding leaders of Ethiopian Jewry in the areas of education and health care and served as effective bridges between the Ethiopians and the larger world community of Jews.

When the State of Israel came into being in 1948, it was intended to be the effective home base for world Jewry which had been scattered for nearly two thousand years. Potentially every Jew can choose to be a citizen of Israel as soon as he or she touches its soil. The new state, guided by its Zionist mission, was to work hard to encourage and support the *aliyah* ("coming home") of Jews from all parts of the world. The Ethiopians were the last community to be recognized as Jews and accorded the privileges of the Law of Return.[6] After World War II, the Ethiopians made frequent, albeit unorganized, attempts to be recognized as Jews by Israel; those who did go to Israel found it nearly impossible to get such recognition. In the mid-1950s, some young people went to Israel for vocational and religious training. Upon completion of their courses, most returned to Ethiopia; only a few joined a *kibbutz*, married, or otherwise settled in Israel as citizens. In a memorandum written in 1966 after a meeting between Yona Bogale and Israel's minister of religious affairs, Yitzhak Rafael, the latter made several promises: to support the training of three to five young Ethiopian Jews in *yeshivot* in Israel, to provide the Beta Israel with religious artifacts as needed, and to arrange for the training of *shohatim* (religious Israeli slaughterers, some of whom were working in Gondar for an Israeli meat-packing company). In 1971, a letter written and signed by seventeen people representing the Beta Israel community of Tigray, led by the ubiquitous Yona Bogale from Gondar, was sent to the Sephardi chief rabbi Yitzhak Nissim. In the letter, the Ethiopians are reported to have said that they desired to be included in the world Jewish community and that they were willing to fulfill whatever requirements the government or religious authorities of Israel deemed necessary in order to gain full acceptance.[7] The Israeli authorities took no immediate action. However, the idea of mass migration came into being.[8]

For a number of reasons, the tempo of action began to pick up around 1973. As mentioned in Chapter 1, the political situation in Ethiopia was rapidly deteriorating, and life for the Jews was becoming untenable.[9] The involvement of international Jewish organizations, particularly those in North America, intensified, and they voiced their concerns about the Beta Israel to the Israeli government. In 1973, one of the two chief rabbis, Ovadia Yosef, ruled in favor of the Ethiopian Jews. His ruling was based on the opinions of other rabbis rather than on secular or scientific evidence.[10] He particularly referred to the ruling of the sixteenth-century chief rabbi of Egypt, David n-Zimra, and his disciple and successor, MaMahari Castro. The rabbis reiterated that the Ethiopian Jews were bona fide Jews, descendants of the lost tribe of Dan. It took another two years before the Ashkenazi chief rabbi, Shlomo Goren, affirmed the decision made by his Sephardi colleague. Having obtained concurrence of the religious authorities, the Begin government passed a law in 1975 declaring that the Beta Israel were indeed bona fide Jews and entitled to immigrate to Israel like any other community of Jews.[11] However, Chief Rabbi Yosef reportedly had made an additional stipulation, which later created problems for the immigrants: "To remove any doubt of the Jewishness of the Falashas—in case at any time they received converts who were not converted according to Halakah—I ordered the conversion ceremony."[12] The conversion consisted of mass public immersion and symbolic circumcision for the males.

At any rate, the decision to recognize the Beta Israel as Jews, even with these reservations, was monumental and opened the door for immigration. But how could the significance of this decision be conveyed to the villagers in Ethiopia without arousing the wrath of the Ethiopian government? In the beginning, the Ethiopian government agreed to allow some Jews legal emigration, provided it was done discreetly. In exchange, the Begin government agreed and, as expected, was ready to grant shipment of arms[13] to enable the Mengistu government to continue the several wars that were raging in different parts of the country and against Somalia. Two planes loaded with munitions left Tel Aviv for Addis Ababa, and on their return the following night, they carried 121 Beta Israel to Tel Aviv. These Beta Israel were the first and last legal Ethiopian immigrants to Israel. Had the secrecy of the operation been maintained, it might have continued until the Ethiopian government became afraid of discovery by other Ethiopians, other African countries (especially from the Arab part of the continent), and Middle Eastern countries. But, thanks to the premature disclosure of the existence of the deal by the Israeli foreign minister of the time, the deal was called off, and the Mengistu regime expelled all Israelis from Ethiopia.[14]

The legal emigration of Jews ended abruptly at the very time when many of the villagers were getting the message to prepare for their departure to Israel. Other nonconventional means were found. Between 1977, when legal emigration stopped, and 1984, approximately seven thousand Ethiopian Jews found their way to Israel. The immigrants were mostly from the southern region of Tigray; a few came from the areas of Wolqait-Tseggede-Tselemit, and Lasta (Wollo region), located between the Gondar and Tigray regions. Families were relatively intact, less maltreated, and in relatively sound physical and mental condition upon their arrival in Israel.

Rabbi David Ben Zimra (Radbaz), the fifteenth-century scholar, spiritual leader, and chief rabbi of Egypt, had declared that the Ethiopians were authentic Jews who could marry other Jews. He based his decision on the accounts of a ninth-century Jewish traveler, Eldad Hadani, who had traced the lineage of the Ethiopians to the lost tribe of Dan.[15] According to the present rabbinate, however, even Rabbi Zimra admitted that the Ethiopian community was innocent of Hebrew and did not include Torah scholars.[16]

Further, the chief rabbinate of Israel reasoned, the Ethiopians had been cut off for long from the Jewish community, and, because of irregularities in divorce procedures, there was a serious problem of mamzerut (Halakic illegitimacy; in Amharic, *dikkala*, "bastard" or *woshela*, "uncircumcised"). According to Jewish law, a *mamzerut* can marry only another *mamzerut*.[17] For such persons and their families, the Amharic and Hebrew terms connote a heavy burden and secular and religious stigma. The person born to such parents has no legitimacy in religious law, which means everything in the context of Israel. Without the complete process of conversion, the person is a nonentity and has no standing whatsoever in Halakah.

Some members of the Ethiopian community were suspected of these irregularities. For instance, if a woman has a child in her second marriage without first following the religiously mandated formula for divorce from her first husband, the child is considered a *mamzer* ("bastard"). The rabbinate, after extensive discussions with religious scholars, found that such irregularities are found among the Ethiopian community of Jews. So, reasoned the rabbinate, to forestall present and future suspicions and to facilitate the free intermingling of Ethiopians with other members of the Israeli community, it would be best to have them undergo mass conversion (note: not reconversion). The process of conversion was to consist of the following main elements: *mila* (circumcision), *tevila* (ritual immersion in the *mikveh*, or bath), and *kabbalat ol mitzvot* (oral declaration of acceptance of the commandments of the Torah). But since the overwhelming majority of Ethiopians are circumcised on the eighth day after birth, the rabbinate deemed that symbolic circumcision, a simple procedure of drawing a drop of blood from the penis and recitation of the appropriate religious passages, would suffice. Although very unhappy with the decision, most of the first wave of Ethiopian immigrants, nearly seven thousand of them, underwent conversion without much resistance.[18]

But this quiet, albeit reluctant, acceptance did not last long. Within a period of about six weeks, between December 1984 and January 1985, Operation Moses brought some eight thousand Ethiopians to Israel. In many respects, this group differed from those who had arrived earlier. Many had languished for up to three years in the refugee camps in the Sudan. They were almost all from the Gondar region and had a different psychological makeup and political persuasion. Their arrival, after the disclosure of the hitherto secret operations, was made public. For the first time since 1977, Israelis got a glimpse of this group of immigrants.

Aware of the complaints of the previous wave of *olim* regarding religious conversion rituals and the growing resistance of the newcomers,[19] the rabbinate appointed Rabbi Glicksberg of Givatayim, a member of the Chief Rabbinate Council, to chair a blue-ribbon committee comprised of forty-eight men from all walks of professional life, to review the requirements once again. In the course of its deliberations, the committee consulted some *kessoch* (Beta Israel religious leaders) and Rabbi Yosef Adane, the son of an Ethiopian *kes* and the only Ethiopian rabbi who was trained and ordained in Israel.[20] Eventually, the committee published the results of its deliberations. The report stated: "The return of the Jews of Ethiopia to the Holy Land was an inspiring act for all Israelis and the entire House of Israel." It reaffirmed the Jewishness of the community but supported the rabbinate's position that the community undergo a "renewal of the covenant, in accordance with established practice," that is, in accordance with Halakah and "would serve the best interests of the community itself." The committee added: "There is a great temptation to solve the problem by postponing it, but the result would be future suffering and contention." The committee made an appeal to a broad segment of the population: "We call upon all who are sensitive to the dignity and future of the Jews of Ethiopia, and who are genuinely interested in their welfare, to strengthen the chief rabbinate in its conciliatory approach. . . . May we all rally around the Torah whose ways are ways of pleasantness and peace."[21] Except for some modifications in the procedures for circumcision, the committee, not unexpectedly, supported the position of the rabbinate. The chief rabbinate accepted the committee's findings and recommendations and dropped the symbolic drawing of blood from the men.[22] The other requirements were not affected.

The Ethiopians rallied to show their total opposition to the conversion requirements. They argued that for thousands of years they had endured untold hardships to maintain their Jewish faith. They followed the injunction of the Law of Moses as they understood it and observed the laws of slaughtering, divorce, marriage, Sabbath, and other holy day celebrations. Although their tradition did not include speaking and reading Hebrew, which they regretted, they were self-sufficient in most other respects. If there were some isolated irregularities, these could be dealt with by drawing upon the knowledge of respected *kessoch* within the community itself. The Ethiopians felt the imposed mass conversion was an insult to their identity and dignity. They could view it only as discrimination for reasons other than religion.[23] They said no previous group had been required to undergo mass conversion.[24] But the rabbinate did not budge. The Ethiopians organized a public demonstration, stopped normal activities, and threatened to return to Ethiopia via Egypt to dramatize their determination.[25] Some threatened suicide, others homicide.[26]

At the same time, the Ethiopians appealed to the government in the person of Prime Minister Shimon Peres, a member of the Labor Party. The prime minister, mindful of the hardships the group might suffer and aware of the political repercussions of such acts, met with representatives of the community in his office in the presence of Absorption Minister Yaacov Tsur. The Ethiopians told him they had left Eretz Yisrael thousands of years ago carrying the Bible and returned carrying the Bible. Yet, by requiring their conversion, the rabbinate denied their Jewishness. The immersion requirement, they said, was degrading. One representative of the community added that seven suicides over the past several years had been related to the pressure of conversion. The prime minister assured the Ethiopians that "we are brothers in all circumstances. . . . Only distance and time, not religion, separated us in the past." He added that the recent conflicts between the immigrants and the rabbinate "should be viewed as a family spat." He promised to find a solution to the problem in a few weeks' time.[27] The Ethiopians agreed to wait; this was in mid-July 1985.

Peres subsequently met with chief rabbis Avraham Shapiro and Mordechai Eliahu, who later would appear before the Knesset committee on immigration. After much negotiation with the rabbis, Peres was able to work out a formula. The statement that came out of the series of negotiations indicated that while the immersion ceremony was not a condition for accepting the Ethiopians as Jews, the personal status of each Ethiopian must be clarified and treated accordingly. In other words, mass conversion might be waived, but any Ethiopian wishing to get married must first submit to ritual immersion.

Other clauses in the statement stipulated that when dealing with the Ethiopians, rabbinical courts must seek advice from the *kessoch*. The agreement reflected the fact that the prime minister did not wish to be involved in matters of Halakah. However, in explaining the agreement to the public, an aide to the chief rabbis added that "all Jews from abroad who want to be married in Israel must prove that they are Jews. The Ethiopians will have to undergo exactly the same procedure."[28] In other words, the situation of the Ethiopians was linked to the perennial question, "Who is a Jew?"[29] This modification in the requirement of mass conversion did not satisfy the Ethiopians. They acknowledged that there were some individuals whose backgrounds might call for immersion, but to require all Ethiopian males to undergo conversion prior to marriage was unfair.[30]

There was a stalemate. A few weeks later, Ethiopians pitched camp outside the headquarters of the chief rabbinate in the heart of Jerusalem. As intended, the event embarrassed the rabbinate.[31] The Beta Israel gained tangible and intangible assistance from the press, the non-Orthodox Jews, and nonreligious political parties, among others. With the high holy days approaching, the rabbinate wanted to reach some agreement so that the Ethiopians would move. Short of complete cancellation of the provisions, however, the Ethiopians would not budge. They maintained their camp in front of the rabbinate for thirty-two days. The event became extremely acrimonious.

As the confrontation intensified, even thoughtful secular Israelis became very concerned. Writing in the *Jerusalem Post*, Elizer Jaffe of

Hebrew University thoughtfully noted that there was a lack of mutual intelligibility among the Ethiopians, and Israeli society. On the part of the Ethiopians there was little grasp of Israeli politics, the rabbinical establishment, judicial procedure, bargaining tactics, and the role of Diaspora Jews in Israeli society. There is no doubt, Jaffe noted, that the immersion-conversion issue "is mortally insulting to most Ethiopians and that they equate immersion with the baptism that hated Christian missionaries tried to force on them in Ethiopia. This is a life-and-death issue for many of them, and it has nothing to do with 'outside agitators,' as claimed by naive Israeli observers." He thought that rather than confronting the rabbinate in a head-on collision, the Ethiopians could use other tactics, as some have suggested in private, such as quietly obtaining marriage certificates from liberal Orthodox rabbis, working toward the ordination of Ethiopian rabbis, making sophisticated use of the courts, and conducting joint Israeli-Ethiopian symbolic immersions in the Kinneret (Sea of Galilee) or the Mediterranean.

By this time, the organizers were demanding the rabbinate's unconditional surrender. Jaffe continued, "they are joined by many Reform and Conservative Jews who for years have been desperately seeking recognition for their rabbis and for their religious innovations and communal religious autonomy." Jaffe felt it was predictable that anticlerical forces in Israel and left-leaning political parties would join camps with the Ethiopians. "Without disrespect for the claims of those who are feeding on the Ethiopian plight," Jaffe noted, "I cannot commend them for their present disservice to the Ethiopians. For instead of encouraging mass *aliyah* of Conservative and Reform Jews in order to strengthen their own case and numbers in Israel, instead of pursuing their own legislative activity in the Knesset and in the courts, and instead of providing realistic, honest counsel to the Ethiopians, these opportunistic political groups have chosen to take a ride on the Ethiopians' backs, and exploit their plight."[32]

Jaffe also thought the power struggle between the Ethiopian leadership and the chief rabbinate was very closely related to the internal communal struggle for control over the Beta Israel community. For whoever delivered the goods would enjoy the popular support of the community. There were respected veteran *olim* whose leadership could be utilized for the good of the community but who had not cast their lots so far with the Beta Israel leadership struggling to emerge.

Crisis in Communal Integrity and Identity

Earlier in July, the Abba Eban of the Labor Party and member of the Knesset had taken the occasion of the controversy to address the larger issues of the state and religion in democratic Israel. Eban pointed out that the collective memory of the Ethiopian Jews reached back to the dawn of Jewish history, long before the establishment of the chief rabbinate with quasi-legal power in Israel. He noted that the chief rabbinate was the creation of the Turkish-British period and had only quasi-legal standing in the eyes of Halakah. As such, he added, the rabbinate should not exercise coercive, executive power. Rather, its powers should derive from excellence in learning and piety, from respect and acceptance by the people of Israel following the tradition exercised by luminaries such as Rabbis Avraham Kook and Isaac Herzog. He added that the giants of modern Zionism such as Herzl, Nordau, and their political followers were "totally unaffected by Halakah." Eban further asserted that "national freedom, democracy, social justice, and scientific rationalism were the ideological roots of modern Zionism." It is true that religious faith has preserved Jewish identity in exile, but that preservation would not have continued were it not for the political and pioneering initiatives taken by secular Zionism, beyond and often against the religious establishment. Although eventually religious Zionism became a respected and organic part of political Zionism, "it was never the leading part." The religious establishment should not press opinions and interests that go beyond what is reasonable and acceptable. "The more so," Eban added, "since there is no absolute truth in the judgments or enactments of any particular religious institution; in many cases, including that of the Ethiopian Jews, for every rabbi with a Halakic opinion there is contrary Halakic judgment by another rabbinic authority." The Ethiopians, now living in a democratic country, he said, had a right to take their case to the elected legislature and government. It was the duty of the government to help them resolve the issues. Eban saw the immersion-conversion issue as primarily political, calling for political solutions.[33] Obviously, this kind of approach led the chief rabbinate to dig its Halakic heels in even deeper.

For Prime Minister Shimon Peres, what Eban said might have been logical. But as a consummate politician, he could afford only to say that the Ethiopians were indeed Jews and citizens of Israel; when it came to Halakah, he was no expert.[34] By publicly deferring to the religious Orthodox establishment, he eventually was able to forge some agreement between the strikers and the chief rabbis during the first week of October 1985.

When at last it came, the agreement was communicated to Peres, who was acting as the mediator, in a letter from chief rabbis Shapiro and Eliahu. Peres then sent a letter to the striking Beta Israel. The tenets of the agreement were similar to those the rabbinate had proposed on the eve of Rosh Hashanah which the strikers had rejected.[35] The agreement left final determination of the Jewishness of Ethiopian couples seeking marriage in the hands of a special rabbinical court which would be made up of rabbis who consider the whole Ethiopian community to be Jewish and in no need of symbolic conversion. However, the strikers wanted their own religious leaders or kessoch to be the judges when an Ethiopian's Jewishness was in doubt. On this count the Ethiopians lost. The *Jerusalem Post* noted: "The defeat on this crucial point must be laid in no small measure to the vociferous support of the well-wishers on the nonreligious left and in the Reform movement. When these two groups, in pursuance of their own aims, took a ride on the back of the Ethiopians, who view themselves as Orthodox, it was a safe bet that the chief rabbis would respond by digging in their Halakic heels and refusing to budge another inch." The editorial went on to say: "This is historically an absurdity, even if laid down by the assemblage of historical scholars [the position taken by this body]. It implies that the rabbinical marriage registrars were right to insist, from the start, that any Ethiopian couple must produce certificates of conversion through ritual immersion before they can be considered marriageable. Moreover, it means that the chief rabbis will be bound—if only to prove freedom from prejudice—to fling the same collective charge of dubious Jewishness in the faces of the next large group of immigrants from antireligious Soviet Russia, where the encouragement of the 'intermingling' of Jews with non-Jews is state policy. . . . It is a frightening prospect."[36]

The agreement further stipulated that an institute would be established within the Ministry of Religious Affairs to study the community's conditions. It would make recommendations about marriages, divorce, and the like. It took a long time before the ministry established the institute, and when it finally did, its membership did not include Ethiopian *kessoch*. The Ethiopians considered this another breach of faith. In the meantime, the rabbinate stipulated that any Ethiopian wanting to marry must follow the process of conversion. The Ethiopians continued to oppose this vehemently. Since that time, liberal rabbis and *kessoch* have officiated over marriages, though some have complied with the conversion requirements. For the majority of the people, especially those who are not married, and for the rabbinate itself, the issues of conversion are still outstanding. The issue has generated a lot of discussion, most of which has been very bitter.[37] It has negatively affected the attitudes of many on both sides and has spilled over into other areas of social and political life.

THE NAMING GAME

Among the many obvious differences between the Ethiopian immigrants and the Israelis were the Ethiopians' names. To make them more Hebraic, to simplify the registration and accounting processes, and perhaps to forestall name-linked discrimination in the future, the Israeli authorities took a number of steps. From the start, a policy was adopted to rework the naming process for the *olim*. As it turned out, the task proved very complicated, controversial, and in the end unsatisfactory to many of the *olim*.

In the Ethiopian context, names usually are loaded with significance. Before assigning a name to a child, parents and relatives consult one another and deliberate over the possibilities. A child may be given several names—one by the father, another by the mother, still another by grandparents, uncles, and significant others. These names signify some special meaning, some hope, or some kind of wished-for relationship between the child and the name giver. This is especially true for the first male child or grandchild in a family. There is always one dominant name by which the individual is known throughout life. This is the first (given) name. The second name, the father's first name, is referred to when double identification is called for. For example, the name of Yakov is given to a boy at birth. Yakov's father's full name is Legesse Nadew. The boy then becomes known as Yakov Legesse, but Yakov is his principal name. Later, when he grows up, he becomes Ato (Mr.) Yakov, Dr. Yakov, Kes Yakov, and so on. When Yakov marries, his wife, Almaz Mazengya, retains her maiden name; she only adds the designation "Woizero" (Mrs.). Ato Yakov and Woizero Almaz Mazengya have a son and a daughter. The boy is given the name Menelik, and the girl Sara. The full names of Yakov's children then become Menelik Yakov and Sara Yakov Legesse, their grandfather's first name or their father's last name, is dropped altogether. The father's first name becomes the second name of his children. Family lineage, then, cannot be traced through family names; there are other ways to trace lineage, however.

When an Ethiopian moves permanently to another society, the naming system creates a number of problems. The names of Ethiopian authors, for example, are listed differently in different library systems; when one tries to consult a particular work, it is often necessary to consult the librarian or the author to know how he or she is classified. It was only after numerous correspondences that I persuaded the librarian at the U.S. Library of Congress to use my last name to catalog my publications. When I was in Ethiopia, my works were entered under my first name, following the Ethiopian system. My family and I also have experienced some confusion at a more personal level. We have lived in two communities since coming to the United States. One community was very familiar with the Ethiopian custom; the other was not. We decided our children would carry my second name (my father's first name) as their last, while my wife kept her maiden name. We thought this would simplify recordkeeping in schools, banks, and municipal offices. Other Ethiopians I have known, now living in the United States, have adopted various other strategies to simplify name-linked identification. To date, however, no single system of naming has been devised that is acceptable to all Ethiopians living abroad.[38]

Given the complex tradition, one can appreciate the problems the Ethiopian *olim* and the Israeli authorities confronted. The Israelis decided to adopt what they thought was the easiest system: assigning to each newcomer a Hebrew name. The meaning of the new name was to correspond, as much as possible, to the original Ethiopian first name. A second name would be adopted for the whole family—father, mother, and children. Since many Ethiopian names are similar to biblical or Hebrew names, this seemed to be a workable approach. For instance, such names as Yakov, Yishak, Sara, Avraham, Yoseph, and Rachel presented no problem. Some other names, such as Mihret (female) or Mihretu (male) could be translated quite readily to Rahamim ("Mercy"). For last names, either a new Hebrew name was assigned to the family, or, in most instances, the name of a dead ancestor, the father or grandfather of the male head of the household, for instance, was adopted. According to this procedure, everyone in the family would have the same last name, including the wife. In most instances, with the assistance of some veteran Ethiopians, names were worked out before the *olim* arrived. The people were informed of their new names at the initial sorting centers.

At first, there was little resistance to the name changes. But resentment slowly developed as the *olim* came to see it as another ploy to deprive them of their authentic identities. For instance, when one man was asked how many children he had, he said that when he arrived he had eight children, three boys and five girls, but now he had only three. The other five, he said, were lost to the family when they married and assumed different names (they carry their husbands' names). To many of the *olim*, the name-changing process is part and parcel of the resocialization process. They resent the fact that this kind of resocialization was deemed necessary. The veteran Ethiopians say it was a mistake to impose this additional burden on the community. The Hebrew names are beautiful and significant; had the people been properly consulted, they probably would have consented to the idea. But they were not consulted. No other *olim* have ever been asked to change their names en masse, although many decided for themselves to adopt Hebrew names. Their individuality and freedom of choice were never in question. To a certain extent, Israeli authorities have recognized their mistake. One group of sixty Ethiopian families who arrived in 1987 was not asked to change their names and did not volunteer to do so. Perhaps in the future, things will be different. For those who have gone through the experience, the misgivings may last for a while.[39]

LEADERSHIP AT BAY

It is inevitable that leaders emerge from an immigrant group during the absorption process.[40] In the case of the Beta Israel, the need for strong, informed, and authentic leadership was obvious, but it was not until the battle lines were drawn between the religious-political authorities representing the absorbing society and the Beta Israel community that the need for leadership became urgent.

Whenever possible, it is preferable that the leadership come from within the group. Anchored in the community, they are more likely to represent the community's aspirations and have their support. Ideally, the leadership also should be conversant with the language and culture of the absorbing society; having lived in the country for some time and having received some education or training there would increase the likelihood that they understand and have the respect of representatives of the absorbing society. Recognized as authentic and credible by both sides, such leaders could act as effective cultural brokers.

For a number of reasons, it took a long time for such leadership to emerge from the Beta Israel community. Many of the leaders in the Ethiopian context became, for all practical purposes, dysfunctional in Israel. *Vatikim* (veteran Beta Israel immigrants) were also few in number, and most were not prepared to assume leadership positions, were out of touch with the migrant community and did not know what the migrant community needed, or did not want to become involved. For their part, the religious and secular authorities of the absorbing society failed to identify, cultivate, and encourage leadership. In all likelihood, the political and religious leadership of the absorbing society was not convinced that continuation of traditional leadership among the group would be in their best long-term interests: it could hamper their absorption and socialization in the new setting and compromise Israel's indivisible, Euro-centered conceptualization of absorption. The weaknesses of this approach, however, overshadow any useful purposes. According to this philosophy, the few seasoned and highly educated Beta Israel leaders, including Yona Bogale, who was intimately knowledgeable about the *olim* and Israeli society and fluent in Hebrew, Amharic, Tigrigna, English, French, and other languages and had made significant contributions to the Beta Israel community in Ethiopia, were practically ignored in Israel.[41]

In the context of traditional Ethiopian and Jewish values, age is revered. In village and family matters, the *shemagile* ("elderly man") and, in some respects, the *baltet* ("elderly woman") are held in high respect, listened to, and often obeyed. Traditionally, when it comes to the governing and control of younger members, there exists an ever-present threat of *irgman* ("curse") which the *shemagile* can use against errant youth. When a curse is made, if the object does not make timely amends and is not forgiven, it is believed to cause untimely death or some other misfortune. Parents and village elders are serious about the proper upbringing of children. At the village level, the *shemagiloch*, especially the *kessoch*, served as leaders in matters related to religious life, administration of justice, and spiritual guidance. According to Leslau, "the priest is not only the confessor but the counselor and the spiritual authority of the entire community."[42] In addition, every person has a *ynefis abat* ("soul father") who is intimately knowledgeable about the individual and family.

Once in Israel, the traditional leadership lost much of its significance because its institutions and religious bases were rendered obsolete.[43] But their influence already had begun to decline before they left Ethiopia. In Ethiopia, especially since the early 1960s, schooled young people have grown increasingly restless, politically radicalized, and defiant toward the established order—family, religion, and government. Primarily as a result of sustained challenges and attacks against the old regime and all the institutions that supported it, the schooled youth undermined the authority and efficacy of the monarchial system (Kebuae Egziabher, or "anointed of God") in the eyes of the traditional public and even the military.[44] When the Haile Selassie government and the thirty-century tradition of imperial rule fell in 1974, it was replaced by a military junta, the Derg, comprised of young military personnel. Eventually, some of the Ethiopian Jews found themselves in Israel. In many respects, the experience of the young leadership that emerged in Israel derived its inspiration from these developments in Ethiopia. So when some Israeli politicians expressed their opinion that some Beta Israel organizers were trained in "communist camps," they were not far from the truth.[45] As a result, there emerged in Israel strong rivalries among a dozen or so organizations led by the youth who were vying for recognition. For a time, this led to confusion among the rank-and-file Beta Israel as well as among the political and religious leadership of the absorbing society. Nevertheless, in the absence of any alternative, the organizations did serve some good purpose in providing a platform on which the Beta Israel could articulate their concerns and convey them to the Israeli authorities.

In terms of the generation and education gaps among the Beta Israel, the community can be divided into two broad categories. On the one side are the older, more conservative, religious, and mostly nonliterate members. On the other side are the younger, more secularly oriented, schooled, and politically active youth.[46] Since the 1940s, the differences between the two groups have increased. As the educated members moved on to find further educational and employment opportunities, the young people became increasingly aware of the need for schooling and responded enthusiastically to Jewish and public schools. But because resources were limited in Ethiopia, particularly in the regions where the Beta Israel lived, students traveled long distances for their education. In most instances, they resided in far-away towns or cities where they came in contact with young people from different backgrounds. These experiences and contacts inevitably influenced their outlook on religion, nationality, and ethnicity. At least in the earlier decades, the traditional Jewish community tried to exclude these young people from effective participation in religious activities in synagogues for fear that they had become contaminated by their association with Gentiles. These were additional factors that contributed to the gaps.[47]

During the first phase of my fieldwork, there were at least a dozen Beta Israel associations, and the Jewish Agency and some government officials complained there were so many that they did not know which ones they should do business with. By the time of my second visit in 1986-87, there were only four organizations left, and two of these were not active. The two active organizations were bona fide Ethiopian grass-roots groups. Most of the previous organizations had been organized and operated by non-Beta Israel groups on behalf of the Beta Israel community (one was run by a Christian church). The latter might have served some useful purposes, but they were condemned by the Ethiopians and urged to cease and desist.[48]

Of the two associations competing for leadership, one was called Beta Yisrael. Located in Ramat Gan, where there was a large group of immigrants, and, at least in the initial years, financially supported by the Canadian Association for Ethiopian Jewry, this organization was more aggressive, more tightly organized, and, according to Jaffe, tended to be "autocratic, isolationist and loath to compromise. One is either with them or against them."[49] This was also the organization that mobilized and led the strikes against the conversion requirements during the months of July through October 1985.

In contrast, the Israel Association of Ethiopian Immigrants, funded for the most part by the Association of Americans and Canadians in Israel and the Zahavi Association of Large Families, has its headquarters in Jerusalem (previously in Haifa) and has branches in many parts of the country. This organization is less aggressive, is more democratic, and assumes no leadership roles in the strikes. Although it supported the goals of the strike, it hoped to achieve the same ends by resorting to the courts. The Beta Yisrael was certified in December 1984, the Israel Association for Ethiopian Immigrants in September 1984. These two organizations overwhelmingly represented the Beta Israel from the Gondar region, with only a few members from Tigray and Wollo.[50] Both organizations resented the non-Ethiopian organizations that tried to speak on behalf of the community. Both strongly opposed immersion and insisted on the unconditional recognition of the Ethiopians as Jews. Both groups also acknowledge the lack of education among the leadership and their supporters.[51] They differed on tactics, organizational structure, and long-range goals.[52]

Beta Yisrael was the stronger of the two. It had been in the forefront of the battle during the conversion controversy and was instrumental in organizing the community for other purposes, such as reuniting families and defending the rights of immigrants to choose which schools their children attended. A number of thoughtful Israelis charged that Beta Yisrael was confrontational rather than conciliatory. Although this might be true, one must look closely at the complex situation of immigration and settlement of the Beta Israel to understand the reasons. Writing in October 1985, at the height of the confrontational period, Jaffe lamented the approach taken by the leadership but thoughtfully pointed out: "Leadership will emerge that is capable of presenting their case in a constructive manner, without losing the identity, pride and respect of this fascinating Jewish community. Only such internal leadership can, over time, prevent exploitation, paternalism, and degradation of the Ethiopian community in Israel."[53]

Now let us turn our attention to the views of the leadership, in particular Addisu Messele, the head of Beta Yisrael since its inception and recognition by the Ministry of Interior since 1984. Addisu Messele is often in the national news, and nearly anyone with some knowledge of the Beta Israel knows the name and reputation of this man. I interviewed him on three different occasions, once in the suburb of Tel Aviv where he lives and twice in Jerusalem. I was also present at two rallies and demonstrations his association organized. One was to demand that the Israeli government increase its efforts for reunion in Israel of relatives left behind in Ethiopia. The other was to commemorate those Beta Israel people who lost their lives in refugee camps while trying to reach Israel. The latter was staged in the presence of high government officials, including the president of Israel.

Addisu Messele is approximately thirty years of age; he is tall, has an aristocratic bearing, wears his hair long, and, except on important public occasions when he wears Ethiopian garb, he does not wear the ubiquitous *kippa* (headgear worn by nearly all Beta Israel males since their arrival in Israel). He uses his Ethiopian names instead of the Hebrew ones that were assigned to him. He received the equivalent of a twelfth-grade education in Gondar. He is articulate in Amharic, Hebrew, and English. He remains attached to the land he left but laments the discrimination, personal and communal, that some of the people in what he refers to as "our country" had perpetrated against the Beta Israel. He does not regret that he came to Israel. He expected, as a matter of right, much better treatment for his people in Israel.

When he was in Ethiopia, Addisu Messele was an active member of EPRP (Ethiopian People's Revolutionary Party). He fled the country when the Derg disbanded the group and began to persecute its members. He went to the Sudan without knowing where he would go from there. In the Sudan, he learned that the government of Israel was allowing the Beta Israel into the country. Eventually, he found his way to Israel. His father came later, but his mother and siblings are still in Ethiopia. Like other Beta Israel who came to Israel during the same period, he went through what he calls *ttilmat* (religious immersion, or *mikveh*) and *gizret* (symbolic circumcision, which he described as painless). He says that when he was in Ethiopia he was very religious. Like most other Beta Israel, he did not even consider drinking coffee made on Sabbath.

After familiarizing himself with the country and the language, he busied himself in Israel. He was employed by the Jewish Agency of Israel to assist in the processing and settlement of those Beta Israel who came after him. With time, he and others became acutely aware that the policies pursued by the absorbing society, such as the conversion requirements and the changing of names, were wrong. He wanted to change the procedures. Failing in his efforts to influence policy, he began to go to the receiving centers to urge the newcomers to refuse to comply with the demands. At registration time, he said, the Beta Israel were presented with stacks of papers containing their new names. Nobody even bothered to ask them what they wished to be called or to explain why it was necessary to change their names. It was all arbitrarily determined by a group of bureaucrats, he said. He told the new arrivals to refuse the name changes. He also told them of their rights, including the right to refuse the conversion demands. Eventually, when the authorities of the Jewish Agency found out what he was doing, he was removed, though he continued to send his representatives to carry out the mission. From that time, on Addisu Messele fought for what he calls the rights of the Beta Israel as Jews and Israelis. He felt that all "this humiliation" was directed at the Beta Israel because they were considered ignorant, powerless, and poor. It is pure and simple politics; it has nothing to do with religion. He maintains that the rabbinate would not dare to do the same thing to the Russians, who were more suspect of intermarriages and other irregularities than the Beta Israel.

Crisis in Communal Integrity and Identity

Addisu Messele thought his people, the Beta Israel, were under tremendous stress, for social, religious, and family reasons. They had thought of Jerusalem as mystical, complete, beautiful, and righteous. Upon arrival, they saw Jewish people doing all sorts of things on the Sabbath. He asserted that the older Beta Israel were disillusioned, while the young had become more sensitized to the political conditions. The conversion demand alienated many of them, he said. As a result, they were willing to join calls for rallies and demonstrations at a moment's notice. The calls were so frequent that once, when he went to the town of Natanya to organize the immigrants against certain actions taken by the authorities, the social worker called him an alien and locked him up in a room. He broke out through the windows. After he had gone a couple of kilometers, the police caught up with him. He told them he was carrying out his duties as a citizen in a democratic society and had not violated any law. Despite his pleas, the police took him to the station. While he was there, two hundred Beta Israel showed up to demand his release. To this day, he has a three-inch scar on his arm from crawling through the broken window.

Comparing the spiritual condition of the *olim* now and before, Addisu Messele is of the opinion that "the Ethiopian community, young and old, men as well as women, are of a very highly religious background. The older people are still very religious. But the young, for the most part, are totally alienated." The stress and alienation, he said, appear in different guises. One symptom is the phenomenon of suicide. From 1984 to 1987, at least thirty-two Beta Israel people had taken their own lives. The reasons were attributed, in the first instance, to the religious controversy which had created much despondency among the group. The second suspected cause was the feeling of inadequacy. Young people were placed side by side in learning situations or at work with other people whose language and culture were that of the absorbing society. When failure ensues, young people become desperate and take drastic actions. The third element was separation from other members of their families. The young came to Israel; many of the old, infirm, women, and children were left behind.

Addisu Messele felt compelled to speak up about the many ills affecting the Beta Israel. If he didn't, no one else would. He said he did this at the expense of his own family. He maintained that the psychologists, social workers, and other service providers who were knowledgeable about the objective conditions of the immigrants but were paid their salaries by the government or the Jewish Agency were not at liberty or would not dare to speak out in public against the shortcomings of their employers. For instance, he said, before he appeared on a national television show with a psychologist who had studied the mental health conditions of the Beta Israel immigrants, to discuss the issues affecting the community's health problems, the psychologist told Addisu Messele that he was not willing to raise the issue of immigrant suicide problems. Instead, the psychologist suggested that Addisu Messele bring up the issue.

I invited him to discuss the charges that have been leveled against the immigrants—that they are not punctual, loyal, or very productive in the workplace. He told me that as farmers and artisans, the Beta Israel are used to hard labor. But in their traditional context they were at relative liberty to organize their own work and time. The farmers and artisans also allowed themselves time to attend weddings and funerals and to visit relatives and friends. Working as an employee of a firm in Israel, laboring at menial tasks for eight hours a day, day in and day out, was very monotonous and tiring. So some would take off to attend weddings or funerals. Supervisors became angry; the tremendous linguistic and cultural obstacles did not make things any easier. The supervisors turned on the workers and called them lazy, unreliable, disloyal, and all the rest. The immigrant workers, in turn, blamed the supervisors because they only demanded punctuality and productivity without understanding the many problems and tragedies in the community. The workers also complained that the wages they received were inadequate. The veteran workers blamed their Beta Israel colleagues for being aloof or unfriendly at the workplace. At the root of the complaints leveled against the Beta Israel, said Addisu Messele, is the absence of shared cultural values.

He thought his organization enjoyed the support of 95 percent of the Beta Israel immigrants.[54] Because of the role he was playing on behalf of the Beta Israel, he said he was fully aware that the Jewish Agency and some departments of the government would like to keep him away. But some of the left-wing or liberal political parties courted him to join their respective ranks. For the time being, he wanted to remain nonpartisan, as far as the established parties were concerned. He evaded discussion of the charges some politicians made that he was a communist.[55] At the personal level, he said he was fatigued. He said it is not easy to lead a community of people who are not sophisticated in matters of politics and personal or group rights and responsibilities in the new setting. He also felt his efforts were not fully appreciated by the immigrants and that the establishment did not wish him well at all. In addition, his father, who was already in Israel, was applying pressure on him to work in league with the Jewish Agency so that they might bring Addisu's mother, brothers, and sisters to Israel. He said the Jewish Agency was helping many other families in similar circumstances, but he thought it was unlikely that they would do the same for his family.

SUMMARY

The receiving society, through its secular and religious representatives, assumed that the Ethiopian *olim* were making *aliyah* for religious reasons. To that end, whatever was done on their behalf to lighten their burdens in the social, cultural, and religious spheres was assumed to be in the best interest of the group. Realizing the good intentions, the *olim* would welcome such actions. Based on these assumptions, processes of reconversion or conversion and the changing of names were carried out. Later, these came to be viewed by the *olim* as injurious to their self-identity, self-respect, and group solidarity. Eventually, when rectifications were suggested, positions already had solidified. Dialogues, which were intended to lead to meaningful compromises, became acrimonious, and the issues remained unresolved. On the whole, the assumptions proved untenable and the actions unsupportable. The people themselves, through their traditional leaders, the *kessoch*, should have been consulted at every stage. But these consultations were rare. In the end, each side developed negative attitudes toward the other, complicating problems relating to the adjustment of the immigrants in Israel and the receptivity of the larger society. Lack of experience on the part of the young emerging leadership among the community might have contributed to the delays that occurred before solutions to the many challenges confronting the community were found.

CHAPTER SEVEN

❖

Primary Education

❖

Both the immigrants and the Israeli society consider education the single most important enterprise in the absorption process. In its variety of forms and organization, education is also the single most important enterprise nearly all Beta Israel are participating in. From the youngest child in the nursery school to the oldest person (as old as eighty-five), men and women, regardless of previous experiences or conditions, all are engaged in learning languages, participating in organized cultural and socialization activities, learning skills of various kinds, and in general preparing themselves to meet the tremendous challenges confronting them in their new environment. We cannot document all the varieties of educational and training activities engaged in by the *olim*, but this and the next two chapters present analyses of some of their major aspects. Learning, by its very nature, is a problem-solving activity. But it also generates frustrations, anxieties, and frictions among and between providers and receivers. The normal challenges to learning are compounded many times over by the many differences between the language, culture, and broad social and psychological makeups of the Beta Israel and the service providers.

STRUCTURE

To get some perspective on the structure and philosophy underlying the system of primary education in Israel, I interviewed several high-ranking officials as well as school inspectors and field representatives. The first was David Pur, head of the secular education division of the Pedagogical Service of the Ministry of Education and Culture. Of Polish descent, Pur was born and raised in Israel. We met in his very modest office on King David Street in Jerusalem.

With respect to the structure of primary education, Pur explained that there are three distinct systems (branches) operating under the general direction of the Ministry of Education and Culture: the state secular, the state religious, and the independent. About 75 percent of all primary-school-aged children are enrolled in state secular schools, 20 percent in state religious schools, and 5 percent in independent schools (4.6 percent are controlled by the Hasidim; the remaining 0.4 percent are controlled by the Orthodox wing).

The two state-sponsored systems receive most of their support from the central treasury. The independent system has unusual features. Although it is administered by the ultra-Orthodox (Agudat Israel), which does not recognize either the efficacy of Zionism or the State of Israel itself, it receives some government subvention. But the Ministry of Education and Culture has very little or no regulatory powers vis-à-vis this system. It has its own unique conceptions, approaches, and methods of teaching and enjoys the power to accept or reject students based on its own criteria. The three systems certify their teachers through the Ministry of Education and Culture, though each has its own teacher-training institutions. At the secondary level, the training and certification responsibilities fall upon the several universities.[1]

The state secular and state religious systems of curricula and matriculation examinations are quite similar. Their differences lie in the biblical, historical, and Talmudic studies, where they differ in inclusion, emphasis and method. For instance, the state secular schools present biblical studies and literature humanistically and in historical context, whereas the religious wing presents them from the perspectives of revelation or divine guidance. In addition, the religious schools include instruction in religious customs and rituals such as meal preparation, holy day observations, and so on. Moreover, students participate in daily worship and other religious activities and are expected to wear appropriate attire (no jeans or short skirts for girls; boys must wear the *yarmulke*). One will generally find more girls than boys in the religious schools. However, in the *yeshivot*, or elite religious academies, males predominate because, according to tradition, religious vocation is restricted to men.

Among Israeli Jews, more than 70 percent are secular. The pioneer Zionists, Pur explained, were products of the Enlightenment of eighteenth- and nineteenth-century Europe. They were either atheists or otherwise nonbelievers in religion. This process of secularization which affected Europeans was wholly absent from the experiences of the Orientals, and this difference in historical experience is manifestly reflected in present-day Israeli society. The 30 percent religious minority draws a significant number of its members from the Oriental population (of Third World background). The majority of students enrolled in the religious schools are from religious homes and are from the Sephardi and mixed sectors of society.[2] Females are also highly represented in religious schools. This group is generally disadvantaged in income, employment, and educational achievement.

In recent years, there has been an observable shift even among the Ashkenazim toward religion and conservative political outlook.[3] However, as far as the schools are concerned, the trend is in the opposite direction. Enrollments in religious schools are declining as more and more parents send their children to state secular schools. The competition these days is not so much between the secular and religious schools as it is between the Zionist and the anti-Zionist religious schools. Both would like to see religious education become the center of educational activity, but they disagree profoundly when it comes to their attitude toward the state. A trend toward theocracy is apparent among the people from northern Africa and the Middle East. These *olim* are susceptible to religious dogmas and charismatic personality cults. Israel is an island of democracy (within the Green Line or pre-1967 borders and for the Jewish population).[4] But, Pur added, the danger for Israel does not arise from the mentality of the Jewish people (Orientals) but from where people live and the period of time people are living in.[5] The secular schools are striving to teach students the efficacy of democratic values, but in the religious schools it is something else,[6] by which Pur meant that the religious branch conducts classes on the bases of divine revelation and guidance, with little if any account given for the human, political dimensions.

We talked about the differences in national and world views among graduates of the various educational systems. Pur admitted that there are differences similar to those found among the general population. Israeli society is pluralistic. Even within the religious, wing there are extremes—extreme nationalists and extreme leftists. Research has demonstrated that those who graduate from the religious schools tend to be conservative. I asked whether such divisions worry him. Pur simply responded, "It is a fact of life." On the other hand, he pointed out the important unifying role played by Jewish tradition, the Hebrew language, holy days, and celebrations. These reflect shared values and encourage some common perspectives which may help bind Israelis together as a national community, he said. He illustrated his point with the example of his membership in a particular *kibbutz*. Although the *kibbutz* is nonreligious, its members do celebrate Passover and other holy days. In addition to these traditions, he said, all share a common destiny.

More than 90 percent of Ethiopian children and youth attend religious schools. To get an understanding of the structure and goals of the state religious administration, I interviewed Ben Yashar, assistant to the head of the state religious education system. Yashar is also in charge of field supervision of the Ethiopian children in state religious schools. He reiterated that the concepts of immigration as understood in the United States and in Israel are entirely different things. In Israel, the concept is better represented by the term *aliyah*, which in Hebrew means "ascent," a return to one's home to reunite with a family. The term *immigration*, on the other hand, connotes economic, political, or other instrumental motives. In other words, he said, in the United States immigrants are looked upon as a burden to be borne; in Israel, the immigration process is a reunion and an opportunity for both the immigrants, and the receiving society. These differences, he said, are very significant, and the education programs that have been forged for the Ethiopian immigrants are grounded in a set of beliefs and assumptions about their homecoming and shared benefits.

In Israel's history of waves of *aliyah*, no group has ever been the target of so much special concern as the Beta Israel. Recognizing the special nature of the Ethiopian olim, the field unit Yashar supervises came into being specifically to address their needs. For the first time, he said, they formulated special curricula and trained teachers for special tasks. In the course of preparations, they consulted the *kessoch*. They also took into account the knowledge left by Emmanuel

Tamrat, Halēvy, Faitlovitch, and others (the list included people who wrote about the religious aspects of the Beta Israel but not historians, anthropologists, and linguists who have written voluminously about Ethiopia and the Jews). Yashar reiterated that 90 percent of Beta Israel education is in the hands of the religious wing, of the Ministry of Education and Culture (including the Youth Aliyah, which is specially coordinated with the Youth Department of the Jewish Agency). The decision to incorporate them initially into the state religious system was made by the Knesset after consultation with Beta Israel leadership. The rationale was to mitigate or lessen the cultural and religious shocks and facilitate their smooth adjustment on the one hand and, on the other, to give the *olim* as much knowledge of the Hebrew language and modern Judaism as quickly as they could absorb it. The special arrangement was to last for a period of one year (until January 1986). Yashar explained that the law stipulates that parents should be given information about the different types of schools so that they can decide where they would like to enroll their children after the first year. To date, most Beta Israel children continue to participate in the religious system.

Reports Yashar had received thus far from teachers, administrators, and others who knew the children were very encouraging. The children were very highly motivated to learn. They often asked teachers for more homework and even remained after school to do additional work. They worked hard. They performed well in basic arithmetic. The problem areas for them were language, literature, reading comprehension, and abstract thinking. Yashar was fairly optimistic that if financial subvention for special tutorials continued, the schools would be able to accelerate their progress. Each child in the primary schools was entitled to 1.8 hours of extra tutorial help per week. At the secondary level, it is 2.2 hours per week. The special tutorials took place outside regular classroom hours. The tutors were either the regular classroom teachers, teachers brought from other schools, or adult volunteers drawn from the community. The school principal had some leeway to make arrangements.

When I asked for Yashar's impressions of Beta Israel response to religious teachings, he said that most insisted on maintaining their own traditions. "We can't do much to force them to go contrary to their wishes," he said. Talmudic and other mainstream Judaic learning were coming very slowly. The young people who lived in the religious dormitories were doing better because they were surrounded by religious precepts and rituals. Those in the grade schools were not progressing as much. The reconversion controversies did not affect the teaching-learning efforts (as far as Yashar's office was concerned). "In our guidance to all our teachers and administrators," he said, "we stress that as far as we are concerned, all Jews are equal." Regarding the goal of full integration of the Beta Israel children, Yashar said that the inhibiting factors were housing and employment availabilities. Parents settled where there was housing and jobs. As a result, the Beta Israel were concentrated in certain communities and absent in others. High apartment vacancies may indicate instability in the community, and so, Yashar said, they had to be very cautious. Within the schools, Yashar observed that there were problems in that some veteran Israeli parents did not want to send their children to study with Beta Israel children. These were usually parents of the lower socioeconomic sector of society.

At this juncture, I turned to David Stahl, our interpreter. Stahl, originally from New York, had come to settle in Israel in 1984. I asked him how he thought race relations in Israel compared to those in the United States. He said there was no comparison. In Israel, problems were very mild. In New York, people talked differently—hypocritically—even when their feelings were against you. The people in Israel, especially the *sabra*, or native-born, may seem hard, rude, and thoughtless on the outside, but inside they were soft and gentle. This included their approach to race relations. Even when they seemed to be talking tough, they did not mean it.

NURSERY AND KINDERGARTEN

Israel has one of the most advanced systems of preschool education in the world. Although attendance is voluntary, nearly all three- and four-year-old children attend some government-sponsored, quasi-governmental, or nongovernmental nursery school. The fees are nominal. Together with their veteran counterparts, the Beta Israel children participate in these programs beginning at an early age. My informants report and my own observations confirm that as far as absorption and socialization processes are concerned, this generation of children will be much better off than the older generations. Other things being equal, one can expect that their early exposure to cognitive and social experiences will enhance their readiness to participate fully in later training opportunities. This may in turn open up other opportunities for social mobility, the attainment of good jobs, and other measures of status and respect. Whether young Ethiopian children come from an intact home or are orphans, these educational enrichment and socialization programs are likely to prove of significant benefit to them in their development.

PRIMARY LEVEL

At the primary level, attendance is universal and compulsory. Special arrangements have been made for the newcomers. Education during their first year in Israel is provided either at the absorption centers or in special classrooms in nearby institutions. During that year, intense attention is given to Hebrew, personal hygiene and health, and a variety of socialization experiences. Mornings are typically devoted to classroom instruction. Under the supervision of adult volunteers, the children spend their afternoons engaged in games, study, or tutorials.

During the second year, pupils attend community schools with other Israeli children. Within these schools, however, the vast majority remain segregated as a group. All Ethiopians are assigned to the same class. They still need intensive support and tutoring in all aspects of the curricula. They also need plenty of exposure to the culture of the school environment—rules and regulations—how to relate to children of different backgrounds, how to play following game rules, and so on. These experiences prepare them to cope better when the time arrives for integrated learning.

SIZE AND DISTRIBUTION OF THE ELEMENTARY SCHOOL POPULATION

Table 2 shows the number of Ethiopian students enrolled in kindergarten and primary classes in Israel's six district as of 1987.

In addition, there were approximately twenty-five hundred high-school-aged students who resided in forty-four Youth Aliyah villages

Primary Education

TABLE 2

Number of Beta Israel enrolled in primary schools by district, 1987

District	Kindergarten	Grades 1–8	Total
Jerusalem	26	235	261
Tel Aviv	—	104	104
Central	70	439	509
Haifa	200	577	777
Northern	550	1,229	1,779
Southern	402	1,030	1,432
Total	1,248	3,614	4,862

Source: Ministry of Education and Culture, State Religious Department, February 1987.

and another sixty who attended state-sponsored secondary schools outside the Youth Aliyah system. Another eight hundred students whose ages ranged from eighteen to twenty-eight participated in the Youth Administration Project. Preuniversity programs included 169 Beta Israel, and approximately one hundred fifty attended universities. All told, about eighty-five hundred Beta Israel or 53 percent of the entire Beta Israel population, were attending school on a full-time basis. Kindergarten through grade eight accounted for 57 percent of the total enrollment. Of the approximately sixteen thousand Ethiopian Jews in Israel in 1987, 30 percent attended primary school.

With this background on the structure and philosophies of the state secular and state religious systems of education and the size and distribution of enrollments, let us now proceed to the field to examine the operation of the schools and the performance of the Beta Israel children. While the cases presented were not randomly selected, they are representative examples of the state-sponsored schools observed.

SINAI SCHOOL

Before my first visit to Sinai School, a state religious school in Ashkelon, I interviewed Eli Dayan, the mayor of that town. He is a young politician of Moroccan origin. He wears a *kippa* and is considered a rising star in the Labor Party.[7] Although he spoke good English, his assistant, Ruth Greenman, a woman of South African background, sat nearby to assist. Rami Davidi, also of Moroccan background, the city's coordinator of immigrants, was also present. According to the mayor, the majority of Ashkelon's sixty thousand residents were of northern African origin —primarily from Morocco, though other groups are also represented. There were approximately one thousand Beta Israel. Ashkelon was one of the few municipalities with budgetary provisions for ethnic and cultural activities. Efforts also had been made to follow a housing policy that would fuse or integrate the diverse communities. But housing shortages made this difficult. Availability was a stronger determining factor than the need to locate people in certain buildings or neighborhoods to achieve the goal of integration. In spite of policy declaration and political and ideological beliefs in the desirability and efficacy of an integrated community, the economic realities of the country continued to favor the "ghettoization" of the immigrants. Efforts to achieve integration also were frustrated by the fact that most Beta Israel wanted to live as close as they can to their relatives and were therefore unwilling to accept the city's assignments, which were based on quite different criteria. The patterns of enrollment in the schools reflected these realities.

Sinai School was thirty years old. The school principal, Shlomo Kabesa, had served as principal for thirteen years. Like most of the teachers and counselors, he was originally from northern Africa. Since it was one of the first schools to take Beta Israel children in 1980, Sinai School was relatively experienced in working with Ethiopian children and their families. Some of the students had attended for six years. Eighty of the three hundred students attending Sinai were Beta Israel. As was the case with most other schools in this region, the majority of students were Sephardi, primarily of northern African background. With the exception of one class of students who arrived during Operation Moses, the majority of Beta Israel children attended classes with their veteran peers. In each class, 25 to 30 percent of the students were Beta Israel. To supplement classroom instruction, the Beta Israel children received approximately one hundred fifty special tutorials per year to help them catch up with their veteran classmates. Materially, the school was very poor. There were chalkboards, the classroom walls were adorned with posters and portraits of current political leaders (President Herzog and Prime Minster Shamir), chief rabbis, the flag of Israel, and some historical Jewish figures. The library, which served also as a study center, was very modest. "We depend on donations and gifts [for the library]," said Sara who had a master's degree in ethnic relations and filled in as part-time school counselor and librarian. The qualifications of the teachers appeared not to be high. Almost all the teachers were Sephardi women. Both administrators (the principal and assistant principal) were men.

Either together with the regional supervisor (of Ethiopian origin) or by myself, I had many occasions to observe the students inside and outside their classrooms. Those Beta Israel children who arrived in the early 1980s related well to their predominantly Sephardi peers. The teachers reported that at first they were quiet, gentle, and softspoken; but now they were as boisterous, rowdy, and carefree as their veteran classmates. They mixed with the other students and joined in the pushing, shoving, and hollering unselfconsciously. In the classrooms, the seating arrangements were random and mixed, perhaps without deliberate effort on the part of the classroom teacher.

Before the first group of Beta Israel arrived in the 1980s, the teachers and counselors were oriented to the task by psychologists and anthropologists. According to the principal, Sinai School, by virtue of its long experience in working with Beta Israel children, prepared handbooks covering such topics as the games Beta Israel children prefer and holiday observations for distribution to other schools. The school personnel also used the children as interpreters to communicate with the parents. Although such experience may boost the morale of the children, it may humble the parents.

Although boys and girls did not share the same benches, the ambiance in the classroom was generally quite casual. In the higher grades, children moved freely in and out of the classrooms without asking permission. At all grade levels, students and teachers addressed one another using first names.[8] This latter aspect of informality is certainly alien to Ethiopian upbringing and may be the reason why one hears young people using the Amharic informal or familiar appellation of *anta* or *anchi* when addressing their male and female elders, respectively, rather than the expected polite form of *irsewa*.

When the school personnel assessed the progress of the Ethiopian students and the advantages their school offered, they tended to stress the social outcomes. The consensus among the teachers and other school personnel was that the Beta Israel children were better off learning with Sephardi children. The Sephardi environment, they said, was especially supportive of the newcomers. As they saw it, the Ethiopians shared more similar cultural values and norms with the Sephardi population than with the Ashkenazim. They did not raise the question of cognitive stimulation that may come from more academically challenging peers who are usually from higher and middle socioeconomic backgrounds, which often translates to mean of Ashkenazi background. But on the whole it is true that classrooms in the southern region, where this school was located, are much more integrated than in any other region, even after the time of arrival from Africa is taken into consideration. Also, the Beta Israel children seemed to be relatively at ease in their relations to classmates. If integration also means progress in learning, this is indeed a big achievement. But there is more to learning than that.

Considerable progress had been made in achieving the objectives of socialization and integration. Most of the Beta Israel children who arrived before Operation Moses were relatively at ease with themselves, with their veteran classmates, and with the school environment. Those who arrived later were not yet attending classes with non-Beta Israel students. Their social adjustment may reflect that they had been there for some three years, that their teachers and veteran classmates were of similar backgrounds, and that there was some proximity in culture and color of skin.[9] Even so, this kind of mixing is very unusual in the annals of Ethiopian Jews in Israel.

The concern was whether these children were placed in classrooms or schools that would facilitate their cognitive development as well. The answer is that while the general environment was relatively conducive to social integration, cognitively it was weak. The ways in which classes were organized and taught were not conducive to optimal learning. When observed in the classroom, the children did not seem to be stimulated, and they were not paying attention to the task at hand. The selection of books in the library was meager and the teaching aids were dull.

Perhaps there was a trade-off for every decision. In the southern region of Israel, and in the religious schools in general, the majority of the population were of Third World background. The region and the schools were administered, for the most part, by first-generation immigrants from northern Africa. This segment of society had been unable to find a place in higher positions by following the regular channels and was now aligning itself with the right-wing religious parties. As one Ashkenazi psychologist from the city of Afula observed, "the religious wing of Israeli society generally breeds narrow concepts and fanatical approaches to life in general and education in particular." Further, the northern African political-cultural background included a dictatorial form of governance without separation of state and religion. Charismatic personality was more important than competence, power more important than compassion. Individual or group perceptions of God were more important than logic, verified knowledge, or reality. This, then, was the environment in which the Beta Israel children were being nurtured. As Chaim Adler observed, the intellectual climate for the Ethiopians was not conducive to rapid cognitive development.[10] The children of the Beta Israel might have been relatively well-off in their social interactions, but cognitively, and for their long-term interests in Israel, they would benefit from an intellectually more stimulating environment. One may argue that the Beta Israel children only shared what existed and that they were no worse off than their veteran classmates. This is true, except that the others were second-generation children who were by comparison relatively well established and well acculturated. In all likelihood, the Beta Israel children would carry a larger burden than the others because they were first-generation immigrants and they were black.

MOREA SCHOOL

Morea School is a religious, coeducational institution, and as far as the Beta Israel are concerned, supposedly an "integrated" one. It covers kindergarten to sixth or eighth grade. Located on the highest point of the town, the school has a commanding view. The elevation also means colder temperatures during the winter months (my visits were in the months of November, December, and April).

The gymnastic classes as well as the others were integrated, according to the instructor, but he said the Ethiopian children had some specific problems. On my visits, I did not observe much integration.

Accompanied by Yafa Chase—a female leader of volunteer social workers from Connecticut who speaks some Amharic and Hebrew, very well trusted by the immigrants of the community, and who had been working for a couple of years in that capacity—I visited the kindergarten class and grades two and three. There were about twenty students in the third-grade biology class I observed. As I sat in this class some of the Beta Israel students rushed in with grass all over their heads and clothing. They were returning from gymnastic activity outdoors. Their appearance may have indicated improper grooming habits or lack of personal pride in looking tidy and attractive.[11] I was told that this class was integrated, but there were only five non-Ethiopian students out of twenty-two. The seating pattern in this classroom was interesting; the Beta Israel gravitated to one side of the classroom and sought out one another's company.

Based on what I had heard earlier about resistance to integration of the Beta Israel in this community, I asked how long the fear that integration would retard the progress of their children would persist among the veteran parents. The teacher answered, "Maybe a couple of years." She told me of her experience the year before with a group of Beta Israel ages seven to nine. At first, she said, it was hard communicating with them. But they worked hard from eight to twelve every day, and they received additional help from volunteers in the afternoons. That brought them to the level where they could function adequately in Hebrew. "They had motivation; that's why they succeeded," she says. This was so despite the fact that they were unable to start school until October on account of the religious strike. She observed that the group of Beta Israel students she taught the year before was more responsible and mature than the one with whom she was presently working.

At the kindergarten level, Beta Israel children would not work without close supervision and encouragement by the teachers. But now they could initiate their own activities. This habit (waiting for adults to give directions) was a carry over from the home, where there was very little a child could do to express himself or herself and where any kind of learning was adult-initiated. The child was accustomed to receiving orders, and, in turn, he or she also learned to give orders to the younger ones. At home, the overriding concern was with the physical security of the child rather than the free expression of self through play or other activities. In the nursery school, on the other hand, safety was provided by the standard regulations governing play equipment and the like; the major concern was to provide an environment that encourages free play of the imagination.

I next visited a kindergarten and a second-grade class. The latter was comprised of students with a wide range of abilities and noticeable differences in their readiness to learn. There were some advanced students who should have been promoted to a higher grade and others who had arrived from Ethiopia only a couple of months earlier and had no grasp of what was going on in the classroom. The newcomers did nothing but clown to amuse themselves and others. This class included students with emotional or learning problems. One child, for reasons unknown, refused to read, write or even open a book. One time he did look over at the book of a seat mate, but the moment the teacher took notice of his action, he withdrew into himself again. Despite the efforts of the classroom teacher, Miriam Avraham, these twenty-two students were not progressing.

The teacher herself was Sephardi. There was another woman assigned to the classroom to assist, but she did not do much during the several visits I made there. After my last observation of this classroom, I felt miserable about the poor quality of the learning environment—the range of problems among the learners, their apparent lack of motivation, and their untidy appearance. Moreover, three of the best Beta Israel students who would benefit from advancement to the next class were being held back for administrative and public relations reasons. The teacher herself felt helpless in the face of the administrative obstacles. The school principal refused to group the children according to their special needs and abilities. When the class was over, I went to meet with the school principal, Avraham Dagan. I was accompanied by Yafa Chase; a few minutes later, the classroom teacher joined us. I briefed the principal on my observations and advanced some recommendations which included the promotion of three Beta Israel students to the next grade and the need to have more teachers in the classroom to attend to the differing needs of these children. The teacher talked to him in Hebrew with much animation. It was not until later that I learned she was agreeing with my assessment of the situation and expressing her dissatisfaction with his inaction or unwillingness to take steps to tackle the problems he himself acknowledged.

The principal concurred with most of our observations and added his own to the list, including the following. Many of the teachers were there because they could not go anywhere else. There were too many Ethiopians in one school—60 percent of the student body were Beta Israel, which hampered integration. The hygiene and personal appearance of the Beta Israel were problems—they arrived at school untidy, their clothing and shoes were dirty and torn, and they often arrived wearing sandals in winter. They were smelly, he said; they shaved their heads, and came to school without lunch. They often had runny noses and sometimes came to school when they were sick. They did not bring pencils, pens, pencil sharpeners, or gymnastic attire. The Ministry supplied money for basic textbooks, but the parents were supposed to supply the rest. The students told their teachers that their fathers did not give them money. When the teachers took the matter directly to the parents, they got some results; otherwise, the parents did not volunteer to provide even the most basic things their children needed to do their school work. As an incentive, some teachers told the children that if they brought one notebook, the school would supply another. But, one teacher commented, "the parents don't care because they don't know the importance of learning. The parents don't know what is important and what is not. They go to the stores to buy sweets and fancy stuff, but are not willing to buy notebooks." The principal planned to talk to the parents on the subject, the teacher added, but the trouble is that "all Ethiopians are like one family. They eat together, decide together, and the like. So I learned that if I can talk to one parent he will tell the others. This means they are 'group-think.' Even then the Ethiopian parents respect the teachers more than they respect the administrators at the absorption centers. When I talk to them, I illustrate what I mean by drawing pictures. Everything begins with the home. The place they come from is very primitive. Every day I tell them how important cleanliness is; I tell them about washing, and with the good weather and sunshine it is easy to wash clothes and get them dry. Sometimes they come to school in winter wearing sandals and without appropriate covers while it is raining. In time, change will come; they will be like the other Israeli children."

Another problem was punctuality. Often children came late to school. The excuses they gave included "Mother wanted me to mind the baby" or "Mother sent me to the store to buy some bread." Another issue was that the Ethiopian children were shy, timid, withdrawn, suspicious, and violent. Referring to the shyness, the teacher remarked that this behavior was sometimes nice.

The resistance of the veteran community to the integration of Beta Israel with their children in the classrooms was a major dilemma. According to the principal, migrant parents wanted to see their children learning in the same classrooms with others, but the veteran Israeli parents refused. Highly segregated classes were maintained because, when pushed, the veteran parents withdrew or threatened to withdraw their children from the school.[12] In addition, the school was worried that it would get a reputation for catering primarily to the needs of disadvantaged children. As a result, most Beta Israel children, even those who came earlier, continued to attend segregated classes. When the volunteer social worker pointed out to the principal that some of the Beta Israel needed promotion, he said, "To what?" When told to the next higher class or the fast track made up of children from veteran Israeli families, he replied that he would not do it. The classroom teacher repeated the names of the children who should be promoted, but he still refused to consider the proposal. He maintained that the promotion of even the best Beta Israel students might make the veteran children feel they were being held back, and that would hurt the reputation of the school. In addition, he reasoned, to stimulate higher achievement, the class needed the presence of these students as models. This was, of course, circuitous reasoning. If a few Beta Israel children were doing so well, they should not be held back with the slow learners, nor should they stay to serve as models for the others. The principal either needed to create a special class for these students or promote them to the other classes made up wholly of veteran Israelis. This is a place where the Beta Israel community needs a strong, knowledgeable advocate. At present, there is no such person.

The dynamics of the triangle involving the school, the home, and the children are very complicated. A major assumption underlying the above complaints conveyed by the principal is that the Beta Israel community—the parents as well as the children—are aware of what the school requires, expects, or demands of them. Is this assumption a fair one? I do not think so. It is important to reiterate that the Beta Israel are mostly of rural origin, nonliterate, and conservative. Since coming to Israel, up to this point they have been sheltered from the outside influences of the new world, perhaps too much and for too long, as one government report pointed out.[13] Until the authorities decided quite suddenly to push them out, the Beta Israel had lived in the protective environment of the absorption centers. With little advance notice or preparation, they were expected to establish themselves in apartments, send their children to community schools, anticipate the requirements of the school culture, and provide for the material, social, and psychological needs of their school-going children. Former care providers and counselors who might have assisted them during this transition already had been dismissed by the Jewish Agency.

School administrators and classroom teachers were also not prepared properly for the Beta Israel. Had they been prepared, the problems of transition would have been expected and the behaviors that led to the complaints of school personnel would have been more understandable. But this is not what happened. The school personnel are also victims of ignorance. They know very little about the background of the migrants or the circumstances that led them to their present situation. The principal agencies responsible for their arrival in Israel and involved in their adjustment during the first year should have been actively involved in the selection of schools for the children. Neither the parents nor the schools were knowledgeable about placement. And, for a period of time, these agencies should have provided guidance and kept tabs on student progress or lack thereof. That such preparation and continuity in services were not provided during the transition phase is a tragedy.

The problems of the migrants as pinpointed by school personnel may be divided into two categories: material and cultural. The Beta Israel migrants live on two types of income: pensions from the government of Israel or wages from employment. The pensions are a very important source of income and are generous. But they are inadequate for the many needs of the people. Incomes from employment are also very limited. Most Beta Israel who find work are in menial jobs that pay the lowest wages. They are beginning from nothing to set up their homes, and there are many things they must buy to furnish their apartments. There is usually not enough money to buy items such as washing machines considered necessary especially during the winter season, the type and amount of clothing deemed necessary by the school for the children, and the like. On the cultural side, the migrants or their children cannot be expected to have a full grasp of the numerous and intricate expectations, requirements, or demands of the schools or of the society in general. Most are unfamiliar with the requirements of modern schooling; a few have had some previous experience, but it is in the context of the society they have left behind. At the same time, the school is under pressure to satisfy many conflicting demands. On the one hand, it is to meet the diverse social and educational needs of the migrants without challenging community perceptions that they are compromising the quality of education provided to the veteran children. Meanwhile, they are trying to guard their turf vis-à-vis the state secular educational system, which is ready and willing to accept the challenge of providing education to Beta Israel students. Up to now, they have had limited opportunity to do. In the absence of mutual knowledge and understanding at the institutional level and without an appropriate central coordinating body capable of providing the requisite guidelines, these competing demands and conflicting expectations inevitably lead to misunderstandings, mistrust, and misgivings as well as the concomitant recriminations and wastes of energy and resources we are witnessing. However, even at the central level, state religious and state secular systems of education do not see eye to eye. Hence, even if it is determined that some children would benefit more from the pedagogical programs provided by the state secular system, it is not easy for school counselors or social workers in the religious system to concur or agree to transfer students. In fact, for political reasons, it may be virtually impossible for them to do so. The few volunteer social workers who worked with the Beta Israel in the absorption centers and who have earned their trust and are still available cannot advise Beta Israel regarding school placement even when they are convinced that they know which would be better for the child. They fear that they would be intimidated by those in the religious school system who may think their interests are under attack.

RAMOT SCHOOL

Ramot, a secular school, is near Morea. The school principal, Yacov Azulos, completing his doctoral program at Hebrew University, was a religious person. He was the only religious person in the country to hold such a position in a secular school. It was true that religious teachers do teach in secular schools (although the reverse was seldom true). This prompted Azulos to comment that "we teach more religion in the secular system of education than they teach in the religious one. The second grade received the Torah here the other day." The religious system is more politics than religion, he said. He is a proponent of secular education. On the whole, he sounded totally different in his sensitivity to the needs of the learners and his openness in talking about the subject from his counterpart in the school several miles away.

With a total of four hundred students at Ramot School, only five were Beta Israel. Azulos would have liked to enroll more Beta Israel students, especially the little ones, in his school, but unless the parents took the initiative he was unable to do so. Besides, if he took the Beta Israel, the other school would become empty. The determined efforts of some social workers, led by an American volunteer, convinced some parents that their children would be much better off attending the secular school. The Morea personnel were angry when the transfers materialized.

The residents in the vicinity of Ramot School were of high socioeconomic status. Because of the large hospital located nearby, the parents of children who attended the school were doctors and other hospital workers. Thus, the school was considered one of the best in the large town—perhaps even in the country. The interaction of the Beta Israel children with their veteran peers was described as excellent.

The principal thought the questions raised by the Beta Israel parents before they made the decision to enroll their children were thoughtful and intelligent. With the assistance of capable social workers, he hoped more Beta Israel parents would come to visit in the future and inquire about the school. Once enrolled, the Beta Israel students received tutoring from American volunteers over and above the 1.8 hours provided by the government. He said that, as a group, the Beta Israel children had excellent skills in mathematics where there was no language involved. It was in the area of language —Hebrew and English—that the five children experienced the greatest difficulty. However, with the help of volunteers from English-speaking countries, they were making progress.

All five Beta Israel students in this school were girls. I talked to three of them as a group and then individually. One of them, Offir (her Hebrew name), said the school that she and the others attended the year before had not provided enough challenge. "We did not progress very much," she said. "This year we are happy." I asked her what language she used at home. She told me that since their parents did not speak much Hebrew, they used Amharic. But to help their parents learn, they sometimes spoke Hebrew with them. At other times, when the children were together, they spoke Amharic so they would not lose it.

Offir experienced many hardships in the Sudan after she left Ethiopia. She had been in Israel for nearly two years. She was the daughter of one of the most articulate members of the Beta Israel community, who had been a man of high status before he left Ethiopia. Her mother looked much younger than her father; this is probably his second marriage. Offir may have been the only child of her parents or at least the only one in Israel. She was very close to her parents and very concerned for their well-being. I saw a letter she had written in Hebrew on behalf of her parents to the regional director of housing. The director said the letter was of high quality and very touching. On the whole, she appeared articulate, pleasant, and mature for her age. The director of housing commented that young people like her sustain hope for the future of the Ethiopian Jews in Israel.

ASSESSING THE SOCIOECONOMIC MILIEU OF THE SCHOOLS

The Morea and Ramot schools presented here are located in one of the two towns where there are large concentrations of Beta Israel and people of northern African background—primarily from Morocco. The mayor and most of the top officials are of Moroccan background. In my effort to understand the character and dynamics of this community and how these may affect the schooling of the migrants, I interviewed community leaders, department heads of the municipality, the head of the community activities center, and a psychologist. The following portrayals of the situation are based on these interviews.

One of the complaints of the Morea School staff was the lack of psychologists who could assess the conditions of the student body. Next door in the secular school, there was no such shortage. I invited one of the school psychologists at the secular school to describe the psychological environment of the schools and the community. The psychologist was a woman of Hungarian origin; she spoke fluent English. Since we had met on several other occasions during my previous visits, we felt at ease with each other. The dialogue began in the school and continued in the coffee shop downtown.

She agreed that the paucity of psychologists was a very real problem in the schools, especially in the smaller towns. Problems were compounded in communities where the Beta Israel were concentrated. Most psychologists served several schools. In the school system where she worked there was one school that enrolled Beta Israel students. Although she had occasion to visit two of the classrooms in the religious school, she did so with great reluctance. She said she didn't want to touch the problems of the Beta Israel students "even if they hung them." To begin with, she explained, there were no appropriate test instruments to evaluate the kinds of problems the Beta Israel presented. Even pencil-and-paper tests that required the child to draw a figure or some object may not be valid for this population. In addition, "there are so many problems with this population that it can drown you. One can devote one's life and still not solve any problems." Another problem confronting the psychologist was that the ages of the children were generally not known, and it was difficult to determine social or psychological criteria for assigning students to appropriate groups. In some respects, the treatment of the Ethiopians was not exceptional. Numerous other *aliyah* had been received negatively. The Romanians, the Hungarians, the Moroccans, the Egyptians, and the Yemenites had all experienced the effects of discrimination. Although the Russians fared better, the Georgians had some problems; they did not mix with others.

Another problem, she said, was that the teachers in the religious schools were inferior. "I do not work with them," she said. "I would not come near that. The teachers in the religious schools are Sephardic; their qualifications are lower than those held by teachers in the secular schools. They are teaching darker and darker generations. Educational levels get lower and lower with each succeeding generation and succeeding *aliyah*. We are still reaping the fruits of the 1950s [the coming en masse of the Orientals]. Now the darker people get to power through the religious institutions. Many of the secular institutions and avenues are closed to them. Therefore, they need to create and enlarge their power through the religious institutions." In the major cities, the schools were of higher standard, but not in the towns and settlement centers. Speaking of the language problem for each succeeding *aliyah*, she said, Bialik, the famous Israeli poet, summed it up well when he said that "Hebrew is the only language taught by children to their parents."

HOME AND SCHOOL

Chapter 4 dealt extensively with the major issues confronting Beta Israel families in their new home. Some major issues impinged on the efforts of the schools as well. To begin, it is important to remember that, over the past forty years in Ethiopia, a general awareness was developed among rural and urban parents of all social and religious backgrounds of the value of secular or "government" education. This awareness did not always lead to enrollment of children in school, because schools were few and, equally important, the parents needed the children to assist at home in various subsistence or economic activities. Among those parents who did send children to school, the feeling was that their sacrifice was substantial and thereafter any additional responsibilities were to be assumed by the school. With the possible exception of some of the educated parents in the major cities, parental involvement and home-school interaction were minimal or nonexistent. The parents assumed that the government provided all the necessary conditions for teaching their children and that the schools would carry out the necessary tasks as best they could. As in other African countries, the schools themselves usually assumed that the parents knew nothing about schooling and therefore neither expected nor encouraged parents to become involved.

Throughout their first year in Israel, there were social workers, house mothers, and a host of others in the absorption centers who catered to the needs of the Beta Israel children. The Jewish Agency provided the necessary material support. The parents came to assume that it was the responsibility of the government which they considered magnanimous and generous. When they left the absorption centers, they were not prepared to participate in the education of their children. After one year in Israel, they were expected to clothe their children in decent materials; to purchase exercise books, pens, pencils, and gym outfits; and to pay small fees for incidental items such as bus fare for class trips. The parents refused. They considered the expectations and demands placed upon them by the school personnel as efforts by local bureaucrats to stand in the way of the government's delivery of services to their children. To further complicate the situation, when parents were asked to attend meetings or conferences at the school, they shied away. School personnel and government officials interpreted this to mean that the parents were detached from or otherwise indifferent to their children's education. These misunderstandings led to acrimonious conflicts which continue to polarize the homes and schools.

Beta Israel parents lack traditions of participation or involvement in the education of their children. They are intimidated by the new environment, and they do not have the language facilities to express themselves or otherwise communicate with school personnel. Some schools use children to facilitate communication, while others prefer to use adult interpreters whom, as noted earlier, the parents do not trust. Moreover, their own young children, those ten years of age and younger, are forgetting their native tongue as quickly as they are learning Hebrew. Parent-child communication is becoming increasingly difficult—further intimidating the parents. School personnel do not fully appreciate the dynamics of these difficulties. The parents are very limited in what they can do, materially and emotionally, in the new environment. Appreciation of these problems by school personnel and government officials is an important first step. Another temporary solution to the dilemma is for the school to provide additional tutoring, study facilities, and so on, for these children to compensate for deficiencies in the home.

SUMMARY

Primary education for Beta Israel children is provided primarily under the aegis of the state religious system. Provisions are made for the parents to exercise their right to enroll their children in the state secular system, but few do so. This suggests either that the parents are satisfied with the state religious schools or that they do not fully appreciate the differences.

Most Beta Israel children are participating in education, in either segregated or integrated classrooms. At this juncture, the pressing question is what conditions benefit the Beta Israel children most. Arguments can be made for both approaches. For those students whose needs are such that they would benefit from, and in fact receive, more focused instruction and intensive support in a segregated learning environment, there is merit in continuing this practice. If their learning, at least in certain areas, would be enhanced in an integrated situation, then that also should be made available.

At this time, the secular and religious systems of education are rivals. The religious schools are most concerned with the precepts and rituals of religion, which may be an important component of education for the children of a people who have been cut off from mainstream Judaism for centuries. However, for intellectual stimulation and cognitive development, the quality of instruction in the secular schools appears to have more to offer. Yet such differences are hardly appreciated on behalf of the education of most of the children. An independent advocating body that understands the situation and is acceptable to all parties concerned should be found to look after the matter. The education of the migrant children is so important that it cannot be left to the petty whims of politics.

In view of the fact that most Beta Israel families are under severe pressure arising from their dislocation and disorientation, parent substitutes, without physical removal from the home, should be considered on behalf of the children to whatever extent possible.

CHAPTER EIGHT

❖

Postprimary Education and Training

❖

Beta Israel youth between the ages of eleven and eighteen have some special concerns, problems, and challenges as they try to negotiate the absorption processes in the new society. In response to the needs and challenges of this age group, a special set of policies has to be put in place; special institutions of socialization, education, and acculturation must be found; and the appropriate teachers, counselors, and other personnel must be recruited and deployed. Even under normal circumstances, adolescents undergo many changes and experience growth pains; many societies recognize and make appropriate provisions for these changes. To facilitate their rapid biological and psychological growth, young people need as much guidance and support as possible from significant persons such as parents, relatives, religious leaders, teachers, and peers. This is also a time when young people have to acquire important skills, attitudes, and knowledge in preparation for lifelong vocations.

For the Beta Israel youth, the processes of normal growth and development have been disrupted. They have been dislocated from their roots, from familiar places and languages, and, even more importantly, for many of them, from their parents and relatives. They have to learn to relate to new people on very basic and important levels, new teachers, surrogate parents or caretakers, religious leaders, and peers whose language, culture and race, are profoundly different. As pointed out in Chapter 1, the absorption process is better facilitated, at least during the critical initial stages, when an individual's primary group is available, functioning, and supportive. In the case of this group of young people, their families and primary group were disrupted by the conditions of their migration, and the support they need so much is either depleted or nonexistent.

In addition to cultural bereavement and deprivation, many young people lost their parents, siblings, or relatives in the course of their long journey to Israel or in refugee camps. Others left their aging parents and younger siblings behind in Ethiopia. Also, although the value of education is very much appreciated among the Beta Israel youth (in terms of material import, it may be overvalued), many of whom had attained some secondary-level education, resources in Ethiopia were limited, and the quality of education was very low.[1] These facts must be kept in mind as we consider the education of Ethiopian youth in Israel.

Attempting to arrange for postprimary or second-level education for migrant youth who had left the land of origin under very unusual circumstances proved to be no easy task. To begin with, the students did not bring with them the educational documents, birth records, and other vital information could guide decisions regarding appropriate individual grade-level placement. Other less reliable means had to be established and utilized, including information provided by the young people themselves.[2] As a result, one inevitably finds that students of various ages and educational levels are learning together in the same classrooms at the secondary level. In addition, one often finds little correspondence between the grade equivalents of the Ethiopian and Israeli school systems. These discrepancies contribute greatly to problems associated with the absorption process.

The absorbing society's response was to categorize the immigrant youth into groups and place them in different learning institutions. Thus, those young people who had been exposed to some kind of advanced schooling before arriving in Israel were placed in boarding schools known as Youth Aliyah, or, in Hebrew, Aliyat Hanoar. Those with little or no previous exposure to schooling were placed in a different sort of educational setting known as the Youth Administration Project, considered in Chapter 9.

In 1986–87, about 98 percent or twenty-five hundred of the Beta Israel between the ages of eleven and eighteen were receiving education and training in forty-four Youth Aliyah villages or centers. In these collective communities, boys and girls studied in the morning and worked in the afternoon. The students received instruction in subjects such as religion, history, geography, and language, but the main emphasis was on the development of vocational and communal living skills. As far as vocational training was concerned, the girls concentrated on home economics (sewing, handicraft, and embroidery, both traditional and modern). The boys received training in agriculture or agro-mechanics and related technical fields such as metalwork, carpentry, and, increasingly, electronics. Few were on the regular academic tracks.

YOUTH ALIYAH: HISTORICAL BACKGROUND

The concept of agricultural schools of the Youth Aliyah type goes back to 1870, when the first modern Jewish school was established in Palestine. The first school, Miqveh Israel ("Hope of Israel," from Jeremiah 17:13), was located about two miles east of what is now Tel Aviv. It was designed to give agricultural education to Jewish children as a part of the Zionist "return to the soil" ideology. In time, several other schools were started. Regarding the scope and mission of these agricultural schools, Bentwich wrote: "These schools have, perhaps, the best claim to the appellation of 'public schools' [for Israel]. They are boarding schools, aiming primarily at the formation of character, with studies only secondary thereto. They are truly 'public,' admitting many of their pupils at nominal fees and with no selection. . . . They have no snobbish attraction; on the contrary, all they can offer is 'toil and sweat,' and a vocation, which, although it may pay, always entails hard work, and does not stand high in the social ladder."[3] The schools were to anchor Jewish youth on the soil through agricultural training schemes.

Youth Aliyah was founded in Israel on March 5, 1933, on the very day Hitler came to power in Germany, to shelter, nurture, and educate the children of distressed Jews from Europe. Since that time, Youth Aliyah has continued to absorb Jewish youth who have experienced either physical or spiritual difficulties in their country of origin and rehabilitate them through education and training in a nurturing and supportive environment. Because of their past experiences and their urgent need to cope with a completely new and strange environment, these children are often under great emotional stress. At these Youth Aliyah centers, which some like to call villages, young people receive special care and attention from experienced teams of education specialists, counselors, psychologists, social workers, and medical personnel.

The number of children living and learning in these villages at any one time has fluctuated over the decades according to world conditions. In 1986–87, for instance, there were nineteen thousand students enrolled in the Youth Aliyah. The majority of these students were the children of first- or second-generation immigrants or children who came from distressed areas in Asia, northern Africa, and the Middle East who had not yet found their way into mainstream Israeli society. More than three thousand of them were newcomers who hailed from the following countries: 398 from the Soviet Union, 98 from Iran, 26 from Romania, 93 from Morocco, 124 from Asia and other northern African countries, and nearly twenty-five hundred from Ethiopia.[4] The numbers have fluctuated, but the total is significant: between the years 1933 and 1986, 232,152 youth have passed through the doors of the Youth Aliyah centers.[5] As immigrants from Europe decreased, children of immigrants from the Middle East, northern Africa, Asia, and, beginning in 1980, Ethiopia have taken their place. Almost three hundred villages are scattered throughout the country. Thus, even though Youth Aliyah was started as an emergency measure, as Bentwich reminds us, it developed special methods that have permanent application and have made it one of the most innovative components of the Israeli educational system. It originated from the need to receive and rehabilitate European youth who were fleeing from tyranny and persecution. It continues to do that even as it tries to respond to changing circumstances. In the villages as well as in the *kibbutzim*, it offers agricultural training in a supportive and nurturing atmosphere which promotes the ideals of communalism. As the young state matures, however, national attention and recognition are increasingly directed toward the professions, the industries, and other "modern" activities. The farm life and farm activities that were such an important component of the Youth Aliyah system are less attractive today. Parents and youth are more enticed by the matriculations that lead to college admission and higher prestige. By now the youth villages are serving young people in modified forms; in recent years, for example, technical courses have been introduced into the curricula. Thus, it may be concluded that this unique and innovative approach to gathering and educating beleaguered youth in a rural setting has been abandoned by many of the better-off members of the society. The ones who continue to participate are recent immigrants, such as the Beta Israel, and youth from disadvantaged homes, who are also poor.

In Tel Aviv, at the administrative headquarters of Youth Aliyah, I interviewed the person in charge of the supervision of Beta Israel along with Akiva Elias, the main trouble-shooter (a veteran Beta Israel), the chief coordinator of medical services, and the chief social work officer. The following information about the Beta Israel youth in the care of Youth Aliyah is based on these interviews.

In 1986-87 Youth Aliyah maintained some nineteen thousand youth in 289 educational settings. There are twenty five hundred Beta Israel boys and girls in forty four centers or villages. Some of these centers are directly owned by the Youth Aliyah organization itself which is a department of the Jewish Agency, but most are owned by independent organizations and societies. Actually, only four centers are completely owned by the Jewish Agency, and these serve the special educational needs of youth who are either physically or mentally impaired. Youth Aliyah also pays the bills for its charges and maintains direct or indirect supervisory responsibilities for all programs and activities. Regardless of ownership, the residential setting remains the heart and soul of the Youth Aliyah's operations. During the initial year, all Beta Israel youth were placed in three centers by themselves. In 1987, two of the centers were desegregated. The third center, Hofim, was not desegregated. This center, located near Akko by the Mediterranean, is unique; it accepts children as well as adults for a period of a year and prepares them to face integrated life in other school and living settings in subsequent years. Under the effective leadership of Rabbi Nahum Cohen, the center has been awarded a medal of recognition by the Knesset for its distinguished services to youth from Ethiopia.[6]

Referring to the general thrust of the Youth Aliyah, the general director, Vizonisky, says: "Our aim is to help the Beta Israel become normal citizens of Israel by helping them become integrated in the educational, professional and other arenas of life." Each of the forty-four centers that enroll Beta Israel students offers some mix of academic, vocational and religious studies; the emphasis placed on each of these areas varies from center to center. At the broader level, boarding schools generally offer both academic and vocational or agricultural training. In the *kibbutzim*, the students study, live, and work together as a group. In the youth day centers, the students have a long day of study and vocational training but return "home" to a boarding village each night.

Youth Aliyah personnel help integrate the youth into society at a pace that is comfortable for them. No pressure is imposed. That is why Beta Israel were completely segregated during their first year. Even in the second year, only about eight hundred were integrated in the classrooms. The rest, although they go to the same centers and villages as veteran Israeli students, attend segregated classes. Boys and girls usually attend separate classes. In the dormitories and dining halls, the Beta Israel have opportunities to mix with students from Poland, Hungary, Georgia, northern Africa, and other lands of origin; opportunities for integration are not lacking. In addition, the director says, efforts have been made to bring some six thousand youth from all over the country together in Jerusalem to become acquainted with the Ethiopians on "Jerusalem Day."[7]

As the director tells it, in the 1950s and 1960s, the veteran Ashkenazi society tried to force its views of integration on the newcomers. This meant that the migrants were expected, even coerced, to behave like Westerners in manners of eating, dress, entertainment, and the like. "But nowadays," Vizonisky told me, "we have concluded that is not Israel. Each form of culture and ethnic behavior brought by the various groups should be treasured. We tell youth in our charge to work out a balance in harmony with themselves. At least, this is what we educators now believe. The politicians may still hold the old views of integration along the unitary, Westernization lines."

As an Orthodox Jew, he added, to be an Israeli means believing in God, the Torah, and Israel. Belief in God has a social mission to help Jews become one nation in the spiritual sense if not in the political sense. To this end, he said, Israel has to educate all its children and youth. Youth Aliyah has an important role in inculcating these beliefs and translating them into action. The largest group of young people in the Youth Aliyah villages are, of course, veteran Israelis; there seems to be a growing number of young people returning to religion. Turning to the issues of bigotry and prejudices, the director said that these could be a problem. He said that although Judaism respects the rights of other people and their ideas, in reality there are extremes of right and left in the society who refuse to see things in perspective.

Regarding specific problems presented by the Beta Israel group, the director listed the following: (1) lack of knowledge about the Ethiopian youth—their wishes and ambitions—among veterans responsible for administering programs and providing assistance to them; (2) insufficient knowledge regarding the assets and different levels of talents and achievements that the Beta Israel brought with them which could be utilized to help them fit into Israeli society or enable them to cope better with the adjustment processes; and (3) the separation of the community. The youth are preoccupied with thoughts and worries about parents and relatives left behind in Ethiopia as well as with the traumatic events that occurred on their journey to Israel. As many have said, "What can I learn here when my heart is there?" The teen years are challenging enough under normal circumstances, but for the Beta Israel, the challenge has been compounded by exposure to tremendous ordeals, for instance, in the camps in the Sudan where they saw much sickness, starvation, and suffering and where relatives and friends died. In addition to these ordeals, Beta Israel youth also are faced with the challenges found in a strange new society, however friendly it may be. It also should be noted that in addition to the strangeness of the material, physical, and social surroundings, it is here that most young Beta Israel saw white people, or *ferenj* in Amharic, for the first time. It is perhaps most difficult for the older male youth, since chronological age is an important factor in determining admission, grade placement, and termination policies. The younger ones will spend more time learning at school, which is what they all want, while the older ones will have less time to learn before they must join the Israel Defense Forces at the age of eighteen. At any rate, the young people must have concluded that they should get as much education as possible because, according to Vizonisky, teachers and administrators complain that the Beta Israel youth want to remain in school longer than their age and other policy and financial constraints allow; they also want to live in apartments on their own rather than in the villages. Some, he said, "do not know their objective situation; they do not know themselves," referring to the limitations that their age, educational background, and abilities might impose on their future job opportunities. They like to do what their age-mates who have different backgrounds are doing. Other character traits attributed to the Béta Israel youth by Haim Yani, inspector of educational programs for the Beta Israel and in charge of individual placement, including young people with special problems, are restlessness, suspicion regarding the intentions or motives of decision makers ("the trait of suspiciousness runs deep in their characters"), stubbornness (not listening to what they are told), and high and sustained ambition for learning. "In this latter characteristic," he said, "they all are united." He also said that they were polite in the beginning but are changing quickly. In dress, wearing makeup, and the like, they have adapted to the Israeli culture very fast. In search of an institution that will allow them to continue to advance their education and training beyond present limits, they try to change schools often. This is understandable but cannot always be accommodated; often, their abilities do not qualify them for the level of studies that they want. Besides, resources are limited. For instance, some want to study for professional careers in medicine, engineering, or computer science. But given their age, background, and the expenses involved, their expectations are unrealistic. "But," Yani added, "I am amazed at the amount of positive change we are witnessing over such a brief period of time." Given the ordeals they went through, the losses they suffered, and the absence of the traditional sources of emotional, cultural, and spiritual support, however, the apparent confusion among the youth is not surprising. Although professional guidance is insufficiently available, the will to help does exist, and the efforts made to date should be fully recognized.

As already mentioned, students at Youth Aliyah are primarily from homes that, for one reason or another, are divided, troubled, or otherwise disadvantaged. Some are orphans and others are the children of recent migrants. In most instances, the disadvantaged are of Asian and African background. Thus when the twenty-five hundred Beta Israel between the ages of eleven and eighteen were placed in more than forty-four such villages (most of which are under the religious organization), in a way they were joining others of less than ideal background in terms of class or other family characteristics.

In the villages, they live in a homelike atmosphere in many ways. The meals, consistently very appetizing and nutritious, are communally prepared and served. As a rule, the housing is not luxurious, but it is comfortable. When asked why they serve their meals on china, Vizonisky replied, "No child should ever say he ate off plastic plates." In many of the villages, the teachers, school principal, and other personnel live on the premises and are accessible to the students at all times. The effort is aimed at maintaining an atmosphere the students can call home. In fact, many, including the Beta Israel, would not have known any other home in Israel except the youth villages.[8] They receive their training in their chosen vocations here; they make friends and are exposed to or immersed in the kind of Israeli culture and language the villages offer. Even after they have joined the army, they return to the villages when they are on home leave.

The cases that follow illustrate the various similarities and differences among Youth Aliyah villages in their educational provision and performance as well as the social and psychological dynamics affecting this group of Beta Israel.

MIQVEH ISRAEL

Located in a beautiful setting two miles outside Tel Aviv is village Miqveh Israel ("Hope of Israel"). I first visited this center in July 1985, in the company of worldwide Youth Aliyah director Uri Gordon and other officials. After meeting with the director of the village, some of the instructors, and some Beta Israel youth, I was taken around the premises and observed the various activities engaged in by the students. Since it was summer, most of the veteran youth were away, so the Ethiopians were very visible.

Most of the Beta Israel youth, male and female, whom I met in 1985 had come to Israel in the Operation Moses group and had been in the centers for only a few months.[9] At that time, they were learning Hebrew and participating in socialization activities in the villages. Although they sat together in the dining room and did not interact much with the other students, they were beginning to assume responsibility for saying the prayer before and after meals and cleaning the dining room and the premises, and on the whole they seemed to be comfortable and relatively pleased with their lot. They appeared very relieved that they had made it safely to Israel, though they were grieving for the loss of relatives and were very worried about those left behind in Ethiopia. They were unsure regarding the expectations others held for them and how the new society, through its representatives in the villages, would react if they openly inquired about friends and relatives living elsewhere. When they wanted to raise issues with me regarding family members in Ethiopia, in the Sudan, or in America or Canada, they would draw me aside to inquire, at times in a whisper, if I knew so-and-so or if I could deliver some message on their behalf. I got the impression then that they did not want other people, including their Ethiopian compatriots, to know about their private concerns. This was also when the religious conversion controversies were beginning to emerge openly.

When I returned in 1987, I found adjustments continuing, though there had been some developments that affected the attitudes of the students as well as those of the center personnel. As I began to interview the same or similar students, I found that their concerns associated with separation from loved ones continued to occupy a dominant place in their thinking. Although many of them are blood relations or had known one another while in the villages of Ethiopia, this did not alleviate their anxieties about those left behind. Their initial euphoria and relief (as well as timidity) had passed; new concerns were emerging about the quality of education and training they were receiving, the security of their careers, and, in general, the kind of future they would have in Israel. Perhaps these concerns became apparent and were expressed openly because, after more than a year in Israel, they knew more about the society. Also, their most immediate needs such as food, shelter, medical care, and safety had been or were being met adequately and were being replaced by an awareness of higher-order needs. At any rate, they seemed to feel secure enough to express their concerns openly and fully without fear of presumed political repercussions.

During this visit, I had the opportunity to meet with Akiva Elias, a very knowledgeable man who spoke Amharic, Hebrew, and Tigrigna. He was assigned to take me around to the various institutions. Akiva Elias is himself a product of Youth Aliyah. On this particular day, we visited a class session on biblical history. Afterward, we met with the head of the department of religious education (the center has a secular and a religious wing, each headed by a different principal), several teachers, a psychologist, a social worker, and several others. There were three hundred youth residing in the village, 40 percent of whom were Beta Israel. The remaining 60 percent are veteran Israelis, most of Oriental origin. The village was coeducational, but classes were segregated by gender. Most of the Ethiopians, as relative newcomers, also were taught in separate classes.

The headmaster was of Yemeni background and had come from that country when he was two years old. He studied in Israel and at a Jewish college in Italy and served as headmaster in other Israeli schools. He was among the first to receive Beta Israel students when they began to arrive in the early 1980s. He and his Ashkenazi wife lived on the village premises. She worked as both a teacher and counselor to the Beta Israel, "like a mother," he told me. The social worker also of Yemeni origin, was married to an Ashkenazi. She had been at the village since 1983. Akiva Elias described her as a dedicated and concerned worker on behalf of the Beta Israel.

There were equal numbers of Beta Israel males and females in the village. Nearly all classes were segregated by gender. Later they were divided according to ability. Meanwhile, the village had accepted youth from other centers. Since decisions about grade level were based on age rather than educational attainment, there was a wide range of abilities at any given level. When necessary, parallel classes were operated to accommodate all youth of the same age. As would be expected, achievement levels and progress rates varied considerably within grades. In spite of their late arrival, a few had progressed very rapidly and had been promoted accordingly. Others were still in transition classes, and a few were in regular classes, appropriate for their age. However, to take advantage of the educational opportunities, some of the young people may have concealed their true ages.[10] In addition to regular classroom instruction, most Beta Israel students received additional tutoring. The amount of extra help provided depended on need but averaged about two hours a day. The instructors admitted that no matter how much help they may have received, there were some who could not progress very far.

The Beta Israel were, of course, all under the religious wing of the village. I was told that the parents or guardians, of those who have them, preferred this. They thought that if their children were educated outside the religious wing they would *balege yihonubinal* ("become immoral or undisciplined"). Whether the students themselves appreciated this kind of concern is another matter. Some, although very few, had joined nonreligious learning institutions in spite of parental or governmental wishes to the contrary. At Miqveh Israel, many of the youth were insisting that they be allowed to transfer to vocational schools where they would begin to earn money sooner (the religious school at which they were then studying was strong in agricultural fields, where employment opportunities upon graduation were not promising). The school personnel wanted them to continue there, perhaps out of fear that they might go to secular institutions. One young student told me he would like to drop out of school right away so that he could earn some money. Since this type of behavior among the Beta Israel is very uncharacteristic, one must wonder whether the real motive was to get transferred to a nonreligious village where he thought the instructional offerings were much better and the religious requirements minimal or nonexistent. But another possible explanation relates to the kind of news these young people heard from Ethiopia, which was very depressing and may have influenced their thinking. Some may have felt compelled to give up their long-range educational and career plans in favor of vocational programs that would enable them to secure paying jobs sooner. It is also possible that they appreciated the fact that ultimately religious education would not help them very much to secure jobs and earn sufficient money to meet their own needs as well as those of their families.

The social worker related that the students were extremely worried about their aging parents still in Ethiopia. They worried that if the remaining sibling were called to serve in the Ethiopian army and met his death, there would be no one to care for the very old and the very young. The Jewish Agency provides some money, primarily through banks in the United States, to help the relatives of young people in Ethiopia, but postal services in Ethiopia are unreliable, and the monies often fail to reach the intended recipients. Some Beta Israel blame the Jewish Agency for not trying hard enough to get the money through. For this reason, then, some youth felt guilty and said they were tired of going to school, and had to secure a job. The social worker added that because they were so worried, they tended to believe anything they heard in connection with this particular concern.

The headmaster complained that the students were more strongly influenced by persons outside rather than inside the school and that, for lack of a strong foundation, some found it very hard to make progress in their education. In addition, he said, they expected the state to provide them with all sorts of assistance indefinitely, when the objective was to make them self-sufficient as soon and as much as possible. "The Beta Israel youth get angry when we tell them this and continue to make additional demands. For instance, when they are asked to do work around the school like any other Israeli, they get angry and tell us that they want to go to school, not work." The trouble, he said, stemmed from the fact that when they first arrived, everything was given to them, "as if they were babies". No one told them about their responsibilities and obligations. Moreover, those who had arrived earlier told the newcomers that it was necessary to pressure the government if they were to get anything. There was a "group-think" mentality among them.[11] At times, they resorted to physical confrontations with care providers in, for example, the absorption centers if their demands were not met. They had learned to become self-centered and nonproductive.

Akiva Elias, troubleshooter for the Youth Aliyah organization, summed up the situation by quoting an Amharic proverb that, roughly translated, says: "A house guest who arrives during a wedding feast thinks there is always going to be a feast." Upon their arrival in Israel, the Beta Israel were showered with attention and generosity. No one told them that the ultimate purpose was to get them to stand on their own two feet in the shortest time possible. At any rate, their present attitude runs contrary to the purposes of centers and schools such as Miqveh Israel.

Policies in the various youth villages or centers differed. Some, for example, did not require the students to do physical work; some provided students with more pocket money than others. Students from the different centers got together and compared experiences, and as a result they built expectations and biases. (Just the previous weekend they had been together at a wedding.) Youth Aliyah provided students with some money to cover incidental expenses such as bus fare to visit relatives every third week or so, haircuts, and other personal necessities, things parents normally would pay for if they were available to do so and could afford it. But every center developed its own policy on the amount of stipends paid. When Beta Israel youth learned they were receiving less than students in other centers, they got annoyed and angry.

The variety of vocational course offerings in the Youth Aliyah centers were limited (different centers specialized in different types of vocational training). What the Beta Israel said they wanted and what Miqveh Israel was able to offer were often at variance. Specialists were coming, he said, to evaluate the students. Based on their assessments, another attempt would be made to match the students' wishes and abilities with the right training centers. As previously mentioned, chronological age was the major determining factor in Youth Aliyah placement. A fifteen-year-old who functioned educationally at the sixth-grade level was nevertheless placed in grade ten or higher because that was where his age cohort should be. Policies were based more on administrative imperatives than on the educational abilities and learning needs of students. As a result, many problems arose when a student's age placed him or her at a level that exceeded his or her ability. This bred complaints and conflict. Center personnel were aware of the issue and hoped one day to find remedies.

On the social side, some of the young Beta Israel women attending Miqveh Israel had either been married or had sexual experiences before they reached Israel. Many "marriages" had taken place in the refugee camps in Sudan. For instance, in the camps, one man might defend his "marriage" to five or more young women by saying that he did so to protect them from other males or to get them out of the country. In addition, many of the young Beta Israel women had been raped in the camps or along the way by *shiftas* (bandits), camp personnel, or their own fellow refugees. In fact, some Beta Israel men were so notorious at the camps for their relationships with young women that at times Israeli secret agents intervened and abducted the troublemakers to Israel.

In the cases of many who were legally married, spouses were left behind for one reason or another, or, even if they were in the country, they were pursuing their education elsewhere. Authorities often were unaware of such marriages. School personnel complained that the Beta Israel youth spent too much time fraternizing with the opposite sex, which sometimes resulted in pregnancies. The social worker, the headmaster, and the house mother are all passionately concerned about this and say that the young women fear the young men would leave them. However, the headmaster emphasized that this was not the place for marriage. The community did not accept it in Youth Aliyah villages. The result was an unacceptably high incidence of pregnancies which, in most cases, were terminated through abortion. According to the headmaster, a psychologist, in cooperation with a nurse and a physician, was going to coordinate a program of sex education to address the problem. When I asked why they had waited to begin this, I was told, "We were not ready."

I asked whether the "reconversion"[12] controversies raging at the time affected the attitudes of center personnel toward the Beta Israel.[13] The headmaster told me they did not. He explained: "We do not agree with the rabbinate's decision; we accept the Ethiopian youth as we accept any other Israeli. But we have noticed that it has affected the students' attitude to some extent. For instance, now some boys come to school without their *kippa* [required headgear or *yarmulke*], and some have started to show defiance toward some of the other religious requirements. This behavior is attributable to the rabbinate's stand on the religious issues." Would they be spiritually affected, too? It was true, said the social worker, that it had brought the identity question forcibly to the front: "For example, when we ask them why they take off their *kippa*, some students reply that this was not a part of their religious tradition in Ethiopia; 'there is no need for us to wear it here since you have told us that we are not Jews.'"

On the question of possible racial discrimination, the headmaster said that it was not a problem, meaning it did not exist. Perhaps he could have said it was not identifiable as such since most of the youth were segregated in classes and dormitories so there were not many occasions for them to interact with the larger body of students. Asked whether his Yemeni background (and brown color) made his work with the Beta Israel any easier, he quoted Golda Meir when she was asked how it felt to be a woman prime minister: "I have never been a man prime minister; I would not know the difference." So, added the headmaster, "I have been brown all my life; I would not know the difference. But the Ethiopians can see that I am brown in color and that my wife is white; they can put one and one together and draw their own appropriate conclusions." But on the whole, he thought being brown was a plus in his work with the Beta Israel youth.

In summary, the Beta Israel, for different reasons, threatened to leave this village for another that would provide them with a technical-vocational program that would train them for suitable employment with good pay so that they could support themselves and their poor families left behind. This means that the Beta Israel at Miqveh Israel did not think they were receiving the sort of training they need to secure a career. It also may mean that they did not appreciate the religious training they were getting at the expense of developing other skills. They also did not see much merit in agricultural work or its relevance to their future lives. Such an attitude put them at crosspurposes with Miqveh Israel's policy. Their demand for continuing support while they pursued their education over a longer period of time was viewed by the institution as a desire to continue to be dependent on the government.

Grade placement continued to be a problem because of a lack of knowledge among the school personnel, who have no records to ascertain chronological age or previous educational attainments and are not familiar with the cultural constructs operating within the community.

Male-female relationships were problematic primarily because of the abnormal circumstances that surrounded the journey to Israel, the separation of the families, and the unavailability of the traditional restraints, such as supervision by family members or early marriages which traditionally resolved issues of sexual relations outside marriage. Other reasons included the need for companionship in the absence of traditional extended family support and the uncertainty on the part of the young women about whether they would get a lifetime partner in the new circumstances where men and women choose each another without the intervention of relatives. Most of these factions have little to do with racial discrimination.

The young people said they were worried about relatives left behind and that they would like to transfer to a school that offered training in technical-vocational fields. Perhaps the greatest concern for the future was the lack of trust between the personnel and the students. The frequent reference to *them* and *us* was indicative of the gulf that still exists between the veterans and the newcomers.

KIRYAT BATYA

Kiryat Batya is a religious village established in 1947 to help children orphaned by the war in Europe. Today it serves youth from different backgrounds. It is located on a vast tract of land beautifully landscaped with a wide variety of shrubs, trees, and flowers. The architectural design is not very impressive, but the buildings are adequate and functional. Accompanied by Akiva Elias, alumnus of the village from the 1950s, I met the director of the village, a large, portly man in his early fifties, originally from Morocco. His office was well furnished. Portraits of several rabbis adorn the walls, and sports trophies the school had won were displayed in cases. Of the 1,250 students at the village, 550 were boarders, and the rest were day students. The Beta Israel youth numbered sixty, thirty boys and thirty girls. Within the school, there was a junior high, a senior high, and a technical-vocational division. Those who graduated from the academic program or stream might try, after service in the armed forces, for college admission. Others might finish high school and proceed to the two-year vocational-technical training program before joining the army. Students who did well in the technical-vocational stream but were not through by the time they reached eighteen years of age could get special permission to postpone army service until after they completed their program. For those who were married or were twenty-four or older, the service requirements were modified.

Placement procedures for the Beta Israel were similar to those discussed already. A student who had completed the equivalent of grade six in Ethiopia studied in an *ulpan* or language training center in his or her first year in Israel, and the following year was placed in grade seven. Those who came from urban-based schools in Ethiopia did relatively well. Those from the rural-based schools had a much more difficult time and were usually placed in segregated classes. Their chances for ever studying in the same classes with the others were extremely limited. But as Akiva Elias put it, "it gives them an opportunity to help one another on their own." This was a religious institution and enrolled only persons of religious persuasion. Others might apply to join the school but must agree to abide by the religious rules and requirements before they were accepted.

There were special concerns and problems particular to the Beta Israel. The following are some of the social, academic, and cultural problems identified in the course of conversations with school personnel and students.

The Ethiopian youth, according to the director, were "gentle and good people. They brought their own civilization with them, as we Moroccans did when we arrived. But we were called uncivilized when we began. We are concerned that the Beta Israel might become poisoned by the Western culture found here. We hope that they will fight to maintain their own culture before it is too late. This includes the issues of sexual morality and respect for parents and elders.[14] We Moroccans came in the 1950s during a time of crisis. We had to live in tents and experienced many difficulties. The Europeans destroyed our culture. We were ashamed to show the best of our culture, and as a result it is lost. We are now trying to rebuild it. I hope that the Ethiopians will not repeat our mistakes." He felt the Ethiopians were in a better position to fight for their cultural and religious identity because the Israeli public had changed its attitude and had more tolerance for some diversity. He added that the requirement to change Ethiopian names to Hebrew ones was wrong. The Ethiopians should fight for their right to decide. For instance, if the individual wanted to change his or her own name or the names of his or her children, that is the individual's business. In the case of the Moroccans, some changed their names and others did not. He himself had not changed his. Many of the Moroccans' names were derived from Hebrew, so problems were minimal. Akiva Elias, graduate of this center whose four children were students at this school, added that when he arrived more than a year earlier in Israel for the second time, they gave him a new name. "I myself do not like that they changed my name. I was not consulted. They just assigned me [a new Hebrew name]." When he was there as a student in the 1950s, the authorities did not try to change his name; the next time they did.[15]

The major obstacle for the Beta Israel at this school related to their low levels of educational attainment before arrival in Israel. It was difficult for these students to make the transition to new situations. Their command of the language was inadequate and their familiarity with basic concepts which underlie industrial training was practically nonexistent. For the most part, all other problems related to their learning were associated with inadequate earlier preparation.

Another problematic area was that the Beta Israel students neither understood nor accepted placement decisions made by school personnel. When they were placed in certain vocational training streams based on test results, they refused to accept the decisions unless they accorded with their own wishes. They thought these decisions were based on discriminatory practices. They refused to accept that placement decisions were made only after careful assessment by trained counselors and psychologists. Akiva Elias said that this was a pervasive problem. Many students asked him to intervene on their behalf. This was a cultural problem based on the premise that test results speak only the language the test makers want them to speak, and through the intervention of a *zemed* (a relative with proper connections), the results could be altered in accordance with the wishes of the test taker. This belief was not limited to the Beta Israel at this institution; it prevailed in many of the other centers.[16]

Still another major problem was a "group-think" mentality among the youth. If one of the villages or centers was reputed to provide more pocket money, better clothing, or better accommodation than others, the news spread quickly, and all the students would want to transfer there. Of course, budgetary allocations were determined on the basis of the number of students served, but otherwise the allocations were similar. Each center was at liberty to allocate its resources as it saw fit according to its particular circumstances; hence the differences in stipends paid.

The headmaster of the senior high school division, a longtime educator at the center (he had been Akiva Elias's teacher in the mid-1950s), said that, based on his observations of the three boys in his division, the Beta Israel were very highly motivated to learn. The trouble was that they either did not know or were unwilling to accept their own limitations. For instance, they planned to take the matriculation examination (which was very competitive and led to university admission if one were successful), when they should know that they could not pass because of their educational backgrounds and language limitations.

At the next stage, Akiva Elias and I met with the house mother who had worked at the center for twenty-three years, the social worker, and the psychologist who visited the center once a week. We continued the conversations about the social issues and concerns of the Beta Israel. Comparing the Beta Israel with other groups of olim, the care providers said the major differences were that the Beta Israel arrived with no previous knowledge of Hebrew and from illiterate backgrounds, which was not the case with other *olim*. They also commented that the Beta Israel who came before 1984–85 were more able to mix with the veteran Israelis than the ones who followed.[17] The numbers in the latter group were larger, and they tended to keep to themselves. Girls were more shy and unwilling to mix with other girls. They said Israeli girls were too pushy and too aggressive. The care providers maintained that Beta Israel girls were stubborn; once they took a position on an issue, they never changed their minds. They never said no, but they did not do what they were asked. Boys and girls studied separately and did not sit together in the dining halls. Two pregnancies had occurred in the center. It had not been easy to provide sex education since there were no female teachers who understood the language and culture of the Ethiopians. But there were plans to initiate a program in the near future. "We try to initiate group discussion with the girls but it is hard to draw them out, "said the care providers. "They never trust us." Except for two classes of girls who were still in *ulpanim*, the rest were in regular classes. Recently, two female students from Bar Ilan University (a religious institution) had been coming to give assistance to the Beta Israel girls. Both boys and girls were doing reasonably well in their education, except for one youth who was not progressing.

TIKVA VILLAGE

Located in the west-central part of the country is Tikva village. Built on a five-acre plot of land, it was small, both physically and in enrollment. It was also different from the other villages I had visited in structure, composition of student body, and level and extent of programs. The village was established in

1958–59 as a day center, but in 1975 boarding facilities were added to accommodate a few students. It was under the aegis of Agudat Israel, the ultra-Orthodox wing of the religious party. The director was of Yemeni background. Of the 200 students learning at the center, 150 were boarders, 25 stayed in rented flats in the vicinity, and 25 commuted from nearby youth villages. The students were all males and were either orphans—which is the case with many of the Beta Israel —or came from broken or otherwise dysfunctional homes. In addition to the Jewish Agency, which sponsors the Youth Aliyah, a number of other organizations cooperated to support the students in this village. Most programs took between two and four years to complete, and, according to the headmaster, the Ministry of Education and Youth Aliyah guidelines were followed in curricular offerings. This means that the programs included subjects such as mathematics, history, English, Bible, and design technology. The students spent an additional fifteen hours a week engaged in laboratory or workshop activities. Furthermore, special teaching methods and instructional materials, developed at Bar Ilan University to address the many learning problems of Beta Israel youth, were tried out and adapted for classroom use. For instance, in the latter part of 1987, it was discovered that the testing instruments that had been designed for veteran Israelis did not work well with the Beta Israel. The Beta Israel performed poorly on these tests, though they did well when the same skills were tested in field situations. This led to the conclusion that the regular instruments of evaluation were not valid measures of the Beta Israel's performance.

The day began at five-thirty in the morning. One hour, beginning at six-fifteen, was devoted to prayer at the synagogues and religious lessons. At seven-fifteen students returned to the dormitories to clean up and have breakfast. Classes began at eight and continued until one p.m. The afternoons were devoted to sports, drama, homework, and counseling activities. For those who needed it, such as the Beta Israel, special tutoring also was provided in the afternoon. Evenings were devoted to handicrafts, music, discussions ranging from the politics and policies of Israel to health issues, including the dangers of drug abuse and AIDS. Sometimes guest speakers were brought in to lead the discussions. There also were opportunities to play video games and watch television. Every three weeks, students went home to visit their families.

There were four groups of Beta Israel in this school. One was comprised of twenty-three nonliterate young men. They were supported by the Student Administration unit, (discussed in Chapter 9), and since they were nonliterate, they should have been placed in another setting. But perhaps for lack of other appropriate centers or because of their age, they were placed here. These young men commuted daily from a nearby village. Learning was very hard and slow for this group. They learned Hebrew and were given a general education about life in Israel; from time to time, they toured the country to become familiar with its history and geography. According to the headmaster, the objective was to prepare them to join a branch of the Israel Defense Forces with the understanding that once in the armed forces they would acquire additional skills which eventually would help them obtain employment and lead a life of dignity. Akiva Elias said the amount of patience and labor these young people required and received from the teachers was staggering. Teachers literally had to hold their hands in order to teach them to write. It would have been impossible to give any group of people this kind and amount of devoted attention in Ethiopia. The second group of Beta Israel was comprised of young men who were more than eighteen years old but very low achievers. They were in *ulpanim*. In the third group were advanced students who attended regular classes. Another twelve Beta Israel youth who studied in a nearby *yeshivah* commuted to take courses in electronics. Some of the Beta Israel had completed their course of studies and were now in the Israeli Defense Forces. According to the headmaster, they were excellent soldiers. From time to time, they returned to visit the village.[18]

The major issues and concerns that applied to most of these Beta Israel may be summarized as follows. According to the social worker, some of the teachers, and the headmaster, learning Hebrew was difficult for them. As a result, even those in the regular classes experienced difficulty in the Bible class. They were better at mathematics. The integration of students in the regular classes was progressing. As of winter 1987, only two classes remained segregated.

Another common problem involved their separation from parents and other relatives. The students sent some money and packages to them, but they didn't always arrive. Meanwhile parents wrote letters about their money problems and asked the children to help. Those students whose parents were in Israel seemed to fare better. They visited them frequently and helped them with their shopping and banking. They also taught their relatives and parents the language, "just as we Yemenite used to do," said the social worker. The difference between the Yemenis and the Ethiopians was that even though some of the adult Yemeni were illiterate, many did know some Hebrew.

Regarding the changing of names, the headmaster who was of Yemenite origin, related his own experiences. He said his original name was Hassan. But with encouragement from his teacher, he changed it to a Hebrew name. His father objected to the change. After much negotiation, a compromise was worked out. Since his father's name was Yehuda, it was appropriate for him to assume the Hebrew name Ben Yehuda ("son of Yehuda"), which was acceptable to his father. The social worker, also of Yemenite origin, said her father and mother never changed their names. But when she married an American, he changed his surname from White to its Hebrew equivalent, which she shares. They all agreed that the Beta Israel should have been offered a choice about whether or not to change their names.

TIVILA TRAINING CENTER

The case of Tivila Training Center was another example of variation on a theme. It had its own peculiarities which present different challenges. Among these was the attempt to take in three different categories of Beta Israel youth and educate them. Also, since it was run by the very Orthodox sector of Judaism, it operated under rigorous religious regulation and students had to meet these additional requirements.

Tivila Training Center, located in the central part of the country, was founded in 1950 in Jerusalem as an institution for older citizens. After it was destroyed by fire, it was rebuilt at its present location and became a center for training young people. Money for the institution came from Jews of Britain. The headmaster was an alumnus of Youth Aliyah, who came from Morocco at the age of twelve, served in the army, attended a teacher-training school, and earned a degree from Bar Ilan University majoring in educational administration with an emphasis on the Hebrew language. He was a teacher and principal in the south before he got married and moved to the northern to a bigger responsibility.

This village was different from others studied. It admitted students who were very high achievers as well as low achievers in the ratio of three to one. The idea was to educate the gifted but not isolate them from the others and to give the low achievers an opportunity to benefit from interaction with better students. For instance, the headmaster explained, one student whose parents were divorced came to the school with emotional and learning problems. In time, there was vast improvements in his behavior and attitudes toward studying. He took pride in himself and began to work hard at his tasks. After leaving, he entered a *yeshiva* and graduated with an average score of 80 percent. The mixing of strong and weak students created a stimulating environment for the latter.

Each grade had four tracks, which made it easy to transfer students from one section to the other according to their progress. If they had to move them between institutions, the headmaster said, it would be much more difficult considering institutional inertia and bureaucratic red tape.

This was also a coeducational institution. Out of a total of 176 students, 52 percent were Beta Israel, of whom 30 percent were female and 70 percent were male. When I visited some of the class activities in tailoring, carpentry, drama, English, and a special class in Hebrew, I noticed that many students did not appear motivated. There was a noticeable lack of enthusiasm for what was being taught. I asked why, if this was a school for both gifted and nongifted students, were most Beta Israel in the vocational stream reserved for those not planning to proceed to academic learning beyond high school? The headmaster explained that in the beginning, most of the Beta Israel students showed a high motivation for learning, but that motivation had waned. One Beta Israel student, Asher Kebede, did join a premilitary training class given in the center for the highly intelligent. Usually, graduates of such classes became officers in the armed forces of Israel. On the other hand, another Ethiopian student, there for three years, was still in the *ulpan*.

The headmaster observed that the Beta Israel were polite and cooperative and had respect for teachers and elders. Lack of punctuality was a problem. When tardiness occurred, and it happened very frequently, they did not bother to apologize. For instance, said the headmaster, it was the custom to pray at sunset. Often they had to wait for the Beta Israel. When they eventually arrived, they offered no explanation or apology. Others did the same, but with the Beta Israel it was more pronounced. The headmaster also observed that they had a great desire to be like the Israelis and within a year had become aggressive and used bad language. Speaking of cultural differences, he continued, on one occasion they found a group of Beta Israel girls huddled together. At first they were frightened but soon learned that it was a harmless act used to comfort one another in times of distress.

The headmaster, the psychologist, and the social worker expressed several concerns. They said the Beta Israel still felt insecure. They did not venture out beyond the village premises. They lacked confidence in their specific Ethiopian Jewishness and tried to adapt to the religious conventions of Israel. "They adopt traits and habits that are not the best Israel has to offer," said the social worker. Such traits included aggressiveness. Their marriages were less stable than they should be, and this was creating problems. The amount of divorce and remarriage among the Beta Israel exceeded that of the veteran population (she was referring to the adult population, not necessarily the youth group).

Another difficulty that kept popping up was the relationship between male and female students. The social worker said that the previous week two of the Beta Israel boys had been absent from some scheduled evening activities. They were found in the room of one of the veteran Israeli girls. This was not permitted.

The young Beta Israel women were very concerned about their future. In the Ethiopian context, arranged early marriages took care of many problems. Here, with the drastically changed conditions, they were not sure what would happen to them. There were no precedents, no role models or mentors, no arranged marriages. The community and the traditional elders were not there or, if they were, they were fragmented and mostly nonfunctional. Two young women had become pregnant. One ultimately married the man responsible. My most knowledgeable informant, who was also present during the interview, himself a veteran Beta Israel, said, "We have difficulty closing the gate which was opened in the Sudan," by which he meant that the many problems, including the sexual ones, that began in the refugee camps of the Sudan still beset the community. The officials now believed that the many sexual activities among the youth occurred in the absorption centers, where the students went every three weeks to visit relatives and friends, and not on the village premises. The social worker informed me that no sex education was being provided. Only simple instruction in personal hygiene was offered to the girls. The social worker insisted that abandoning their traditional culture would continue to lead the Beta Israel into a lot of trouble. "We who came from Morocco," she said, "lost our traditional culture; we are now trying to recover it. I hope the Ethiopians will do better."

BEN YAKIR

Ben Yakir, which means "beloved child," was another sort of village that exclusively serves youth with learning disabilities. Akiva Elias, the headmaster, the social worker, and I first sat together to discuss the program and later visited some of the classrooms and field activities. I learned that the village was coeducational. Of the 130 students, 30 were Beta Israel boys. There were no Ethiopian girls in attendance. The age range was mixed but most of the students appeared to be of primary school age, not high school age, which was atypical for a Youth Aliyah village (except at Hofim in Akko, where there were people of varying ages). These children were mentally "weak" and had been rejected by other Youth Aliyah villages but were classified as "educable" or "trainable" since the organization did not accept severely handicapped people. At this center, they received two or three years of training before being transferred to other centers for additional training and then drafted into the army. "They may not be sent to the front lines, but at least they will be able to work in the kitchens and sweep the hallways," said the British-born Israeli social worker.

At the village there was a large animal farm with ponies, sheep, goats, cows, a variety of wild animals (in enclosure), and birds. "These animals help to rehabilitate the children," said the deputy headmaster of the village. The children were responsible for looking after the animals. They also decided who should be responsible for the different types of animals. Every week they rotated the responsibilities so that every child had a chance to be in charge. Adult supervision was provided on an as-needed basis. The children appeared to be well cared for, well groomed, cheerful, and comfortable.

GIVAT WASHINGTON

For the slight variation it represents, we must include here another village, Givat Washington, a large establishment by Israeli standards. It had two major sections—a regular Youth Aliyah type of program and a teacher-training wing. The social worker and the house mother were of Yemeni origin; the housing director was Tunisian; the director of the village and the school principal were from Germany and Poland, respectively. Although this was primarily an institution for female students, all top administrators were male.[19] They were also all *sabras* (born in Israel).

Of the eight hundred students enrolled, two hundred were in the teacher-training programs, 10 percent of them men being trained as physical education teachers. Of the one hundred Beta Israel women enrolled, 70 percent were in *ulpanim*. When they finished their intensive language program, they would join either the high school track or the technical-vocational track or, if they were able and within the age limit, the teacher-training track. In 1986–87, some of the Beta Israel girls were already in the ninth and tenth grades of the high school track. Another twenty were expected to join the high school track in 1987–88.

Akiva Elias and I sat down with the headmaster, the house mother, and the social worker. From our conversation, I learned that since 1986, some of the Beta Israel students had been "mainstreamed" into the dormitory and dining hall with their veteran peers. Also just that year, the first Beta Israel girl had joined the teacher-training program.

The major problems were administrative and psychological. On the administrative side, the budgetary cut was hurting. Tutorial assistance had been reduced, and youngsters without parents who used to get monthly spending money were no longer receiving it. Without these stipends, it was feared, their morale would suffer.

Another major area of concern was finding the appropriate fit between the individual and the programs of training and education available. For instance, the policy of Youth Aliyah does not allow mixing students of different ages in the same classroom. The students would rather leave school than be in the same class with others younger than themselves. But what could be done with a woman of twenty-five who had neither a husband nor any job skills? The students wanted to join the Youth Administration Project (a project designed for adults who had little or no exposure to formal schooling), and they wanted to live in apartments of their own. This was tried, but other problems cropped up, such as looseness in sexual morality. In addition, when it was suggested that they take courses that would enable them to become nurse's aides in hospitals or nursing homes, they refused. They wanted to become doctors, or, failing that, they wanted to get married, when in actual fact marriage issues were quite complicated for this group of Beta Israel women. For instance, the social worker said that she was aware of at least seven who had been married before. The most knowledgeable source in the field, who still works with the youth, said that as many as 80 percent were married before they arrived in Israel. The problem was that there were many complications with the marriage arrangements that had taken place in Ethiopia—most were arranged marriages and were negotiated when the women were very young. Now, either because the women wanted to continue their education or the men had been away for too long or they wanted to choose their own husbands, some of the women were changing their minds about previous marriage arrangements. In an attempt to untangle or regularize this complicated issue, the Israeli rabbinate established an office in Jerusalem that was responsible for negotiating some kind of order and regularity out of this mess.

The marriage procedure followed in certain parts of Ethiopia, which included the Beta Israel community, was very complicated and required some explanation. Marriages in Ethiopia were by tradition arranged by a girl's parents and relatives, and typically girls married very young. If the girl was underage, which was often the case, the marriage ceremony might be carried out, but the marriage was not consummated until she reached the age of majority (thirteen or thereabouts). Until the girl reached that age, she lived with the husband's family, though she frequently visited her parents. The provision that put restraints on the consummation of the marriage in regard to sexual relations was known as *gieyed* in Amharic. This means that the parents of the husband promised that their son would not know his wife sexually for the duration of the specified period of time. Usually this promise was kept, although circumstances, such as the girl's desire to be intimate with her husband with or without the knowledge of the parents, or the death of the parents might be cause enough for altering the agreed-upon arrangement. In the case of the Beta Israel women under discussion, the husbands in most instances either did not come to Israel with their wives or, if they did come, did not register their relationship when they entered the country. They may have withheld this information from the authorities to enhance their educational chances. But when some of the men began to show up asking for their wives in an effort to reestablish relations, some of the young women became reluctant or were unwilling to agree. If the marriage has been "forced" upon the woman, or was never consummated, the rabbinate is in favor of annulling it.[20] In some respects, the woman's refusal is contradictory or in the long run may even be self-defeating, since finding and marrying the person of choice may not be easy in the Israeli context. Also, since many of these women may not be able to go far in their education, it will be difficult for them to lead independent single lives.

In addition, since arriving in Israel some of the young women may have come to know other men. In other instances, some women and men have come to view arranged marriages as obsolete and nonbinding in Israel. Some feel free to explore and experiment with alternatives available in Israel.

Regarding sex education in the school setting, the informants told me that if they taught contraceptive methods they would be giving the students the message that it is all right to engage in illicit sex. In a religious institution, they said, they could not justify this and therefore did not teach about it. At the absorption centers, the *olim* may have been told it was permissible to use birth control, but not at the school.[21] The informants reported that there had been two pregnancies in the village. At the young woman's request, one was terminated by abortion, which the center financed. In the second case, the couple married and lived together with their two children in their own apartment in another part of the country.

How were the women doing educationally? The headmaster reported that they had a great motivation to learn with purpose. They were willing to spend a lot of time on their lessons. Ironically, this was one of the problems; most young Beta Israel women wanted to continue to study for a longer period of time, while the institution told them this could not be allowed because of mandates concerning length of study and resource constraints. Those in the academic stream were given additional tuition to help them progress as much as possible before the deadline. They were also given extra drills and allowed to take their tests orally rather than in writing. In spite of these additional efforts, not all would achieve the necessary competencies before they had to leave.

The Beta Israel women who were in *ulpanim* were divided into three groups. The first group included seventeen young women with the ability to proceed to high school (academic track) but who were too old (seventeen or older). This group required special programs which the center could not provide. The Ministry of Education could arrange alternatives for them elsewhere. The second group of thirty women would ultimately enter the vocational-technical track. For academic reasons, they could not proceed anywhere else. The third and largest group was also older and very weak in abilities and knowledge. These women could be helped so that in the near future they might find employment in factories. On the whole, about twenty of the women who performed well academically felt good about themselves though they were worried about what the future held for them. If Youth Aliyah allowed, this group of women could be helped to finish high school.

So far, then, the main problems identified included: absence of the students' parents and, in some cases, spouses; discrepancies in their abilities and ambitions; the low level at which they started their education, which made progress very hard; and limitations of the center to provide what the students were asking for or what they needed.

Regarding the social life of the women, as reported earlier, the Ethiopians would like to appear and act like the veteran Israeli girls, but at the same time they felt the Israelis were aggressive and pushy and kept their distance from them. For the first time, the authorities in the village tried to integrate the dormitories. Students in the ninth and tenth grades were assigned to share rooms, two veterans together in the same room with two Beta Israel. The eleventh-graders and *ulpanim* students were placed in the same buildings as veteran Israeli girls, but not in the same rooms. They had started to mix in the dining halls also. Outside the dormitories and dining halls they had opportunities to get together to celebrate holidays. On such occasions, the school personnel worked hard to bring together students from the high school, *ulpanim*, and vocational tracks. Sometimes the Beta Israel assumed some specific responsibilities, and when they did, they gained better acceptance from the veteran Israelis. Especially in the beginning, it was difficult for the girls to carry out daily responsibilities and interact. During the 1985 school year, for instance, one veteran father of a girl came to the school to complain that he did not like the idea that his daughter was sharing a dormitory room with an Ethiopian girl. He was told to go away with his daughter. Now no one said openly that she did not want to share a room with an Ethiopian girl. Also the behavior of the Ethiopian girls had improved over time. During 1985–86, a lot of fighting and pulling of hair occurred, especially around the telephones. Veteran Israeli girls used to say to the Beta Israel, "You are strangers, you are not Jews. You return to Ethiopia," or "You stink, and your food stinks." On one occasion, a psychologist had the students close their eyes and say whether the person who had just come in through the door was an Ethiopian or a veteran Israeli. They could not tell the difference, according to the report, which demonstrated that Ethiopians don't stink.

On another occasion, one girl cut off the hair of a Beta Israel girl when the latter was asleep. Another veteran Israeli girl woke up a sleeping Ethiopian girl and said, "I'm sorry, I didn't mean to wake you up." When physical fights broke out between the two groups of girls, the school personnel would complain to Akiva Elias that the Beta Israel were the ones who provoked the fights. He told them the problems were on both sides. The veteran Israelis had the advantage of knowing the language and where to go to complain. The Beta Israel did not. The only avenue left to them was to fight physically for what they thought were their rights. When the school first experimented with putting two Ethiopians in the same room with two veterans, there were many petty squabbles. For example, the Beta Israel girls would clean their side of the room and leave the rest messy. The Ethiopian girls did not usually complain about the squabbles and fights; rather, they would complain of severe stomach and headaches.[22] But in recent months there had been more acceptance on the part of the Israeli girls. They no longer felt that the Ethiopians did not belong in Israel, especially since they learned that many of them were orphans.

For the Beta Israel women in particular, there were a number of other health and social problems. The health problems included hysteria, tuberculosis, and asthma. Some attempted to jump from windows, and others simply disappeared for weeks before they were found in some other town.[23] Some had been consulting a *tenuity* (literally, "one who points out"; here it means a healer) or *balezar* (Amharic for "sorcerer" or "one who is possessed of spirits that have power to tell fortunes, present or future, or diagnose illnesses and prescribe medicines"). For instance, one girl would not eat and was wasting away. She insisted that her parents, who were still in Ethiopia, be brought to Israel; otherwise she was going to die. Finally, upon the recommendation of a trained Israeli psychologist, the school secured the services of Aleka Yaacov,[24] an elegant elderly Ethiopian gentleman who believed he had special powers that enabled him to heal the sick through traditional divination methods. In this case, the proper ingredients, such as incense, must be present for the process to work, so the girl was taken to his home near Tel Aviv. Some of the girls reported having been healed in this way. Fortunately for the believers, others in the country were renowned for their possession of the same healing powers, including Aleka Sibhat of Beersheba and Aleka Tiruneh of Afula. There were several other less well-known individuals as well. As a reminder, the social worker said, although these kinds of sicknesses were common there, 40 percent of the Beta Israel women were not sick.

SEPARATION FROM LOVED ONES AND ITS EFFECT ON LEARNING

The separation of young people from parents and other relatives was a constant source of anxiety, guilt, and remorse. Soon after they heaved their first sigh of relief for their safe arrival in Israel, they began to look back on those they had left behind in Ethiopia, usually the very old, the very young, and the infirm. As a rule, older parents in Ethiopia rely on youth for material and social support. Rural parents always looked forward to the days when their children would be old enough to relieve them of their economic burdens. Children were about the only old-age insurance they had. Now, in the confusion and turmoil of Ethiopia, where droughts, wars, and famine were taking unprecedented tolls among the population, the young people would have helped the infirm and the old. Knowledge of these expectations and conditions, then, became a constant worry for most of the young people. The worries and concerns in turn tended to interfere with their optimal functioning in Israel. When one of the students said, "How can we learn here when our hearts are there?" he was speaking for many of his peers in Israel. To illustrate how this painful process continued and interfered with meeting the challenges of absorption, three letters were selected from among the many that parents and other relatives in Ethiopia had sent to young people in Israel. The letters were not easy to translate into English; they were dictated by adults to a young child, who may be one of the few in the family who can write. Often the indication "written by" appears at the end of a letter. The first letter quoted below, however, might have been written by an adult not as literate as the authors of the other two.[25] The messages of these letters are clear and persuasive.

LETTER 1

May 4, 1986

Dear our daughter, whom we love and think of constantly, day and night,

How are you? We are very well, thanks be to the God of Israel, except for the fact that we miss you very much. After my greetings, I would like to remind you that the letter you sent has reached us, and we are very glad for it. Since we had not heard from you, we were very worried. You have told us that the first cheque you had sent us was returned to you. Now you are telling us that the nine hundred birr [Ethiopian currency, $0.40 U.S. = 1 birr] you sent us has been lost. It is news to us. When was it sent? Clarify this, and please write and tell us. If it has been lost for good, like the death of a child, we shall never get over it. Others [a list of names follows] who had similar misfortunes sent other cheques when they learned of the loss. But in your case the cheque has been returned to you. Nowadays the matters are under control; nobody steals the monies [anymore]. We feel you have forgotten our problems [sufferings]. If you were like your former self, you would have sent us another cheque.

If you were to come to visit our country [village] once, you would learn that as a result of the help from Israel everyone has not only enough to eat but to buy cows, oxen, and wristwatches. But as for me, instead of blaming you, I only blame my own bad luck and God. Even [two names are mentioned], who left only this year for Israel, have called their parents twice. But I only say I am glad that you got what you wanted. We only pray for your health; we don't want to say anything else. Everyone here is basking in daylight [happiness] day in and day out [they are happy because of the money received], but for us we are lower than the living and higher than the dead. It is wonderful to see others eating. During my troubles I had borrowed [money] from others, hoping that you would help me out. But now I cannot pay it back, and in addition I have been asked to pay 50 birr and 30 kilos of grain for *assrat* [tithe]. When I was not able to pay, I was jailed. Eventually I had to sell the donkey at a cheap price in order to pay what the government demanded of me. But now, together with our [economic] troubles, the grief is coming back anew. Last year during the horrible season I did not till my land. This year, too, since I do not have seeds, I will not be able to plant. If my children [the younger ones still living at home] survive the hunger this year, I will be very lucky. Since I have no donkey, I don't even have anything for transporting food.

We received the photograph and letter of M, but the important thing is to send us the address of A, her mother is killing herself crying. I had written to T and A, but I have not received any reply. Up to now there was a telephone station . . . but from now on we will not have enough money to call.

I heard about that *gobatta's* [hunchback's] tricks [someone known to the parties; not identified by name but disliked]. Man [humankind] is wet, he cannot go up in smoke, otherwise I would have burned up to ashes; he burned me [I am fuming with anger over what he did].

I am your father who is left alone, longing, poor father, and your mother who misses you and loves you.[26]

LETTER 2

March 15, 1986

Dear our beloved children [two names, followed by a long salutation],

After my greetings, I would like to remind you that after giving birth to you I brought you up [supplied you with all your needs]. I carried *mugogo* [a utensil like a frying pan made of clay used for baking *enjera*, the Ethiopian bread, usually manufactured and marketed by Beta Israel women] from our village for fifteen kilometers to Azezo [the marketplace] while carrying you on my back. But I would have been happier if you had stayed with me here. On the other hand, I am glad you have been able to go. When I noticed how different you have become from your letters and pictures that you have sent me, I was overwhelmed with joy. It was this year for the first time that I began to feel happy over your going away. In the first place the necklaces that Yiftusira sent, in the second instance the money that both of you sent me, reminded me that suffering to bring up good children pays.

Even now, remember, my children, that I do not have anyone else to fetch me *kubet* [dry cow dung used for fuel] or firewood. I am laboring by myself working on my usual vocation to bring up those little ones who were born after you [younger siblings]. I therefore like to remind you that the money you have sent me was enough only to pay the government *assrat*. Traveling the same distance to bring *arbacha* [soil material taken from anthills and used to make household utensils] and walking long distances to gather firewood for the winter [Ethiopian rainy season, July to August] is becoming too much for me. To save me from all these, send me some money to buy grain for the family; also money to buy clothing for your sisters, your father, and myself. I appeal to you my, children; we don't have anything to eat or anything to wear. I have lots of troubles. Etati [perhaps a sister] is not well. Tell Tessema [the sister's son] I said hi and ask him why he does not send her money. May the Lord help us to be together.[27]

LETTER 3

Dear beloved [a long salutation follows],

You have written us frequently, but we have not been responding even as often as once a month. Of the two letters you sent us recently, one was delivered by a *ferenj* [a white foreigner][28] and the other through the post office. I came to understand that my letters sent through Dinku's address [a relative] have not been reaching you. As Huluager told me, you have *ferenj* friends who are helping you as father and mother. I am very glad. Send me their address, and if possible their photograph as well, so that I can send them a letter of thank you. The reason is I know that some children who have *ferenj* friends have been able to help their relatives in Ethiopia. For example, HE's *ferenj* friend was able to send a cheque for one thousand dollars to AE [a father]. This is [the equivalent of] 2,500 birr. These people are now out of poverty. They can buy cows, oxen, mules, and other things. Poverty is vanished from their house. As for me, Dinku sent me 25 dollars in November which enabled me to buy some clothing for my children and send them to school. Other people are now happy buying replacements for the cows and oxen they had sold or lost.[29]

We stop here for now. Write us as soon as you have received this letter. May the Lord help us to get together. Amen.[30]

Among other things, these letters reveal the very poor material and cultural conditions in which the villagers find themselves. It is also unmistakably clear from the letters that the parents have concluded that their children are well-off in Israel. Once in a while, they ask, "How are you?" but these are perfunctory expressions. The assumption on the part of the parents is that their children are in a strong position to help them. If the children are not sending money, it is only because of lack of concern. The parents also grieve that their children are not around and not physically helping when needed. But the abiding concerns of the relatives, as seen in the letters, are for their own material survival. They are asking for money for their many needs. To get the message across, the parents use a variety of subtle and not so subtle psychological tactics such as recalling what they went through to bring their siblings up, what they have to do now for the younger children, the kind of deprivation the parents are now suffering because there are no grown children around to help with chores, how the government is milking them of the small incomes they get from abroad, and then by comparing their lots with other parents in the village who are receiving more assistance from their children who live in Israel. The deprivation of love of children is there also, but the parents are convinced that their children are doing much better, in both material and educational terms, and thus concentrate on how the children can share these benefits with those left in Ethiopia. The struggles the young people go through in order to find their way in a new society are, of course, not within the field of vision of the parents.

While the concerns of the parents for survival and their open appeals for help are understandable, the effect such letters have is tremendous. The young people feel guilty for abandoning their aging parents and younger siblings in time of need. The Ethiopian youth in Israel have many concerns of their own regarding absorption—whether they are going to succeed in their education, what careers to choose, and so on. Normally, such concerns are enough to occupy their total attention. But they are saddled by additional concerns for relatives left behind. In fact, it is the greatest single concern that cuts across almost all groups of these *olim*. Rightly or wrongly, they feel that had they been able to stay in Ethiopia with their relatives, they could have done much more than what they are doing for them from Israel. The Jewish Agency is aware of this and is trying to ascertain the needs and provide some relief, though not all Beta Israel would agree with this assessment. Unfortunately, the monies do not always reach the intended recipients, and that is where the problems lie.[31]

Young people have enough challenges handling the learning and relearning processes in the Youth Aliyah setting. These institutions and their personnel could further facilitate the learning and adjustment processes. But many of the fundamental factors that affect the functioning of youth are beyond the control of the learning institutions. Although the centers may be able to lighten the burden, they can do little to solve the problems. Even the entire society, through the government, cannot resolve the central problems. All the same, the young Beta Israel collectively raise their issues with government officials. Sometimes they organize demonstrations and put the government on public notice. The government responds that it is doing all it can to resolve the problems of separation, by itself or in cooperation with other countries interested or more influential with the Ethiopian authorities. As long as the young *olim* are troubled by these concerns, however, their learning will be negatively affected.

CONCLUSION

Arriving in Israel after their long ordeals, which left many of their families fragmented, most of the immigrant Beta Israel youth between the ages of eleven and eighteen are placed in boarding villages such as those in the Youth Aliyah system. Youth Aliyah was conceived to serve as a "home for the homeless" and as a center for learning and living. Both in conception and in application, it tries to combine the functions of two of the most important institutions for the socialization and education of youth: the family and the school. In many ways this concept is unique to Israel,[32] and, as Bentwich reminds us, perhaps will never be replicated anywhere else. The centers or villages where the Beta Israel youth are found are different from one another in the particulars of viewing and discharging their respective responsibilities regarding the Ethiopians.

There are problems such as the Israelis' lack of knowledge about the *olim*, their achievement levels before they arrived in Israel, their motivations, and their ways of viewing the world. This is all complicated by linguistic and cultural differences and the awesome burden of the separation of families. Impressive progress has been made to help the migrant youth settle down and begin their training. But it is also very obvious that much more needs to be done. The young people are insecure regarding their training and careers and, more generally, their future in Israel. In their search to secure a good future for themselves and their families, they people want to explore alternatives. This kind of search is manifested in their desire to continue their training beyond the allotted time and to gain entry into programs at other centers they perceive to be more promising. A number of them outside the *yeshivot* think the religious schools are very deficient in preparing them for vocations in the technical fields, and they would like to transfer to secular schools. On the other hand, primarily for political and policy reasons pertaining to these particular *olim*, they find it practically impossible to get permission to transfer.

More importantly, as a reflection of the disorganization of the *olim* in the process of migration and settlement, the traditional moral and social values together with the institutions under which such values had operated are no longer functional and are not being replaced rapidly enough by new ones. Hence, the problems of extramarital pregnancy and the mistrust of authority figures in the schools are evident in many centers. Perhaps more needs to be done in the latter area on the part of the authorities so that the young people can learn to have confidence in the leadership. As a start, the existing, though limited, educated manpower among the Beta Israel (veteran and newcomers) must be given visible responsibilities so that they can serve as authentic leaders and role models. At another level, family unification in Israel would help the absorption and learning processes. In a short while, many of the eighteen-year-old males will join the IDF. It is thought that their education will continue there. In addition, given the warrior tradition in the culture they came from and the value Israeli society attaches to its fighting men, the Ethiopians may distinguish themselves in the military. That would enhance their opportunities for full acceptance, learning, employment, and absorption. A very small number may proceed to postsecondary education.

CHAPTER NINE

❖

Adult and Continuing Education

❖

The adult population of Ethiopian Jews can be divided into four broad categories. The first consists of those between the ages of eighteen and twenty-eight and is the focus of this chapter. In the second category are those between the ages of twenty-nine and forty-five, within the employable age range. After their first year of language instruction, they can receive training either on the job or outside working hours. The third category includes those between the ages of forty-six and sixty-five. Most persons in this group are retired or otherwise pensioned, although they engage in some kind of learning activities. In the fourth category are those sixty-six and older. This group, which is small, perhaps not more than 6 percent of the total, is also engaged in some kind of language instruction and learning programs to develop basic skills to cope with the new environment.[1]

The vast majority of the adult Beta Israel population that came to Israel is nonliterate even in its own languages of Amharic and Tigrigna. The exceptions are religious leaders who had some training in religious and ritualistic matters and a few of the young adults who were exposed to some kind of learning as a result of the literacy campaigns initiated in Ethiopia in the mid-1970s.[2] Israel confronted a tremendous challenge in its efforts to absorb these segments of the Beta Israel population. At one time, it was suggested that these adults should be written off as the "lost generation."[3] But to write off such a large number of citizens is admitting defeat before the battle even starts. Further, the majority of the adult migrants were relatively young, with many years of life ahead of them. The choice was either to find means of preparing these young adults for participation in productive, democratic living or to accept their dependence on the state for the remainder of their potentially long lives.[4]

YOUTH ADMINISTRATION PROJECT

As a partial response to the challenge, Israel developed a special program known as the Youth Project Administration for single Beta Israel between eighteen and twenty-eight who had little or no prior experience with formal schooling or any training that would enable them to function in an industrialized society such as Israel. The ministries of Education, Labor, and Absorption cooperate with the Jewish Agency in the administration of the programs; supervision is provided by a joint committee. Soon after completion of their *ulpanim*, these young adults were given the opportunity to enroll in either religious or secular institutions of learning. Those who chose religious institutions later wanted to transfer to secular ones but were not permitted to do so. In 1986, approximately eight hundred Beta Israel were enrolled in Youth Project Administration programs. What follows are several case studies that depict the operation, curricula, and kinds of problems encountered in the centers and the steps taken toward their resolution. The case studies do not cover all shades of issues revealed during fieldwork but are representative enough to depict patterns of some of the major issues.

BOYS TOWN

In November 1986, I visited Boys Town, a large institution located outside Jersusalem. With the assistance of international Zionist organizations, Boys Town was founded in 1950 to train the Oriental youth who were arriving in large numbers. Over the years, it continued to attract a large amount of support from international Jewish organizations and has grown in terms of enrollment, physical size, and budget. It looks like a small town. It has a well-appointed public relations office which employs a full-time staff. It offers technical-vocational training in a variety of areas such as metalwork and carpentry.

There were 120 Beta Israel youth here, divided into two groups: 40 were in the junior high school section and 80 in the technical-vocational areas. The junior high students lived on the school grounds; the others were bused daily from a nearby absorption center and teacher-training school for a few hours of instruction in technical and vocational subjects. The rest of their training was provided in another school operated by the religious wing of the education system. The previous year (1985–86), these youth were living and learning near one of the largest towns in the southern part of the country. When I asked them why they had transferred to this school, they replied, "The environment was not conducive where we were, so we requested to be transferred here, and we succeeded." About the problems they had in their previous school, they told me, "They [the veteran Israeli youth] insult us. They call us *kushi* [equivalent to the American term nigger]." Half-heartedly, they told me they liked Boys Town better. When I asked whether it was better for them here in Israel than in Gondar, they said, "Yes. If we had stayed in Ethiopia, we would not have gained anything else but serve in the army." Although they were going to serve in the army here as well, they said that serving in Israel was different. Here they would serve as soldiers, but at least they would receive instruction in other job skills which would ultimately free them to assume different careers. They added that they had run away from Ethiopia because of the conscription laws that were put into place in 1979.[5] They had seen many of their compatriots lose their lives, and they saw no sense in serving in that kind of army.

At Boys Town, I was able to observe two groups of young men working and learning in the metal and carpentry workshops. In the metal shop, they were huddled around a large machine, at times standing in one another's way. They did not know what to do and were obviously not getting anywhere. Although the instructor was nearby, he made no effort to guide or assist the men with the problem. What I saw indicated to me that the students had no grasp of the seemingly rudimentary tasks they were supposed to perform. The instructor seemed as puzzled as the students, though for different reasons, but he did not say much.

In the carpentry workshop the young men were more spread out, working either alone or in pairs at a table full of equipment. However, here, too, there seemed to be a lack of directed movement that usually comes from knowing what is to be accomplished and how to do it. Given that this was their second year of training, the situation was disconcerting (the first year of training was spent in another institution, where, because of personal and communal problems, they did not learn much and were transferred to this institution).

Before I visited the workshops, the director of the school had told me everything was proceeding smoothly and that the Beta Israel students were doing well. My observations, however, indicated otherwise. I interviewed the supervisor of instruction in the metal shops. He was very straightforward in his answers. He told me that the young men were not progressing well at all. The students only recently had joined the institution, and the teachers had been neither informed about nor oriented to their special needs. He was of the opinion that the students were wasting time. Because of time constraints, I was not able to visit those Beta Israel students who were in the junior high section of the school.

Boys Town is one case where there was obvious confusion arising both from the students' and the institution's lack of experience, knowledge, and abilities. The officials who made the decisions about student placement did not effectively inform the staff about the background, abilities, and special learning needs of the students. This may be an example of bureaucratic bungling that has serious consequences for the young men involved. It illustrates the problems that arise when representatives of the receiving society charged with training a great influx of immigrants with complex needs are ill informed or ill prepared. As a result, efforts are misguided, and valuable time is lost. When, in two months' time, these young men were to leave the institution, one wonders what skills they would have to carry them through life. Many of the young men hoped they would be able to get respectable employment, but many others feared that their lack of skills would relegate them to menial, low-paying jobs for the remainder of their productive lives.

WIZO GIRLS VOCATIONAL SCHOOL

Also in November 1986, I visited WIZO Girls Vocational School, located in a suburb of Jerusalem. I was accompanied by Dr. Haim Rosen, an Israeli anthropologist who had done some fieldwork in the 1960s among the Tigray people in Ethiopia, speaks some Amharic and Tigrigna, and is well accepted by the Beta Israel.[6] Upon our arrival at the school, the principal, Odet Paroblo, and several members of the staff briefed us on the operations of the center and the performance of Beta Israel students. The center was financed by the Women's International Zionist Organization. It included a nursery school program which charged user fees according to rates determined by the Department of Labor. The center was a huge learning complex. It provided a variety of educational, recreational, and cultural programs for people ranging in age from three to ninety. Efforts were made to bring the young and the old together on special occasions so that they could interact and learn from one another. On Hanukkah, for example, young and old gathered to sing, dance, and play; the children presented flowers and fruit baskets to the elderly. "In this way," said Odet Paroblo, "we can teach kids to respect old age." The Beta Israel women participated in these activities. Although it was a nonboarding facility, it served hot meals to eight hundred people daily. In addition to the Ethiopian girls, the center also catered to veteran Israeli girls between the ages of fourteen and eighteen who, for emotional or cognitive reasons, had missed out on schooling and were being given a "second chance." There were also provisions for children and adults with special mental or emotional problems. The staff included psychologists and social workers. Although the motto was "take care of the mother and child," males also participated.

There were thirty-five Beta Israel women in the eighteen-to-twenty-eight age group, though some appeared to be older. A few had some kind of primary education, but the majority had no schooling. According to their teachers, those with some education and those who came from towns in Ethiopia did better than those with no schooling and those from rural areas. Many of the Beta Israel students, particularly those from the rural areas of Ethiopia, were married at one time; a few still were married, and some had children.[7]

At this center, the Beta Israel women studied Hebrew, arithmetic, and some social studies. They also took vocational courses such as sewing, child care, cooking, and secretarial training. On the walls of the sewing classroom were pictures of exotic women in beautiful dresses, but the needlework the girls were doing was very rudimentary. Some were clustered together in small groups around the sewing machines, while others were doing traditional Ethiopian embroidery work (which, although it fetches a good price in the market, was not being produced in sufficient quantity). Some of the girls were smartly dressed in either traditional Ethiopian or European dresses and appeared neat and alert; others were untidy and sullen. Compared to other similar groups, these young women appeared more subdued and lacked zest in their actions and expressions. When I asked them how they liked the school, one replied in Amharic: "We labor until we go [die]." When I asked her what she meant, she told me that learning the Hebrew language was very hard. Another woman, fiddling with an obsolete sewing machine, added: "It is a struggle, especially learning the language." Yet in their interactions with their teachers and the school principal, they appeared to be at ease and familiar. For example, when addressing their teachers, they used first names or *Moha* ("Teacher"); they were also on a first-name basis with the principal or called her *Safta* ("Grandmother"). Unless there is sufficient familiarity and comfort, Ethiopians do not address persons in authority in this way.

Rosen, who had visited the group the previous year, remarked that the girls were completely transformed. "Last year," he said, "they were timid, fearful, and withdrawn." His observations suggest that, over time, some of the women's inhibitions may subside, and they may be able to make more rapid progress in their learning. However, perhaps their opportunity to talk to a fellow Ethiopian in Amharic, their native language, led to their openness. That evening, I recorded in my notebook: "These girls seem to be fighting a difficult battle. Some had no exposure of any kind to formal learning before coming to Israel under Operation Moses. The extent to which they will be able to develop their social and academic skills remains a question. Perhaps most of them will end up having jobs in service-related areas

—as cleaners in industrial establishments or as helpers in nursing homes, hospitals, and nurseries. At any rate, the efforts on the part of Israeli society are highly commendable." Of course, there were individual differences. Some might continue their training after leaving the institution and eventually might attain positions in accordance with their aspirations.

ONIM SCHOOL

Also in early November, Zeev Chernov (the general-director of Youth Project Administration), a veteran educator from the Ministry of Labor, and I set out north from Tel Aviv to Onim, where eighty Beta Israel between the ages of eighteen and twenty-eight were studying. Some of these young adults had gotten as far as the eighth or ninth grade before leaving Ethiopia. The majority, however, had little or no exposure to education. The center had many other students, males as well as females, from a variety of ethnic groups. With the exception of one or two Beta Israel who were participating in a couple of courses with non-Ethiopian students, the Beta Israel were in segregated classrooms. Moreover, men were segregated from women. Of the eighty Beta Israel students at this center, thirty were women and fifty men. Except for the few who were married, the students lived in dormitories on campus. The men and women resided in opposite wings of the same building. Four students were assigned to each room. The rooms were neat, the beds were made and the floors swept, but the walls were barren. During the day the young men and women could interact with one another on the school grounds, but in the evenings they were restricted to their respective wings of the dormitory. They were supervised by house parents who ensured their separation at night. Although the school year officially began in September, because of the high holy days, which were in October in 1986, and the strike by the Beta Israel who were protesting reconversion requirements, for all practical purposes, school was just getting under way. On the day of my visit, however, classes were not in session because of to a general nationwide strike organized by the National Secondary School Association against the Ministry of Education and Culture. It was also the third day of a strike among the female students, who were demanding assurances of appropriate certification upon completion of their courses.

As I walked around the campus chatting with students and school personnel, visiting some of the dormitories, and sharing meals in the common cafeteria, I observed that the Beta Israel did not interact much with the other students. Moreover, the Ethiopians also voluntarily segregated themselves by gender. In general, they appeared healthy and showed good personal taste in grooming and cleanliness, but they did not engage themselves in constructive activities. Rather, they seemed to just mill around. After talking with some of the students, I met with key administrative personnel and teachers from the school, the regional supervisor for girls' education, and the general-director of Youth Project Administration from Tel Aviv to exchange views, assess progress, and identify important issues relevant to the situation of the Beta Israel students.

The teaching-learning problems encountered with Beta Israel boys were outlined for me as follows. According to the teachers who were trying to teach them technical-vocational skills, these young adults had no concept of an angle or a line, they had difficulty drawing parallel lines, and they did not know how to handle workshop tools. Without mastery of these concepts, they could not become good mechanics or technicians. The teachers reported that they followed Bloom's taxonomy of cognitive learning. Although they began with rudimentary mathematical concepts and principles, the teachers found that it could take nearly forty hours to teach Beta Israel students what five-year-old Israeli children could learn in less than five minutes. Teaching also was affected by a lack of trust. The controversy over the "conversion" mandated by the Israeli rabbinate, which led to the general strike of the Beta Israel community, had generated attitudes of mistrust between the Ethiopians and veterans. These attitudes affected relationships between Beta Israel students and their teachers. Trust, which is essential to sound teacher-student relations, was lacking and must be regained before meaningful education can take place.

Initially, male students were taught courses in metal and woodworking so they could later choose a single trade for concentrated training. Before they made their choices, they were informed of the proficiencies required for the different trades. For instance, students were told that electronics required more preparation and special talent than carpentry. Usually, a student's choice of a trade for concentrated study coincided with the teachers' evaluation. At other times, students were helped to choose a trade that more closely matched their abilities. Most students preferred electrical engineering; carpentry was the least preferred field. Their choices reflected the prestige values attached to the different occupations in the larger society. In the first year, students received ninety hours of workshop experience. One of the problems with this group, which may account for the slow progress, was that they arrived in the middle of the previous school year, which could not have facilitated their transition and introduction. However, their problems are similar to those reported at other centers.

The teachers and administrators expected that twenty-six or so of the young men would complete the equivalent of a grade eight education certificate for proficiency in literacy skills from the Ministry of Education. They expected that approximately 10 percent would proceed to the next level (the equivalent of grade nine). Those in the latter group would be in a better position to enter apprenticeships and eventually secure good jobs. Since most of the Beta Israel at this center were overage, they would not join the army.

Like the men, the women were enrolled in classes for Hebrew literacy, Bible study, history, and geography. But the technical-vocational subjects were different. The women took cosmetology, home economics, and sewing, so that they could eventually work as beauticians, nurse's aides, and seamstresses. On the day I was visiting, however, the women were on strike because three days earlier they had been informed that they would not be granted certificates of proficiency upon completion of their literacy and vocational courses. Presumably, the authorities did not think their performance warranted certification. Some of the Beta Israel men had struck in sympathy with the women.

The young women were very agitated and appeared pensive, confused, and helpless. They told me they were doomed without the certificates. They were very much aware of the fact that they would be unable to secure meaningful employment without the coveted certificates; for the remainder of their lives, they would be sweeping floors and cleaning streets. They complained that the authorities had reneged on their promises regarding certification. They were not sure what to do next. When I approached the teaching staff and administration to discuss the issue, I was met with silence. The man in charge of the program of studies for the Ethiopians told my associates, however, that the women were doing the right thing. "They have nothing to lose," he said.

Combined with problems internal to the learning institution, some of the complaints the students had about their studies may be related to characteristics inherent in the learning process itself. Learning itself can provoke anxiety. Had these young people not been exposed to the educative process, they would not be so acutely aware of the different shades of quality of education, work, and prospects for earning a living. Education, even in its more limited forms, has the potential to inflate aspirations and heighten frustration when attainments fall short of expectations. Other student complaints related to issues that are either beyond the control of the center or not directly related to their central responsibilities. However, since the full attention of the learner is requisite to effective teaching and learning, it is very difficult to determine what is and what is not directly related to the learning process. If the educational institution does not cooperate with other agencies to help the students solve problems, optimal learning is not likely to occur.

The young men and women at this center said they were worried about their relatives in Ethiopia; money enclosed in letters was not reaching them, or at least they were not getting responses. One student told me: "My father died in the civil war [involving the provinces of Eritrea and Tigray and the state of Ethiopia], leaving my mother with a twelve-year-old child. No one is left to care for her and the child. I was able to help them much better when I was in the camp in the Sudan [letters used to reach their destination from there]." They told me that Israeli authorities were doing little to bring their relatives to Israel. Only those few who had good connections with the proper Israeli officials had succeeded in arranging to have their relatives brought to Israel, they told me. The students were frustrated because they were not in a position to earn enough money to send to relatives. Some regretted ever having left Ethiopia; others said, "Take us to America so that we can work and support our families." These complaints, of course, had nothing to do with the school. However, given that these concerns distracted the students from their studies, they became an educational problem. Another complaint was voiced by some of the better students who stated that they were not being taught English. To them, proficiency in English was as important as proficiency in Hebrew if they were going to get ahead.

I returned to the center about two weeks later. This time, I was accompanied by NA who oversees the field supervision for the nationwide project. The students were still on a partial strike and very agitated. No progress had been made toward resolution of certification issues.

The students told me they often got sick and many suffered from asthma (a frequent complaint among the *olim* in general). They reiterated concerns about their parents and relatives left behind in Ethiopia and complained that they were not getting the kind of education and training they wanted. In their words, "We are not making it here. We are better off returning to Ethiopia." I continued to chat with them in the dormitories, in the dining halls, and in the street. They seemed depressed. They told me how worried they were about their future in Israel and about their aging parents and younger siblings in Ethiopia.

I asked the woman in charge of the students' training and welfare, who also teaches language, whether she thought the teachers were prepared to handle the issues presented by the Beta Israel youth. She told me that many of the teachers had been *ulpan* teachers the previous year and were not unfamiliar with the Ethiopians and their conditions. She herself had four years of experience. Moreover, before coming to this center, the teachers had been given special training in how to teach youth who had little education. Their training stressed the need to make the materials and concepts as concrete as possible. She told me that teachers should talk less and give more demonstrations and that they should help the Beta Israel students cope with their constant worries about their families left behind in Ethiopia. She said that teachers should encourage independence among the Beta Israel women. Veteran Israelis feared that when these young women left the center, they would not be able to stand on their own feet. She added that the women were primarily from rural Ethiopia and had no experience with the kind of urban life that exists in Israel.

The center aimed to teach the students to speak Hebrew which would assist them in their everyday lives. Also, in preparation for their lives independent of the center, they were being taught how to apply for jobs, where to go for insurance protection, how to cook and sew, and how to take care of families. Three times a week, the women were taken to nearby hospitals and nursing homes, where they received nurse's aide training. The teacher told me she hoped that at least some of the students would achieve the equivalent of an eighth- or ninth-grade education before leaving the center. Those who did might proceed for further training. However, most would end up as low-skilled workers in either hospitals or industry. She noted that housing would be a problem since there were few alternatives for single people in Israel. Most likely, they would live in hostels.

These young people were being given training that was not available to them in their land of origin. Their appetites had been whetted, and they were anxious to improve the quality of their lives through education, however rudimentary it might be. They lacked the sort of guidance that could temper their expectations to fit the realities of their situation. Persons of their age and skill level were bound for menial jobs with limited opportunities for promotion or income improvement. It is possible that they understood the reality of their situation but were not yet ready to accept it.

NOURIM SCHOOL

Nourim School is the largest school in Israel. There were six hundred students in grades nine through twelve, sixty of whom are Beta Israel males between the ages of eighteen and twenty-eight. Although the school was coeducational, there were no Beta Israel females. The Beta Israel students lived apart from the others and attended separate classes. In the dining hall and on the playground, where opportunities for socializing with the other students existed, there seemed to be little interaction between the Beta Israel and veterans.

About one-third of the Ethiopian students had no schooling before they came to Israel. The teachers described one student of ethnic minority origin in Ethiopia (perhaps the son of a former slave) as impossible to teach.[8] "He simply does not cooperate," one of his instructors told me. Most students had difficulty understanding abstract concepts in mathematics. The teachers and the students were deeply frustrated by the fact that they did not share a common language. The students could not yet express their deepest thoughts and articulate their concerns in Hebrew, the language of their teachers. The students were delighted to have the chance to speak with someone in my position in their native language. Among the teachers, there was a consensus that some of the Beta Israel were gifted in language acquisition, but most were learning it very slowly. They noted that, although the students said they understood instructions, their actions indicated that they did not.

Overall, learning was a difficult process for them. Certain information, concepts, and skills which the teachers took for granted when instructing veteran Israeli children were simply absent among the Beta Israel. According to the workshop teacher, who had twenty-five years of experience: "Among the Beta Israel, some very basic experiences are missing. But when we try to teach them the basic concepts in mathematics, for example, they complain that we underestimate their abilities and are not teaching them 'real' mathematics. They tell us that they are tired of that kind of thinking and teaching." The students thought the training they were receiving was more limiting than enabling. Their expectations associated with education, of course, reflected the Ethiopian context. The teachers' and administrators' perceptions of the reality of their situation in Israel, however, were not readily aligned with the students' expectations. The results fueled conflict.

The staff also contended that these young men denied paternity and did not accept responsibility when they got young women pregnant. The field supervisor added that this problem was widespread among Beta Israel youth. In three years, there had been some one thousand unplanned pregnancies among the Beta Israel population. This rate greatly exceeded that reported for Israeli youth in general and, I might add, certainly exceeded the rate among Ethiopian youth under normal circumstances.[9] This incidence of unplanned pregnancy was a result of several factors: the absence of traditional parental supervision and control; the students' fear of loneliness and need for close relations and friendships among young people of similar cultural backgrounds, including the opposite sex; and inadequate knowledge of birth control. The issue was very sensitive, especially since most of the young people were living, studying, and working in institutions controlled by religious organizations. Naïveté and ignorance about the sexual act and its consequences were also at work here. One professional told me that when one of the pregnant girls was asked why she was not careful, she said, "It is not me; it is God who did [willed] it." Like the boys, the girl was trying to deny personal responsibility for the situation. The authorities were beginning to acknowledge this behavior which created problems for the young people, the institution, and the society. The physician in charge of medical services at the training schools told me that the Jewish Agency had developed program materials to teach the Beta Israel about the biological, social, and psychological significance of sexual activity.

Another informant, directly involved in dealing with these problems, told me that when a schoolgirl became pregnant she was taken to one of two centers, where she continued her education. Once the child was born and the young mother had sufficiently recovered, she was transferred to another training center. Responsibilities for child care were assumed by the center. The rationale for these procedures was that since these young people were without relatives, the center must function in loco parentis. It is humane; it is caring. But it is no substitute for teaching the young people about prevention and responsibility in relationships.

Students at Nourim were entitled to two years of training. This was official policy, and resource constraints did not allow for extensions. According to the teachers and administrators, the Beta Israel refused to accept these parameters. Their persistent demands were annoying. As was the case with Beta Israel throughout the country, these students were acutely aware of the value of education and training for their future careers and well-being. Although they complained about the quality of the education and training they were receiving, they wanted as much of it as possible. According to school personnel, they wanted to change from one line of vocational training to another, for instance, from carpentry to electronics, to make sure that if one specialization proved unsatisfactory the other could be utilized. This strategy also may have been intended to enhance their own prestige by changing to a more prestigious vocation. When students asked to extend their education beyond the two-year limit, they were told they must be employed and able to meet all their own tuition and living expenses.

I visited some classes and talked to some of the students. As elsewhere, the students had a litany of concerns and complaints. The first related to mathematics instruction. They told me that they were not being taught the kind of math they would like to learn. They were being taught the watered-down, practical version in lieu of formal, recognized mathematics provided to other students. A second complaint was that the teachers did not make allowances for individual differences. For instance, one student told me: "Some of us completed grades five, six, or even higher levels of schooling before we even left Ethiopia. Yet the teachers lump us all together and expect us to proceed at the same pace in mathematics, language, and other subjects. When we complain about this, we are told that this is the way that we can learn best—helping and learning from one another. We do not trust them. They refuse to listen to our suggestions and complaints. If they want us to progress in our education, they have to take our opinions and feelings into account. For instance, although we are learning to become mechanics and technicians, they do not even let us to try the simplest things such as turning the engines on and off."[10] One class of fifteen Beta Israel showed complete mistrust of the intentions of the teachers, particularly the administrator in charge of the Ethiopian students. On that day, I wrote in my field notes: "The mistrust and misgivings run very deep."

With a few exceptions, most students found Hebrew difficult to learn. The students complained that they did not always understand what the teachers were saying. "We wish we had a teacher who would speak our language as you do. Things would be different," commented one. They also told me that they wanted to continue their education beyond that year: "We just need more time than the two years allotted to us."

Following the class visits, I joined some teachers, Odeda Tamir (the administrator in charge of the Ethiopians), Schmuel, the shop supervisor, and the field supervisor, Amnon Nave, who accompanied me from Tel Aviv to the school, for lunch in the school cafeteria. The food was tasty and nutritious. At the table, we had time to exchange ideas, impressions, and suggestions for improvement. The school personnel were anxious to know the concerns of the students and my impressions. I provided them with a brief summary of my observations and interpretations. They were not surprised.

The youth at this center were worried about their future life in Israel. They felt that both the quantity and the quality of education and training they were receiving were inadequate. They wanted the center to prepare them for a secure future. They also wanted to know what they would be doing when they left the center at the end of the year. They knew that some would be drafted into the IDF, but they had not yet been informed about who would be required to join and who would not. The students said they were struggling and fighting for their future security and well-being; there was no one else to look after their interests. They utilized various strategies to get the attention of the administration. Odeda Tamir, the administrator, told me that from time to time the students threatened to leave the school en masse. One student did leave but returned two weeks later. Tamir insisted that she did not have the budget to meet the students' desires. She appeared very defensive and adamant on this issue. There was strong evidence of polarization. The staff, certainly the administrator, were on one side, the students on the other. This was reflected in the frequent use of the pronouns they and we. As was the case at the Onim School, several of the Beta Israel youth at this center expressed their regrets about having left Ethiopia in the first place.

The youth may have been demanding too much or even expecting too much by way of education and training. They brought with them from Africa a strong belief that education was the best guarantee of a secure future. In a way, their attitudes and behaviors reflected a determination to fit into modern Israeli society and a confidence in their ability to do so eventually. One might not expect this from young people who had experienced such traumatic and overwhelming changes in the circumstances of their lives. Perhaps such attitudes should be cherished and nurtured. But what they perhaps did not understand, and there was no one to help them understand it, were the realities of their situation in Israel. Most of these young men arrived in Israel with little or no formal education or skills relevant to a modern industrialized country like Israel. Because of their age, they would not have the opportunities to progress in education and develop the higher-level skills younger persons might. It was also very likely that they would not be aware of or would not fully comprehend prevailing conditions in Israeli society. The resources that might be reasonably allocated for their training and education were limited; the economy was small, and there was already a glut of highly educated people. With some understanding of their situation in the context of Israel, these young people might be more likely to make the best use of whatever opportunities they were offered and accept the fact that their generation, at least, would enter the Israeli work force at the bottom of the ladder. Their children and subsequent generations might fare better. But even within these proscribing circumstances, there were many things the administration and center staff could do to improve and enrich the learning environment of the Beta Israel and to help them understand Israeli society and their place in it. They were not doing them.

When I suggested that perhaps the legalistic aspects of administration might have to bend a little in favor of relevant education for this group, Tamir stressed the importance of holding to bureaucratic rules and regulations; resource limitations demanded this, she said. She did not seem to be open to suggestions based on my field observations. That evening, I made the following entry in my field notes: "There is a lack of empathy, warmth, and humane feeling at this center. Relationships are adversarial." The administrative staff, including Tamir, seemed inflexible. In situations that called for humane, generous, understanding, or helpful attitudes or approaches, they responded in a bureaucratic, impersonal, mechanical, and legalistic fashion. In sum, they left the impression that the bureaucratic functions of their office overshadowed their roles as educators, counselors, and mentors. Tamir and others in responsible positions could learn a lot from the experiences and approach taken at Hofim Center. One cannot help but empathize with the young people when they say they regret leaving their homes in Ethiopia. There they would not be subjected to so much emotional and mental anguish. They could at least express their problems to their elders, teachers, or other relatives in their own language and in a familiar environment.

Regarding the three cases discussed thus far, there are some common issues and challenges; there are also differences. Some of the issues are under the purview of the centers and therefore can be controlled, changed, or modified. Others are beyond the control of the institution since they emanate from external sources. In such cases, the institutions can at least provide counseling, information, and emotional support. Among the common issues are: (1) the Beta Israel's strong desire to study in school and the attendant belief that it will lead them to better career opportunities and a secure life in the future; (2) dissatisfaction with some of the learning programs or the way they are administered; (3) separation from loved ones and inability to do anything to assist them; (4) dissatisfaction with social relations at the centers; and (5) the desire to prolong the length of training to improve proficiency.

In terms of education and training, the Israel Defense Forces were in some respects expected to be extensions of all civilian educational institutions, such as the technical and vocational schools. Young people would continue to advance their skills and learn new ones which would help them secure and retain jobs upon discharge from the armed forces. At the age of eighteen, every able-bodied man served in the IDF for three years. Every woman served for two years, unless she was married or religious. Young men in *yeshivot* were either fully exempt from service or allowed to fulfill their obligation in some other way. During my fieldwork, there were ten thousand young men in this group; very few were Ethiopian Jews. There were complaints from the secular population that the number of exemptions was growing too large. Further, all able-bodied Israeli men (except as noted above) were on reserve duty until the age of fifty-five. Until then, they were obligated to serve forty-two days per year (sixty days during the disturbances of 1988-89).

The field supervisor, Amnon Nave, a retired army colonel with twenty-seven years of experience as a soldier, told me that the Beta Israel men would join the army for varying lengths of time. Those who were between the ages of eighteen and twenty-one would be drafted for three years; those between the ages of twenty-two and twenty-eight would serve for only four months, though they would remain on reserve until they reached the age of fifty-two; and those who were exempt would be given job placements. The exceptions were those who were physically or mentally impaired and those in the *yeshivot*. Beta Israel women are classified as religious and are exempt from service in the armed forces. While in the army, the Beta Israel may continue training in their chosen vocation, though changes may be made depending on the needs of the army. I never met a Beta Israel man who objected to the prospect of joining the army. A few hundred of them are already serving. One young man, a graduate of the Orde Wingate Youth Village on Mount Carmel, became an officer in the paratroopers. His promotion was widely announced by the media, and his alma mater prominently displays pictures taken of him at the ceremony.

TEL AZAR VOCATIONAL SCHOOL

Tel Azar Vocational School, located in yet another metropolitan center, was one of the largest secular schools of its kind. It did not exactly fit either the Youth Aliyah or the Youth Administration model. Here there were three groups of Beta Israel, organized into two classes. The first group was small, only three men. Two were in their late twenties, and one in his early forties. They all had families and had completed twelfth grade before leaving Ethiopia. The second group consisted of seventeen young men who lived and studied at a nearby religious school, but were bused to Tel Azar for vocational-technical training. The third group consisted of twenty-eight men bused from another religious school. Students in the latter two groups studied Hebrew, religion, social sciences, and mathematics from eight a.m. to one p.m. every day at their respective religious schools. Afterward they came to Tel Azar for vocational training until six p.m. The first group of three men had been at Tel Azar for two years and were just finishing their program of studies at the time of my visit. The other two groups were to be there for another two years. Except for the three men who were too few to warrant a special class, the Beta Israel students learned in classes of their own; they did not attend classes with veteran Israelis. It is these three men we will concentrate on in an attempt to understand the kind of challenges they had to confront and the outcomes that occurred.

The enrollment of these three men in technical-vocational classes at Tel Azar was mandated by the Joint Distribution Committee (JDC), which funded their education. The religious authorities were not pleased with the mandate but complied after the JDC threatened to stop funding for the project if the religious authorities interfered. The director, a jovial man of Oriental origin, told me that if it were possible, the students would like to study at Tel Azar full-time. The students would prefer to learn skills that would translate into career and job opportunities in the future. The religious schools did not provide such programs.

The director sent for the three senior Beta Israel students to join us in the discussions. When they arrived, the director introduced us and asked them to brief me on what they were learning. The director knew English as well as Hebrew; the students spoke Amharic, Hebrew, and some English. The three students and I engaged in an animated and warm exchange of views in Amharic. At first, the director appeared uneasy, but he relaxed when we briefed him on our exchanges. About their training, they told me they liked their courses and also liked learning with veteran students. They added that the going was tough, especially in the beginning. Many of the problems they experienced were related to language.[11] They were sure they would not pass the final practical and theoretical examinations. They thought that at this late stage nothing could be done to prevent their failing. They could only hope those following in their footsteps would benefit from their experiences. They explained that the examination was controlled by an outside body, and the school could do nothing to alter its administration. They knew that if they failed the exam and did not get a certificate, they would be doomed to a lifetime of menial work. Perhaps for reasons of language and culture, the students did not feel comfortable discussing these profound concerns with school personnel. The director was taken aback, as he was hearing this for the first time. Genuinely shocked and concerned, he tried to reassure them that they would pass their examinations and get certificates. He said he felt confident that they would pass the practical part of the exam and that he would do his best to provide translators for the theoretical part. The students appreciated his concern but remained doubtful that they would succeed. The director turned to me and expressed deep appreciation for my bringing this situation to his attention. The success or failure of these Beta Israel, as well as the others, depended in a major way on the quality of concern and support that administrators and other school personnel offered them. These three students did not blame any individual or the institution for their situation. They seemed to have a realistic understanding of their circumstances and prospects. Several months later, I learned that two of them had passed the examination and earned the coveted certificates. The forty-one-year-old, the one least proficient in language, did not get through. Perhaps the students in the other two groups would see that success is possible and will otherwise benefit from the experiences of their pioneer compatriots.

CASE OF BET EL

Twelve Beta Israel boys were enrolled at Bet El, a center located about thirty kilometers from a large metropolitan area. It was a religious center, which means that the school personnel as well as students were religious or had to follow strictly the religious requirements of dress, food, Sabbath, and other holiday observations. It happened that a nonreligious organization had been inviting the Beta Israel students and their veteran peers for weekends away from the premises. On these trips, the students participated in workshops and learned more about the history and geography of Israel. The young people enjoyed these activities very much. The principal of Bet El, however, began to complain the weekend retreats were not conducted according to religious requirements. The hotel where they stayed did not serve kosher food, the teachers leading the workshops were not religious, and the students were participating in secular activities on the Sabbath. The boys liked these retreats and wanted to continue them. Friction continued, and some of the boys reported that the principal called them names that denigrated their race and their form of Judaism.[12] There was no independent verification to substantiate the second accusation. Eight of the twelve Beta Israel students went on strike; the four who abstained from the strike were threatened with physical harm if they did not join in the class boycott. These four students were quickly transferred to another center. The eight threatened to boycott classes until the principal was removed. They repeated that he was racist and closed-minded, and did not have their welfare or best interests in mind. The man in question had many years of experience as a teacher and administrator in the religious school system, and it was not easy for the authorities to dismiss him lightly in good conscience. Meanwhile, much instructional time was wasted. Eventually, with the help of the central administration, a compromise was worked out whereby all students were to return to class and the principal was to be transferred to another institution at the end of the term.

TERTIARY-LEVEL EDUCATION

The number of Beta Israel youth who qualified for higher education was very small and reflected the poor educational condition in highland Ethiopia. Those few who were fortunate enough to have completed high school and who passed the matriculation examinations may have attended one of the colleges in Ethiopia before migrating. Although the secondary schools in Ethiopia operate as though all students will continue their studies at the higher levels, only about 2 percent of their cohorts actually do.[13] The desire for college education on the part of students and their parents is tremendous, as there is a deeply held belief that a college diploma opens the gate to money, power, lifelong security, and high status. Whether this was actually the case was another story; the important thing was that the Beta Israel brought these expectations and hopes with them to Israel, where the opportunities for college education for poor immigrants were limited.

Many of the young men left Ethiopia in circumstances of urgency. Either they fled when the Ethiopian People's Revolutionary Party was defeated and its members were being hunted down by the government agencies, or they left suddenly when the 1979 draft law was promulgated by the Ethiopian regime. The net effect of these sudden departures was they did not carry any documents such as school certificates. For the most part, therefore, the placement officers had to rely on their own hunches or what the individuals told them. In light of the tremendous thirst Ethiopians have for education, including college education, it is likely that some of the young men overstated their past accomplishments. Those who had completed the twelfth grade in Ethiopia and some others who had sat for the matriculation examination there might have reported that they wanted, and were entitled to, admission to college.

Whatever their educational background may have been, other problems affect their ability to perform at the tertiary level in Israel. The language of instruction was primarily Hebrew, with some English; the educational system combines aspects of pre-World War II English and German university life and Ashkenazi cultures; and some of the students, especially those from the rural high schools, were weak even by local standards. At first, plans were made to place some of these students in preuniversity programs for a year and then to give them the admission tests; later, the period was extended for two years. But the going proved to be very tough for both personnel and students, at least during the initial years. In the summer of 1985, when I visited the Hebrew University, I learned that both sides were experiencing many frustrations. The students articulated their fear that they would not succeed, and there would be no future for them. The authorities, admitting the weaknesses of the students, told them there were alternative types of programs for college admission. The students thought the authorities did not want them to proceed to college. There were severe frictions and many frustrations.[14] Eventually, of thirty-five students who sat for the matriculation, only one was able to pass. The rest were directed to other sub-college training institutions. The following year, when the period of pre-college preparation was extended to two years, thirteen passed the matriculation examination for admission to Hebrew University.

In 1986–87 there were about two hundred Beta Israel students in the various colleges and universities in the country, including one young woman in the Technion. Perhaps most of those in the Youth Aliyah branch may learn to temper their ambitions and accept the fact that their hopes for a college education are not realistic. It is possible, however, that those Beta Israel children who are now in the lower primary schools may not only achieve fluency in Hebrew, but also in the educational culture which will give them a better chance at the university level. But judging from the experiences of other non-European immigrants, the Beta Israel may either have to temper their ambitions for some time to come or, as some of the more determined ones are already doing, leave Israel to pursue opportunities in the United States or Canada.

CONCLUSION

How should this discussion of the education and training aspects of absorption be summarized? First, in regard to achieving the objectives of literacy and numeracy to the equivalent of grade eight or nine as well as sufficient vocational skills for employment, formal evaluations were either not completed at the time of this writing or were not available. But a minimum 60 percent success rate was expected. As far as the broader, long-term goal to improve the life chances of this segment of the Beta Israel population is concerned, the effort is noble and worthy of the tremendous expenditure. There are no shortcuts known to mankind which can help people attain a life of dignity. Appropriate education and training or induction are essential. If it were not for the Youth Administration Project, this segment of the population would have been left in darkness for the rest of their lives. This would have been a tremendous loss, not only for the individuals and their families but also for the society. Although they may not become truly fluent, at least they are learning to speak Hebrew. This is important. Helping young adults attain literacy and numeracy, especially in a second language, is no small achievement. Even if the aspirations of both the authorities and the students are not fully realized, the young people's appetite for further learning has been whetted to unexpected levels. In fact, one of the major complaints of the administrators and teachers was the students wanted to stay in school longer, wanted to learn more, and were not confident that they had enough education to go out and start working. Equally important, experiences in other lands show that the children of parents with even rudimentary literacy skills are far more likely to gain literacy. This means that these young adults are more likely to become active supporters of the education of their own children. In many families communication between parents and children is a problem because the latter have become more fluent in Hebrew than their parents and have forgotten their native language. With this group, that problem will at least be reduced. Another important outcome is that the learners now have the basis for further learning, formal or informal, inside or outside their places of work. They are also more prepared to participate in civic activities as fully-functioning members of a democratic society.

There are, of course, many problems as the young adults try to adjust to their new home and engage in learning. This is not surprising. Some of the problems could have been reduced with proper management and understanding on the part of the authorities and some patience on the part of the learners. It appears, at least in some of the cases, that those working with the Beta Israel community as teachers adminstrators were not carefully selected, oriented, and supervised. Allowances should be made for such realities. Otherwise, the small problems become magnified or exaggerated, interfering with the central mission of the whole enterprise and eventually threatening to defeat the very purposes of the undertaking.

CHAPTER TEN

❖

Community, Race, Modernity, and Work

❖

Up to now, we have considered the issues of absorption primarily in the context of institutions such as the initial absorbing and learning centers and in relation to the interaction between the immigrants and the personnel or caregivers working in those centers. To the extent that they are intended to prepare the *olim* for life in the larger society, these centers are in many ways contrived and limited. As alluded to earlier, although necessary, the absorption centers tend to isolate the immigrants from the larger society and circumscribe, distort, or under certain conditions even work against the ultimate goals of successful absorption. The sooner the immigrants move out and learn to function in the real and larger world, the better. At the time of my initial fieldwork (1986–87), most of the pre–1984 arrivals and about half of the 1984–85 arrivals were out of the sheltered centers and living on their own in apartments. Some seven hundred of them were holding full-time jobs in factories and service industries. In other words, the community was in transition from the secluded, limiting conditions of the absorption centers to life in the mainstream of society. This phenomenon is in a way the beginning of the ultimate test of whether successful absorption beyond the centers and beyond association with the primary group is occurring or not.

This chapter examines the various issues that arise as the immigrants interact with the larger community, observing the dynamics of their interactions in towns, villages, schools, and workplaces. In these contexts, issues of modernity, race, work habits, and gender relations are also examined.[1]

RACE AND MODERNIZATION

Other groups of darker-skinned people with their own traditional cultures such as the Yemenites and the Benei Israel (from India) had migrated to Israel before the Ethiopians came. There are also those from northern Africa who now constitute a large sector of the Jewish population. These people, although not strictly white, are often classified as such.[2] In terms of color, there are different shades of people from white to dark brown that have migrated to Israel. In general, the Ethiopians are unique neither in skin color nor in levels of modernity.[3] However, in a number of other specific ways, they are different from other *olim*. The extent to which these differences might affect their successful absorption needs to be analyzed. Among the differences, the following are most conspicuous: (1) they are the only group to hail from sub-Saharan Africa and are therefore also darker than others, though not uniformly; (2) the vast majority are of peasant or small holder origin, with no other skills in trade or craft; (3) compared to other communities of Jews in the Diaspora, they were isolated from their coreligionists in Europe, Asia, and northern Africa for the longest period of time; (4) the Western aspect of Israeli culture is totally alien to most of them; (5) until recent decades, they had no tradition of the Hebrew language or the rabbinic laws (Halakah) in their twenty-seven hundred year history; (6) they are the last community to be recognized by Israel as bona fide Jews entitled to avail themselves of the Law of Return and, as a community, the last arrivals as well; and, (7) for the vast majority of Beta Israel, the departure from Ethiopia and the torturous journey through other countries en route to Israel resulted in traumatic separation of family members, loss of several thousand lives, and other experiences that will scar their memories for a long time to come.⁴ These characteristics and experiences, then, distinguish the Beta Israel from other *olim* and must be kept in mind as the issues of race relations and modernity in the absorption process are analyzed.⁵

In considering the absorption of the Beta Israel into Israeli society, the first questions that come to mind pertain to race and modernity.⁶ Does race present a problem for the Beta Israel? Is it possible to untangle problems that arise from race from those that arise from their level of modernity? In other words, can the two issues be examined separately to see how they operate?

The Hebrew term *aliyah*, which refers to migration to Israel, is not synonymous with the English term *immigration*, for example, to the United States, Britain, or France. *Aliyah* literally means "to ascend" or "to go up" to Israel. It is associated with the concepts of *kibbutz a galuyot*, or ingathering of exiles, and *mizug a galuyot*, or the fusion or amalgamation of exiles. For the *edot* (Jewish communities), immigration means coming home to Israel and connotes redemption from life in the Diaspora.⁷ Whenever a Jew leaves his or her home of origin, he or she finds a new home in Israel as well as cultural, national, and religious fulfillment. This is part and parcel of the ideology of Zionism, which was the driving force in the conception and establishment of the Jewish state and has influenced thinking about policies and practices pertaining to immigrant absorption. Such an ideology does not leave much room for discrimination among the communities of Jews—including discrimination based on ethnic origin, level of modernity, and skin color. Thus, when many knowledgeable Israelis say that there is no room for racism in Israel or Judaism, they may have this ideology in mind. Many believe that the tenets of this cultural and political ideology of the family serve to guide the thinking and interactions of citizens. Although it negates the possibility of de jure or doctrinal discrimination, uncritical belief in the doctrine may unintentionally camouflage racial or cultural prejudice and discrimination when they arise.

Before the Beta Israel began to arrive in Israel, questions about their race entered many discussions about their Jewish authenticity and rights under the Law of Return. Some, arguing from the position of racial purity, said it was not possible that the Ethiopians could be Jews because they do not physically resemble any other Jewish community.⁸ The World Jewish Organization, among others, argued bitterly that the Israeli government was dragging its feet because the Ethiopians happened to be blacks from Africa.⁹

There were other immigrants, such as the Benei Israel from India, whose right to intermarry was questioned by the rabbis because of possible contamination from mingling with Gentiles during the years of the Diaspora. At the time, the Benei Israel community argued bitterly that this attempt at discrimination by the rabbinate was because of their color (black or brown) more than anything else.[10] Although the Benei Israel had traditions that included the Hebrew language and rabbinic law, these questions were raised, and recommendations for administration of special rites were made. After much delay and many arguments involving the Knesset, the Ministry of Religious Affairs, and the rabbinate, which were tinged with demonstrations of anger on the part of the Benei Israel (including camping out in front of the chief rabbinate's office and burning an effigy of Chief Rabbi Nissim), the Benei Israel were successful in their challenge of the establishment.[11] For the Beta Israel, the situation is even more complicated because of the characteristics that distinguish them from all other *edot*.

In an effort to sort out the possible effects of race on the absorption of Ethiopian Jews into Israeli society, I canvassed a number of Israeli professionals for their perceptions. Two educators at Jerusalem's Adult Education Department agreed that the Beta Israel do have problems relating to language, culture, education, and technology. However, they told me the question of race is not talked about because, as one put it, "we think we are an open society." The educator went on to say: "Closer contact will do away with the race problem. The Ethiopians who came fifteen years ago think, talk, and act like us; we do not see them as different. To the extent that it exists, the color bar is mutual. Barriers may arise for reasons of class rather than color. Educational level is what brings the difference, not race." To this the other educator added, "If a rabbi tells me they are Jews, it is okay for my child to marry an Ethiopian."[12] According to the views of these two educators, then, the color issue exists but is not independent of cultural, religious, and socioeconomic factors. If the Ethiopians think, act, and talk like the veterans, they will be accepted. This assimilationist perspective is prevalent in Israel. It suggests that racial discrimination, independent of other factors, may not be a formidable issue; but as it often gets entangled with issues of culture, educational attainment, and religion, it becomes one.[13]

I posed similar questions to Zvi Klein, a highly respected professor of psychology at Hebrew University. He said he had heard that the Ethiopians are one of the groups most amenable to assimilation.

About the presence of racism in Israeli society, he said he thought that to the extent that it exists, it is embedded in other issues and may not be readily apparent to the casual observer. "Besides that," he added, "middle-class people would be embarrassed to admit to themselves or to others that they harbor racist attitudes against fellow Jews. Moreover, the Jewish bond in Israel is very inclusive and all-embracing to the extent that most of the people may not mind differences in skin color." When I told him that some educated Beta Israel say there is no racial prejudice in Israel, he replied that their position is unrealistic. By that he meant that one cannot conclude that there is no racial prejudice in society; it exists but is moderated by the absorbing society's ideology and other cultural affinities.

Veteran Israelis openly admit that every group of *olim* has experienced some form of discrimination. As Micha Feldman tells it, the German Jews were discriminated against when they first arrived in Israel because, among other things, they dressed formally. The Romanians, Georgians, Egyptians, and Yemenites had similar experiences. The Moroccans, in particular, were subject to racial discrimination.[14] So, to the extent that they encounter racial discrimination, the Ethiopians are not different in this respect.[15] There are also jokes told about each group of immigrants. One joke about the Beta Israel, for example, is: "Q: Why did Israel bring the Ethiopians? A: They needed spare parts for the Yemenite."

Steve Kaplan of Hebrew University, a specialist in the history of Ethiopian religions and coordinator of the Ben-Zvi Institute's research project on Ethiopian Jewry, put the problems of race, modernity, and culture of the Beta Israel into a broader perspective. In an interview with a reporter from the *Jerusalem Post* in 1985, Kaplan said he was not surprised by the misconceptions about the Ethiopians: "They have inherited all the slurs which were cast at earlier immigrant communities. The stories of dirt, disease and ignorance which were peddled about the Moroccans and the Georgians will soon be told about the Ethiopians."[16] In the case of the Ethiopians, he added, the situation is even more complicated because of the traumatic experiences they had en route to Israel. The confusion among the Beta Israel immigrants might be attributed to fear and bereavement rather than culture shock. Commenting on a social worker's refusal to distribute sophisticated toys and games among Ethiopian children in one of the absorption centers, Kaplan said the decision was illogical. "If she thought they were behind in their development, the solution would be to give them additional stimulation—not to deprive them."

He added, "It may be more than a generation before the rest of Israel is convinced that Ethiopian Jewry can hold its own in keeping pace with the 21st century."[17] "It is unfortunate," he continued, "that the Beta Israel immigrants' confrontation with modern technology was getting so much attention, because that will be the easiest thing to overcome. What will be more difficult is maintaining the balance between social integration into the wider society and preserving their own social traditions." The media have compounded the simplistic image of blacks held by the public, which is largely derived from Tarzan films. To begin with, far from being "primitive," as much of the public media report, many Ethiopian Jews are literate in several languages, and most had seen electricity, cars, and running water. They did not live in jungles.

As a result of such misperceptions, some people have asked Kaplan in all seriousness about the possibility of the Ethiopians' contribution to Israeli sports. Some enthusiasts already were dreaming that the Beta Israel would bring gold medals to Israel from the 1988 Olympics, he said. Still other Israelis who perceived of the Ethiopians as unskilled and illiterate believed their coming would lessen Israel's dependence on West Bank and Gaza Strip Arabs in the construction industry and would produce a new source of maids for cleaning and other household work.[18] Among the Israelis, Kaplan observed, there is a lack of understanding of the Ethiopians, overgeneralization about their lack of skills and abilities, and undervaluation of their cultural contributions. One problem is the Israelis' lack knowledge of the cultural history of the *olim.* To overcome this, Kaplan is cooperating with others to catalogue information on the community. He is concerned that, being under pressure and eager to become part of the mainstream of Israeli society, the Beta Israel may lose their cultural heritage. He saw a strong need for Israeli schools to include aspects of Beta Israel culture and history in their curricula.

In June 1986, arrangements were made for a group of American professors, including myself, to visit a large town where about one thousand Beta Israel immigrants were living.[19] Because the mayor was noted for his managerial skills, the city was included in our itinerary. Upon arrival, we were told the mayor had left for Jerusalem on urgent business and that we would be briefed by the deputy mayor. During the briefing, the deputy mayor (an Ashkenazi; the mayor is Sephardi) went out of his way to inform us that the Ethiopians were lazy, unwilling to work, and uncooperative. He compared them unfavorably with the one hundred Vietnamese refugees who had settled there. In the short time they had been there, he said, the Vietnamese had shown tremendous progress in adapting to the Israeli situation compared to the Ethiopians. For instance, he added, some of them have already joined the city orchestra and are working in other advanced areas of social endeavor. He pointed to a black girl who was sweeping the hallways of his office and commented that she was the exception; she was a hard worker. Even after he learned that there was an Ethiopian professor in the audience, he made no effort to alter his posture of disdain.

The next day, arrangements were made for us to meet with four people who had knowledge of the *olim*: a historian, an anthropologist, and two educated Ethiopians (one a veteran of fourteen years in Israel who had obtained all his secondary and college education there; the other, a relative newcomer who had been a teacher in Ethiopia). After their initial briefing, one of the professors raised the issue of racism. The non-Ethiopian Israelis deferred to the Beta Israel representatives. The Ethiopians denied that there was any discrimination based on race. One of them, citing experiences with his own small children in nursery schools, said he had observed no discrimination.[20] On the other hand, he and the other Beta Israel complained bitterly about some ridiculous manifestations of cultural slights shown by some sectors of the public media. Recently on television, for example, a five-year-old Beta Israel child had been shown learning how to use a toothbrush for the first time in her life. As far as the commentator and the managers of the show were concerned, the fact that a child of this age did not know how to perform such a rudimentary act as cleaning her teeth with a toothbrush and toothpaste was something sensational and newsworthy. The Beta Israel argued that in Ethiopia "we use different methods to achieve similar ends."[21] Besides, they could see no reason for broadcasting such an event other than to poke fun at the young girl and, through her, at the community of recent immigrants. As annoyed as they were, the two Beta Israel implied that the slights were directed at the group's level of modernity, not race.

At the community level, veteran parents expressed fear that the Beta Israel would pass on exotic contagious diseases to their children in school. A school counselor in one of the first areas where the Beta Israel had settled informed me that before 1979, there were no black pupils in Israel.[22] When the Beta Israel began to arrive, the veteran parents and their children had problems accepting the newcomers.[23] Their fears were ameliorated when the Ethiopian children were placed in schools of their own for at least the first year. When it came time to transfer them to schools attended by veteran children, though not necessarily in the same classrooms, parents complained that the Beta Israel might retard the progress of their children.[24] Some threatened to withdraw their children, and others actually did. The religious schools, which were already experiencing declining enrollments for other reasons, were very much worried about the threats and in most cases made provision for parallel classes. This meant there were at least two classes for each grade so that the Beta Israel children would not be mixed with the veteran children.[25] While these concerns might be attributed to the natural desire of parents to have optimal learning environments for their children, they also may be interpreted to have racial overtones, as was true with other immigrant groups.

The following account further illustrates the complex issues of culture, race, religion, and levels of modernity in the absorption process. In the winter of 1985, the ultra-Orthodox Habad Hasidic movement's Uziel School in Beersheba refused to register two Ethiopian girls for the following year. Further, the school announced that it was going to examine the status of those children already enrolled. The reason given was that one-third of the one hundred-eighty students enrolled in the school were Ethiopian, and adding more would impede the educational progress of the other students. In fact, the compelling reason was that parents representing the children of the majority insisted, and the religious "authorities" instructed them not to accept any more Ethiopians immigrant children before they had gone through the conversion rites and were certified as bona fide Jews by the rabbinate.[26] The chief rabbi of Beersheba, Eliahu Katz, supported the position of the school. He added: "We have regulation from the chief rabbinate [of Israel] that Ethiopian immigrants are to undergo ritual immersion. Only very recently, seventy of them did undergo immersion in the ritual bath here without any difficulty. There was no bitterness."[27] In the meantime, the Ministry of Education and Culture sent letters to the parents of the one hundred-eighty students children in the school which stated that the school was part of the religious school system supported by public funds and is under the jurisdiction of the ministry. Therefore, the school must accept all Beta Israel children. The ministry's representative saw the school's position as "a serious case of revolt." He added that the case smacked of "racism where 'skin color and other unsuitable criteria' took the place of equality before the law." If the school did not alter its position, the ministry would take back the school building from the Hasidic movement. The ministry further advised the parents that they could transfer their children to another school. Having made its position clear, the ministry referred the matter to the high court. The high court ruled that the Beersheba municipality (representing the Ministry of Education and Culture) must take steps to ensure that the Beta Israel children are enrolled in school without difficulties. At the same time, the court rejected the petition of those parents who had complained that the change in the status of the school would rob them of their right to register their children at a Habad school. In their opinion, Uziel did not come under the jurisdiction of the municipality. The court ruled that the municipality, which had fired the school principal and closed the school, had no authority to treat the school like any other state religious school, adding, "It cannot be forced to accept the Ethiopian Jewish children."[28] The court also said that only the ministry's director-general has the obligation and responsibility to give instructions on enrolling children.

The preceding case is a clear example not only of the issues involving the Beta Israel in relation to their status as immigrants but also of the unclarified—still evolving—delineation of administration, control, power, and authority among the religious and secular parties and institutions in Israel. Apparently, the experiences gained from other times involving similar groups and circumstances have not been taken advantage of by the authorities.[29]

In another setting, a group of young Beta Israel men in the midst of their training requested a transfer from the vocational school they were attending because the conditions had become unbearable. Their specific complaint was that the veteran students insulted them.[30]

At the community level, a number of towns have refused to accept Beta Israel; others have tried to limit the number of families allowed to settle. The reasons for these actions might be economic, but they could be racial as well. The city council of one town, Benyamina, complained when additional Ethiopians settled there because, a few Beta Israel families who had settled earlier were having difficulties with the veterans. In some instances, windows of apartments belonging to Ethiopians were smashed; there also had been physical fights between veterans and newcomers. While the town was in the midst of this conflict, the Ministry of Immigrant Absorption brought more Beta Israel families in at night and settled them there. The local people refused to accept them. One Beta Israel who followed the case informed me that the fight was really between the town and the absorption ministry—the Ethiopians were caught in the middle.[31] Even if this generous interpretation is applied, the consequences are the same: attitudes between veterans and newcomers had been poisoned.[32]

The mayors of some of the larger cities complained that the government had asked them to bear too heavy a burden. In many of the larger settlements and cities, racial and cultural relations are less than cordial. The mayors openly admit this. Smaller settlements, such as Kiryat Arba, have handled the situation much better.[33] Admitting that many problems exist along the lines described above, one veteran administrator added that 99 percent of the problems are not related to race. He thinks the government and the Jewish Agency have much work to do by way of orienting the veteran Israeli communities regarding tolerance of the Beta Israel.[34]

Although racial discrimination against the *olim* exists, it is not as prevalent or as conspicuous as some might think. Israeli society is very sensitive about this issue. The history of Jews in the Diaspora was that of minorities oppressed many times for their racial, cultural, or religious differences. Zionist ideology is based on the principles of egalitarianism, socialism, and justice. Mindful of the 1975 United Nations resolution that equated Zionism with racism,[35] Israeli society does not ignore discrimination for any reason, including race. Racial discrimination occurs, but so far its magnitude is manageable. The Ethiopians themselves are not capitalizing on the concept of racial discrimination; either they do not recognize it when it is manifested in a milder or isolated form, or they are not willing to admit that it could exist among the Jewish Israeli community.[36] However, recognizing the existence of racial discrimination is only the first step. Unless responsible authorities at different levels confront it and provide appropriate interventions, the problem may grow. Only when the issues are brought into the open is it possible for members of the respective communities, in cooperation with the officials, to come to grips with them. Careful monitoring and management are needed at every stage.

As indicated earlier, community conflicts are more likely to occur in places where there is a large concentration of the immigrants. This is not surprising. In places where the relative number of immigrants is larger than the resources of the community, antagonism is more likely. In one town where there was a community of fifteen hundred Beta Israel (reduced from sixteen hundred at the time of my first visit in November 1986), the deputy mayor, of Moroccan origin, gave the following account of the conditions precipitating conflict in his town of about sixty thousand people. He said that although the town was glad to have Ethiopian residents, too many had settled there. Four years earlier, when the first Ethiopians came to the city, he said they were ready for them. But by the time the second wave of immigrants arrived, the city no longer had the resources to cope with the influx. The government initiated the settlement of the Beta Israel and assumed responsibility for housing. However, other aspects of the program required additional resources which no agency provided sufficiently. For instance, based on the assumption that the Beta Israel were making a religious *aliyah*, they were channeled into the only religious school in the community. The two secular schools were not required to share the burden. This created problems for the Beta Israel as well as the veterans in the community. Provision of nursery schools was another problematic area.

Why did so many of the Beta Israel settle in this town? In the beginning, said the deputy mayor, housing was available. "Secondly, the good reception we gave to the first wave gave the impression to the government authorities and the immigrants alike that we could take more. In many instances," he continued, "the government dumped many of them here without our consent." When pressed to be specific about the problems, he listed the following: (1) 30 percent of the Ethiopian households are headed by single parents; (2) there is a perception that the Beta Israel either are not motivated to work or do not understand how to hold jobs; and (3) there is a lack of resources and facilities such as nursery schools.

"There are jobs in the city," he said, "but the Ethiopians do not like to work." In addition, they lacked nursery schools. When they resorted to innovative approaches, they were told by the immigrants that their efforts were inadequate. In the case of the nursery school, they lacked adequate space, so they moved the children with cerebral palsy to another facility and converted the place into a nursery school for the Beta Israel. But the Beta Israel parents at once rejected it for fear that it was previously occupied by children who might have contagious diseases. The deputy mayor thought the priorities of the Ethiopians and veteran Israelis were different. As an example, he told me that the Ethiopians were not willing to buy their children schoolbooks or pay for field trips organized by the school. The social worker who accompanied me to the interview added that this was a problem in other places. Another problem mentioned by the deputy was that the Beta Israel "like to stay on the outside, and the Israelis want them to begin to become involved and become a part of the solution of the many problems associated with immigration and settlement. But," he continued, "there is a sense of isolation on the part of the immigrants which the authorities are aware of.... This is why we are trying to involve them and bring about broader interactions with the larger community through sports, vocational training programs, and cultural activities which are organized and operated by the city in cooperation with Project Renewal."[37] The conflicts, he said, are primarily a result of cultural differences. In his opinion, race has nothing to do with the problems. He referred to other brown people such as the Benei Israel and the Yemenites who have settled in Israel successfully.[38] Interestingly, he did not include the Moroccans, his own group, in the list of people of color.

Following these encounters with the mayor and his colleagues, I interviewed the Beta Israel in their settlements. They denied that they were not interested in paying whatever is necessary to support their children's education. They argued that they were constrained by lack of money. They maintained that the checks they received, whether from the pension fund or wage employment, were inadequate; their income did not allow them to do all they would like to do for their children. In addition, they could not involve themselves in their children's education because they did not speak Hebrew well enough.

The social workers and others, including educated members of the Beta Israel community, agree that the parents are truly limited in what they can do for their children's education. Despite their limitations, they say they could do more, but they believe that since the government brought them here and has, up to now, provided for all their individual and family needs, there is no reason why it should not continue to do so as long as such needs are there. Now that the children are in school and the parents are living outside the absorption centers, they think it is the government's responsibility to continue to support them. For the *olim*, the government is a benevolent source of power and money. They see these new or additional requirements as devices used by local bureaucrats to advance their own careers at the expense of the welfare of the immigrants.[39] Once again, we are witnessing misunderstandings and misinterpretations of motives and a general absence of mutual trust.

THE CULTURE OF WORK

At this time, most Beta Israel either are involved in training or education programs, have already retired, or are waiting for an assignment.[40] Most of the men and women have neither the experience nor the skills needed to participate in a modern, industrialized setting. Some seven hundred out of a total population of sixteen thousand are fully employed by industry or government. Employment is encouraged. In addition to the financial benefits, it offers opportunities for broader interaction, development of friendships, and bolstered self-esteem. However, since most Beta Israel lack sophisticated training or skills, they have difficulties finding a job. When they do find one, it is typically on the bottom rung of the ladder, and upward mobility is difficult. Industry is not ready to jump in and offer them meaningful jobs, the sort the Beta Israel would like to have.[41] The government encourages prospective employers to provide qualified Ethiopians with job opportunities. Assisted by quasi-governmental institutions such as the Joint Distribution Committee, the government usually assumes responsibility for job placement, housing, training, and salary subsidy. The subsidy pays the salary for one year or so while employees receive on-the-job training. At the end of the training period, the heretofore subsidized employees must convince the employer that they have all the skills required to do the job and that it is in the latter's best interest to employ them.[42] The employer usually is expected to pay the employee's salary, though this is not always what happens. The government may continue to pay part of the salary beyond that period if prospects for a permanent job exist.

The expectation is that all able-bodied men and women should hold jobs and become self-sufficient, tax-paying members of society in the shortest possible time. But the realization of this objective is, for a number of reasons, taking more time than had been anticipated. To begin with, although the Ethiopians were mostly peasant farmers, they have proved unwilling to work and live on farms in Israel. Almost no Ethiopians live in a *kibbutz* (communal village) or a *moshav* (cooperative village). At one time, the government tried to encourage about a dozen Beta Israel men to establish a cooperative, but without success. Since that time, no further thought has been given to the possibility that the Beta Israel may agree to farm. Another problem is that agricultural production in Israel, as in the United States, has become a technologically sophisticated enterprise. The Beta Israel do not have the requisite knowledge or technical skills. Another reason the Beta Israel reject agricultural work may have to do with the fact that only a small fraction of the Israeli population works in this sector, and the *kibbutzim* have difficulty keeping themselves solvent. In Ethiopia, the Beta Israel had been subsistence tenant farmers for many generations. Farming in general, and tenant farming in particular, was an arduous and increasingly unrewarding occupation in the parts of highland Ethiopia where they lived. The land was overworked, and yields had become diminished.[43] Of the little they were able to harvest, a disproportionate share had to be paid to the landlords.[44] It is not surprising, then, that so few Beta Israel have joined the agricultural sector in Israel.

With time, other traditional occupations of the Beta Israel, such as blacksmithing, carpentry, masonry, weaving, and pottery making, lost their significance. Their skills and markets were displaced and overtaken by modern machinery and more efficient methods of distribution in Ethiopia's towns and cities. Their traditional mainstays were no longer adequate. By the time they reached the Promised Land, they had even less enthusiasm for these occupations. They had been told stories about the land that flows with milk and honey, where minimal labor for a small part of the year yields more than enough to live on. They expected to escape from everything—political, cultural, and economic oppression as well as occupational drudgery. Indeed, throughout their first year in Israel, their needs had been generously met, which reinforced and verified their expectations.[45] It will take considerable time before both sides understand that these are indeed distorted perceptions of reality.[46]

If the Beta Israel are not in absorption centers, they are in the settlement towns (areas designated for immigrants). Of those who have secured employment, most find themselves in the service or production sectors of the economy which require minimal skills and where the pay is low.[47] Many see that their chances for promotion or salary improvement are slim. They complain about their status and worry about those who will follow them, though they do realize that those in Youth Aliyah or vocational schools will have better chances. On the whole, they realize that it will be another fifteen or twenty years, when their children begin graduating, before their children's prospects for attaining high-status jobs will improve.

Historically, the Beta Israel are disciplined and hard workers. In predominantly Christian regions of Ethiopia, where in the name of religion an overabundance of holidays is observed and where occupations are rigidly hierarchical, the Beta Israel were relatively unhampered by these strictures and toiled most days of the year in arduous labor. I was surprised to hear several Israeli employers and coworkers complain that the Beta Israel were unreliable workers. More specifically, the complaints about male factory workers are that (1) they are cliquish at workplaces; (2) they give a variety of weak excuses to leave their workplaces to attend to private matters; and (3) they are easily offended by their bosses or coworkers. On their part, the Beta Israel men complain that they are not respected in their places of work, they are pushed around too much without consultation or consent, and so on.

Accustomed as they are to hard labor, and now receiving regular cash wages, the immigrants, one might presume, should be happy to do any work. But, although survival demanded that they labor long and hard in their land of origin, they did have some control over their activities. Their agricultural work was seasonal: planting, weeding, and harvesting activities predominated at different times of the year. Attached to this cycle of activities were rich cultural traditions which included get-togethers with neighbors to feast and celebrate good times. There were also two long seasons for recreation and other nonfarm work. The jobs held by the Ethiopian Jews in Israel, on the other hand, tend to be repetitive and monotonous. Out of boredom, the immigrant may take any opportunity to be absent from work. There are also cultural expectations that interfere with work attendance. Often, they miss work either because a neighbor has died or because of *merdo*, the occasion when one is told that a relative who lived far away (in this case, in Ethiopia) has died. The bereaved stays at home to receive condolences from friends and relatives.[48] This phenomenon is compounded by the fact that in Ethiopia, when a relative or friend dies, the occasion is serious enough to warrant the stoppage of most work for several days. In their new home, the Beta Israel worker may be absent from the job for several days without contacting the foreman, not imagining, perhaps, that the boss does not understand the situation. They may also stay home from work because they are sick or another member of the family is ill. Furthermore, for reasons of language and culture, interaction with coworkers is minimal, which leads others to believe that they are clannish.

To illustrate some of the dilemmas encountered by the male Beta Israel worker, let us consider the case of Yaphet. Yaphet and his family have lived in Israel for about six years. He is in his early forties. He lives with his wife and three young children in a three-room apartment. There are other Beta Israel in the same apartment building, and most of them also have small children. As he took me around the apartment complex near a very large absorption center (which by now was half empty), it was clear that he was very familiar with the personalities and the circumstances among this large community of Ethiopians. Before he got his present position as a factory worker, Yaphet, one of the first arrivals and proficient in Hebrew and familiar with Israeli culture, served as one of the interpreters at the absorption center. The newcomers felt animosity toward him, as they did toward many other interpreters, because they suspected that he somehow worked in league with the center administrators against the interests of the *olim*. When I visited some of the other apartments I invited him to join me. He declined, saying that he did not feel well and that I should visit him in his own apartment. According to my social work informant, the reason for his reluctance to visit other apartments, was that he knew he was not welcome.

When I visited his apartment, his wife and children were watching, on a large color screen, a video tape of Ethiopian folk music and dance they had recently obtained from Addis Ababa.[49] The apartment was well furnished, and, from all appearances, his children and wife were healthy and well dressed. Since leaving his job as interpreter at the absorption center, Yaphet had been employed in one of the local factories for a salary of about six hundred shekels per month ($400 U.S. in 1986) which was considered a good salary for a person of his qualifications. When asked to describe his work situation, he said the conditions were all right but he felt unfulfilled. He said that because of his low level of formal education and skills, he feared relegation to menial jobs for the rest of his life. He said that when he contemplated his situation he felt depressed. He said he was too old to begin going to school and too young to retire. He saw only limited prospects for himself, but hoped conditions would be different for his children. His concerns were qualitatively different from those expressed by the other workers I interviewed. Whereas they were concerned about being accepted at their place of work, Yaphet was concerned about his future.

For the Beta Israel women, the situation is different. To begin with, this is the first time in their lives that they have been able to work away from the home or farm. More importantly, this is the first time they have been able to earn their own income and control its expenditure. For these reasons, perhaps, they seem to be more reliable and disciplined workers. They not only work as hard as expected, they also get along with their supervisors and coworkers. This does not necessarily mean they are immune to community expectations regarding attendance to matters that require absence from work, but at least the employers do not seem to hold it against them. This suggests that the complaints against the male workers may include factors other than their mere absence. It may be that men are less likely to inform their foreman that they will not be in for work, and so on.[50] The differences in work-related behavior and attitudes may result in employers' preference for hiring women, which, among other things, may aggravate the existing husband-wife conflicts that were discussed in Chapter 5.[51]

SUMMARY

As the immigrants leave the sheltered absorption centers and begin to interact with the larger society, issues of acceptance or rejection based on culture and race have emerged. Informants report that discrimination based on culture, class, levels of modernity, or education does indeed exist. But they are ambivalent on the question of racial discrimination. While some of their descriptions of experiences or events do contain elements of racial discrimination, they do not fully admit that certain actions have to do with race or identify them as racially based. Their convictions mirror the ideology underlying Israeli law and convention that the state cannot discriminate against any community of Jews. For this reason, it is not easy for anyone to admit that he or she discriminates against other Jews because of their race. The Beta Israel vaguely refer to racism in society but do not dwell on it. They attribute their difficulties to differences in culture and level of modernity.

Regarding employment and apartment living (beyond the absorption centers), there are problems. In the work place, employers complain that Beta Israel employees lack punctuality and loyalty. The Beta Israel complain that their employers do not make allowances for cultural requirements. As of 1987, not much interaction in either the workplace or the neighborhoods occurred between the veterans and the newcomers. Neither group was going out of its way to initiate communication. Interaction may evolve if, in the meantime, problems that contribute to the development of negative attitudes are alleviated.

CHAPTER ELEVEN

❖

Epilogue

❖

                          This concluding chapter summarizes the developments up to the summer of 1992 that took place since the main report was drafted; highlights briefly some of the progress (or lack thereof) made by the immigrants toward establishing themselves in the new country; and indicates some suggestions policymakers may wish to consider for priority action.

When the huge, dramatic, and daring airlift of the Beta Israel from the Sudan refugee camps was concluded in the spring of 1985, many thought that under prevailing regional and global political circumstances, any hope for additional migration of the Beta Israel would have to be postponed indefinitely. Indeed, for the next five years, the flow of Ethiopian refugees slowed to a trickle. In most cases, the few who were able to leave departed from Addis Ababa with the clandestine assistance of individuals and organizations from abroad. Still, half of the known Beta Israel population remained stranded in Ethiopia. But the plight of the Beta Israel who remained in Ethiopia was never far from the minds of their relatives in Israel, or of the government and the Jewish Agency of Israel, or of the various Jewish organizations in the United States, especially the American Association for

Ethiopian Jews (AAEJ).[1] The Ethiopian Jews themselves, now divided even more between Ethiopia and Israel, began to work hard to end the intolerable conditions with a reunification of the families in Israel.

As far as I am aware, compared to the Beta Israel no migrant group from Ethiopia or elsewhere in Africa has ever drawn so much attention, so much concern from the international community, either for or against the migration. In the United States, concerned organizations included the AAEJ, which lobbied Congress, the one hundred-fifty-member Congressional Caucus for Ethiopian Jews, and the Reagan and Bush administrations. At times, these and other organizations facilitated visits to the United States by Beta Israel representatives, who presented the case for the African Jews. One of these representatives was Rachmim Elazar, chairman of Israel's National Council for Ethiopian Jews, who was flown to Washington in March 1989.[2] At a meeting in the White House, Elazar thanked Bush for the help he had provided when he was vice president and asked him to apply pressure to the Ethiopian government, perhaps by offering new forms of aid with strings attached. The Israelis, Elazar told the president, were doing their best, but they needed help. The president and his national security adviser, Brent Scowcroft, assured Elazar that State Department officials would press for the emigration of Ethiopian Jewry at the appropriate diplomatic meetings.[3] Shortly afterward, other American Jewish organizations reversed their erstwhile policy of quiet diplomacy and supported Elazar's position. The National Jewish Community Relations Advisory Council (NJCRAC) decided to circulate petitions, addressed to U.S. government officials, on behalf of Ethiopian Jewry, and the Congressional Caucus for Ethiopian Jews urged Congress to pass a joint resolution in support of reuniting Ethiopian families in Israel.[4] Thus, the full range of political pressure was mounted on behalf of the Beta Israel.

Of course, there were always those who did not believe in selecting the Beta Israel for special treatment and leaving the fate of millions of other suffering Ethiopians to nature and the capricious Mengistu regime. Among these critics were Americans and non-Beta Israel Ethiopians. For example, the University of Michigan student newspaper in Ann Arbor staged debates and published an editorial that condemned the whole process.[5] Mesfin Woldemariam, a prominent professor at Addis Ababa University, presented a paper criticizing the manner and circumstances of the Jews' departure from Ethiopia. He described the exodus as part and parcel of the Mengistu regime's abuse of human rights and an affront to human dignity.⁶ No doubt, his views were shared by many other Ethiopians who were aware of the whole story.

Even after the 1985 disruptions, the emigration process, in one form or another, continued at the rate of about three thousand people annually. By 1989, the total population of Ethiopian Jews in Israel was about twenty thousand.⁷ This rate of emigration was far from satisfactory, however, given the plight of the Beta Israel families who had been divided between Israel and Ethiopia and the political and economic circumstances prevailing in Ethiopia. Those already in Israel continued to insist that the most important single problem they faced was the separation of their families. Those still in Ethiopia continued to plea for reunification. In their traditional society, the young people were gone, leaving relatives exposed to psychological and economic suffering in Ethiopia. The guilt these young people felt about the situation was so severe that it interfered with their ability to function normally.

In their desperation, the Ethiopian Jews in Israel even claimed that favoritism influenced the pace of family reunification, that Ethiopians with access to high authorities in the Israeli government were able to bring their relatives to Israel more easily than others.⁸ But these types of arrangements were obviously ad hoc and insufficient to meet the tremendously pressing needs for family reunification of the estimated twenty thousand to thirty thousand Beta Israel who remained in Ethiopia.⁹

The Beta Israel continued to demonstrate against what they perceived to be Israeli inaction and demanded increased efforts to speed up the reunification process. The government of Prime Minister Yitzhak Shamir tried to inform them that in concert with all its friends, Israel was doing all it could to step up the pace. It told demonstrators that some efforts on behalf of the Beta Israel were confidential and could not be divulged for fear that they would be jeopardized by public disclosure. At one point, in an attempt to show the Ethiopians that the matter was being actively pursued through secret negotiations, Israeli newspapers published photographs of Beta Israel leaders meeting with the Israeli political leadership without divulging the substance of the conversations.¹⁰

For a while, reports circulated to the effect that the Ethiopian government, besieged by the continuing precipitous decline in the economic, military, and political arenas and under pressure from the Soviets, who had informed the Ethiopians that their military and economic agreements with the U.S.S.R. would terminate by 1990, to seek peaceful solutions with the rebel groups and improve its relations with the West, was making desperate overtures to the noncommunist world, including Israel. In November 1989, these reports gained credibility, when the governments of Ethiopia and Israel announced they were reestablishing formal diplomatic relations.[11] This was quite a dramatic development. It is known that the two governments had been secretly conducting some kind of military relations for some time. But the Ethiopian regime's open acknowledgment of relations with Israel left it vulnerable to criticism from the Arabs, including Libya, the Sudan, Syria, and Iraq. Libya had vacillated between siding with the Eritrea and perhaps, even Tigrean rebels and the government of Ethiopia. Iraq and Syria had been helping the Eritrea and Tigrean liberation fronts. For its part, Israel was very pleased with this turn of events. But before agreeing to resume diplomatic relations, the Israelis set forth their own demands. One of these was that the government of Ethiopia permit the orderly emigration of the remaining Ethiopian Jews to Israel. The Ethiopian government, in spite of the inevitable domestic and Arab political repercussions, relented.[12]

Though this agreement was well known at the time, the Ethiopian deputy foreign minister, Tesfaye Dinka (who became prime minister in April 1991), equivocated on the Israeli-Ethiopian agreements, including the understandings regarding emigration of the Beta Israel. As late as June 1990, he said that no mass exodus of Beta Israel had been agreed upon, only that some might be allowed to leave to join their families. He also asserted that his government had sought assurances from Israel that the emigrants would not be settled in the West Bank, and, he said, "we are looking at the implications of how our neighbors would look at it Lieutenant."[13] Regarding the rumors of arms-for-people deals, Tesfaye added: "Up until now, in spite of what has been said, there have been no military deals, no weapons, no particular military assistance, no groups to train. These reports are absolutely false."[14] Not unexpectedly, in spite of the Mengistu regime's cautions and denials, Ethiopia's Arab neighbors were alarmed by its decision to resume diplomatic relations with Israel.[15]

This shift in the diplomatic and political balance created disquietude among the leaders of the Horn of Africa and other observers of the region. As the rivalry of the superpowers in the region subsided, the medium-sized and smaller powers were creeping in to fill the void. Israel, Iraq, Libya, and others were filling the vacuum created in

Somalia, Ethiopia, and the Sudan. The latter countries, decimated by civil wars, drought, famine, and ethnic strife, were fast becoming fertile grounds for power plays. As one astute student of the area's politics observed: "Many people in the Horn—Ethiopia, Somalia, and the Sudan—view this hasty superpower retreat with alarm and despair, because Israel, Libya, and Iraq are stepping into the vacuum. Jerusalem has already sold large quantities of arms and sent military advisers to Colonel Mengistu. In response, President Saddam Hussein of Iraq and Libya's leader, Muammar el-Qaddafi, are pumping weapons into Somalia, the Sudan, and Eritrea for the rebels." He added that "the militarization of the Horn is so advanced now that it is easier for many people to buy Kalashnikov rifles than a loaf of bread." The author of the article concludes by observing further that "wars in the Horn know no borders; neither do refugees. There is [an urgent need] . . . to work for a regional solution."[16]

Soon after the resumption of diplomatic relations, Ethiopian Jews began to emigrate for Israel in greater numbers. Uri Gordon, head of the Department of Immigration of the Jewish Agency of Israel, reported in 1990 that within less than a year, nearly four thousand had arrived in Israel, and another one thousand would be coming in the following weeks. In the meantime, another twenty thousand Beta Israel had moved from the Gondar region to Addis Ababa, where they were waiting for transportation to Israel.[17]

As Flora Lewis of the *New York Times* rightly observed, Israel has no love for Mengistu; it was pursuing its national interests on the same basis on which it had maintained relations with non-Arab states such as Turkey and Iran. In the case of Ethiopia, the Red Sea coast was at stake. (It is no secret that some of the powerful Arab states would like to transform the Red Sea into an Arab lake.) As part of its new relationship with Ethiopia, Israel reportedly began providing munitions, including cluster bombs, that could be used against the several Ethiopian rebel forces, particularly the Eritrea People's Liberation Front. It also supplied advisory and more tangible assistance that allowed the Mengistu regime to continue its battle against the insurgency.[18] This displeased the U.S. government, which for its part had long been disgusted with the Ethiopian regime. In this instance, the global interests of the United States and the regional, more immediate interests of Israel clashed.

Then, once again, the emigration was disrupted, and the normal monthly flow of five hundred or more Ethiopian Jews came to a halt. According to the Ethiopian government, Israeli representatives working in Ethiopia were following improper procedures. It did not spell out what the improper procedures were, but diplomats in Addis Ababa and two U.S. congressmen, Howard Wolpe, chairman of the House Subcommittee on Africa, and Gary Ackerman, who had visited Ethiopia and followed developments closely, agreed that Mengistu was upping the price for releasing the Beta Israel. They alleged that during a visit to Israel on July 4 and 5, 1990, Mengistu did not get all he wanted and was therefore holding the Beta Israel hostage. The Israeli government, on the other hand, has consistently denied both an arms deal and the Mengistu visit. The Israeli ambassador to Ethiopia, Meir Joffe, asserted that the emigration suspension was part of an agreement between the two governments designed to stem the influx of non-Jewish people who had recently traveled from Gondar to Addis Ababa in the hope of joining the exodus to Israel.[19]

Despite the government's efforts to the contrary, the general public in Addis Ababa soon learned of the operations in behalf of the Beta Israel, and the exodus became somewhat controversial in Ethiopia. Other Ethiopians saw the new arrivals from the countryside being housed and taken care of very well in every respect, but no one bothered to explain why they were thus favored. Kassa Kebede, Mengistu's Israeli-educated uncle and confidant, who had not only favored the emigration under the pretext of family reunification all along but also had worked very hard on its behalf, allowed the AAEJ and other Jewish organizations to set up refugee camps in Addis Ababa without having to go through the normal government procedures administered by the relief and rehabilitation commission of his country. The U.S. embassy collaborated fully in transporting the Beta Israel from Gondar and providing tents and food for the camps.[20] Understandably, other Ethiopian government officials who were not consulted as the process unfolded protested the mass emigration, saying that it was an "embarrassment for Ethiopia to have so many of its people leave."[21]

Israel attempted to organize this latest exodus differently. After announcing they had established diplomatic relations with Ethiopia primarily to extricate the Beta Israel from that country and reunite them with their families in Israel, the Israelis pursued two strategies. The first was to facilitate the emigration of those who had been waiting in line to leave, and the second was to prepare the majority of the other Jews in Ethiopia for eventual emigration to Israel. There must have been considerable discussion among the Israeli, American, and other volunteer organizations working in Ethiopia about whether the preparation activities should be conducted in the provincial city of Gondar or the Beta Israel should be brought to Addis Ababa. Some of the volunteers, among them representatives of the Joint Distribution Committee (JDC) of the United States, thought it would be more convenient, less expensive, and less disruptive for the emigrants if the preparations were carried out as much as possible in Gondar. Others, mainly the AAEJ, insisted that, given the civil strife raging in the Gondar area, Addis Ababa was the better choice. Eventually, the decision was made to transport the Beta Israel to the capital.[22]

These procedures were quite different from those followed in earlier emigration efforts. Previously, Ethiopian Jews were taken to Israel, either secretly or legally (as happened for a brief period in 1977), where they were processed for health and documentation reasons and placed in absorption centers for ten months or more. That process generated numerous problems for both the emigrants and the care providers. In addition, it was hoped that the new procedure of screening people to establish their Jewishness before their departure from Ethiopia would forestall the earlier unpleasant experiences with mandatory conversion and the refusal of some Ethiopians to comply.

This time, even within Ethiopia, the task, for both the Beta Israel and the care providers, was tremendous. Logistical and travel arrangements, securing housing in the crowded city, and providing the necessary health, education, and other facilities presented a daunting challenge. Many helping hands were needed, and financial and personnel assistance poured in from private and governmental sources in Israel and North America. Doctors, nurses, and other support workers were recruited locally. Tents were pitched in the Israeli embassy compound in Addis Ababa. Training in nutrition, healthful living, language, and other essential skills was provided. Since it was thought that there were many non-Jews in the refugee camps, the Ethiopian and Israeli governments cooperated in screening the emigrants. Soon, those deemed ready for departure were leaving for Israel at the rate of between five hundred to one thousand a month.

THE CONDITION OF THE EARLIER EMIGRANTS

It may be helpful to digress briefly to describe how the Ethiopian Jews in Israel were doing before the current wave of new emigrants arrived. On the whole, the Beta Israel have acclimated fairly well to Israeli economic, social, and cultural conditions. But there are still problems. "Five years after Operation Moses," one observer recently wrote, "Ethiopian Jews are embroiled in religious turmoil and heartsick for family members left behind, but making it economically in Israel."[23] As of April 1991, this was probably an accurate summary of their condition. Finding enough housing and jobs for the immigrants also continued to be problematic.

When the Ethiopians began arriving in the late 1970s, they could not have done so at a more opportune time. Migration from other areas of the world to Israel was practically nonexistent, and the organizations, personnel, and institutions dedicated to helping new arrivals were nearly idle. So when the Beta Israel arrived, their reception was relatively warm and competent, and housing and other facilities were forthcoming. Not long after they had settled into their new lives, however, dramatic changes on the world scene (the collapse of communism in Eastern Europe and the rise of *glasnost* in the Soviet Union) led many other heretofore oppressed people to seek new opportunities elsewhere, including in Israel. All of a sudden, in addition to the other problems they faced, the Beta Israel found themselves in competition with newcomers from the Soviet Union for housing, jobs, and training opportunities.

Not unexpectedly, complaints have been voiced by the Ethiopians and their Israeli supporters. The complaints include, for instance, that Ethiopians located in Kiryat Gat, one of the older settlements, have been abandoned in the absorption centers, with no jobs, no further training, and inadequate housing. According to the complaints, this situation was complicated by the arrival of the Russian Jews, which made orphans of the Ethiopians. One Israeli official said, "What really galls me is that the Ethiopians never saw Israel as a second choice. This is where they always wanted to be," in contrast to the Soviets, most of whom preferred other countries as their first choice.[24] Many of the Beta Israel and a number of their supporters believe the Beta Israel have been forgotten and that they have many problems that need to be resolved if their continued search for effective adjustment in Israel is to succeed. Indeed, it may be true that the Ethiopian emigrants need more education, training, and material assistance than the Russians and other refugees from relatively developed societies. This needs to be taken into full account. At the same time those from the former Soviet Union also needed jobs appropriate to their training and skills, but enough jobs were not available.

Epilogue

Though there have been many success stories among the Ethiopian emigrants (for example, some of the younger generation have joined the Israeli armed forces, where they have distinguished themselves in valor and intelligence),[25] and others were doing very well at their studies, many others are unemployed or underemployed. In spite of the official policy of the Israeli government and the Jewish Agency to scatter the Ethiopians throughout the country to avoid the creation of "African ghettos," many of the absorption centers, which were intended to be temporary measures, were converted to apartments. They became permanent residences because of a lack of appropriate housing. Though many of the emigrants, especially the elderly, had a strong desire to live as near as possible to relatives and friends, many younger Beta Israel who remained in the converted absorption centers complained about their lack of employment opportunities, and the older people felt isolated from their children, who, they said, came to visit only during the weekly Sabbath or even less frequently. The authorities had tried to provide housing arrangements that kept children and their parents together; the small size of the apartments had led to overcrowding, conflict, and even divorce. The lot of the older generations seems unlikely to improve in the near future, given their limited language and other coping skills. The younger generations, who had not secured the kind of work and living conditions they desired, were also dissatisfied.[26] Nevertheless, these earlier arrivals have acquired many useful language and social skills that will be shared gladly with the newcomers.

OPERATION SOLOMON

The 1989 agreement between the governments of Ethiopia and Israel provided for a plan to complete the Beta Israel exodus in two years. This program of gradual, orderly departure was intended to benefit the two governments and the Beta Israel themselves. It would allow the Israeli immigration authorities sufficient time to thoroughly screen and certify the emigrants before they arrived in Israel. It gave the Ethiopian government time to make sure that non-Jews were not taking advantage of the opportunity to emigrate. And it allowed the Israeli and North American volunteer agencies to establish and coordinate the training programs required to equip this rural people with the rudimentary skills they needed to function reasonably well after their arrival in Israel. Because total monthly departures were relatively small, the program also could be portrayed to the Ethiopian general public and the international community as a limited operation undertaken mainly for the purpose of family reunification. For a time, these mutual advantages encouraged the cooperation of all parties concerned, but in Ethiopia military events were overtaking political plans.

In early March 1991, it was becoming common knowledge that the Ethiopian insurgents were making steady gains in their struggle against the increasingly demoralized government forces, and foreign residents in Addis Ababa were being told by their embassies to leave the country. At this juncture, the Israelis must have decided to review other options. The first alternative they began to consider was initiation of a massive Beta Israel airlift similar to Operation Moses in 1984–85, with or without the cooperation of the host country. But proceeding without the active support of the Ethiopian government was considered very risky from all points of view. When the United States was consulted, it must have advised caution. Israel demurred but continued its airlift preparations.

The Israeli authorities must have known also that there was no assurance that a new Ethiopian government would be sympathetic to or easily bought or influenced to allow the continuation of Beta Israel departures. In fact, given the reported Israeli provision of military supplies to the Mengistu government, equipment that was eventually used against the Eritreans in the port city of Massawa and elsewhere, it was possible that once the insurgents gained power they would want to take revenge against Israel and refuse to permit the Beta Israel exodus.[27] In addition, the leadership of the Tigrean and Eritrean rebel forces had maintained friendly relationships, at one time or another, with a number of Arab states, including Iraq, Saudi Arabia, Syria, and Libya. So all the evidence indicated that drastic measures might be required to accelerate the exodus before the insurgents took power.

The Israeli plans proved prudent. On May 21, 1991, Mengistu Hailemariam, who had ruled Ethiopia since 1977, resigned his presidency and fled the country for Zimbabwe.[28] His vice president, Lieutenant General Tesfaye Kidane, who had been appointed to that position two weeks before, assumed power as acting president. Before Mengistu's dramatic flight, President George Bush, at the urgent request of Prime Minister Yitzhak Shamir of Israel, had written a letter to Mengistu asking him to permit unusual Israeli measures to get the

Beta Israel out of Addis Ababa. Mengistu had relented, but he fled the country before the request was implemented. Now, the Israeli government wanted to put its plans into full operation. In order to forestall any unpleasant confrontations with the forces of the government now headed by Tesfaye, Shamir contacted his friend in Washington again, and, on Thursday, May 23, the president directed a renewed request to Tesfaye. The request was granted.

The next afternoon, an assortment of unmarked Israeli military and civilian planes began to descend on the international airport at Addis Ababa. The first plane carried armed security forces, the second doctors and other support personnel. Operation Solomon, as it came to be known, was in full swing. Less than thirty-six hours later, 14,087 Ethiopian Jews had been airlifted to Tel Aviv. At one point during the operation, there were twenty-eight planes in the air between Israel and Ethiopia (at least one Ethiopian airliner also took part in Operation Solomon). About five hundred people who were considered non-Jews were left behind in the refugee camps in Addis Ababa. Another two thousand Beta Israel, unable to reach Addis Ababa in time to join the exodus, were still in the Beta Israel villages in Gondar.[29]

For all intents and purposes, the decades-old saga of Beta Israel emigration and many of the problems associated with it are over. Fully aware of the need for large amounts of financial aid to rehabilitate, educate, house, and provide jobs for this huge number of rural people, and the fact that appeals for help would be directed to the U.S. government, the Jewish Agency of Israel has stated that, following the express wishes of the United States, as long as the Ethiopian Jews are under its care, it will not settle any of them in the occupied West Bank.[30]

Over the last decade, the emigration of this humble community of Africans, a process so full of drama and local, regional, and international political intrigue, shrouded with great tragedy and finally crowned with a measure of triumph, had become a gripping story. The great challenge for the future will be how to settle, educate, and eventually help the Beta Israel to become productive citizens of their new home. Judging by the experiences of those who emigrated to Israel in the mid-1980s, formidable challenges await the new arrivals, especially the older generation.[31] But this latest group of emigrants from Ethiopia has one important advantage. They will realize significant moral and psychological benefit from the presence of some twenty thousand compatriots who had preceded them to Israel and can be expected to welcome the Operation Solomon refugees with joy and relief.

The immigrants from Ethiopia, the last Jewish group to arrive, came from very rural areas of Ethiopia. Their economic, social, and cultural needs are many and complex. They have to be educated, socialized, trained, housed, and eventually provided with meaningful jobs. To carry out such tasks is very expensive, and Israel does not have unlimited resources. But on the positive side, the Ethiopians by and large are very eager to learn. They still have unbelievably high confidence in their identity and their abilities to succeed in Israel. These assets need to be nurtured and developed by policymakers and society in general. If the authorities continue to insist on putting time limits on the amount of schooling to be provided, for instance, or on the kind of educational and training provisions in policies formulated for another group of immigrants, they would have missed the opportunity of facilitating the early and orderly integration of the community into the mainstream of society. The Ethiopians are a very small minority even by Israeli standards. They will not be a viable group on their own as other immigrant groups are. As they seek to grow and join the mainstream of society, they need constant financial and psychological support from governmental and private organizations. To the extent that the necessary supports are forthcoming and informed by enlightened understanding, the Ethiopian immigrants will emerge as worthy citizens of their new home.

Notes

CHAPTER ONE

1. The only ones still in Ethiopia, as far as can be determined, are those who had been converted to Christianity and are now seeking to reclaim their ancestral identity. Some three thousand of these people are still in camps in Addis Ababa waiting for favorable decision from Israel. In Israel, the debate about whether to let them come in or not is continuing. Whether the new Labor government headed by Prime Minister Rabin will be favorably disposed remains to be seen.
2. See Rivka Bar-Yosef, "Desocialization and Resocialization: The Adjustment Process of Immigrants," in Ernest Krausz, ed., *Migration, Ethnicity and Community* (New Brunswick and London: Transaction Books, 1980), pp. 19-37.
3. S. N. Eisenstadt, *The Absorption of Immigrants* (London: Routledge & Kegan Paul, 1954).
4. Erik H. Erikson, *Childhood and Society* (London: Imago, 1957).
5. R. K. Merton, *Social Theory and Social Structure* (Glencoe: Free Press, 1957).
6. See note 1 above.
7. Eisenstadt, *The Absorption of Immigrants*, pp. 1-26.
8. Edward Ullendorff, *The Ethiopians: An Introduction to the Country and People* (London: Oxford University Press, 1960).
9. The *Kibre Negest*, originally rendered in Ge'ez and whose last part was completed in the early part of the fourteenth century, is held in great esteem by the people of highland Ethiopia and it has been the source of legitimacy for the political and cultural arrangements that prevailed for a thousand years. See Donald N. Levine, *Greater Ethiopia* (Chicago: University of Chicago Press, 1974), pp. 92-112.

NOTES

10. In his recent book journalist Graham Hancock argues that the Ark of the Covenant was transferred from Jerusalem to the Egyptian island of Elephantine, from there to an island on Lake Tana in Ethiopia, and eventually to Axum where it resides now. He also quotes a leading Beta Israel *kes* (priest), Raphael Hadane (Adane), who is living in Israel, to support this thesis. See Graham Hancock, *The Sign and the Seal* (New York: Crown, 1992), pp. 425-27.

11. Refer to Zephaniah, 3:10.

12. Eric Payne, *Ethiopian Jews: The Story of a Mission* (London: Olive Press, 1972).

13. Acts of the Apostles, 8:26.

14. See Ullendorff, *The Ethiopians*; Wolf Leslau, *Falasha Anthology* (New Haven and London: Yale University Press, 1951); David Kessler, *The Falashas: The Forgotten Jews of Ethiopia* (London: George Allen & Unwin, 1982); Robert Hess, ed., *Proceedings of the Fifth International Conference of Ethiopian Studies*, Session B (Chicago: University of Chicago, 1978); Arnold Jones and Elizabeth Monroe, *A History of Ethiopia* (London: Oxford Clarendon Press, 1955); and Henry A. Stern, *Wanderings among the Falashas in Abyssinia*, 2nd ed. (London: Frank Cass & Co., 1968).

15. Ullendorff, *The Ethiopians*. See also Kay K. Shelemay, *Music, Ritual, and Falasha History* (East Lansing: Michigan State University Press, 1986), 197-226.

16. Robert L. Hess, in Stern, *Wanderings among the Falashas*, pp. xxi-xxxi.

17. Ibid. For the background on the struggle between the Muslim and Christian forces and the coming of the Portuguese, see Richard Pankhurst, *An Introduction to the Economic History of Ethiopia*, (London: Lalibela House, 1961), pp. 75-89.

18. Payne, *Ethiopian Jews*, p. 12.

19. Pankhurst, *An Introduction to the Economic History*, pp. 284-86.

20. Edward Gibbons, *The Rise and Fall of the Roman Empire*, Vol. II, (Chicago: Encyclopedia Britannica, 1952), pp. 159-60.

21. Kessler, *The Falashas*.

22. Leslau, *Falasha Anthology*; see also Wolf Leslau, "A Falasha Religious Dispute," *Proceedings of the American Academy for Jewish Research* 11 (1947): 71-95.

23. See Stern, *Wanderings among the Falashas*. For a general understanding of the historical relations between the state and religion, see Taddesse Tamrat, *Church and State in Ethiopia* (1270-1527, London: Oxford University Press, 1972).

24. Payne, *Ethiopian Jews*.

25. For an evaluation of the mission's activities see Steven Kaplan, "The Falasha and the Mission: A Note on an Encounter," *Proceedings of the Ninth International Congress of Ethiopian Studies* (Moscow: The USSR Academy of Sciences, 1988), pp. 116-22.

26. Joseph Halevy, "Excursion chez le Falacha en Abyssinie," *Bulletin de la Société de Geographie* 17 (1869): 270-94. See also *Travels in Abyssinia*, enlarged translation from Halevy's account by James Picciotto, 1877.

27. Halevy, *Travels in Abyssinia*, pp. 324-25.

28. Leslau, *Falasha Anthology*.

29. Ullendorff, *The Ethiopians*.

30. Halevy, *Travels in Abyssinia*, p. 227.

31. H. Nahum, "Mission chez les Falachas," *Bulletin de l'Alliance Israelite Universelle* 33 (1908) 110-37.

32. This does not mean that there was no discrimination against them; there was. In the school context, discrimination is subtle and most of the time passes unnoticed by the non-Beta Israel.

Notes

33. Leslau, *Falasha Anthology*.
34. See Leviticus, 6:25, 22:6-7.
35. Payne, *Ethiopian Jews*, p. 23.
36. Leslau, *Falasha Anthology*, p. xix.
37. For traditional conventions, protocols, and role expectations among the various elements of traditional Ethiopian society, see Mahitemeselassie Gebremaskel, *Zikra Neger*, (Addis Ababa: Berhanina Selam, 1942 E.C. [Ethiopian Calendar].
38. Leslau, *Falasha Anthology*.
39. Both Rabbi Yosef Adane, the only Beta Israel rabbi who was trained and ordained in Israel, and Addisu Messele, the most prominent young leader of the community in Israel, related to me how they were subjected to harassment by their fellow students in the city of Gondar.
40. G. J. Abbink, "The Falashas in Ethiopia and Israel: The Problem of Cultural Assimilation," doctoral thesis, Institute for Cultural and Social Anthropology, 15, Nijemegen, Neth., 1984.
41. Saladin, who drove the Crusaders from Jerusalem in 1187, was successfully persuaded by King Lalibela of Ethiopia, who had just come to power to grant the Ethiopian Christian community a piece of the holy place. See Sergew Hable-Selassie, *Ancient and Medieval Ethiopian History to 1270* (Addis Ababa: Haile Selassie University, 1972), p. 262; Hancock, *The Sign and the Seal*, pp. 86, 106-8, 359; David Buxton, *The Abyssinians* (London: Thames & Hudson, 1970), p. 44.
42. See Teshome G. Wagaw, "Ethiopia, Israel, and the Resettlement of the Falashas," *CAAS Newsletter* (Winter 1986): 1-11. For their ordeals during the emigration process see Teshome G. Wagaw, "The International Political Ramifications of Falasha Emigration." *Journal of Modern African Studies*, 29, 4 (1991): 557-81.

CHAPTER TWO

1. Judah Matras, "The Jewish Population: Growth, Expansion of Settlement, and Changing Composition," in S. N. Eisenstadt, Rivka Bar-Yosef, and Chaim Adler, eds., *Integration and Development in Israel* (New York: Praeger, 1970), pp. 308-39; and S. N. Eisenstadt, *The Absorption of Immigrants* (London: Routledge & Kegan Paul, 1954), pp. 47-104.
2. Sammy Smooha, *Israel: Pluralism and Conflict* (Berkeley and Los Angles: University of California Press, 1978), p. 181.
3. Matras, "The Jewish Population," p. 310.
4. See H. H. Ben-Sasson, ed., *A History of the Jewish People* (Cambridge, Mass.: Harvard University Press, 1976), pp. 991-1000.
5. See Matras, "The Jewish Population," pp. 314-15.
6. However, the number of Jews who have migrated to Israel is disappointing to those who had hoped for mass relocation. As R. B. Schmerl observed after reading this chapter: "That hasn't happened. By far the largest Jewish community in the world is American, with over five million Jews. Only an insignificant number of American Jews have emigrated to Israel. I suspect that more Israelis have come to the U.S. than Americans have moved to Israel."
7. Smooha, *Israel: Pluralism and Conflict*, p. 381.

NOTES

8. S. N. Eisenstadt, *Israeli Society* (New York: Basic Books, 1967), p. 61; Yakov Imram, "Changing Patterns of Immigrant Absorption in Israel: Educational Implications," *Thirtieth Annual Conference of the Comparative and International Education Society*, Toronto, March 1986, pp. 3-5.

9. The perspective contained in this paragraph was suggested by R. B. Schmerl of the University of Hawaii.

10. See Matras, "The Jewish Population," pp. 319-321.

11. Imram, "Changing Patterns," p. 6; and Matras, "The Jewish Population," pp. 317-19.

12. There are also small Jewish sects which are often referred to as marginal. Such groups include the Karaites and the Samaritans. It is not clear from my sources, however, how these groups are classified for census purposes. The details of the history, beliefs, and practices of the two sects are found in Alan D. Crown, "The Samaritans in 1984," *Yod* 10, 20 (1984): 9-31; and Mordecai Roshwald, "Marginal Jewish Sects in Israel II," *International Journal of Middle East Studies* 4 (1973): 328-34.

13. *Modernization* is often synonymous with *Westernization* as defined and used here.

14. See Smooha, *Israel: Pluralism and Conflict*; Alex Weingrod, Israel: Group Relations in a New Society (London: Pall Mall Press, 1965); Rivka Bar-Yosef, "The Moroccans: Background to the Problem," in Eisenstadt, Bar-Yosef, and Adler, *Integration and Development* pp. 419-28; and Jeff Halper, "The Absorption of Ethiopian Immigrants: A Return to the Fifties," in Michael Ashkenazi and Alex Weingrod, *Ethiopian Jews and Israel* (New Brunswick: Transaction Books, 1987), pp. 112-36.

15. For a critique of such policy, see Halper, "The Absorption of Ethiopian Immigrants."

16. Rivka W. Bar-Yosef, "Desocialization and Resocialization: The Adjustment Process of Immigrants," in Ernest Krausz, ed., *Studies of Israeli Society* (New Brunswick: Transaction Books, 1980), pp. 19-37.

17. Vivian Z. Klaff, "Residence and Integration in Israel: A Mosaic of Segregated Groups," in Krausz, *Studies of Israeli Society*, p. 58.

18. Michael Selzer, *The Outcasts of Israel: Communal Tensions in the Jewish State* (Jerusalem: Council of the Sephardi Community, 1965); and Halper, "The Absorption of Ethiopian Immigrants."

19. Percy Cohen, "Israel's Ethnic Problems," *Jewish Journal of Sociology* 9, 1 (June 1967).

20. Judith T. Shuval, "Self-Rejection among North African Immigrants in Israel," *Israel Annals of Psychiatry and Related Disciplines* 4, 1 (1966): 101-10; Klaff, "Residence and Integration" pp. 53-71.

21. Weingrod, *Israel: Group Relations*, p. 39.

22. Roberto Bachi, "Effects of Migration on the Geographical Distribution of the Population of Israel," *Proceedings, Conference of the International Union for the Scientific Study of Population*, Sydney, Australia, 1967, p. 746.

23. See Klaff, "Residence and Integration," p. 63.

24. Ibid., p. 62.

25. Refer to Erik Cohen, "The Black Panthers and Israeli Society," in Krausz, *Studies of Israeli Society*, pp. 147-63; and Imram, "Changing Patterns," pp. 8-9.

26. Sammy Smooha and Yochanan Peres, "The Dynamics of Ethnic Inequalities: The Case of Israel," in Krausz, *Studies of Israeli Society*, pp.: 165-81; Cohen, "The Black Panthers," pp. 147-63.

Notes

27. Ibid., pp. 165-81.
28. See Imram, "Changing Patterns."
29. Ibid., p. 6.
30. Chaim Adler, "School Integration in the Context of the Development of Israel's Educational System," in Yehuda Amir and Miriam Rivner, *School Desegregation: Cross Cultural Perspectives* (Hillsdale, N.J.: Lawrence Erlbaum Associates, 1983), pp. 21-45.
31. Imram, "Changing Patterns."
32. Ibid., pp. 16, 18-19.
33. The Ministry of Education and Culture also supervises a parallel education system for Israel's Arab population. The Jewish and Arab populations agree that they prefer having separate systems of education for their communities to accommodate their respective linguistic, religious, and cultural traditions. Hence, with the exception of tertiary-level education, the two communities send their children to their own schools. Arabs comprise 17 percent of the total population of Israel. Among the Arab population, 80 percent are Muslim and the remainder are Druze and Christian. The languages of instruction in the Arab schools are Arabic and English; Hebrew is taught as a third language. The disadvantage of this arrangement is that at the university level, Hebrew is the primary language of instruction and examination. As a result, Arabs are underrepresented at this level. Because of a lack of qualified teachers, insufficient teaching-learning aids, and inadequate buildings and facilities, the quality of Arab education in Israel is below the standard enjoyed by the Jewish population. National laws such as compulsory education and the education of girls as well as boys apply equally to the Arab and Jewish populations.
34. Eisenstadt, *Israeli Society*, p. 267.
35. Adler, "School Integration."
36. Smooha, Israel: *Pluralism and Conflict*, p. 265.

CHAPTER THREE

1. The term *Falasha* has been commonly used within and outside Ethiopia; it derives from the Ge'ez or Amharic word *meflas*, "to remove."
2. The monarchy was periodically challenged by some *agew* usurpers such as those of Lalibela fame who ruled between the tenth and thirteenth centuries. In 1270, the throne was restored to the Solomonic line and, with a few exceptions in the nineteenth century, continued until the overthrow of Emperor Haile Selassie in 1974 and his mysterious death while under house arrest a year later.
3. The Ethiopia of that time, or Abyssinia proper, was confined to highland Ethiopia, which became the strong home base of the two major monotheistic peoples, the Jews and Christians.
4. One of the difficulties for the Beta Israel people has been and continues to be this lack of total recognition of their full Jewishness both by the people in their land of origin and by other Jews in Israel. The continued controversy over reconversion issues in Israel is directly linked to this vital question.
5. Some speak of the Beta Israel *versus* the Amharas. This contrast is misleading. The Jews are Amhara. It should be, rather, the Jews versus the Orthodox Christians.

NOTES

6. The Beta Israel as a minority were for the most part landless. In a society where land was highly valued not only for its economic worth but for its psychological importance and prestige as well, to be without land was more than being poor; it made one subject to severe exploitation. To compensate for their poverty, the Beta Israel concentrated on developing and perfecting skills in areas in which the other members of society were not interested but which were vital to the community and appreciated as such. Nonetheless, the perfection of skills also aroused other types of problems, such as the *taib* syndrome mentioned above.

7. The Democratic Charter, announced in 1976, simply states that all religious, linguistic, and ethnic groups of Ethiopia will enjoy freedom and equal rights without any interference by the government. This means that the power of the state church was no more and that the Beta Israel, as one such group, presumably would enjoy equality in all sectors of national life. See Teshome Wagaw, "Emerging Issues of Ethiopian Nationalities: Cohesion or Disintegration," *Journal of Northeast African Studies* 2, 3 (1980-81): 69-75; and Teshome Wagaw, *The Development of Higher Education and Social Change: An Ethiopian Experience* (East Lansing: Michigan State University Press, 1990).

8. See David Kessler, *The Falashas: The Forgotten Jews of Ethiopia* (New York: Schocken Books, 1985).

9. For the politicization of the students and their roles in social change, see Teshome Wagaw, "The Burden and Glory of Being Schooled: An Ethiopian Dilemma," in Seven Rubenson, eds, *Proceedings of the Seventh International Conference of Ethiopian Studies*, University of Lund, 26-29 April 1982 (Uppsala: Scandinavian Institute of African Studies, 1984), pp. 487-96.

10. The strength of the armed forces has grown by leaps and bounds in the last decade. For instance, in 1974, the combined total was fifty thousand men, including the police force. By the mid-1980s, that number had grown to a three-hundred-thousand-man standing force, making one of the poorest countries in Africa the first in military power after Egypt.

11. Payne and Parafit both assert that during this period, the Israeli government also was assisting in development projects among the Beta Israel areas until it was frightened by what this might eventually entail, i.e., the desire on the part of the Ethiopians to want to immigrate en masse to Israel, for which it was not prepared even to imagine. Eric Payne, *Ethiopian Jews: The Story of a Mission* (London: Olive Press, 1972), pp. 30-60; and Tudor Parafit, *Operation Moses* (London: Widenfeld and Nicholson, 1986) pp. 39-41.

12. As noted above, under the new Marxist government of Ethiopia, the special privileges of the Ethiopian Orthodox Church as a state church were done away with. From now on, presumably all religions would be treated on the same footing without any partiality. This change might have inspired hope on the part of the minority religious communities, including the Beta Israel.

13. This information was provided in July 1985 by Michael Baruch Eshkol, who was part of the leadership, and is now living in Kiryat Gat, Israel. Ironically, ORT's activities (improving the lot of the Beta Israel in Ethiopia) also were opposed by certain Jewish organizations, such as the American Association for Ethiopian Jews, for trying to subvert the plans to help the Ethiopians migrate to Israel. Also see Leon Shapiro, *The History of ORT* (New York: Schocken Books, 1980), pp. 321-24.

14. Payne, *Ethiopian Jews*.

15. Edward Ullendorff, *The Ethiopians: An Introduction to the Country and People* (London: Oxford University Press, 1972) pp. 110-12; Wolf Leslau, *Falasha Anthology* (New Haven and London: Yale University Press, 1951) p. xli; G. J. Abbink, *The Falashas in Ethiopia and Israel: The Problem of Cultural Assimilation* (Nijemegen, Neth.: Institute for Cultural and Social Anthropology, 1984) doctoral thesis, pp. 110-11.

16. The term *legal* here is used in the sense that the act was carried out with deliberate cooperation of the constituted government even if that government itself was not constituted legally. Otherwise, there was no statute that provided for the act of emigration.

17. Parafit, *Operation Moses*, pp. 35-62.

18. These early conflicts continue to influence current alliances and government policies in the region. See "In Sudan, Tide Turns against the U.S.," *New York Times*, April 29, 1986.

19. The maltreatments are reportedly from Sudanese camp officials as well as from non-Jewish Ethiopians. To the extent that they were identified as Jews in an Arab country, perhaps this was not surprising. The motive of the Ethiopians who might have participated in the maltreatment of the Beta Israel may lie in the need to survive amid very limited resources and/or may be a result of traditional religious prejudices brought with them from Ethiopia.

20. Interviews with the survivors in Jerusalem, July 1985.

21. Major Melaku Teferra was born and raised in Debre Tabor, Gondar region, and is a graduate of the elite Harar Military Academy. His relatives were important government officials throughout the reign of Haile Selassie. He, however, is not only one of the original members of the Derg but a very fanatical one. This might have stemmed from either his need to prove himself a radical Marxist in the eyes of other Derg members or, as some have suggested, his will to avenge past grievances his relatives might have had against the Beta Israel. At any rate, in his positions as governor of Gondar and, more recently, regional representative to the Communist party, he has done more physical, mental, and property damage in the area than any of the other Derg members, with the exception of Lieutenant-Colonel Mengistu Hailemariam, the Derg's chairman and later president of the country. When the Mengistu government was overthrown in May 1991 and he fled to Zimbabwe as a refugee, many of his cronies were apprehended and as of June 1992 were languishing in prison awaiting trial. Melaku Teferra, however, escaped, and his whereabouts are unknown.

22. The Reagan administration already had committed some resources for the operation, but these were neither large nor public up to this time.

23. Nimeiri was right to fear what this might entail. As a member of the Arab League, he could not have taken steps that might seem cooperative with Israel and hope to stay in power. His country was not Egypt, and Egypt, though it might have sympathized with his conditions, could not openly have supported his actions. How much empathy he was getting from the American and Israeli governments was never clear.

24. Parafit, *Operation Moses*, p. 96.

25. This exchange was dramatized during the official trial of Momar Tayeb in the fall of 1985 in the Sudan. See note 37 below.

26. Most of the major Israeli and international papers scrambled for the news. See "An Airlift to the Promised Land," Time, February 14, 1985; "Politicians Wrangle over Secrecy Breakdown," *Jerusalem Post*, January 7, 1985; "An Unfinished Rescue," *Jerusa-*

lem Post, January 6, 1985; "Ethiopians Upset and Bitter over Airlift Halt," *Jerusalem Post*, January 6, 1985; "Airline Stops Ethiopian Rescue," "U.S. Officials Angered by Lifting of Censorship," and "Belgian Charter Firm: 'Publicity Stopped Us,'" *Jerusalem Post*, January 7, 1985.

27. "An Exodus Mired in Politics," *Macleans*, January 21, 1985.

28. Mengistu Hailemariam, TV interview, Canadian Broadcasting Service, May 1985.

29. See "Sudanese Officials to Visit Moscow," *Washington Post*, January 18, 1986.

30. See "In Sudan, Tide Turns against U.S.," *New York Times*, April 29, 1986.

31. "Ex-Sudan Aide Gets Two Jail Terms for Role in Ethiopian Airlift," *New York Times*, April 6, 1986.

32. In December 1985, at an international conference in Nigeria, I had a chance to discuss the issue of the trials with one university chancellor and two professors of political science. They were unanimous that the cooperation of Sudan in the airlift was wrong. But each gave different reasons. The chancellor maintained that Sudan should not have helped Israel in any way. The second man maintained that the major crime was making the Sudanese security apparatus available to the service of foreign governments. The third one, admitting that the trials were the most popular entertainment in the country then, said that for Nimeiri's government to have accepted money for cooperation in the airlift was an insult to the Sudanese people. All three said they had nothing against the Ethiopian Jews themselves.

33. See, for example, "U.S. Fearing 'Another Tehran' Plans Partial Pullout from Sudan," *New York Times*, April 17, 1986; "Embassy Threatened," *New York Times*, April 17, 1986, p. 9; and "Sudan: Qaddafi Calling," *Newsweek*, April 14, 1986.

CHAPTER FOUR

1. In May 1991, another massive airlift known as Operation Solomon, brought about 14,500 more immigrants to Israel. This latest addition is not treated in this book. It will be mentioned in the final chapter.

2. In some of the youth centers where the two groups live together, the differences are apparent. On occasion, there have been fights between the two groups. The rural youth accuse those coming from the urban centers of wanting to have it both ways. That is, because of their good education and the modernizing influences of the cities, the urban youth were relatively well off and well accepted in Ethiopia; now, once in Israel as Jews, they continue to enjoy relative advantages over youth of rural background. The latecomers also tend to maintain greater positive feelings and pride for their cultural heritage, and tend to maintain more attachment to Ethiopia in general. Where such misunderstandings occur, the authorities at such centers have tended to side with the majority, those who originate from the rural areas, on the grounds that they are more genuine Beta Israel than the others. However, veteran Ethiopians brought in to deal with such cases have warned the authorities against such discriminatory attitudes.

3. Demographic information is based on the 1986 report of the Jewish Agency in Jerusalem.

Notes

4. Once in Israel, the traditional skills men possessed, such as farming, masonry, weaving, and the like, have become nonfunctional. Therefore, in the new situation, the lack of usable skills applies to men as well as women.

5. Based on data obtained from a publication of the Jewish Agency and the Ministry of Immigrant Absorption, Government of Israel, titled, "The Absorption of Ethiopian Jews: A Master Plan," Jerusalem, August 1985, pp. 23-26. The total 1988 Ministry of Immigrant Absorption estimate of the Beta Israel population was sixteen thousand. This total takes into account, as the document does not, the number of Beta Israel already in the country before 1980 (about four hundred), those who arrived in small groups or individually since 1985, and those born in Israel subsequent to immigration.

6. S. N. Eisenstadt, *The Absorption of Immigrants* (London: Routledge & Kegan Paul, 1954), pp. 1-26.

7. J. Faitlovich (interviewed), "The Falashas," *Jewish Chronicle*, October 27, 1905, p. 22.

8. Joseph Halevy, *Travels in Abyssinia*, 1867, translated from the French and published in English by James Picciotto, 1877. The passage quoted here is from the English version, p. 227. Halevy visited some of the Beta Israel villages in the Lake Tana area in the winter of 1864. He seems to have mastered the Amharic language well enough to understand and converse with the local population. Since his stay in Ethiopia did not exceed a year, it can be presumed that he had studied the Amharic language and perhaps Ge'ez as well (the language of liturgy at the time) before arriving in Gondar.

9. See, for instance, Donald Levine, *Wax and Gold* (Chicago: University of Chicago Press, 1965).

10. For studies regarding values and practices associated with child rearing in rural Ethiopia, see Teshome Wagaw, "Attitudes and Values concerning Children among the Menz in Rural Ethiopia," *Journal of Psychology* 94 (1976), pp. 257-60.

11. A considerable body of literature exists in this area. In the case of Ethiopia, see Teshome Wagaw, "The Burden and Glory of Being Schooled: An Ethiopian Dilemma," in Sven Rubenson, *Proceedings of the Seventh International Association of Ethiopian Studies* (Lund, Sweden: University of Lund, 1982), pp. 487-96. Also Teshome Wagaw, *The Development of Higher Education and Social Transformation: An African Experience* (East Lansing: Michigan State University Press, 1990), chapters 7-9.

12. Ibid.

13. Although these skills are not actively taught to young women in Israel because of lack of time on the part of the girls, the older women who practice them receive a handsome price for the products.

14. Rachel Astman, in charge of the planning and research department of the Ministry of Immigrant Absorption, gave these estimates. The information is consistent with that from the Jewish Agency. See the plan document of the Government of Israel, "The Absorption of Ethiopian Jews: Master Plan," Jerusalem, Summer 1985, pp. 1-151.

15. Although the establishment of the committee was known to the public, its reports remained confidential. The information was supplied to me by a committee member.

16. For the significance of this loss, see, for instance, Emanuela T. Semi, "The Beta Israel (Falashas): From Purity to Impurity," *Jewish Journal of Sociology* 27, 2 (December 1985) pp. 103-14.

17. Ibid.

NOTES

CHAPTER FIVE

1. Uri Gordon, interview, July 1985, Tel Aviv.
2. Ministry of Immigrant Absorption, "The Absorption of Ethiopian Jews: Master Plan," Jerusalem, 1986, p. 1.
3. These accounts are based on data supplied by individual informants and the Jewish Agency and, more importantly, on the report of the comptroller's office of the Israeli government, a watchdog of departmental activities. The part of the latter document entitled "Initial Absorption of the Ethiopian Immigrants," pp. 127-68, was released in 1986. Information was updated to 1987-88 by way of telephone interviews with people who have continued to be closely involved with the absorption and adaptation processes in Israel.
4. This is in addition to the forty-four or so Youth Aliyah villages that house and educate young people of high school age. (See Chapter 8 of this book.) Several other centers were especially established to care for younger orphaned children as well.
5. The authorities were acutely aware of these realities, at least at the planning stage. See Ministry of Immigrant Absorption, "The Absorption of Ethiopian Jews," pp. 3-4.
6. This analysis benefits from the evaluation of the Office of the Comptroller as outlined in its 1986 report entitled "Initial Absorption of Ethiopian Immigrants," pp. 127-68, and the reply to the same document by the Jewish Agency under the same title, February 1987, pp. 29-35.
7. Ibid., p. 131.

CHAPTER SIX

1. See Chapter 1 of this book; also S. N. Eisenstadt, *The Absorption of Immigrants* (London: Routledge & Kegan Paul, 1954), pp. 1-21.
2. For the major religious works of the Beta Israel, see Wolf Leslau, *Falasha Anthology* (New Haven: Yale University Press, 1951).
3. When they are told that the kind of Judaism they practiced in Ethiopia is outdated or has been modified by the teachings of the Oral Law, some Beta Israeli mischievously reply, "We did not know that we were to add to God's Law." They say this in spite of the fact that they made their own modifications. (Ibid.)
4. See David Kessler, *The Falashas: The Forgotten Jews of Ethiopia* (New York: Schocken Books, 1985), pp. 106-29.
5. Ibid., pp. 74-80.
6. It has been said that the resistance to grant the Beta Israel the right to immigrate to Israel for so long relates to race more than any other single factor. Other communities such as the Samaritans and the Karaites, which not only are non-Talmudic but actively refuse to be instructed in Talmud, have been accepted in Israel. The Ethiopians, while admitting that they were not versed in the Halakah or Oral Law, were at least willing to learn about it. See Kessler, *The Falashas*, pp. 58-73.
7. The contents of the memorandum and the letter are reported to exist in the files of the chief rabbinate's office. Although I was not able to review the original letters, I have no doubt that they exist and that the contents conveyed by the spokesman of the rabbinate, Rabbi Eliahu Ben Dehan, are, barring translation errors, accurate.

However, as an anthropologist who has followed the case closely stated, those were very hard days for Ethiopian Jewry. They might have promised anything. See Haim Shapiro, "Chief Rabbinate Says Documents from '66 and '71 Show: Ethiopian Jews Promised to Convert," *Jerusalem Post*, November 17, 1985.

8. Tamrat Emmanuel, a highly learned Beta Israel, suggested in the 1950s that mass migration was inadvisable. He favored sending select youth to Israel and other countries for the purpose of education and training; other changes would follow.

9. Actually, in relative terms, the lot of the Beta Israel and other minorities in Ethiopia improved. The 1976 charter established the equality of all religious and linguistic or ethnic groups in Ethiopia and abolished state support for any religious group. For a time, optimism among the Beta Israel and their supporters prevailed. Implementing the ideals embodied in the Charter proved difficult, however.

10. Secular scholarship maintained that the Beta Israel were one of a number of groups found in Ethiopia whose religious beliefs had elements of Judaism. Among the secular scholars who are often cited are Edward Ullendorff of the University of London and Wolf Leslau of the University of California. The rabbinate used this position when it demanded conversion of the *olim* in the 1980s. See Yedidya Atlas, "Rabbinical Perspective," *Jerusalem Post*, November 8, 1985.

11. For a more complete analysis, see Teshome Wagaw, "Ethiopia, Israel, and the Resettlement of the Falashas," *CAAS Newsletter* (Winter 1986): 1–11.

12. See Haim Shapiro, "Goren Himself Had Ethiopians Convert," *Jerusalem Post*, February 28, 1985.

13. See Teshome Wagaw, "The Emigration and Settlement of Ethiopian Jews in Israel," *Middle East Review* 20, 2 (1987/88): 41–48.

14. Ibid.

15. Dr. Michael Corinaldi, an Israeli lawyer who specializes in the legal affairs of marginal Jews and represents them in Israeli courts, asserted, in an interview, that the Jewishness of the Beta Israel is not the question. Their physical characteristics and religious books are similar to those obtaining in earlier Jewish traditions. The only difference is that, for a long time, the Ethiopians lacked a spokesperson who could defend their interests effectively.

16. In 1985, when the issues of conversion surfaced, two new chief rabbis—Ashkenazi Chief Rabbi Avraham Shapiro and Sephardi Chief Rabbi Mordecai Eliahu—were installed. The two former chief rabbis, Ovadia Yosef (Sephardi) and Shlomo Goren (Ashkenazi), concurred between 1973 and 1975 that the Ethiopians were Jews. Both rabbis based their judgment on the works of Eldad Hadani and, more importantly, Rabbi David Ben Zimra. Also during the tenure of Yosef and Goren *giyyur* (certificates of conversion) were issued. However, when the former chief rabbis declared in 1985 that the Ethiopians did not have to undergo mass conversion, their successors said they had contradicted themselves. The former chief rabbis denied that they had reversed themselves; if they had issued giyyur, it was only to certify the facts already in existence. See, for instance, Shapiro, "Goren Himself Had Ethiopians Convert."

17. For a more complete explanation of the chief rabbinate's position, see the article written by the spokesman for the chief rabbinate, Yedidya Atlas, "Rabbinical Perspectives."

18. The early wave of immigrants were persuaded that since they did not have the Talmud or Hebrew in their tradition, and since there might have been irregularities regarding marriages and divorce, it would be to the immigrants' long-term advantage to accept mass conversion, which they did. But even then, the Israeli public was fully

aware that other immigrants, such as the Russians, who intermarried and knew nothing about Judaism, were unconditionally accepted as Jews upon arrival in Israel. Such discrepancies contribute to ill feelings. For a more complete discussion, see Louis Rapoport, "Black Jews in Crisis," *Jerusalem Post*, international edition, April 19, 1986. For an explanation of the position of the chief rabbinate, see Atlas, "Rabbinical Perspective."

19. By now, young Beta Israel youth such as Addisu Messele, who had migrated a few years earlier with the first wave and had gone through the rituals as required, were having second thoughts about the whole issue. They began to urge the newcomers to refuse the reconversion demands.

20. The ordination of Adane antedated the migration of the Beta Israel. It was also logical that he should be consulted by the rabbinate. But politically, it proved lethal for him. The Beta Israel viewed him as a lackey of the chief rabbinate and effectively rejected his services. This was unfortunate for the community and for this intelligent, unassuming, and pleasant young man. For Adane's views of his position in relation to the Beta Israel community, see Rapoport, "Black Jews in Crisis." Adane is a young, very highly educated Beta Israel. However, since he sided with the chief rabbinate in its decisions to require the Beta Israel to go through the ritual immersion, he was effectively excluded from having any kind of influence on the immigrants. The rabbi complains that his advice is completely ignored by the Ethiopian community. See Haim Shapiro, "Ethiopian Rabbi Laments 'Strike' Damage," *Jerusalem Post*, international edition, January 18, 1986.

21. The report and recommendations of the blue-ribbon committee are in, "Public Statement," *Jerusalem Post*, September 29, 1985.

22. Ibid.

23. Actually, some of the more thoughtful citizens thought that, contrary to reports in the media dominated by liberal secularists, "there was no groundswell of support for the Ethiopian cause." For an articulate assessment of this and other aspects of the controversy, see Rapoport, "Black Jews in Crisis."

24. This assertion is only partially true. As the rabbinate points out, some five hundred immigrants a year undergo the conversion requirements. Also, in the 1960s, the Benei Israel (Jews from India) were required to undergo reconversion. After bitter protests, however, the requirement was dropped. Many Russian immigrants who intermarried with Gentiles and knew very little, if anything, about Halakah and other aspects of Judaism, were admitted without the conversion requirements. The Beta Israel are aware of these cases and effectively use them to advance their cause. See S. N. Eisenstadt, *Israeli Society* (New York: Basic Books, 1967), pp. 312–16; and Elizer Jaffe, "Ethiopian Politics," *Jerusalem Post*, October 1, 1985.

25. I was in Kiryat Arba, a Jewish settlement in the historic city of Hebron, when the protests were beginning to emerge. The Ethiopians were confused. Some veteran Israelis were urging them not to sit and wait but to get up and march.

26. See "Ethiopians Threaten Suicide," *Jerusalem Post*, July 19, 1985.

27. Judy Siegel, "Ethiopians Meet Peres," *Jerusalem Post*, July 22, 1985.

28. Haim Shapiro, "Ethiopians Are Cautious about Peres' Formula," *Jerusalem Post*, July 24, 1985.

29. The question of who is a Jew is the subject of much discussion and disagreement. The generally accepted definition is that anyone born of a Jewish mother is a Jew. But there are problems involving conversion. Until 1989, the Israeli rabbinate resisted recognition of anyone converted by Reform and Progressive branches of Juda-

ism. Yet the overwhelming majority of Diaspora Jews are members of these movements. The case of Shoshanna Miller, who was converted to Judaism in the United States and wanted to migrate to Israel, is instructive. The Israeli minister of interior refused to register her as a Jew. After months of legal battles, the high court ruled in her favor. It was not until 1989 that the Israeli Supreme Court ruled that persons converted to Judaism by non-Orthodox rabbis have the right to migrate to Israel as Jews. See "Israeli Supreme Court Rules on 'Who Is a Jew' Argument," *Ann Arbor News*, July 25, 1989.

30. It is standard procedure that all Jewish women are immersed before marriage. It is the immersion of the prospective groom that is problematic.

31. The Beta Israel must have gotten their inspiration from the Benei Israel, who had similar grievances in the 1960s. See Eisenstadt, *Israeli Society*, pp. 312-14.

32. Jaffe, "Ethiopian Politics."

33. Abba Eban, "Religious Challenge," *Jerusalem Post*, July 19, 1985.

34. The rabbinate was always sensitive to what it considered its prerogatives vis-à-vis the office of the prime minister. See Atlas, "Rabbinical Perspectives"; and Eban, "Public Statement"

35. Many supporters of the Ethiopians now believe the strikers made a gross blunder by not accepting the terms offered. With the holy days coming, the rabbinate was more likely to be conciliatory, and the strikers would have gained much more public support. In part, this is attributed to the lack of sophistication about political realities in Israel on the part of the strike leaders.

36. "Till the Next Time," *Jerusalem Post*, October 4, 1985.

37. In Israel, for a long time, only the Orthodox stream of Judaism had the right to interpret, decide, and implement the rules governing marriage and divorce and determining who is a Jew. The others, including the Reform and Conservative branches, remained powerless. In 1987, the highest court of Israel ruled that persons converted to Judaism by non-Orthodox rabbis have the right to come to Israel as Jews. See "Israeli Supreme Court Rules."

38. In addition, mostly in highland Ethiopia, there are other names given to older brothers and sisters, uncles, aunts, grandparents, and older people. See Susan Hoben, "Kin Terms of Reference and Kin Terms of Address in Amharic of Menz," in Harold Marcus, ed., *Proceedings of the First U.S. Conference on Ethiopian Studies*, East Lansing, Mich., 1973, pp. 279-89.

39. Some Ethiopians continue to use their original names when they introduce themselves to strangers. Others use both names. A few have reverted entirely to their original names.

40. Eisenstadt, *The Absorption of Immigrants*, pp. 1-26.

41. When I visited Bogale at his home in July 1985, he let me feel and understand that he was very concerned with the plight of the immigrants in Israel. He said leadership was lacking and the immigrants were adrift. As in Ethiopia, the Ethiopians in Israel were ungrateful and suspicious of the motives of others. He compared his efforts on behalf of the Beta Israel to those of Haile Selassie on behalf of Ethiopia. With dedication, both did what they could for their people, though the efforts were not appreciated. I came to feel that he wished the Israeli authorities would give him some well-deserved recognition for his accomplishments and allow him to continue to provide leadership. This feeling of not being recognized in Israel has been mentioned by others. See, for instance, Ruth Gruber, *Rescue* (New York: Atheneum, 1987), pp. 99-133.

42. Leslau, *Falasha Anthology*.

43. For an interesting analysis of the relationships and significance of rituals and leadership, see T. E. Semi, "The Beta Israel (Falashas): From Purity to Impurity," *Jewish Journal of Sociology* 27, 2 (December 1985): 103–14.

44. Official announcements and declarations by the emperors, including Haile Selassie, began with *"Mo anbessa Ze-imnegede yihuda. . . . Kibuae egziabher, nigusa-negest Ze-Ethiopia"* ("Of the tribe of Judah. . . . Anointed of God, king of kings of Ethiopia").

45. The leaders of student organizations in Ethiopia were leftist, and some individuals may have been communists. It would not be surprising if the Beta Israel youth now leading their respective organizations in Israel are of similar persuasion. One of the leaders, Addisu Messele, did not disavow the claim.

46. There are exceptions, of course. For instance, some young people are conservative and nonliterate, and some older nonliterate members are progressive in their outlook. In general, however, the categorization applies. It should be remembered that the schooled youth are still in the minority—they represent about 37 percent of the relevant age groups and an even smaller percentage of the entire Beta Israel population.

47. See Leslau, *Falasha Anthology*, p. xxiii.

48. As of 1985, seven such *amutot*, or nonprofit, organizations were registered with the Ministry of Interior.

49. Jaffe, "Ethiopian Politics."

50. This can be explained in terms of ethnic disharmony and conflict of interest. The Tigray and other groups had arrived in Israel before 1984. They went through immersion and other requirements and had some additional time to adjust to the environment. As a result, their concerns are a little different from the others, and they are less involved in many of the activities.

51. These views were expressed during a series of interviews with the respective leaders in Jerusalem and Tel Aviv in the spring of 1987.

52. See Jaffe's excellent analysis of the leadership dilemma in "Ethiopian Politics."

53. Ibid.

54. Addisu Messele's critics maintain that he exploits the sentiments of the uneducated segment of the Beta Israel population; they also challenge his estimations of the number who support him.

55. At one juncture, some Knesset members expressed a need to investigate the communist influence among the leadership. The idea was quickly rejected by other politicians.

CHAPTER SEVEN

1. Several of the seven universities have teacher-training components. The most important for the religious system is Bar Ilan University, which is a religious institution. Most of the religious secondary schools are supplied with teachers educated by this institution.

2. Before I discovered the reasons for this disproportionate representation in religious schools, I shared my observation with one of the school principals;. He responded that it is God's will; "we have no say in that matter."

3. The phenomenon of religious fundamentalism in the Middle East is not limited to Islam. Israeli youth also are moving in that direction.

Notes

4. Israel's population is composed of Jews and Arabs. Within the Arab group there are Muslims, Druze, and Christians.

5. Information provided by David Pur (Ashkenazi), director of pedagogical services, Ministry of Education and Culture, Jerusalem; and Amram Melitz (Oriental), director of the religious schools of the southern region. Their views are identical regarding the general operational structure of the educational systems, although their philosophies differ for the obvious reason.

6. Israel is a democratic state within the Green Line (pre-1967 boundary) and for the Jewish segment of society. Being made up of Jews and Arabs, the State permits different types of obligations and responsibilities for Muslim, Druze and Christian citizens. For instance, for obvious reasons the Muslims do not serve in the Israeli Army.

7. The interview with Eli Dayan took place in his office in Ashkelon with the help of a translator on March 28, 1987.

8. The only exception I noticed was an American who taught English in a high school in Kiryat Arba, who insisted that the children address her as "Doctor."

9. The relationships between the northern Africans and the Ethiopians are not consistent. In the northern settlement towns, northern Africans consistently refer to the Ethiopians as "they," and this is not always said in favorable tones. Orientals in the southern region are more likely to point out the cultural affinities between themselves and the Ethiopians. They are of the opinion that the Beta Israel children are better off in schools attended mostly by Oriental children, most of whom attend religious schools. The Beta Israel do not express any preference between the Ashkenazim and Sephardim or Orientals, at least not at the verbal level.

10. Adler, one of Israel's most knowledgeable senior scholars, has studied migrant education and thinks that segregated learning, at least in the initial periods, may not be bad in itself. However, it is bad if the Beta Israel children are not exposed to the sort of stimulating experiences that come from peers who are socially different and motivated to learn.

11. In traditional Ethiopia, students were not supposed to call attention to themselves by investing time in making themselves physically attractive. Such attitudes might have spilled over to modern times.

12. The religious schools are losing students without the additional complication brought about by the presence of the Beta Israel. Personnel in the religious schools are therefore careful to avoid any situation or decision that may alienate veteran parents. But these political and practical survival considerations do not help fulfill the urgent learning needs of the Beta Israel.

13. A report issued by the government comptroller's office in 1986 indicated that although research has shown that early integration in housing resulted in an accelerated rate of absorption, the Jewish Agency kept the Ethiopians in the sheltered, protected environment of the absorption centers for too long.

CHAPTER EIGHT

1. See Teshome Wagaw, "Education and Society in Contemporary Ethiopia," *Proceedings of the Ninth International Congress of Ethiopian Studies*, Moscow, 1986, pp. 34–43.

NOTES

2. Birth records are not kept in the parts of Ethiopia where most of the Beta Israel come from. School records are not available because many left the country secretly.

3. B. Bentwich, *Education in Israel* (London: Routledge & Kegan Paul, 1965), p. 121.

4. Jewish Agency, "Youth Aliyah: Graphic Report," Jerusalem, 1986-87, pp. 1-7.

5. Nadine Caspi ed., *Bulletin* (Jerusalem: Jewish Agency, June 1985).

6. Hofim is sponsored by the Canadian Hadassah-WIZO and is operated by the Youth Aliyah Department of the Jewish Agency. Rabbi Cohen and his wife were awarded the Knesset Speaker's Prize in 1985 for their leadership in the institution that contributed the most to the quality of life in Israel, specifically for services to the Ethiopian youth and children.

7. In May 1987, this occurred in the context of Jerusalem Day as a part of the celebration of the twentieth anniversary of the reunification of the city following the 1967 war and the defeat of Jordan.

8. No one says these institutions are adequate substitutes. But in the absence of the primary educative forces that intact homes usually provide, institutions such as Youth Aliyah may represent the next best alternative.

9. See Teshome G. Wagaw, "Ethiopia, Israel, and the Resettlement of the Falashas," *CAAS Newsletter* 2, 2 (1986): 1-11.

10. In addition, other vital documents such as marriage and divorce records were lacking which caused havoc and confusion in the delineation of legal family relationships, lineage, etc.

11. Using expressions like *group-think*, this complaint is commonly made by personnel in many of the villages.

12. The rabbinate calls it conversion; the Beta Israel and the media call it reconversion.

13. This question was raised because in some of the other institutions controlled by religious institutions, including one university, Beta Israel students had reported that faculty had become hostile toward them as a result of their refusal to follow the rabbinate requirements for reconversion. The ultra-Orthodox organization Agudat Israel has refused to accept Beta Israel students to its primary schools because of doubts raised about the authenticity of their Jewishness.

14. The Moroccans regret the loss of their culture. They came in the 1950s, when the country was under great stress, and they feel now that they were unfairly required to adopt European culture of the state and that they gave in too readily to the seduction. Today they are trying to revive their former culture which is no easy task. They hope the Ethiopians do not succumb to the "melting pot" trap.

15. The changing of names may have some rationality if done properly, that is, in consultation with the person involved or, better yet, if the concerned person initiates the change. The official reason given for the name changes is that many of the names reflect the conditions of the Diaspora, and so, once a person is in Israel, the name should fall in line with the new realities. Many well-known Israelis, such as David Ben-Gurion and Golda Meir, changed their names. Others changed their first names but retained their surnames. In the case of the Beta Israel, however, the change was complete, including those who already had Hebrew names such as Abraham, Yakov, and Sara. In retrospect, many Beta Israel consider the act an affront to their person and culture.

16. Like any other Ethiopians, the Beta Israel believe that through the intervention of the right people nearly any policy or decision can be changed. In this case, the situation was compounded by the fact that the concept of ability to learn or intelligence was not in their vocabulary. Anyone can learn, or at least earn a passing grade, goes the assumption, if only the teacher is understanding or is well disposed toward the individual. Seldom do the children or their parents say an examination was failed for lack of ability or study. Instead, phrases such as "The teacher failed me" or "The teacher failed my child" are used.

17. Those Beta Israel who migrated before 1984-85 were relatively more able than the latecomers to mix and interact with veteran Israelis perhaps because they were fewer and the circumstances of their migration were much less traumatic. This also may reflect the cultural expectations and other differences between the two groups. Most of those who came early were members of ethnic minorities in Tigray.

18. Since this observation was made, I heard (in a telephone conversation with Haim Rosen at the end of April 1989) that the Beta Israel youth who have joined the IDF are doing so well that some have been subjects of a documentary film. In a society that values its armed men so highly, this kind of distinction will serve the Ethiopians very well in terms of public relations and acceptance in the mainstream of society.

19. This is not exceptional. Although most schoolteachers and center workers are women, it is rare to find them in administrative positions. When a question about this was posed to the village director, he smiled and said nothing. I have heard no one complaining about the absence of women in administrative positions.

20. Actually, this is much more complicated than it appears. By tradition, almost all young people enter into marriages arranged by their elders. Is one then to conclude that all marriages are "forced" upon the couples and therefore subject to renegotiation at a later time?

21. As a rule, the absorption center social workers are young and progressive in many respects, including regarding sexuality. They do openly tell women how to practice family planning and avoid unwanted pregnancies.

22. It is a common phenomenon reported by many center personnel that the Ethiopians often get headaches or stomach aches. These ailments are associated with their emotional states.

23. Among the general population of Beta Israel, thirty-two people, most of whom were young, took their own lives between 1985 and 1987. Most informants think this is a higher incidence than that among the larger Jewish population in Israel.

24. *Aleka* (Amharic, meaning "chief," "learned," or "leader") is a respected title usually given to a man of high learning in the religious or secular realms. But it is also used by sorcerers, or *tenuity* or *balezar*, who as a rule also claim to have a higher calling because they can communicate with the spirit world and heal the sick. The three men mentioned in the text are highly respected personalities in the Beta Israel community. A *tenuity*, by the way, could be a man or a woman, but the woman does not assume the title *Aleka*, only the practice. Psychiatric experts do not discount the merit of such practices for the people who believe in them.

25. I am grateful to the authorities in Israel for letting me have access to the archives for scholarly purposes.

26. At the end of the letter, besides the names of the senders, a Muslim name is listed, which perhaps serves as a code name for purposes of bank account transactions between Ethiopia and outsiders.

27. The names of the mother, the father and the one who composed the letter (most likely a relative) are listed as senders.

28. The *ferenj* referred to here is most likely a white Israeli or American who had come as a tourist or through some other guise to assess the situation of the Beta Israel in Ethiopia and carry some money from the Jewish Agency to the people stranded there.

29. This refers to the fact that at one time in the mid-1980s, many of the Beta Israel community sold their animals and belongings thinking they would come to Israel. When they failed to get out, they were faced with formidable problems. The Jewish Agency tried to send money to help them become reestablished. The children and relatives who made it to Israel were very helpful in supplying the necessary information so that the monies would get to the right people.

30. The father, mother, a sister, and a brother are listed as senders of this letter. Usually, the one who composes such letters is one of the younger members of the family who, as a rule, may be the only literate one. The adults either dictate or tell what they want to convey to the young writer. As a general rule, the writer identifies himself or herself by adding "written by" at the end of the letter.

31. When, for political reasons, it is impossible to send money directly from Israel to Ethiopia, third countries such as the United States are used. Even with this route, the problems of nondelivery persist.

32. There are institutions serving similar purposes in other societies, such as the United States, but these are often local ventures sponsored by religious organizations, not national commitments as in the Israeli case.

CHAPTER NINE

1. My categorization of the immigrants is similar to that used by the Ministry of Immigrant Absorption in, "The Absorption of Ethiopian Jews: Master Plan," Jerusalem, August 1985. Also refer to Table 1 in Chapter 4.

2. This dismal lack of even rudimentary education affects all groups of Ethiopians—Jews, Christians, Muslims, and others—in the traditionally conservative regions of Tigray and Gondar, where the vast majority of Beta Israel lived before coming to Israel. Yet these very regions, particularly the cities of Gondar and Axum, are renowned for their eminence in classical literature, theology, music, and the arts. For background on the problems of literacy, see Teshome Wagaw, "Appraisal of Adult Literacy Programs in Ethiopia," *Journal of Reading* 21, 6 (1978): 504–8; and, in the same journal issue, Fay Starr and Deretha Starr, "Learning to Read in Ethiopia," pp. 509–13.

3. In speaking of the generation of those older than forty-five, Uri Gordon, the director-general of Youth Aliyah used the term *lost generation*, by which he meant that these people would not be able to learn the skills related to language, society, and the world of work.

4. This problem exists in much of the Third World, where large segments of the population are nonliterate. The Israeli approach is interesting in its own right and for its possible application in other societies facing a similar challenge.

5. Since that time, for fear of conscription and more importantly because of a loss of hope in the future of Ethiopia, young people have been leaving the country in droves. As one Ethiopian official recently stated, "Ethiopian youth, even those in the

fourth grade, talk and dream of nothing else except to leave the country." This is a new phenomenon that indicates the unbearable political and social conditions in the country since the mid-1970s. Up to that time, Ethiopians have always preferred to stay home; the "brain drain" that afflicted many other Third World countries was never a problem for Ethiopia.

6. Haim Rosen, his wife Esther, and I traveled to a number of Beta Israel settlements together. Esther is of Yemeni background, and Haim speaks some Tigrigna and Amharic. Both are well accepted by the Beta Israel.

7. Although the rules exclude married people from participating in the Youth Administration Project programs for reasons that their participation may interfere with family life, a few have managed to slip in.

8. The Ethiopian Jews, like many others in the area, kept slaves. When slavery was abolished during the reign of Haile Selassie, the practice de facto continued. Although it has been almost completely eliminated in recent decades, the offspring of the former slaves are identifiable. It is reported that the Jews who were left behind in the Sudanese camps when Operation Moses was interrupted were mostly members of this ex-slave group.

9. Traditionally, this kind of situation did not arise too often because of close supervision, the social stigma attached to a girl's loss of virginity, and the lack of privacy, among other things.

10. The administrator in charge said that she did not have the budget or the instructors to allow such activity.

11. This relates to another problem I observed in the field. The young adults (ages eighteen to twenty-eight) who had become literate for the first time learned the vocabulary of their trade in Hebrew. Although many of these terms have Amharic or Tigrigna equivalents, those who had not attended school in Ethiopia were not familiar with them. Now, when they tried to converse in their native languages, they included many of the Hebrew terms, and after a while the communication would become tiring or unintelligible.

12. The term the school principal is reported to have used was the Hebrew word for "uncircumcised." The Beta Israel are very sensitive to such nuances, because they were challenged in Israel that some irregularities in the area of religious rituals might have taken place during the long centuries of isolation from the mainstream of Judaism. The fact of the matter is that the Beta Israel are circumcised on the eighth day after birth, as are their Christian and Muslim counterparts.

13. For background on the Ethiopian education system, see Teshome Wagaw, *Education in Ethiopia* (Ann Arbor: University of Michigan Press, 1979). Issues pertaining to higher education are more fully discussed in Teshome Wagaw, *The Development of Higher Education and Social Change: An Ethiopian Experience* (East Lansing: Michigan State University Press, 1990). Changes since the 1974 revolution are analyzed in Teshome Wagaw, "Ethiopia: Systems of Education," in T. Husen and T. Postlethwaite, eds., *The International Encyclopedia of Education* (New York: Pergamon Press, 1985), pp. 1723-29.

14. For detailed analysis of the kinds of problems this group faced initially, see Teshome Wagaw, "Ethiopia, Israel, and the Resettlement of the Falashas," *CAAS Newsletter* (Winter 1986): 1-11; and T. Wagaw, "The Emigration and Settlement of Ethiopian Jews in Israel," *Middle East Review* 20, 2 (1987/88): 41-48. For the reaction of the regional and international community to the immigration, see T. Wagaw, "The International Political Ramifications of the Falasha Emigration," *The Journal of Modern African Studies* 29, 4 (1991): 557-81.

NOTES

CHAPTER TEN

1. As anthropologist Bronislow Malinowski observed, once a community has opened itself to interaction with other communities, the resulting culture is neither like the first nor like the second. Rather, it assumes a character of its own. So it is with the case at hand. By virtue of the fact that Israel has brought in the Beta Israel community, and in spite of the fact that the paradigm of incorporation is assimilatory by design, the Beta Israel community will leave its imprint on the host society.

2. The Jews from northern Africa are classified as either Orientals or Sephardim. Both terms are inadequate, but since they have been used almost universally in the literature, I followed the established appellations.

3. The fact that other people of color had migrated to Israel does not mean the Ethiopians are not conspicuous. On the whole, most of them are darker in skin color than most of the other Israelis, and the texture of their hair is different. Anyone who wants to discriminate based on such superficial nuances will find ample opportunity to do so.

4. Estimates of the number of Beta Israel who lost their lives in the refugee camps in the Sudan or during the journey range from thirty-five hundred to five thousand or more.

5. The separation of the immigrants from relatives and some of the other hardships endured by the Ethiopians were also the experience of most of the European Jews who migrated between 1939 and 1945, and even later.

6. When I travel to different parts of the world, the first question many people ask is how the Falasha are doing. Are they discriminated against because they are black? Most often, such questions come from Africans or African-Americans. When I respond to such queries, some conclude that there must be more than I am willing to divulge. The assumption is that racial discrimination must be very flagrant in Israel. The position I take, based on my research, is that, yes, race is a factor and racism exists, but this is mitigated by the fact that the Ethiopians are Jews. In the eyes of most Israelis, it is unacceptable to discriminate against fellow Jews on account of the color of their skin. Further, the *olim* have not been in the country long enough for prejudicial attitudes, on both sides, to emerge and solidify their positions.

7. The prevailing view in Israel is that a Jew cannot possibly lead a truly Jewish life as long as he or she lives among a majority of Gentiles. According to this conception, fulfillment can be found only by making *aliyah* to Israel.

8. See, for instance, David Kessler, *The Falashas: The Forgotten Jews of Ethiopia* (London: George Allen & Unwing, 1985), p. 154. Kessler argues that the situation for the Falashas was a great deal harder because they not only were innocent of rabbinic teachings but also did not conform to the popular notion of racial purity. Yet, in April 1987, when I interviewed Michael Corinaldi, a noted lawyer in Jerusalem who defends the rights of the Beta Israel in Israeli courts, he suggested that the Ethiopians' physical features do conform to the notion of Jewishness.

9. The American Association for Ethiopian Jews has used this line of argument several times in its effort to get the attention of the Israeli government. Other writers, including journalists, have argued similarly. See, for example, Louis Rapoport, "Black Jews in Crisis," *Jerusalem Post*, international edition, April 19, 1986; and Kessler, *The Falashas*, pp. 66–67.

Notes

10. It was extremely difficult to support the objections of the rabbis in the case of the Jews from India who had some knowledge of Halakah and were not as isolated as the Beta Israel for such a long time. Even then, the Indians were required to undergo conversion. They refused, and the matter was left at that. See Kessler, *The Falashas*, p. 154; and S. N. Eisenstadt, *Israeli Society* (New York: Basic Books, 1967) pp. 312-14.

11. Eisenstadt, *Israeli Society*, pp. 312-14.

12. Some Ethiopian Jews have married Canadians, Americans, and Israeli veterans. Two men who married North American women left Israel to live in their wives' country of origin. I am aware of two Ethiopians (a woman who had lived in Israel for a dozen years and a man) who married veterans and live in Israel.

13. This is in reference to the controversy over reconversion. Ethiopians are accepted as Israelis the moment they arrive. But to get there in the first place, they must have been accepted as Jews. Once in Israel (for reasons given in Chapter 4), however, they were required to go through ritual reconversion. In the eyes of many religious Jews, this requirement might have cast doubt on their authenticity or fidelity to their religious principles.

14. For discussion of the Moroccan immigrants, see Rivka Bar-Yosef, "The Moroccans: Background to the Problem," in S. N. Eisenstadt, Rivka Bar-Yosef, and Chain Adler, eds., *Integration and Development in Israel* (New York: Praeger, 1970), pp, 419-28. See also , Harvey Goldberg, "The Mimuna and the Minority Status of Moroccan Jews," *Ethnology* 27, 1 (1976): 75-87.

15. Micha Feldman worked in the department of the Jewish Agency responsible for the settlement of the Beta Israel. He is fluent in Amharic and very much respected among the olim. He also has visited the Beta Israel villages in Ethiopia on more than one occasion. Feldman's views were corroborated by Sarah Rachmani, a school psychologist in Afula.

16. Kaplan's views were given in an interview with Greer F. Cashman and appeared under the title "Recording a Culture," *Jerusalem Post*, January 11, 1985.

17. Ibid.

18. Ibid.

19. The study group, under the auspices of Professors for Peace in the Middle East, included American professors from a number of different universities. We visited a variety of institutions where talks were given by distinguished politicians, academicians, and private individuals in Israel proper and in the West Bank. The two-week tour was intended to help the professors become acquainted with the issues of war and peace in the Middle East.

20. Ethiopians in general, and those in the highlands in particular, have been spared the humiliating experiences other Africans were subjected to during the period of European colonialism. Hence, it is possible that when confronted with the issue outside their land of origin, either they fail to be sensitive enough to notice it or they are unwilling to admit racial discrimination.

21. People in Ethiopia use the small branches of plants known as *yettirs mefakiya* to clean their teeth. Modern science is now telling us that some of these plants have the effects of fluoride. Not only do they clean the teeth, they also provide some protection against certain diseases of the gum.

22. This is not quite true, since the Benei Israel and the Yemenites have been settled in Israel since the early 1950s. She might have been referring to the area where she was now working.

NOTES

23. The Beta Israel who came in 1979 were not as destitute as those who came in 1984–85. The latter had devastating experiences in refugee camps. Yet the issues of race and health were of concern to the veteran community, especially the parents.

24. Beta Israel children were integrated into schools with veteran children, but this does not mean they attended the same classes. This is a first step toward eventual integration at all levels. The rate of progress is dependent on the readiness of the Beta Israel children and local circumstances, including the willingness of the school headmaster and the veteran parents.

25. There are some problems connected with this, as observed in the field. Some of the brightest children, who could have been placed in more advanced classes, were held back because places were not found for them.

26. This is the so-called independent branch or the third part of the school system. Although it gets government subvention, it operates its school very much on its own terms. It is under the control of the ultra-Orthodox religious wing which barely recognizes the validity of the Rabbinate Council. Nonetheless, it used the excuse of the council when it wanted to exclude the Beta Israel. The other branches of the educational system regard the Beta Israel as Israelis and Jews who are entitled to enroll in their schools. For the controversies surrounding the case, see, "Habad School Still Won't Register Ethiopians," *Jerusalem Post*, March 14, 1985; "Beersheba Fights Habad," *Jerusalem Post*, May 5, 1985; "Parents Taking City to Court," *Jerusalem Post*, August 25, 1985; and "Habad School Must Take Ethiopians," *Jerusalem Post*, August 30, 1985.

27. "Habad School Still Won't Register Ethiopians."

28. See "Parents Taking City to Court in Row over Habad School," *Jerusalem Post*, August 8, 1985.

29. Eisenstadt, *Israeli Society*, p. 313.

30. This report was given on November 19, 1986, by a group of Beta Israel students attending classes at Boys Town, Jerusalem, but commuting from another center. Haim Rosen, who was with me, thought the other boys rejected the Beta Israel because they thought they were better off materially than the others and this aroused jealousy. Rather, the problem was that the Beta Israel were finding it difficult to catch up with the activities required both in the classrooms and outside, and this reflected negatively on them.

31. My informant did not deny the possibility that the reason could have been racial or cultural prejudice. But he feels these prejudices could have been minimized had the ministry acted prudently.

32. As is the case with many other attitudes, racial attitudes are often learned in context. Unless the two groups have lived in close proximity, opportunities for forming opinions are few. So the Israeli veterans might not have been racists, and may still not be, but the roots of racism are taking hold.

33. Kiryat Arba is located near the historic city of Hebron in the West Bank. The five thousand Jewish settlers, most of whom came from North America and Europe, are politically conservative and ideologically motivated. When the first group of Beta Israel were settled there in 1985, the United States and Egypt protested. Since then, some Beta Israel families have settled there permanently, others temporarily. Under the leadership of the dynamic Yanai Elchanan, an immigrant from South Africa, the integration of the *olim* is proceeding very well.

34. Ami Bergman, who made the comment on November 25, 1986, is the head of the American Joint Distribution Committee in Jerusalem.

Notes

35. This is UN Resolution No. 3379 of November 10, 1975, which refers to the Jewish and Arab communities of Israel and Palestine. This resolution has been decried by World Jewry and its supporters but still remains on the books.

36. On November 6, 1986, in the city of Afula, Aleka Tiruneh, a highly respected member of the Beta Israel community, informed me that in Ethiopia he had nine oxen, many cattle, and was a highly respected upper-middle-class *neftegna* (a leading member of the Ethiopian resistance forces during the short-lived Italian occupation of 1936-1941). He said he lost all this when he came to Israel. He added that in Israel they look upon him as one of the illiterate Africans who happens to be living there in comfort. He said that although he was one of the few lucky ones—he lost no close relatives in the process of migration—he regrets coming to Israel. I asked him if he had plans to return to Ethiopia. He replied that it was unlikely he would return. He was not necessarily referring to racial discrimination; he was concerned with cultural deprivation and loss of status.

37. Project Renewal is supported by American Jewish organizations to rehabilitate and revitalize depressed areas so that their inhabitants can become healthy and self-sufficient.

38. There have been complaints of racial discrimination by other *olim*. See, for instance, Ernest Krausz, ed., *Studies of Israeli Society* (New Brunswick: Transaction Books, 1980), pp. 147-63, 165-81. A number of my informants, however, seem to be unaware of historical antecedents. They think that incidents are unrelated to the issues of race or they tend to forget about them.

39. The concept of government as a father image, certainly as it pertains to education, is in part a carryover from the earlier years in Haile Selassie's reign in Ethiopia. Parents were induced to send their children to "modern" schools, and sometimes payments were made to parents to do so. But in recent years, as the demand for education accelerated, that kind of largesse was withdrawn. Public education for those who can get in, however, remains free in Ethiopia. The Beta Israel expect even more from the government in their new home.

40. Stephen Donshik, the United Israel Appeal's director of program evaluation, expressed concern that the training the Beta Israel are getting may prove inadequate for a changing world and called for a reassessment of training methods and programs. See his article, "Ethiopian Immigrants—Completing the Task," *Jerusalem Post*, July 13, 1986.

41. Plenty of manual and construction jobs in Israel are held by the Arab segment of the population. The Beta Israel could do these jobs, but since other Jews have shunned that kind of work, the immigrants may consider the jobs unfit for persons of their cultural background.

42. This information was supplied by Amnon Nave, an official in the Ministry of Labor.

43. Regarding the life of the peasant in highland Ethiopia, see Donald Levine, *Wax and Gold: Tradition and Innovation in Ethiopian Culture* (Chicago: University of Chicago Press, 1965); Joseph Halevy, *Travels in Abyssinia*, 1877; Teshome Wagaw, "The World of Work in Ethiopian Culture," unpublished paper, Addis Ababa: Haile Selassie I University, October 1971.

44. In the parts of Ethiopia where the Beta Israel lived, more than 90 percent of the general population owned land. The landless were primarily the Muslims, Addis Christians (New Christians), and Beta Israel. The landholding system was communal, and no single individual *balabat* (landlord) derived much benefit from tenants. Since

the land tenure reform in 1975, individuals now may rent land from the state, but no one owns land in perpetuity.

45. Still, many Beta Israel think the government, in its benevolence and generosity, wants to continue to support them at the levels they enjoyed during their first year in Israel. *Idmae lemengist*, or "Long live the government," is the expression they frequently use. They cannot say enough good things about the government (Israel) and America, whose population, they think, is mostly Jewish.

46. Many think it is this realization that prompted the Jewish Agency to terminate their stay in the absorption centers abruptly in the winter of 1986. This sudden act precipitated much rancor on the part of the Beta Israel community and many of the workers.

47. In the early period of immigration, it was thought best to encourage employment of Beta Israel in the production rather than the service sector of the economy. In reality, this is not possible, at least at this stage.

48. Although efforts are made to break the news during weekends or other holidays, it is not always possible to do so. Even if it is, the individual may stay away for more than a day or two, depending how closely he was related to the deceased. If a relative or friend dies in Israel, tradition requires that a large number of community members must attend, and the close relatives sit in ritual at home for about seven days. This latter custom is also observed in Israeli Jewish tradition.

49. One of the criticisms leveled against the *olim* by the veterans is that they spend too much money on televisions and furniture, which the veterans claim are unnecessary.

50. Among the male workers, it is possible that Gondar pride enters the picture. The Gondarese are known to take pride in asserting their independence. In Israel, where they are told what to do and how to do it and are required to report their comings and goings to a *ferenj* (Amharic for a white or strange person) supervisor, they may feel affronted. This is my interpretation based on knowledge of how the Gondarese male ego operates. At any rate, the smallholder in Ethiopia is self-directed and self-regulated and may find working in a bureaucratic situation a nuisance at best, unacceptable at worst.

51. This is not unlike what is happening among the black minorities in the United States, African-American females are obtaining more higher education, better employment, and higher wages. At least in the short term, this trend tends to disrupt family relations.

CHAPTER ELEVEN

1. The Chicago-based American Association for Ethiopian Jews continued its effective work: raising the necessary funds, recruiting some facilitators within Ethiopia (both government officials and private individuals), and pressuring the Israeli and U.S. governments to maintain diplomatic pressure on Mengistu through the United Nations and its member governments.

2. Rachmim Elazar was brought to Israel in 1972 when he was a very young boy. Since then, he has graduated from Tel Aviv University and become very fluent in Hebrew as well as his native language, Amharic. He is one of the few Beta Israel who are very well acculturated to Israeli society. For some time, he was in charge of the Amharic radio program produced for the new immigrants.

3. This set the tone for subsequent State Department actions. For instance, Herman Cohen, assistant secretary of state for African affairs, pressed the Mengistu government at every opportunity to release the Beta Israel if it wanted improved relations with Washington. It must be recalled that George Bush had been very active during 1984 and 1985 in persuading the Sudanese leader to permit, even to facilitate, the exodus of the Ethiopian Jews to Israel.

4. The American Association for Ethiopian Jews, which has been active on behalf of the Beta Israel for a long time, often has been accused of ignoring the physical safety and political considerations associated with its work. But it has continued its activities in Israel, the United States, and Ethiopia. It asserts, with a measure of justified pride, that without its lobbying of Congress, the administration, and other private organizations and its fund-raising efforts, the migration outcome would have been very limited at best. For example, the association's newsletter, *Release: A Report from AAEJ*, vol. 9, no. 1, lists many successful activities. While some of this information may be self-serving, most of the achievements on the list are true. For an updated list of the AAEJ's achievements and the tasks remaining, see a letter sent to the membership of the association from its president, Nate Shapiro, dated December 1990. For the meeting at the White House, see Joel Rebibo, "A Long Way from Gondar," *Moment*, 4, 5: 44-45.

5. "Ethiopians Exploited," *Michigan Daily*, vol. 1C, no. 80.

6. Mesfin Woldemariam, "An Ethiopian Peace Initiative," presented at the XIth International Conference of Ethiopian Studies, April 1-6, 1991, Addis Ababa.

7. There were about seventeen thousand immigrants by 1987. With an increase of approximately five hundred per year over four years, the total reached the vicinity of twenty thousand.

8. I have not been able to verify this, but I have in my files numerous letters, obtained in the field in Israel, in which Beta Israel complain about their situation in graphic detail. See also the description of a prominent, controversial leader, Addisu Messele, in Rebibo.

9. The reader must keep in mind that there has never been an accurate census of the Beta Israel.

10. In April 1987, I witnessed a march by a large number of Beta Israel to the prime minister's office in Jerusalem. The marchers, men and women, young and old, carrying placards with signs saying "Let my people come," shouted repeatedly for reunion with mothers, children, and other relatives in Ethiopia. Such demonstrations occurred frequently. See Elizabeth Brown, "Waiting in Gondar," *Reform Judaism* (Winter 1989): 6-7.

11. I heard about the resumption of diplomatic relations when I was in Philadelphia on a research fellowship. There were Israeli professors there as well, so the Israeli consulate transmitted a series of messages from Israel. On November 6, 1989, Giddeon Allon reported in *Ha'aretz* that a special delegation from Ethiopia, led by Kassa Kebede, the Israeli-educated uncle of Mengistu Hailemariam, had been received by Israeli Prime Minister Yitzhak Shamir and the defense minister, Moshe Arens. According to Allon's report, Shamir expressed appreciation for Ethiopia's desire to establish formal relations, noting that the two countries had been friends for a long time, and a resumption of formal relations was proper and timely. This meeting was held just as the Ethiopian president declared a national mobilization to resist rebel forces marching toward the capital from the north. The implication surrounding the hasty reestablishment of relations was that Ethiopia was desperately hoping Israel would serve as a sig-

nificant asset by providing military hardware and advice, and that it would urge the U.S. administration to agree to an exchange of ambassadors between Washington and Addis Ababa.

12. Indeed, on January 17, 1990, Prime Minister Shamir stated that as soon as the Israeli embassy was organized in Addis Ababa, all the fifteen thousand (sic) would emigrate to "their country." See *Almishmar*, January 17, 1990.

13. The Ethiopian public was told repeatedly by the government-controlled media that the Beta Israel had been abducted by the Israeli government and that given a chance they would like to return to Ethiopia. As far as the general Ethiopian public was concerned, the thought that groups of Ethiopians were leaving the country because they found life unbearable was another, perhaps most disgusting, manifestation of the government they were living under. Even the intellectuals who were aware of the government propaganda to the contrary objected to the way in which the Beta Israel were leaving the country. See Woldemariam, "An Ethiopian Peace Initiative."

14. See Mary A. Fitzgerald, "How Ethiopian Rebels Turned Struggle Around," *San Francisco Chronicle*, July 4, 1990; "Ethiopia Mulls Exodus of Black Jews," *Washington Times*, June 12, 1990.

15. Ibid.

16. Abdul Mohammed, "Power Games in Africa's Horn," *New York Times*, June 11, 1990.

17. See "Ethiopian Exodus Starts Again," *Washington Times*, November 23, 1990.

18. For a detailed account, see Flora Lewis, "Ethiopia Peers West," *New York Times*, January 30, 1990; "Friends Like Us," *Economist*, January 27, 1990, p. 39.

19. The whole operation of bringing the Beta Israel from Gondar and placing them in Addis Ababa for proper certification and exit purposes was done in an extralegal manner. See the very useful article by Jane Perlez, "Strain on Ethiopian City: Stranded Jews," *New York Times*, July 14, 1990, p. 3.

20. Ibid.

21. Ibid. Kassa Kebede, one of the most prominent government officials (and Mengistu Hailemariam's uncle) during the reign of Haile Selassie, served as the main link between Mengistu and the Israeli authorities. He traveled to Israel to reestablish diplomatic relations and later bypassed the government's normal channels to transport the Beta Israel to Addis Ababa. He was later rewarded, just in the nick of time. He and two other officials were taken to Israel during Operation Solomon. For the circumstances of their fight, see Joel Brinkley, "Two Ethiopian Officials Given Asylum by Israelis," *New York Times*, May 30, 1991, p. 7.

22. Most of this information was obtained through private communication with Ethiopians and Americans who worked directly with emigrants in Addis Ababa. Also, information was obtained from some of the volunteer organizations at headquarters in Washington or Chicago and from their regular publications. I am grateful for the information provided by Gary Miller of the Jewish Distribution Committee of America, who visited the Beta Israel between January and February 1991. His untitled report, which he kindly made available, was very extensive and informative..

23. Rebibo, "A Long Way from Gondar," p. 42.

24. Larry Derfner, "Forgotten Immigrants," *Jerusalem Post* international edition, March 31, 1990, p. 10.

25. Yaiel "Jack" Edelstein, who returned to the United Stated after spending a few months in Israel, communicated this to me on May 5, 1991, in Ann Arbor, Mich. For a

Notes

brief but otherwise excellent account of the issue, see Rebibo, "A Long Way from Gondar," pp. 42-55.

26. See Derfner, "Forgotten Immigrants."

27. But the Israeli government should have known that whoever might assume power in Addis Ababa would wish to establish and maintain good relations with the United States and the Bush administration would sooner or later use its good offices to influence the Addis Ababa regime.

28. This news was a surprise in that many people assumed that Mengistu would commit suicide rather than flee. See Clifford Krauss, "Ethiopia's Dictator Flees; Officials Seeking U.S. Help," *New York Times*, May 22, 1991.

29. I was in direct telephone contact with Addis Ababa during Operation Solomon. One excellent source of information was a nurse in the Addis Ababa refugee camps. See Clifford Krauss, "Israel Begins Airlift of Ethiopia's Jews," *New York Times*, May 25, 1991; also, in the same issue by the same reporter, "Eritrea's Capital Reported Seized." See also Clifford Krauss, "Ethiopian Jews and Israelis Exult as Airlift Is Completed," *New York Times*, May 26, 1991.

30. This issue also was raised by the United States and Egypt during the 1985 exodus of Ethiopian Jews to Israel. Although very mindful of this, some families eventually settled in at least one occupied area, Kiryat Arba, near the historic city of Hebron.

31. See Teshome Wagaw, "Ethiopia, Israel and the Resettlement of the Falashas," *CAAS Newsletter* 2, 2 (Winter 1986): 1-11; "The Immigration and Settlement of Ethiopian Jews in Israel," *Middle East Review* 20, 2 (Winter 1987/88): 41-48.

Glossary

ETHIOPIC

abba—title of a monk.
addis mette—newcomer.
agew—term for the indigenous people who practiced Judaism before the fourth century.
aleka—chief or leader (scholar).
assadagih ayideg—used when a child has done something seriously wrong. It means "May the one who brought you up be destroyed."
astergwami—interpreter.
atinkugn—do not touch me.
Ato—Mr.
balege—uncouth.
bale-ij—artisan, one who uses his or her hands to make a living.
baltet—elderly woman.
buda—one with the "evil eye".
debtra (woch)—deacon(s) or cantor(s).
dejmettinat—waiting at the gate in expectation of a favorable outcome.
Derg—a committee or junta that ruled Ethiopia from approximately 1978-1990.
Egziabher—God. Lord of the universe; a term used by Ethiopian Jews and Christians alike.
enjera—Ethiopian bread.
ferenj—foreigner, white people.
Falasha—Beta Israel or Ethiopian Jews, a term used most by outsiders.

gieyed—covenant regulating sexual consummation with an underage bride.
gizret—circumcision.
gobbatta—hunchback.
gojo mewttat—establishing a home by a couple.
irgman—curse.
ittan—incense.
kayla—another name for Ethiopian Jew.
kes or *kahin*—priest.
Kibre Negest—the Ethiopian equivalent of the Talmud.
kibuae Egziabher—anointed of God.
Kimant—a religious community found in the Gondar region.
Kubet—dry cow dung used for fuel.
libam—a wise or thoughtful female in family or community matters.
merdo—breaking news of the death of a family member.
mesgid—place of worship.
mugogo—frying pan.
Orit—the Old Testament or Torah.
Seged—religious holiday observed by Ethiopian Jews.
Sharia—a Muslim term meaning Islamic Law.
shemagile—elderly man.
shifta—vagabond.
Tabot—the tablets on which the Ten Commandments were inscribed.
taib—derogatory name applied to Ethiopian Jews.
Tezaz Sanbat—commandments of the Sabbath.
tezkar—a feast in remembrance of a dead person.
Tigray—north-central region of Ethiopia.
ttilmet—religious immersion.
Woizero—Mrs.
yebalege lij—an uncouth child or child of an uncouth parent; a child of improper upbringing.
yechiwa lij—a child of proper or gentle upbringing.
yejegina lij—son of a brave parent.
Yedem or *yemergem gojo*—hut of curse or malediction.
yenjera lij (och)—stepchild (ren).
yeset lij—a child of unmanly behavior, "son of a woman."
yetebareke—meat of a slaughtered animal (blessed).
yezemed irdata—help of a relative.
ynefis abat—soul father or confessor.

HEBREW

Agudat Israel—the ultra-Orthodox religious group.
aliyah (aliot)—immigration.
aliyat hanoar—boarding schools, youth *aliyah*.
Beta Israel—The House of Israel, another name for Ethiopian Jews.
edot—ethnic community or tribe.
Halakah—Religious Law.

GLOSSARY

Hovevei Zion—lovers of Zion.
Histadrut—Israeli Labor Federation.
kabbalat ol mitzvot—oral declaration of acceptance of the commandments of the Torah.
kibbutz galuyot—gathering of exiles.
kibbutz—communal village.
kippa or *yarmulka*—head cover worn by religious Jewish males.
Knesset—parliament.
kushi—derogatory term equivalent to "nigger."
mamzer—bastard.
merkaze kilta—absorption center.
mikveh—ritual bath.
mila—circumcision.
Mishna—the oral laws.
moha—teacher.
mizug galuyot—the fusion and integration of exiles.
moshav—cooperative village.
olim—immigrant.
ozrot—maid.
sabra—Israeli-born.
safta—grandmother.
shohatim—religious (Israeli) slaughterers.
tevila—ritual immersion in a bath.
ulpanim—Hebrew language schools.
vatik (im)—veteran Israeli(s).
yeshivot—religious colleges (seminaries).

Bibliography

Abbink, G. J. "The Falashas in Ethiopia and Israel: The Problem of Cultural Assimilation." Doctoral thesis, Institute for Cultural and Social Anthropology, Nijemegen, Netherlands, November 15, 1984.

———. "Seged Celebration in Ethiopia and Israel: Continuity and Change of a Falasha Religious Holiday." *Anthropos* 78 (1983): 789–810.

Adler, Chaim. "School Integration in the Context of the Development of Israel's Educational System." In *School Desegregation—Cultural Perspectives*, edited by Yehuda Amir and Shlomo Sharan. Hillsdale, N.J.: Lawrence Erlbaum Associates, 1984. pp. 21–45.

———. "Social Stratification and Education in Israel." *Comparative Education Review* 18 (February 1974): 10–23.

———. "Twenty-Five Years of Israeli Schooling: The Perspective of Absorption." In *Cultural Transition: The Case of Immigrant Youth*, edited by Meir Gottesman. Jerusalem: Magnes Press, Hebrew University, 1986. pp. 17–24.

"An Airlift to the Promised Land." *Time*. February 14, 1985.

"Airline Stops Ethiopian Rescue." *Jerusalem Post*. January 6, 1985.

Albaum, Melvin. "Agrarian Settlements." *Growth and Change* 1, 3 (1970): 45.

Amir, Yehuda. "Perceptual Articulation in Three Middle Eastern Cultures." *Journal of Cross-Cultural Psychology* 7, 1 (1976): 37–48.

Amir, Yehudah Aharon Bizman, and Miriam Rivner. "The Effects of Interethnic Contact on Friendship Choices in the Military." *Journal of Cross-Cultural Psychology* 4, 3 (1973): 361–80.

Antonovsky, Aaron, and David Katz. "Factors in the Adjustment to Israeli Life of American and Jewish Immigrants." *Jewish Journal of Sociology* 12, 1 (June 1970): 77–88.

BIBLIOGRAPHY

Aronoff, Myron J. "The Politics of Religion in a New Israeli Town." *Eastern Anthropologist* 26, 2 (1973): 145–71.

———. "Ritual Rebellion and Assertion in an Israeli New Town." *Jewish Journal of Sociology* 15, 1 (June 1973): 79–105.

———. "Ritual Rebellion and Assertion in the Israeli Labor Party." *Political Anthropology* 1 (March 1976): 3–4.

Ashkenazi, Michael, and Alex Weingrod. *Ethiopian Immigrants in Beersheva: An Anthropological Study of the Absorption Process.* Highland Park, Ill.: American Association for Ethiopian Jews, 1984.

Ashkenazi, Michael, and Alex Weingrod, eds. *Ethiopian Jews and Israel.* New Brunswick and London: Transaction Books, 1987.

Atlas, Yedidya. "Rabbinical Perspective." *Jerusalem Post.* November 8, 1985.

Avi-Hai, Avraham. "Israel: Centrism and Diasporism." *Jewish Journal of Sociology* 18, 1 (June 1976): 43–56.

Avraham, Shmuel, and Arlene Kushner. *Treacherous Journey: My Escape from Ethiopia.* New York: Shapolsky Publishing, 1986.

Bar-Yosef, R. Weiss. "Desocialization and Resocialization: The Adjustment Process of Immigrants." In *Migration, Ethnicity and Community,* edited by Ernest Krausz. New Brunswick and London: Transaction Books, 1980. Pp.19–37.

Barak, Azy, and Elchanan I. Meir. "The Predictive Validity of a Vocational Interest Inventory-RAMAK: A Seven-Year Follow-Up." *Journal of Vocational Behavior* 4, 3 (1974): 377–87.

Barinbaum, Lea. "Role Confusion in Adolescence." *Adolescence* 7, 25 (Spring 1972): 121–27.

Becker, Tamar. "Self and Social Responsibility: A Comparative View of American and Israeli Youth." *American Journal of Psychoanalysis* 36, 2 (1976): 155–62.

Beckingham, Charles F., and George W. B. Huntingford. *The Prester John of the Indies.* London: Hakluyt Society, 1954.

Beke, C. T. "Remarks on the Matshafa Tamar." *Jewish Chronicle.* March 31, 1848.

———. "The Samaritans." *Jewish Chronicle.* February 5, 1847.

"Belgian Charter Firm: 'Publicity Stopped Us'." *Jerusalem Post,* January 6, 1985.

Ben Shaul, D'vora. "Absorption by Default." *Jerusalem Post.* January 24, 1985.

Ben-Dor, Shoshana. "Hamekomot hakedoshim shel yehudei Ethiopia [The Holy Places of the Jews of Ethiopia]." *Pe'amim* 22 (1985): 32–52.

Ben-Ezer, Gadi. "Cross-Cultural Misunderstandings: The Case of Ethiopian Immigrants." *Israel Social Science Research* 3, 1–2 (1985): 69–84.

Bentwich, Joseph S. *Education in Israel.* London: Routledge & Kegan Paul, 1965.

Bilski, R. "Basic Parameters of the Welfare State." *Social Indicators* 3, 3–4 (1976): 451–70.

Blackstone, Tessa. "Education and the Under-privileged in Israel." *Jewish Journal of Sociology* 13, 2 (December 1971): 173–87.

Bruce, James. *Travels to Discover the Source of the Nile.* Edinburgh: G. G. J. and J. Bobinson, 1970.

Budge, Ernest Alfred Wallis. *The Queen of Sheba and Her Only Son Menyelek.* London: Medici Society, 1922.

Carmi, Shulamit, and Henry Rosenfeld. "Immigration, Urbanization, and Crisis: The Process of Jewish Colonization in Palestine during the 1920s." *International Journal of Comparative Sociology* 12, 1 (March 1971): 41–57.

Bibliography

Cohen, Erik. "The Black Panthers and Israeli Society." *Jewish Journal of Sociology* 14, 1 (June 1972): 93–109.
Cohen, Erik, and Menachem Rosner. "Relations between Generations in an Israeli Kibbutz." *Journal of Contemporary History* 5, 1 (1970): 73–86.
Cohen, Percy S. "Israel's Ethnic Problems." *Jewish Journal of Sociology* 9, 1 (June 1967): 100–107.
Comay, Yohanan, and Alan Kirschenbaum. "The Israeli New Town: An Experiment in Population Redistribution." *Economic Development and Cultural Change* 22, 1 (October 1973): 124–34.
Cox, Oliver C. *Caste, Class and Race: A Study in Social Conflict*. New York: Doubleday, 1948.
Crown, Alan D. "The Samaritans in 1984." *Yod* 10, 20 (1984): 9–31.
Crummey, Donald C. *Priests and Politicians: Protestant and Catholic Missionaries in Orthodox Ethiopia, 1830–1868*. London: Oxford University Press, 1972.
D'Abbadie, Antoine. "Responses des Falashas dits Juifs d'Abyssinie, aux questions faites par M. Luzzatto." *Archives Israelites* (1851): 179–85, 234–40, 259–69.
De Jong, Gerald F. "Population Redistribution Policies: Alternatives from the Netherlands, Great Britain, and Israel." *Social Science Quarterly* 56, 2 (1975): 262–73.
Deshen, Shlomo. "The Varieties of Abandonment of Religious Symbols." *Journal for the Scientific Study of Religion* 11, 1 (1972): 33–41.
Devereux, Edward C., Ron Shouval, Urie Bronfenbrenner, Robert R. Rodgers, Sophie Kav-Venaki, Elizabeth Keily, and Esther Karson. "Socialization Practices of Parents, Teachers, and Peers in Israel." *Child Development* 45, 2 (1974): 269–81.
Doresse, Jean. *Ethiopia*. Paris: P. Geuthner, 1971.
Dreman, S. B., and Charles W. Greenbaum. "Altruism or Reciprocity: Sharing Behavior in Israeli Kindergarten Children." *Child Development* 44, 1 (1973): 61–68.
Eban, Abba. "Religious Challenge." *Jerusalem Post*. July 19, 1985.
Eichhorn, David M., ed. *Conversion to Judaism*. New York: Ktav, 1965.
Eisenstadt, Shmuel N. *Absorption of Immigrants*. London: Routledge & Kegan Paul, 1955.
———. *Israeli Society*. New York: Basic Books, Inc., 1967.
Eisenstadt, Shmuel N., Rikva Bar-Yosef and Chaim Adler. *Integration and Development in Israel*. New York: Praeger, 1970.
Eliade, Mircea. *Myth, Rites, Symbols: A Mircea Eliade Reader*. New York: Harper and Row, 1976.
———. *The Sacred and the Profane: The Nature of Religion*. New York: Harcourt Brace, 1959.
Elon, Menachem. *Ethos and Identity: Three Studies in Ethnicity*. London: Tavistock, 1978.
———. "Jewish Law." In *Religious Life and Communities*. Jerusalem: Keter Books (Israel Pocket Library), 1971.
"Embassy Threatened." *New York Times*. April 17, 1986. P.9.
Erikson, Erik H. *Childhood and Society*. London: Imago, 1957.
"Ethiopians Upset and Bitter Over Airlift Halt." *Jerusalem Post*. January 6, 1985.
Etzioni-Halevy, Eva. "Patterns of Conflict Generation and Conflict 'Absorption': The Cases of Israeli Labor and Ethnic Conflicts." *Journal of Conflict Resolution* 19, 2 (1975): 286–309.
"An Exodus Mired in Politics." *Macleans*. January 21, 1985.

BIBLIOGRAPHY

"Ex-Sudan Aide Gets Two Jail Terms for Role in Ethiopian Airlift." *New York Times*. April 6, 1986.

Faitlovich, Jacques. *Masa el HaFalashim* [Journey to the Falashas]. Tel Aviv, 1959.

———. *Notes d'un voyage chez les Falashas*. Paris: 1905.

Feuerstein, Reuven D., D. Krasilow, and Yacco Rand. "Innovative Educational Strategies for the Integration of High-Risk Adolescents in Israel." *Phi Delta Kappan* 55, 8 (1974): 556.

Fishman, Joshua. "Introduction: The Sociology of Language in Israel." *International Journal of the Sociology of Language* 1 (1974): 9–13.

Flad, J. Martin. *The Falashas of Abyssinia*. London: William Macintosh, 1869.

Friedlander, Dov. "Family Planning in Israel: Irrationality and Ignorance." *Journal of Marriage and the Family* 35, 1 (February 1973): 117–24.

Gamst, Frederick C. *The Qemant: A Pagan-Hebraic Peasantry of Ethiopia*. New York: Holt, Rinehart, and Winston, 1969.

Gidney, William T. *The History of the London Society for Promoting Christianity amongst the Jews*. London: London Society for Promoting Christianity amongst the Jews, 1908.

Glazer, Nathan, and Daniel Moynihan. *Beyond the Melting Pot*. Cambridge: MIT Press, 1970.

Goffman, Erving. *Encounters: Two Studies in the Sociology of Interactions*. New York: Bobbs-Merrill, 1961.

———. *The Presentation of Self in Everyday Life*. New York: Anchor Books, 1959.

Goldberg, Harvey E. "Cultural Changes in an Israeli Immigrant Village: The Twist in Evan Josef." *Middle East Studies* 9, 1 (1973): 73.

———. "The Mimuna and the Minority Status of Moroccan Jews." *Ethnology* 17, 1 (1976): 75–87.

Goldman, Ronald. "Cross-Cultural Adaptation of a Program to Involve Parents and Their Children's Learning." *Child Welfare* 52, 8 (1973): 521.

Goldscheider, Calvin. "Out-of-Wedlock Births in Israel." *Social Problems* 21, 4 (1974): 550–67.

Goldschmidt, E., et al. "The Karaite Community of Iraque in Israel." *Social Problems* 28, 3 (1976): 243–52.

Gottlieb, Irving. *Ethiopian Falasha Music*. London: Kensall Rise, 1976.

Gross, Morris B. "The Israeli Disadvantaged." *Teachers' College Record* 12, 1 (1970): 105–10.

Gruber, Ruth. *Rescue: The Exodus of the Ethiopian Jews*. New York: Macmillan, 1987.

Haber, L. "The Chronicle of the Emperor Zara Yaqob 1434–68." *Ethiopia Observer* 5, 2 (1961).

Halevy, Joseph. "Excursion chez le Falacha en Abyssinie." *Bulletin de la Société de Geographie* 17 (1869): 270–94.

———. *La Guerre de Sarca Dengel contra Falashas*. Paris, 1907.

———. *Te'ezaza Sanbat Commandments du Sabbath*. Paris: Bouillon, 1902.

———. *Travels in Abyssinia*. Translated from the French (1869) by James Picciotto. London, 1877.

Halper, Jeff L. "The Absorption of Ethiopian Immigrants: A Return to the Fifties." In *Ethiopian Jews in Israel*, edited by Michael Ashkenazi and Alex Weingrod. New Brunswick and Oxford: Transaction Books, 1987. Pp.112–39.

Bibliography

Halper, Jeff L., and Henry Abramovitch. "The Saharanei as a Mediator of Kurdish-Jewish Ethnicity." In *Jews of Moslem Countries*, edited by S. Deshen and M. Shokeid. Tel Aviv: 1984. Pp.104-28.

Hancock, Graham. *The Sign and the Seal: The Quest for the Lost Ark of the Covenant*. New York: Crown, 1992.

Hess, Robert L. "An Outline of Falasha History." In *Proceedings of the Third International Conference of Ethiopian Studies*, 1969.

Hess, Robert L., ed. *Proceedings of the Fifth International Conference of Ethiopian Studies*, Session B. Chicago Circle: University of Chicago, 1978.

Hoben, Allan. *Land Tenure among the Amhara of Ethiopia: The Dynamics of Cognatic Descent*. Chicago: University of Chicago Press, 1973.

———. "Social Stratification in Traditional Amhara Society." In *Social Stratification in Africa*, edited by Arthur Tuden and Leonard Plotnicov. New York: Free Press, 1973.

Hoben, Susan. "Kin Terms of Reference and Kin Terms of Address in Amaric of Menz." In *Proceedings of the First U.S. Conference on Ethiopian Studies*, edited by H. G. Marcus. East Lansing: Michigan State University, 1973.

Hofman, Joseph E. "The Meaning of Being a Jew in Israel: An Analysis of Ethnic Identity." *Journal of Personality and Social Psychology* 15, 3 (1970): 196-202.

Imram, Yacov. "Changing Patterns of Immigrant Absorption in Israel: Educational Implications." Paper presented at 30th Annual Conference of the Comparative and International Education Society, Toronto, March 1986.

"In Sudan, Tide Turns against U.S." *New York Times*. April 26, 1986.

Inbar, Michael, and Chaim Adler. *Ethnic Integration in Israel*. New Brunswick: Transaction Books, 1976.

Israel Central Bureau of Statistics. *Statistical Abstract of Israel*, no. 37. Jerusalem: Bureau of Statistics, 1986.

Jencks, Christopher, Marshall Smith, Henry Acland, Mary Jo Bane, David Cohen, Herbert Gintis, Barbara Heyns, and Stephan Michelson. *Inequality: A Reassessment of the Effect of Family and Schooling in America*. New York: Basic Books, 1972.

Jones, Arnold H. M., and Elizabeth Monroe. *A History of Ethiopia*. Oxford: Clarendon Press, 1955.

Kahane, R., and L. Starr. "The Impact of Rapid Social Change on Technological Education: The Israeli Example." *Comparative Education Review* 20, 2 (1976): 165-78.

Kaplan, Steven. "Al hashivut limudei ethiopia l'heker haFalashim" [On the Importance of Ethiopian Studies in Falasha Research]. *Pe'amim* 21 (1984): 141-47.

———. "The Beta Israel and the Rabbinate: Law, Ritual and Politics." *Social Science Information* 27, 3 (1988): 357-70.

———. "The Falasha and the Mission: A Note on an Encounter." *Proceedings of the Ninth International Congress of Ethiopian Studies*. Moscow: USSR Academy of Sciences, 1988. Pp.116-22.

———. "Histoire et tradition: Les Chefs communautes Beta Israel et leuer evolution." *Les Temps Modernes* 41, 474 (1986): 80-100.

———. "Leheker Toldot Beta Israel b'heksher haYehudi-Notsri beEthiopia" [On the Research of the History of Beta Israel in the Jewish-Christian Context in Ethiopia]. *Pe'amim* 22 (1984): 17-31.

———. "Letoldot Beta Israel (HaFalashim), mitoch 'haHayim' shel Abuna Takla Hawaryat" [Toward a History of Beta Israel According to the 'Life' of Abuna Takla Hawaryat]. *Pe'amim* 15 (1983): 112-25.

Katz, David, and Aaron Antonovsky. "Bureaucracy and Immigrant Adjustment." *International Migration Review* 7, 3 (Fall 1973; Fall): 247-56.
Kessler, David. *The Falashas: The Forgotten Jews of Ethiopia*. London: George Allen & Unwin, 1982.
Kirwan, L. P. "The Christian Topography and the Kingdom of Axum." *Geographical Journal* 138 (1972).
Kleinberger, Aharon F. *Society, Schools and Progress in Israel*. New York: Begram Press, 1969.
Koestler, Arthur. *The Thirteenth Tribe: The Khazar Empire and Heritage*. New York: Random House, 1976.
Krausz, Ernest. "Edah and 'Ethnic Group' in Israel." *Jewish Journal of Sociology* 28, 1 (June 1986): 5-17.
Krausz, Ernest, ed. *Studies of Israeli Society*. New Brunswick and London: Transaction Books, 1980.
Kupor, Leo, and Michael G. Smith. *Pluralism in Africa*. Berkeley and Los Angeles: University of California Press, 1969.
Kushner, Gilbert. *Immigrants from India in Israel: Planned Change in an Administrative Community*. Tucson: University of Arizona Press, 1973.
Leacock, Eleanor B., ed. *The Culture of Poverty: A Critique*. New York: Simon and Schuster, 1971.
Leslau, Wolf. *Coutumes et croyances des Falacha (Juifs d'Abyssinie)*. Paris: Institut d'Ethnologie (Travaux et Memoires LXI), 1957.
———. *Documents Tigrigna: Grammaire et Textes*. Paris: Klincksieck, 1941.
———. *Falasha Anthology*. New Haven: Yale University Press, 1951.
———. "A Falasha Religious Dispute." In *Proceedings of the American Academy for Jewish Research*, 1947.
———. "Taamrat Emmanuel's Notes of Falasha Monks and Holy Places." *Salo Wittmayer Barron Jubilee Volume, American Academy for Jewish Research* (1975): 623-37.
Levine, Donald N. *Greater Ethiopia: The Evolution of a Multiethnic Society*. Chicago: University of Chicago Press, 1974.
———. *Wax and Gold: Tradition and Innovation in Ethiopian Culture*. Chicago: University of Chicago Press, 1965.
Lewins, Frank. "Religion and Identity." In *Identity and Religion: International Cross-Cultural Approaches*, edited by Hans Mol. London: Sage, 1978.
Lewis, Arnold. *Power, Poverty, and Education: An Ethnography of Schooling in an Israeli Town*. Ramat Gan, Israel: Turtledove Publishing, 1979.
Lewis, Herbert S. "Yemenite Ethnicity in Israel." *Jewish Journal of Sociology* 26, 1 (June 1984): 5-24.
Lewis, Oscar. "The Culture of Poverty." *Scientific American* 215 (November 4, 1966): 19-25.
Liebman, Charles S. "The Diaspora Influence on Israel: The Ben-Gurion-Blaustein Exchange and Its Aftermath." *Jewish Social Studies* 36, 3-4 (1974): 271-80.
———. "Religion and Political Integration in Israel." *Jewish Journal of Sociology* 17, 1 (June 1975): 17-28.
Littman, Enno. "The Legend of the Queen of Sheba in the Tradition of Axum." In *Bibliotheca Abessinics*. Leyden: Brill, 1904.
Luzzato, Paola C. "Memoire sur les Juifs d'Abyssinie ou Falachas." *Archives Israelites* 12-15 (1851-1854).

Bibliography

McCarthy, Daniel J. *Old Testament Covenant: A Survey of Current Opinions*. Oxford: Blackwell, 1972.
McNab, Christine. *Language Practice: Implementation Dilemmas in Ethiopian Education*. Stockholm: University of Stockholm, 1989.
Mahiteme-Selassie, W. Maskal (Blatengeta). *Zikra Negar*. Addis Ababa: Berhannena Salam Printing Press, 1946.
Marcus, Harold G., ed. *Proceedings of the First United States Conference on Ethiopian Studies*, East Lansing: Michigan State University, 1975.
Marcus, M. L. *Notice sur l'epoque de l'etablissement des Juifs dans l'Abyssinie*. Paris, 1829.
Marx, Emanuel. "Communal and Individual Pilgrimage: The Region of Saints' Tombs in South Sinai." In *Regional Cults*, edited by Richard P. Werbner. London: Academic Press, 1977.
Matras, Judah. "On Changing Matchmaking, Marriage, and Fertility in Israel: Some Findings, Problems, and Hypotheses." *American Journal of Sociology* 79, 2 (September 1973): 364–88.
Mead, George H. *On Social Psychology*. Chicago: University of Chicago Press, 1957.
Merton, Robert K. *Social Theory and Social Structure*. Glencoe: Free Press, 1963.
Messing, Simon D. "The Highland-Plateau Amhara of Ethiopia." Ph.D. dissertation, University of Pennsylvania, 1957.
——. "Journey to the Falashas." *Commentary* 22, 1 (1957): 28–40.
——. *The Story of the Falashas: "Black Jews" of Ethiopia*. Danbury, Conn., 1982.
Minkovich, A. *Evaluation of the Educational Achievements of the Elementary School of Israel*. Jerusalem: Hebrew University, 1978.
Murray, A. *The Life and Writings of James Bruce*. Edinburgh, 1808.
Nahum, H. "Mission chez les Falashas." *Bulletin de l'Alliance Israelite Universelle* 33 (1908): 110–37.
Oded, A. *The Bayudaya: A Community of African Jews in Uganda*. Tel Aviv: Tel Aviv University, 1973.
Ortner, Donald J., ed. *How Humans Adapt*. Washington, D.C.: Smithsonian Institution Press, 1983.
Ottaway, David, and Marina Ottoway. *Ethiopia: Empire in Revolution*. New York and London: Africana, 1978.
Pankhurst, Richard. *An Introduction to the Economic History of Ethiopia*. London: Lalibela House, 1961.
Parafit, Tudor. *Operation Moses*. London: Widenfeld and Nicholson, 1986.
Parkes, James W. *The Foundations of Judaism and Christianity*. London: Valentine Mitchell, 1960.
Parkyns, Mansfield. *Life in Abyssinia*. London: Cass, 1966.
Payne, Eric. *Ethiopian Jews: The Story of a Mission*. London: The Olive Press, 1972.
Philby, Harry St. John. *The Queen of Sheba*. London: Quartet, 1981.
"Politicians Wrangle over Secrecy Breakdown." *Jerusalem Post*. January 7, 1985.
Porten, Bezalel. *Archives from Elephantine*. Berkeley: University of California Press, 1968.
Quirin, James. "The Beta Israel (Falasha) in Ethiopian History: Caste Formation and Culture Change 1270–1868." Ph.D. dissertation, University of Minnesota, 1977.
——. *The Evolution of the Ethiopian Jews: A History of the Beta Israel (Falasha) to 1920*. Philadelphia: University of Pennsylvania Press, 1992.

———. "The Process of Caste Formation in Ethiopia: A Study of the Beta Israel (Falasha), 1270-1868." *International Journal of African Historical Studies* 12, 2 (1979): 235-58.
Rabinowitz, Louis. "Rabbinate." In *Religious Life and Communities*. Jerusalem: Keter (Israel Pocket Library), 1974. Pp.122-270.
Rajak, Tessa. "Moses in Ethiopia." *Journal of Jewish Studies* 29, 2 (1978).
Rapoport, Louis. "Exodus of the Black Jews." *Jerusalem Post*, International Edition. September 9, 1984. P.15.
———. "Frightening Crisis for Ethiopian Jews." *Jerusalem Post*. April 7, 1986.
———. *The Lost Jews: Last of the Ethiopian Falashas*. New York: Stein and Day, 1983.
———. *Redemption Song: The Story of Operation Moses*. San Diego, New York, London: Harcourt Brace Jovanovich, 1986.
Rathjens, C. *Die Juden in Abessinien*. Hamburg: W. Gente Verlag, 1922.
Redfield, Robert. *The Primitive World and Its Transformation*. Ithaca: Cornell University Press, 1965.
Reminick, Ronald A. "The 'Evil' Eye among the Amahara of Ethiopia." In *The Evil Eye*, edited by Clarence Maloney. New York: Columbia University Press, 1976. Pp.85-101.
Rosen, Chaim. "Encountering the Ethiopian Jews: Questions of Culture and Behavior." Jerusalem: Jewish Agency, 1985.
Rosen, Charles B. "Tigrean Political Identity: An Explication of Core Symbols." In *Proceedings of the Fifth International Conference on Ethiopian Studies*, edited by Robert Hess Chicago Circle, University of Chicago, 1979.
Roshwald, Mordecai. "Marginal Jewish Sects in Israel (II)." *International Journal of Middle East Studies* 4 (1973): 328-54.
———. "Who Is a Jew in the State of Israel." *Jewish Journal of Sociology* 12, 2 (1970): 233-66.
Roumani, Maurice. "From Immigrant to Citizen. The Contribution of the Army to National Integration in Israel: The Case of the Oriental Jews." *Plural Societies* 9, 2/3 (1978): 145-58.
Saidel Wolk, Rachael. "The Falashas Must Be Saved." *Jewish Veteran* (March-April 1980): 5-6, 25-26.
Schoenberger, Michelle. "The Falashas of Ethiopia: An Ethnographic Study." Ph.D. dissertation, Cambridge University, 1975.
Selzer, Michael. *The Outcasts of Israel: Communal Tensions in the Jewish State*. Jerusalem: Council of the Sephardi Community, 1965.
Semi, Emanuela Trevisan. "The Beta Israel (Falashas): From Purity to Impurity." *Jewish Journal of Sociology* 27, 2 (December 1985): 103-14.
Sergew, Hable Selassie. *Ancient and Medieval Ethiopian History to 1270*. Addis Ababa: United Printers, 1972.
———. "The Problem of Gudit." *Journal of Ethiopian Studies* 10, 1 (1972): 113-24.
Shaki, Anvar. *Who Is a Jew in the Jurisprudence of the State of Israel*. Jerusalem: Mossad haRaz Kook, 1976.
Shama, Auraham, and Mark Iris. *Immigration without Integration: Third World Jews in Israel*. Cambridge: Schenkman, 1977.
Shapiro, Leon. *The History of ORT*. New York: Schocken Books, 1980.
Shelemay, Kay Kaufman. *Music, Ritual, and Falasha History*. East Lansing: Michigan State University African Studies Center, 1986.

Bibliography

———. "Seged: A Falasha Pilgrimage Festival." *Musica Judaica* 3, 1 (1980): 42-62.
Sherman, A. "The Falashas in Israel." *Israeli Magazine* (February 1973): 58-62.
———. *In Search of Rachmim*. Jerusalem: La Semana, 1977.
Shipler, David. "Torture Reported of Ethiopian Jews." *New York Times*. November 15, 1981.
Shuval, Judith T. "Self-Rejection among North African Immigrants in Israel." *Israel Annals of Psychiatry and Related Disciplines* 4, 1 (Spring 1966): 101-10.
Simon, Rita J., and Michael Gurevitch. "Some Intergenerational Comparisons in Two Ethnic Communities in Israel." *Human Organization* 30, 1 (Spring 1971): 79-88.
Smooha, Sammy. *Israel: Pluralism and Conflict*. Berkeley and Los Angeles: University of California Pre
Smooha, Sammy, and Yochanan Peres. "The Dynamics of Ethnic Inequalities: The Case of Israel." *Social Dynamics* 1, 1 (June 1973): 165-81.
Soen, Dan. "The Falashas - Black Jews of Ethiopia." *Bulletin of the International Committee on Urgent Anthropological and Ethnological Research* 10 (1968): 67-74.
Stanner, Ruth. *The Legal Basis of Education in Israel*. Jerusalem: Ministry of Education and Culture, 1963.
Stark, Freya. *The Southern Gates of Arabia*. New York: E. P. Dutton, 1936.
Steinberg, Bernard. "Education and Integration in Israel: The First Twenty Years." *Jewish Journal of Sociology* 30, 1 (June 1988): 17-35.
Stern, Henry A. *Wanderings among the Falashas of Abyssinia*. London: Wertheim, MacIntosh, and Hunt, 1868.
"Sudan: Kaddafi Calling." *Newsweek*. April 14, 1986.
"Sudanese Officials to Visit Moscow." *Washington Post*. January 18, 1986.
Taddesse, Tamrat. *Church and State in Ethiopia, 1270-1527*. Oxford: Clarendon Press, 1972.
Teske, R. H., Jr., and Bernard H. Nelson. "Assimilation and Acculturation: A Clarification." *American Ethnologist* 1, 3 (1974): 351-67.
Thomas, Murray R., ed. *Politics of Education*. Oxford: Pergamon Press, 1983.
Turner, Victor. *Dramas, Fields and Metaphors: Symbolic Action in Human Society*. Ithaca and London: Cornell University Press, 1974.
———. *Process, Performance, and Pilgrimage: A Study in Comparative Symbiology*. New Delhi: Concept, 1979.
———. *The Ritual Process: Structure and Anti-Structure*. Chicago: Aldine, 1969.
"U.S. Fearing 'Another Tehran' Plans Partial Pullout from Sudan." *New York Times*, April 17, 1986.
"U.S. Officials Angered by Lifting of Censorship." *Jerusalem Post*. January 6, 1985.
Ullendorff, Edward. *The Ethiopians: An Introduction to the Country and People*. London: Oxford University Press, 1960.
———. *Ethiopia and the Bible*. London: Oxford University Press, 1968.
Ullendorff, Edward. *The Semitic Languages of Ethiopia*. London: Taylor's Press, 1955.
"An Unfinished Rescue." *Jerusalem Post*, (January 6, 1985).
Valentine, Charles. *Culture and Poverty: Critique and Counter Proposals*. Chicago: University of Chicago Press, 1968.
Van den Berghe, Pierre L. *Race and Racism: A Comparative Perspective*. New York: Wiley, 1978.
Wagaw, Teshome G. "Access to Haile Selassie I University." *Ethiopia Observer*, 14, 1 (1971).

BIBLIOGRAPHY

———. "Appraisal of Adult Literacy Program in Ethiopia." *Journal of Reading* 21, 6 (1978): 504-508.

———. "Attitudes and Values Concerning Children Among the Menz in Rural Ethiopia." *Journal of Psychology* 94 (1976): 257-260.

———. "The Burden and Glory of Being Schooled: An Ethiopian Dilemma." In *Proceedings of the Fifth International Association of Ethiopian Studies*, edited by Sven Rubenson. Lund: The University of Lund, 1983.

———. "Child Health Care in Rural Africa." In *For Children: Their Education and Development* edited by J. Schwertfeger and T. M. Tice. Ann Arbor: School of Education, University of Michigan, 1981.

———. *The Configuration of Education and Culture: An African Experience*, Ann Arbor: The University of Michigan, Center for Afroamerican and African Studies, 1984 (ERIC Document Reproduction Service, No. 250 239).

———. "The Descendants of Dan: A Lost Tribe of Israel Goes Home." *Michigan Alumnus* 93, 1 (September/October 1986): 31-40.

———. *The Development of Higher Education and Social Transformation: An African Experience*. East Lansing: Michigan State University Press, 1990.

———. *Education in Ethiopia: Prospect and Retrospect*. Ann Arbor: The University of Michigan Press, 1979.

———. "Education and Society in Contemporary Ethiopia." *Proceedings of the Ninth International Congress of Ethiopian Studies*. Moscow: The USSR Academy of Sciences, 1988. Pp.34-43.

———. "Emerging Issues of Ethiopian Nationalities: Cohesion or Disintegration?" *Journal of Northeast African Studies* 2, 3 (1980-81): 69-75.

———. "The Emigration and Settlement of Ethiopian Jews in Israel." *Middle East Review* 20, 2 (Winter 1987/88): 41-48.

———. "Ethiopia: The Educational System." In *The International Encyclopedia of Education*, edited by Thursten Husen and T. Neville Postlewaite. Oxford and New York: Pergamon Press, 1985.

———. "Ethiopia, Israel, and the Resettlement of the Falashas." The University of Michigan *CAAS Newsletter* 2, 2 (Winter 1986): 1-11.

———. "The World of Work in Ethiopian Culture." Unpublished paper, Addis Ababa: Haile Selassie I University, October 1971.

———. "The International Ramifications of Falasha Emigration." *Journal of Modern African Studies*, 29, 4 (1991) pp. 557-581.

Waldman, Menahem. *Yehuday Ethiopia. Adat Beta-Israel*. (The Jews of Ethiopia). Jerusalem: 1985.

Weil, Shalva. "Bene Israel Indian Jews in Lod, Israel: A Study in the Persistence of Ethnicity and Ethnic Identity, Ph.D. Dissertation." Sussex University, 1977.

Weinfeld, Moshe. "The Loyalty Oath in the Ancient Near East." *Ugarit Forschunger* 8 (1976): 379-414.

Weinstein, Brian. "Ethiopian Jews in Israel: Socialization and Re-education." *Journal of Negro Education* 54, 2 (1984): 213-224.

Weller, Leonard. "A Research Note on 'Delayed Gratification' and Ethnicity and Social Class in Israel." *Jewish Journal of Sociology* 17, 1 (1975, June): 29-36.

Weller, Levinbok, Rina Maimon, and Asher Shaham. "Religiosity and Authoritarianism." *Journal of Social Psychology* 95, 1 (1975): 11-18.

Winston, D. *The Falashas: History and Analysis of Policy Towards a Beleaguered Community*. New York: National Jewish Resource Center, 1980.

Bibliography

Wurmbrand, Max. *The Falasha Arde'et* (the Book of Disciples). Tel Aviv: Friends of the Faitlovitch Library, 1961.

———. "Falashas." *Encyclopedia Judaica* 5 (1971): 1143-1154.

Yinger, J. M. "Toward a Theory of Assimilation and Dissimilation." *Ethnic and Racial Studies* 4, 3 (1981): 249-264.

Yogev, Abraham. "From Decentralization to Centralization in Israeli Education: A Model for Examining Restructuralization of Emergent Educational Systems." Paper presented at the International Sociological Association, Paris, 1980.

Yosef, Ha Rav Ovadiah. "Letter on the Falashas." Jerusalem: Chief Rabbi's Office, 1973.

Young, Allan. "Why Amhara Get Kureynya: Sickness and Possession in an Ethiopian Zar Cult." *American Ethnologist* 2, 3 (1975): 567-584.

"Youth Aliyah: Graphic Report." Jerusalem: The Jewish Agency, 1986/87.

Zehavi, Alex Rivka Hanegbi and Haim Shalom, eds. *The Integration of Immigrant Adolescents.* Jerusalem: The Jewish Agency, 1984.

Ziv, Avner and M. Luz. "Manifest Anxiety in Children of Different Socioeconomic Levels." *Human Development* 16, 3 (1973): 224-232.

Zloczower, Avraham. "Occupation, Mobility and Social Class." *Social Science Information* 11, 5 (October 1972): 329-357.

Index

Abbadie, Antoine d', 14
Absorption and Sorting Base, 94
Absorption centers. *See* Immigrant absorption centers
Abyssinia, 249 n. 3
Ackerman, Gary, 238
Adane, Rabbi Yosef, 113, 247 n.39, 256 n.20
Addis Ababa, 21
Adler, Chaim, 51, 141, 259 n.10
Afro-Asians. *See* Orientals
Afula, 82-85
Agudat Israel, 47, 173; exclusion of Beta Israel from schools, 222-23, 260 n.13, 266 n.26
Aksum Tsion (Zion), 56
Aleka, 261 n.24
Aliyah (*Aliyot*), 32-34, 110; defined, 217; difference from immigration, 133
Aliyat Hanoar. See Youth Aliyah
Alliance Israelite Universelle, 15
Allon, Gideon, 269 n.11
Amede Tsion, Emperor of Ethiopia (1314-1344), 10
American Association for Ethiopian Jews (AAEJ), 61, 64, 233-34, 239, 250 n.13, 268 n.1, 269 n.4

Amharas, 24, 56, 74, 249 n.5
Amharic language, 1, 17, 23
Arab-Israeli War of 1973, 54
Arab League, 68, 69, 251 n.23
Ark of the Covenant, 7, 246 n.10
Arons, Moshe, 269 n.11
Ashkelon, 138
Ashkenazim, 38; differences from Orientals, 40-41; educational values, 45; migration to Israel, 31-36, 39; perceptions of Oriental immigrants, 42-43; shift toward religion, 132
Association of Americans and Canadians in Israel, 124
Astergwami, 104
Astman, Rachel, 253 n.14
Ati, Omar Abdel, 70
Avraham, Miriam, 143
Axum, 7, 246 n.10, 262 n.2
Axumite Kingdom, 7
Azulos, Yacov, 147

Bachi, Roberto, 44
Balfour, Arthur, 33
Balfour Declaration, 33
Bar Ilan University, 173, 258 n.1
Bar-Josef, R. Weiss, 3

INDEX

Basel Missions, 15
Begin, Menachim, 61
Ben Dehan, Rabbi Eliahu, 254 n.7
Benei Israel, 95, 216, 218, 256 n.24; refusal of conversion, 265 n.10
Ben-Gurion, David, 260 n.15
Benjamin of Tudela, 14
Bentwich, Joseph S., 156, 189
Ben Yakir, 178
Benyamina, 223
Ben Zimra, Rabbi David (Radbaz), 112, 255 n.16
Ben-Zvi Institute, 219
Bergman, Ami, 266 n.34
Beta Israel, EDUCATION—ADULT STUDENTS: expectations, 204, 206; family separation problems, 200; Hebrew language problems, 196, 205, 209; Israel Defense Forces service, 207-8; lack of trust for teachers, 198, 204; literacy, 191; perceptions of training, 203, 205; qualification for tertiary education, 211-12; sexual activity, 203; teaching-learning problems, 198, 199, 202-3, 204-5; *Ulpanim*, 96, 170; Youth Administration Project, 155, 192, 213, 263 n.7
Beta Israel, EDUCATION—POSTPRIMARY STUDENTS: academic difficulties, 174; aspirations, 160, 164, 171; cultural bereavement and deprivation, 155, 160, 161; dissatisfaction with education, 161, 168, 171; expectations, 165-66; family separation problems, 160, 162-63, 165, 174, 184-88; health problems, 182-83; inadequate educational preparation, 171; placement, 155; pregnancy, 167, 172; sexual activity, 166-68, 177, 181; social problems, 176-77, 182-83
Beta Israel, EDUCATION—PRIMARY STUDENTS: cognitive development, 140-41, 142; home-school problems, 150-52; placement, 266 n.24, 266 n.25; population, 136-37; religious education, 134-35; segregation, 144-45; social integration, 138-39
Beta Israel, EMIGRATION, 53-54, 61-62; airlift to Israel, 65-66; condition upon arrival, 77; death toll, 264 n.4; final (1990) mass emigration, 237-39, 241-44; hardships of, 77, 247 n.42; international reaction, 263 n.14; reasons for emigration, 56-59; routes to Israel, 55; in Sudanese refugee camps, 63-66, 251 n.19
Beta Israel, EMPLOYMENT: cultural effects in the workplace, 229, 231; employment levels, 227; employment prospects, 228; employment skills, 253 n.4; rejection of agricultural work, 227-28; training adequacy, 267 n.40; women in the workplace, 229; workplace problems, 128
Beta Israel, IN ETHIOPIA: *Buda* concept, 20-21, 23; child rearing, 78-80, 253 n.10; circumcision practices, 263 n.12; culture, 23-24; defeat by Susenyos, 11-12; dietary practices, 18; early accounts of, 14-17; economic deterioration, 59; education's effect on family, 80-81; and Ethiopian emperors, 8-12, 21; ethnic differences, 23-24; exclusionary lifestyle, 12; family life, 77-81; gender-role expectations, 79; geographical centers, 7, 9, 22; Gondares, 268 n.50; history, 5-8; identity, 4; Jewishness, 109, 249 n.4; lack of Halakah tradition, 216, 254 n.6; landlessness, 12, 250 n.6, 276 n.44; language, 23; marriage procedures, 180-81; nonemigrants, 245 n.1; nonuse of Hebrew, 17, 216; occupational identity, 5, 12; persecution, 12-13, 20-22, 56; religious culture, 17-19; ritual purity, 19; sabbath practices, 18; and student movement, 21
Beta Israel, IMMIGRANTS: birth control, 85-87; competition with Russian immigrants, 240; cultural deprivation and loss of status, 267 n.36; cultural preservation problem, 220; cultural problems, 146-47; *Dejmettinat*, 107; demographics, 73-76; differences from other immigrants, 216-18; distrust of local authorities, 105-6; divorce rate, 82; emergent leadership, 121-29; ethnic differences, 252 n.2; expectations of government, 101-2, 267 n.39, 268 n.45; family disruption, 82, 83, 88-90; family reunification efforts, 233-35, 269 n.10; financial problems, 103, 146, 226; gender-role disruption, 81-82; generation gaps, 123-24; in the Israel Defense Forces, 261 n.18; Jewishness question, 217, 249 n.4; loss of spiritual support, 84, 87; loss of traditional leadership, 121-

Beta Israel, IMMIGRANTS *(continued)* 29; loss of traditional values, 189; physical identity, 216, 264 n.3, 264 n.8; population before 1979, 72-73; population in 1988, 253 n.5; psychosomatic complaints, 261 n.22; reaction to name changing, 121, 260 n. 15; relations with Northern African immigrants, 259 n.9; resistance to reconversion, 113, 115-16, 256 n.19, 257 n.35, 260 n.13; ritual purity problems, 88; rival youth organizations, 123-29; settlement problems, 102-6; suicide, 127, 261 n.23; support needs, 244. *See also* Gondares; Tigreans
Beta Yisrael, 124-29
Bet El, 210-11
Bethlehem, 31
Bialik, Hayyim Nahman, 150
Bilu, 32
Book of Baruch, 54
Book of the Angels, 17
Boys Town, 193-95, 266 n.30
British Mandatory Government, 35, 37
Bruce, James, 14
Bush, George, 64, 234, 242, 243, 269 n.3

Canadian Association for Ethiopian Jewry, 124
Castro, MaMahari, 111
Chase, Yafa, 142
Chernov, Zeev, 197
Chieger, Emanuel, 86
Christian Missionary Society, 15
Church's Ministry among the Jews, 15
Circumcision, symbolic, 113, 114
Cohen, Herman, 269 n.3
Cohen, Percy, 44
Cohen, Rabbi Nahum, 158, 260 n.6
Congressional Caucus for Ethiopian Jews (U.S.), 234
Conversion requirement, 111-18, 255 n.18, 256 n.24, 256 n.29, 265 n.13; Beta Israel resistance, 113, 115-16, 256 n.19, 257 n.35, 260 n.13; conversion vs. reconversion, 260 n.12
Corinaldi, Michael, 255 n.15, 264 n.8

Daffa-Allah, Gizzuli, 69
Dagan, Avraham, 143
Dahab, Suwar, 69
Dan, Lost Tribe of, 57, 112
Davidi, Rami, 138

Dawit I, Emperor of Ethiopia (1382-1411), 10
Dayan, Eli, 138, 259 n.7
Dayan, Moshe, 61
Death of Abraham, 17
Derg, 24, 56, 58-59, 251 n.21; freezing of legal migration, 61; treatment of Beta Israel emigrants, 63-64
Discrimination: toward immigrants, 44-45, 144-45, 168, 217-24, 231, 264 n.6
Dominitz, Yehuda, 67
Donshik, Stephen, 267 n.40

Eban, Abba: on conversion issue, 117
Edot, 217
Education. *See* Beta Israel, EDUCATION—ADULT STUDENTS, POSTPRIMARY STUDENTS, PRIMARY STUDENTS
Egypt, 62, 69, 251 n.23; aid to Sudan, 70
Eisenstadt, Shmuel N., 3, 50
Elazar, Rachmim, 234, 268 n.2
Elchanan, Yanai, 266 n.33
Eldad the Danite (Hadani), 14, 112, 255 n.16
Eliahu, Chief Rabbi Mordecai, 255 n.16
Elias, Akiva, 158, 163, 164, 166, 170, 174, 178
Elijah of Ferrara, 14
Emigration. *See* Beta Israel, EMIGRATION
Erikson, Erik H., 3
Eritrean rebels, 242
Eritrea People's Liberation Front, 237
Eshkol, Michael Baruch, 250 n.13
Ethiopia: armed forces, 250 n.10; Christian tradition, 12; civil war, 58-59; conscription law, 59; Declaration of the Democratic Charter (1976), 57, 250 n.7, 255 n.9; diplomatic relations with Israel, 236, 269 n.11; drought, 57, 58; emperors, 249 n.2, 258 n.44; isolationism, 8, 13-14; Land Reform Law (1975), 59; military aid from Israel, 61, 237; naming practices, 119-20, 257 n.38; political instability, 237, 242; response to Sudanese airlift, 70; Revolution of 1974, 25, 58; slavery, 263 n.8; student organizations, 258 n.45; wars against Muslims, 10, 246 n.17; youth exodus, 262 n.5
Ethiopian Jews. *See* Beta Israel
Ethiopian Orthodox Church, 20, 54, 250 n.12; persecution of Beta Israel, 56
Ethiopian People's Democratic Revolutionary Front, 27

INDEX

Ethiopian People's Revolutionary Party, 58, 126
European Airways, 65
European Jews. *See* Ashkenazim

Faitlovitch, Jacques, 16, 77-78, 110, 134
Falasha. See Beta Israel
Feldman, Micha, 219, 265 n.15
Flad, J. Martin, 15

Garang, John, 64, 69
Ge'ez, 1, 16, 23
Ghazi, Ahmad ibn Ibrahim, 11
Gibbons, Edward, 13
Givat Washington, 178-83
Giyyur (certificates of conversion), 255 n.16
Glasnost, 240
Glicksburg, Rabbi, 113
Gobat, Samuel, 15
Gojo mewttat, 100, 101
Gondar (city), 12, 21, 262 n.2
Gondar (region), 262 n.2; civil strife, 239
Gondares (peoples), 23, 24, 74, 124, 268 n.50
Gordon, Uri, 91-92, 162, 237, 262 n.3
Goren, Chief Rabbi Shlomo, 111, 255 n.16
Green Line, 132, 259 n.6
Greenman, Ruth, 138
Gudit, Queen (Judit), 8
Gutleman, George, 65

Hadane, Raphael, 246 n.10
Haile Selassie I, Emperor of Ethiopia (1930-1974), 12, 21, 25, 58, 249 n.2, 267 n.39
Halakah, 112, 117
Halakic illegitimacy (*Mamzerut*), 112
Halevy, Joseph, 15-17, 109, 134, 253 n.8
Hancock, Graham, 246 n.10
Hebron, 31
Herzl, Theodor, 32, 117
Herzog, Rabbi Isaac, 117
Histadrut (Labor Federation), 46
Hofim, 260 n.6
Hovevei Zion, 32
Hussein, Saddam, 237

Immersion-conversion requirement. *See* Conversion requirement
Immigrant absorption centers, 92-99, 259 n.13; absorption center personnel, 95-97; conversion to permanent housing, 241; isolation of immigrants, 215; social workers, 261 n.21
Immigrants: factors determining integration, 76-77; measures of absorption, 4. *See also* Beta Israel, IMMIGRANTS
Immigration: of Jews to Israel, 37-39; of Jews to Palestine, 31-36; of Orientals to Israel, 39-42. *See also Aliyah;* Beta Israel, EMIGRATION; Migration
Iraq, 236
Islamic Law (Sharia), 65
Israel: Arab population, 249 n.33, 259 n.4; diplomatic relations with Ethiopia, 236, 269 n.11; discrimination toward immigrant groups, 44-45, 144-45, 168, 217-24, 231; ethnic distribution patterns, 44-45, 51; family planning, 85-87; misconceptions about Beta Israel, 220-26; Oriental-Ashkenazim inequalities, 50-51; pluralism, 41-42, 133; pre-immigration relations with Beta Israel, 110-11; race relations, 135; racial discrimination, 217-25, 231, 264 n.6; recognition of Beta Israel as Jews, 57, 111; religious minority, 132; Zionism, 30-31, 110, 132, 217

Israel, EDUCATIONAL SYSTEM: adult and continuing education, 191-211; Arab schools, 249 n.33; independent systems, 131; lack of cooperation between religious and secular systems, 146, 152; as means of political recruitment, 46; as means of social integration, 47; personnel training, 150, 214, 258 n.1; postprimary education, 155-56; preschool education, 135-36; preuniversity programs, 212; primary education, 131-33, 136; psychological climate of schools, 149-50; School Reform Law (1968), 48-49; secular system, 131, 147-48; state religious system, 131-33; testing instruments, 173; trend system, 46. *See also* Youth Aliyah

Israel, IMMIGRANT POLICY: *Aliyah* concept, 133, 217; assimilation concept, 43, 218; educational policy, 133-34, 154-55; efforts at reunification of Beta Israel, 234-39, 241-44; financial aid to Sudan, 65-66; ingathering and settlement concepts, 30-31; integration efforts, 138; media depiction of Beta Israel, 92-93; military aid to

290

Israel, IMMIGRANT POLICY *(continued)*
Ethiopia, 61, 237; name changing, 120-21, 260 n.15; resistence to Beta Israel immigration, 254 n.6; settlement process, 93, 95, 100-101, 259 n.13; war aid to Ethiopia, 61. *See also* Conversion requirement; Immigrant absorption centers; Jewish Agency for Israel
Israel Association of Ethiopian Immigrants, 124
Israel Defense Forces, 207-8
Israeli-Arab War of 1973, 54

Jaffa, 31
Jaffe, Elizer, 116; on Beta Israel, 124, 125
Jeremiah, 7
Jerusalem, 31
Jewish Agency for Israel, 67, 93, 243; absorption center personnel, 96-97; aid to Beta Israel remaining in Ethiopia, 262 n.29; termination of absorption centers, 98-99, 268 n.46
Jewish Distribution Committee of America, 270 n.22
Jewish population, 37-38. *See also* Immigration
Joffe, Meir, 238
Joint Distribution Committee (U.S.), 94, 209, 239
Judit, Queen (Gudit), 8

Kabesa, Shlomo, 138
Kaplan, Steve, 219
Karaites, 17, 248 n.12, 254 n.6
Kassa Kebede, 238, 269 n.11, 270 n.21
Katz, Eliahu, 222
Kesoch, 18, 84, 87, 113, 122
Kessler, David, 264 n.8
Kibbutz, 133, 227
Kibbutz galuyot (ingathering of exiles), 37, 217
Kibre Negast ("Glory of the Kings"), 5-6, 56, 245 n.9
Kimant, 13
Kiryat Arba, 224, 256 n.25, 271 n.30
Kiryat Batya, 169-72
Kiryat Gat, 240
Klaff, Vivian Z., 43, 44
Klein, Zvi, 218
Kook, Rabbi Avraham, 117

Lake Tana, 11, 22, 246 n.10
Lalibela, King, 24, 247 n.41

Law of Return, 2, 37, 57
League of Nations' Mandate for Palestine, 33
Leslau, Wolf, 16, 19, 122, 255 n.10
Lewis, Flora, 237
Libya, 62, 68, 69; aid to Sudan, 70; relations with Ethiopian rebels, 236
Lost Tribe of Dan, 57, 112

Mahdi, Sadik, 62
Makeda, Queen of Ethiopia (Sheba), 1, 6, 54
Malinowski, Bronislow, 264 n.1
Mamzerut (Halakic illegitimacy), 112
Matras, Judah, 33
Meir, Golda, 260 n.15
Melaku Teferra, 63, 64, 251 n.21
Melitz, Amram, 259 n.5
Menelik I, Emperor of Ethiopia, 1, 6, 54
Menelik II, Emperor of Ethiopia (1889-1913), 12, 21
Mengistu Hailemariam, 24, 27, 68, 251 n.21; and Beta Israel release, 237-38; flight from Ethiopia, 242, 271 n.28
Merton, Robert K., 3
Mesfin Woldemariam, 234
Mesgid, 18
Messele, Addisu, 125-29, 247 n.39, 256 n.19, 258 n.45, 269 n.8; on Beta Israel community, 127-29
Migration: challenges of, 2-3; defined, 2; theories of, 2-4. *See also* Immigration
Miller, Gary, 270 n.22
Miller, Shoshanna, 256 n.29
Minas, Emperor of Ethiopia (1559-1563), 10
Ministry of Education and Culture, 49-50, 131, 134, 249 n.33
Ministry of Immigrant Absorption, 93-94, 100-101, 253 n.5, 253 n.14
Miqveh Israel, 156, 162-69
Mizug galuyot (fusion and integration of exiles), 43, 217
Morea School, 141-47
Morrocan immigrants, 44, 260 n.14
Moshav, 227
Mossad, 62

Nahum, Rabbi Haim, 16
National Council for Ethiopian Jews (Israel), 234
National Jewish Community Relations Advisory Council (U.S.), 234
National Religious Party, 50

Nave, Amnon, 205, 207
Nazareth, 31
Nimeiri, Gaffar, 62, 63, 64–65, 251 n.23; repercussions of Beta Israel airlift, 69–71
Nissim, Yitzhak, 110
Nordau, Max Simon, 117
Nourim School, 202–8

Old Testament, 7
Onim School, 197–202
Operation Joshua, 53, 66
Operation Magic Carpet, 39
Operation Moses, 53, 66; disclosure of, 67; repercussions, 67–71
Operation Solomon, 71, 241–44, 252 n.1
Organization of African Unity, 54
Organization for Rehabilitation and Training (ORT), 60, 250 n.13
Orientals, 264 n.2; birthrate, 40; differences from Ashkenazim, 40–41; educational progress, 47–48; educational values, 45; immigration to Israel, 39–42
Orit (Torah), 14, 17; in Ethiopian Orthodox Church, 54

Palestine: Christian community, 31; Jewish community (*Yishuv*), 31–36, 41–42; partition of, 37
Parafit, Tudor, 250 n.11
Paroblo, Odet, 195
Payne, Eric, 12, 60, 250 n.11
Peres, Shimon, 64, 68; and conversion issue, 114–15, 117–18
Prester John, 14
Professors for Peace in the Middle East, 265 n.19
Project Renewal, 82, 267 n.37
Pur, David, 131, 132, 133, 259 n.5

Qaddafi, Muammar, 62, 237
Qozmos, 10

Rachmani, Sarah, 265 n.15
Racial discrimination: in Israeli society, 217–24, 231, 264 n.6
Rafael, Yitzhak, 110
Ramot School, 147–49
Reagan Administration, 251 n.22
Reconversion requirement, 111–18, 255 n.18, 256 n.24, 256 n.29, 265 n.13; Beta Israel resistance, 113, 115–16, 256 n.19, 257 n.35, 260 n.13; reconversion vs. conversion, 260 n.12

Religious fundamentalism: in the Middle East, 259 n.3
Rosen, Esther, 263 n.6
Rosen, Haim, 195, 261 n.18, 263 n.6, 266 n.30
Russia: emigration of Jews, 31–32

Sabra, 135, 179
Safed, 31
Saladin, 24, 247 n.41
Samaritans, 17, 248 n.12, 254 n.6
Sarsa Dangal, Emperor of Ethiopia (1563–1597), 11
Schmerl, R. B., 247 n.6, 248 n.9
Scowcroft, Brent, 234
Seker, 47
Selzer, Michael, 44
Semien Mountains, 1, 7, 22
Sephardim, 31, 264 n.2
Sephardim-Orientals, 37–38. *See also* Orientals
Shamir, Yitzhak, 64, 235, 242, 243, 269 n.11, 270 n.12
Shapiro, Chief Rabbi Avraham, 255 n.16
Sharia (Islamic Law), 65
Shuval, Judith T., 44
Sibhat, Aleka, 183
Sinai School, 138–41
Skewed, 18
Smooha, Sammy, 51–52
Solomon, King of Israel, 1, 6
Somalia, 237
Stahl, David, 135
State Education Law (Israel), 46
Stern, Henry A., 15
Student Administration unit, 174
Sudan, 236; aid from Israel, 65–66; aid from Libya, 70; aid from United States, 65, 70; and Beta Israel refugees, 63–66; coup of 1985, 69; economic deterioration, 64; economic interest to West, 68–69; political alliances, 62; political instability, 237; trial of Nimeiri government, 69–70
Sudanese People's Liberation Army, 64, 69
Susenyos, Emperor of Ethiopia (1607–1632), 11, 13
Syria, 236

Tabot, 54–55
Taib, 20
Talmud, 17
Tamir, Odeda, 205, 206

292

Index

Tamrat Emmanuel, 110, 133–34, 255 n.8
Tayeb, Omar Mohammed, 70, 251 n.25
Tekazai River, 7
Tel Aviv, 31
Tel Azar Vocational School, 208–10
Tesfaye Dinka, 236
Tesfaye Kidane, 242
Testament of Abraham, 17
Tewodros II, Emperor of Ethiopia (1855–1868), 12, 15, 21
Tezaz Sanbat (Commandments of the Sabbath), 17
Tiberias, 31
Tigreans, 24, 73–74, 242, 258 n.50, 261 n.17, 262 n.2
Tigrigna, 23, 73
Tikva Village, 172–75
Tiruneh, Aleka, 183, 267 n.36
Tivila Training Center, 175–77
Torah. See *Orit*
Tsegga, Abba, 10
Tsur, Yaacov, 114

Ullendorff, Edward, 6, 16, 255 n.10
Ulpanim, 96, 170
United Nations, 37; Resolution No. 3379, 267 n.35
United States: aid to Sudan, 65, 70; intervention in Beta Israel migration, 64; support for reunification of Beta Israel, 234–35
Uziel School, 222–23

Vatikim (Veteran Ethiopians), 95, 122

Walters, Vernon, 64
Weingrod, Alex, 44
Weizmann, Chaim, 33
White Paper on Palestine, 35
"Who Is a Jew" controversy, 256 n.29

Wilson, Woodrow, 33
WIZO Girls Vocational School, 195–97
Wolpe, Howard, 238
Women's International Zionist Organization, 193
World Jewish Organization, 217
World Zionist Organization, 32, 33

Yaacov, Aleka, 183
Yani, Haim, 160, 161
Yashar, Ben, 133–35
Yemen, 8
Yemenites, 95, 174, 216
Yeshaq, Emperor of Ethiopia (1412–1429), 10
Yeshivot, 132
Yishuv, 31–36, 41–42
Yohannis I, Emperor of Ethiopia (1668–1678), 11
Yona Bogale, 110, 122, 257 n.41
Yosef, Chief Rabbi Ovadia, 57, 111, 255 n.16
Youth Administration Project, 155, 192, 213, 263 n.7
Youth Aliyah, 86, 260 n.8; Beta Israel dissatisfaction, 165–66, 168, 171; Beta Israel enrollment, 155–56, 158–59; Beta Israel problems, 160–61; history, 156–57; homelike atmosphere, 161–62; placement policies, 166–67, 169–70, 179

Zahavi Association of Large Families, 124
Zara Yakov, Emperor of Ethiopia (1434–1468), 10
Zemed, 171
Zephaniah, 7
Zionism, 30–31, 110; and concept of *aliyah*, 217; secularism, 132

www.ingramcontent.com/pod-product-compliance
Lightning Source LLC
Chambersburg PA
CBHW070607170426
43200CB00012B/2615